D1757105

Due for return on or before last date
stamped below

THE ELIZABETHAN JESUITS

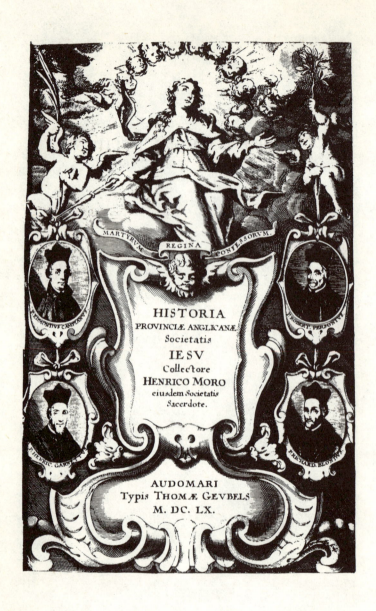

MARTYRUM REGINA CONFESSORVM.

F. EDMVNDVS CAMPIANVS

P. ROBERT. PERSONVS

HISTORIA
PROVINCIÆ ANGLICANÆ.
Societatis
IESV
Collectore
HENRICO MORO
eiusdem Societatis
Sacerdote.

P. HENRIC. GARNETVS

P. RICHARD. BLOVNT.

AUDOMARI
Typis Thomæ Geubels
M. DC. LX.

THE ELIZABETHAN JESUITS

Historia Missionis Anglicanae Societatis Jesu (1660)
of Henry More

edited and translated by

FRANCIS EDWARDS, S.J.

F.S.A., F.R.Hist.S.

PHILLIMORE

1981

Published by
PHILLIMORE & CO. LTD.,
London and Chichester

Head Office: Shopwyke Hall,
Chichester, Sussex, England

ISBN 0 85033 375 X ✓

9001583935

136810   271.53
MOR

Printed and bound in Great Britain at
The Camelot Press Ltd, Southampton

CONTENTS

FOREWORD

AT A MEMORABLE HIGH MASS in Saint Peter's, Rome, on Sunday, 25 October 1970, Pope Paul VI solemnly canonised 40 English and Welsh martyrs. For many people in Britain, it was a highly controversial act: a not very welcome reminder that England has not always been a land of liberty, nor one ready to welcome every kind of seeker after truth. Indeed, much of the 16th century, and most of the 17th, meant for English and Welsh Catholics, not to enlarge the context by speaking of Scots and Irishmen, a time of darkness and persecution. From it they emerged slowly and gradually. Not until the 19th century, in fact, were Catholics fully accepted into the national community, and even then it was often with reservations. Their point of view took a long time to win acceptance.

We know what contemporary Catholics are like from meeting and living with them. What were the papists really like in the 16th century? What were their leaders like, and the more influential among them? Some of them have always been considered highly controversial figures, and among these the most controversial were, perhaps, the Jesuits. Ten Jesuits are named among the newly canonised. Not enough has yet been published in English to enable us to arrive at a balanced picture of this Order. Most of what has been published in English on the subject has been hostile rather than otherwise. Considerable quantities of documents must still be published in their entirety before we can begin to arrive at a final judgment. The complete letters of Robert Persons, S.J., and Henry Garnet, S.J., for example, will need to be made available to students. This task, fortunately, is already in hand.

It is important to know what others thought of Jesuits. It is also interesting to know how they saw themselves. The present history, then, deals with the Elizabethan Catholics from the viewpoint of an important group among them. Or more exactly, it sees them through the contemporary eyes of one of the abler members of that group. The contemporary view is always important. Indeed, history that is not based on the evidence of its own times is not history at all, merely propaganda.

These are ecumenical days. Disagreements on religion remain, and will continue to do so. But Christians with religious differences do not now pursue one another with the vigour of St. George chasing dragons. It can do no harm, however, to re-examine the roots from which contemporary persuasions grew, taking fanaticism as a warning, but not failing to admire heroism and sincerity wherever they appear. Certainly, there can be no doubt about the heroism or sincerity of those Catholics who braved the authority of the Elizabethan state in matters of religion.

INTRODUCTION

FAIRLY NUMEROUS Elizabethan and early Jacobean
works have been re-published over the past century of
specifically Roman Catholic interest. A few of these have
been by Jesuits or represented the Jesuit viewpoint. They
include Robert Persons's *Christian Directory*, Edmund
Campion's *Ten Reasons,* and more recently William T.
Costello's *The Judgment of a Catholicke Englishman
living in Banishment for his Religion* of 1608 (facsimile
edition, Gainsville, Florida, 1957). Such studies only
touched particular problems, and that rather briefly.
A translation of Henry More's *Historia* makes available
a contemporary, or near contemporary, attempt to write
a complete, systematic and scholarly history of the time
from this important viewpoint.

Henry More had access to many who acted and wrote
the drama of his day and whose experience would otherwise have been lost along with many contemporary
documents. His work is also a contribution to the history
of historiography. True, it is not simply history from
the Jesuit viewpoint so much as the viewpoint of a Jesuit.
His production does not provide a simple answer to all
the difficulties of the Jesuit position. Any student of the
documents of the period will recognise at once how much
condensation and summarisation sometimes shrink into
a few paragraphs. The appointment of the archpriest
and the question of equivocation alone produced docu-
mentation which could each fill a volume far larger than
this. But More's conclusions and summaries represent
a useful contemporary attempt to distil many gallons of
source material into a litre or two of concentrated
narrative.

The fact that More's work is in some sense a classic
does not put it beyond criticism. Some of More's faults

as a historian were searchingly discerned by his 'revisers', or fellow-Jesuits and scholars, to whom his history was referred by the authorities of the Order before it was allowed to be printed in 1660. The interesting document they drew up, of which a copy exists in the state archives in Brussels (Varia, S.J., Carton 31), points out that there are 'some grammatical mistakes and infelicities of language. His style is variable and crabbed'. There are other criticisms, and 'at least one of the revisers is inclined to the view that this edition of the history should be held up until times are more suitable rather than published now. For it contains many things which could offend royalists and also those who now rule England with no little harm to the Catholic cause'.*

There is always a contemporary fear not that a historian of his own times will not tell the truth, but that he will tell too much. This will hardly be considered a serious objection in our own age to reprinting More.

Apart from relying on the best printed works of his day (*see* page 357), More made considerable use of manuscript sources published and unpublished. Indeed, some of the letters and documents he quotes would appear to be no longer extant so that his work sometimes acquires special value as a unique and virtually original source. Here and there, perhaps, he may even lean too heavily on lengthily-quoted documents. But this is a pardonable fault to those who appreciate the importance of sources. Piety, poetry, mystical experience and plain historic fact sometimes flow together in a fashion not to the taste of our own times. Some attempt has been made to edit this so that legend is removed and history remains. Nothing in the original of historical interest has been omitted. Omissions, in any case, are always indicated.

This first half of More's history has never before been published in English, although use was made of it by Henry Foley, S.J., in his *Records of the English Province, S.J.* (London, 1877 to 1883). Many of the longer omissions

---

*The present editor has used a Farm Street transcript of this verdict in a volume entitled *Excerpta ex Archiv. Bruxellis*, p. 125.

from More in the present volume can often be found in Foley. They usually consist of pious anecdote and passages of devotional rather than historical interest.

More's narrative, as one would expect, is that of a highly committed believer. This emerges clearly in the translation. But while attempting to observe fidelity to the original, it seemed unnecessary to reproduce turns of phrase adopted by both Catholic and Protestant writers of this period which seem offensive to modern ears. More, by the standards of his contemporaries, is usually moderate in tone and normally generous to adversaries. But this is not an 'ecumenical' work, any more than John Foxe's *Book of Martyrs*. By the middle of the 17th century, attitudes and terminology of rival Christian groups had hardened. The present translation has attempted to round the edges of contemporary expressions without losing the sense.

More's original tenses and moods have been retained in translation wherever they were consistent with euphony. Where two words in Latin convey the same meaning, one English word serves for both (e.g., 'exerceat et conturbet' on page 67). Sometimes a phrase has been given contemporary accuracy. So when More speaks (page 9) of the 'whole world' it has been translated as 'the western world'. The shortest equivalent word or phrase is used to convey the Latin so that 'the Church of Christ', for example, becomes simply 'the Church'. Phrases like 'as will be said in its place' are usually omitted as adding nothing to the sense. The original tends to pass from the telegrammatic to the prolix. Sometimes when describing incidents or narrating, More omits detail to the point where the story only becomes intelligible from other sources. He sometimes omits important dates, even from quoted letters (cf. Allen to Bayley, p. 123). Perhaps it was the fault of the printer that it is not always clear where quotation begins and ends (e.g., Sir William Cecil's letter, p. 193). The convention of the day allowed considerable freedom in the matter of quotation. Passages are sometimes indicated as such which are really précis or paraphrase, or even omitted without any indication. At all events, where one can check his documents against the original, More conveys the sense accurately. The translator has discovered no instance of falsification, or undue dragging of the sense of an original to suit any purpose of his own. Only in one place would he appear to have been unaware of sources which led him to a wrong conclusion, namely in his over-optimistic portrayal of the relations which prevailed between Robert Persons and Gaspar Haywood, both Jesuits (Book IV, para. 11). It is no mean feat in a work of such length that More has written what modern scholarship can often expand but rarely contradict.

GENERAL NOTES

1. **Jesuit terminology**: A period of postulancy, short for prospective priests, was followed by a noviceship normally lasting two years. A man's 'grade'—whether he should be a priest or a lay-brother—was decided at entry. After the novitiate, three simple but perpetual vows of poverty, chastity and obedience were taken. Then there might follow a further period of study for priest-students, known in England as the 'juniorate': after this, three years' philosophy were followed by university studies for younger members, and then 'regency', or a period of teaching in the colleges. Four years' theology followed; ordination to the priesthood normally taking place in the third year. A year's ascetical discipline and study—the 'tertianship', or third probation, completed training. The last step was 'profession'. There were temporal coadjutors—lay-brothers—and spiritual coadjutors, or priests who pronounced solemnly the three vows of the religious life. There was also an inner élite, so to speak, of Fathers who added a fourth vow of obedience to the Pope—the 'professed of the four vows'.
2. Round brackets in the text indicate marginal notes in More's printed history. Square brackets denote matter contributed by the translator and editor.
3. An asterisk indicates a note at the back, which will be found under More's chapter and paragraph number.

LIFE OF HENRY MORE

HENRY MORE was the second son of Edward More of Barnborough, and great-grandson of Sir Thomas. He was born most probably at Leytonstone in 1586. Henry began his education at St. Omers in 1597, continuing at Valladolid from 1603 as the protegé of the Countess of Medinaceli. Joining the Jesuits at Louvain on 19 November 1607, his life was lost to public view for some years. In 1614, John Gerard, the Jesuit who wrote an account of the Gunpowder Plot, was master of novices. He asked the Prefect of the Jesuit Mission, resident in Rome, for More's services as his 'socius' or assistant. In spite of the fact that More's good academic record suggested employment in one of the colleges, he was sent to help Gerard. The novitiate was then being transferred from Louvain to Liège.

Gerard and More did not get on notably well. Indeed, Gerard describes More as 'of a close and hidden disposition; not friendly . . . I have found . . . that any one thing he mislikes . . . will lose him more than all that one can do to him, or for him, will gain him. And then he keeps it to himself, and one shall not know what it is he mislikes' (Stonyhurst MSS.: Anglia, IV, No. 41). More was a scholarly and reserved man who did not open easily to others.

'He hath also a kind of slowness in answering when his advice is asked in anything which is very troublesome, as in consultations. When it comes to his time he will be more long before he speaks than any other'. However, there was no 'show of contention that others perceive in this house; nor past four or five times hath there been in private any expostulation, and then it was without any falling out'. Jesuits were only human even in an age

1

that demanded of the extraordinary heroism for much
of the time.

In 1622, More crossed to England to work among the
Catholics in the London district. He was among those
in the Jesuit house and noviceship at Clerkenwell who
were arrested after a notorious raid of 15 March 1628.
Seven Jesuits were arrested with More, including the
rector of the district, who was found 'hiding in a cellar
under the ground with the altar equipment' (More:
History, Book 10, paragraph 14). All those captured
were eventually released, although one who confessed
his priesthood was condemned to death, if only for form's
sake. More spent his next few years in prison. He was
released officially in 1633. We need not suppose the
experience was particularly arduous, for these, after all
were the days of Charles I not of James I. More's release
may have occurred earlier, although the written record
suggests not. He next became chaplain to Robert, Lord
Petre of Ingatestone and Thorndon Hall, Essex. Petre was
a considerable benefactor of the Society, and while More
was chaplain, endowed a district for them with an anual
income of some £250 to last until his death.

From November 1631, More was appointed a 'consultor' or advisor, to the English Provincial. This office
further obliged him to correspond regularly with Rome.
The General's letters in reply are still extant. More's
advice was acknowledged on various occasions in such
phrases as 'most welcome', and 'remarkably opportune'.
Perhaps the greatest difficulties at the time were connected
with finding suitable superiors and officials for the various
English Jesuit establishments in Europe. The persecution
in England was not a serious obstacle. Indeed, it now
amounted to little more than exclusion from public life,
and the 'right to open worship'.

That the General's appreciation of More was more
than courtesy was proved by his appointment in 1635
to succeed Richard Blount as Provincial. Vitelleschi
expressed his complete confidence in More's 'outstanding
prudence, charity and zeal for God's glory'. More, as might

have been expected, was not overjoyed at the honour, being far from convinced of his own adequacy. His period of office covered the last few years of peace in England before the civil war. The Jesuit houses in Europe had been long if intermittently troubled by the Thirty Years' War. They were also ruffled by internal disagreements and national differences between English and Walloon Jesuits. The General reported, 'at Liège it is said that at no time is there any lasting harmony. The professors dig at one another more sharply than charity allows'. (Generals' Letters: Mount Street photocopies, 1605/41, f. 419v.) The new Provincial crossed to Flanders at the end of 1635 to deal with the situation more effectively on the spot. More's appointment seems to have been popular with his subjects. Much of his time was taken up with routine affairs; demolishing molehills, and kicking pebbles from the path of day-to-day administration. It is amusing to hear Vitelleschi exhorting More in a letter of 2 August 1636, 'The use of tobacco, especially smoking, is said to be so much on the increase that, apart from the great waste of time involved, which they lose in taking the smoke, they take too little heed of the small edification they give. Your Reverence should do away with this abuse'. Such matters could be allowed time and attention in circumstances which were 'half-way between war and peace and persecution'. (Arch. S.J., Rome, Anglia. 33/I, f. 55v.) Larger difficulties were on the way.

Bishop Richard Smith left England for France in 1631. He thus created a problem of government for the Catholics, and another of communication, which were solved as far as they could be by the presence in England of papal envoys to Queen Henrietta Maria, the Catholic bride of Charles I. George Conn took up this post in July 1636. As upholder of papal policy and authority, Conn found much in common with Henry More, but More true to himself, was not a tool that was particularly pliable. Moreover, Conn hoped to establish good relations with all shades of Catholic opinion in England, and to mediate between them and King Charles. The latter was not anti-Catholic, as his father had been, but he was opposed to Jesuits. However, he was ready to negotiate a form of oath or external expression of loyalty which, if possible, would not contravene the faith of his Catholic subjects. Hence he must be humoured and even indulged. The vexed question of the papal deposing power continued as a theoretical obstacle to real understanding. Nevertheless, to the very eve of civil war, conditions of living continued to improve for the papists. Indeed, Conn could proclaim, 'The peace which Catholics enjoy in these regions has never been greater or more universal' (Vatican Library; MS. Barberini Latin, 8642, f. 240r.) The papal envoy was only afraid that Catholics were growing reckless in the incautious exercise of their growing liberties.

More was succeeded as Provincial by Matthew Wilson, *alias* Edward Knott, a writer and scholar of note in his day. For a time, however, More carried on his administration in England while Knott, like his predecessor, began his period of office with a visitation of English-speaking Jesuit houses in the Low Countries. This was not altogether a matter of choice. Charles I was opposed to Knott's appointment, and Conn could not welcome it, since Knott had offended in the matter of at least one book published secretly in England a short while previously. While Conn could scarcely disapprove of an effective controversialist for the Catholic and papal cause, he could not usefully take Knott's part openly against the King. The Jesuit General did not wish to offend the latter, but neither did he wish to change the appointment. By way of compromise, Knott stayed in Europe, while More virtually fulfilled his functions in England, as vice-Provincial, until he himself was called to Ghent in 1642.

The civil war brought a hardening of attitude and arteries on all sides. Persecution of Catholics recommenced, at all events where the Roundheads had their way. Meanwhile, in July 1641, More had to remind his colleagues that it was 'unlawful to take the oath of allegiance, even with protestations, or to go to church'—that is, the non-Catholic churches—'So I hope none of ours will be found to think or to deliver their mind otherwise' (Cardwell transcripts, Mount Street copy, vol. iii, ff. 107-111). More's transfer to Flanders in 1642 saved him not only further grim experience of civil war, but also further brushes with Henry Silisdon, S.J., a fellow-Jesuit with whom he and others did not see eye to eye. Both men, it seems, possessed an individualism which conflicted with the same quality in the other. Master of Tertians—Jesuits in the last year of their ascetical training—in 1643, More was later sent to make a report on St. Omer's College for the General. Both tasks were carried out with More's customary painstaking competence. In the autumn of 1644, More was sent to London as rector of the district to replace Silisdon. So far More's career had been one of steady progress: a reliable man who carried out his duties conscientiously and well. He was now to come up against a difficulty from which he and his reputation would only recover after much time.

In 1645, the Jesuits in England were once again the storm-centre of persecution. This was normal for them. Ralph Corby had been executed at Tyburn on 7 September 1644. Henry Morse followed him on 1 February 1645. Henry Silisdon, who had expressed his own wish to become a martyr, was appointed Provincial in 1646. More was now pinned between a superior whom he did not find congenial, and a task which was becoming daily more impossible. He wrote of his district to General Caraffa on 17 July 1646, 'From a purely human point of view the place is quite wretched, where you see nothing but the darker side of humanity . . . there is a continual fear that all Catholics will be expelled. Almost every day there is news of our men in prison, exile or full flight' (Stonyhurst MSS. Anglia, A, V. No. 24).

By 1647, however, the situation had changed somewhat in so far as the Independents had now a clearer ascendancy over the Presbyterians. Independents were inclined to be more tolerant of Catholics; and when the latter made a secret approach to them in 1647, they held out a hope of toleration although on conditions. Henry More entered eagerly into negotiations, writing a treatise, among other activities, to show that Catholics could live peaceably even under governments which were formally heretical. George Ward, a Jesuit theologian, was no less forward than More. They joined with the heads of other religious Orders and Congregations, and a group of influential laymen to form a negotiating body for the Catholics. Eventually, the Council of War drew up three propositions to which the Catholics must consent immediately in return for toleration. There was no time for More or the others to have recourse to Rome. More had not even time to approach his Provincial, who was then in Flanders. With Ward, he therefore represented the Jesuits in the negotiation, and on their behalf consented with the rest. More made it clear in a preamble, as he thought and later claimed, that the consent of the Jesuits to the propositions was not over a matter of doctrine, but only one concerning practical procedure. In this sense, they agreed that the Pope could not absolve persons from obedience to the civil power, not allow anyone lawfully to kill or injure another because he was excommunicated for heresy; nor could the Pope allow a person to break faith with someone else who had fallen into heresy. More, Ward and the rest were prepared to admit that, whatever the Pope's theoretical powers, they would certainly not use or invoke them in a sense contrary to their agreement to the propositions. Two forms of the preface or preamble, however, reached Rome, one by way of Brussels and the other by way of Paris. That which went through Brussels was rather less cautious than that which went by Paris. The latter More and Ward later claimed as alone authentic.

Subsequent reactions among the Jesuits to all this, especially those on the Continent, were mixed. Their Roman theologians upheld More's decision. Edward Knott, however, as heartily denounced it, claiming that the preface—presumably he saw the one that went by Brussels—was not sufficient to remove the controversy from the arena of doctrine as such. In short, More, Ward and their friends had erred in faith. Indeed, they had betrayed the position formerly insisted on by Pope Paul V when he rejected the oath of allegiance devised by or for James I in 1606. The English Jesuits were divided in the controversy. Innocent X appointed a special commission of Cardinals which reached a decision on 15 November 1647. It was unlawful for the English Catholics 'to bargain with the heretics' (ARSJ., Anglia, 34, f. 187r).

Caraffa, the Jesuit General, had no intention of victimising More, who had acted in good faith, in transferring him to the Continent. His period of office as rector had, in any case, almost run out. On 15 January 1648, the Pope decreed it unlawful for the Catholics 'to subscribe in the negative' to the three propositions. However, it was about this time that the discrepancy in the various documents sent to Rome began to come to light. More was called to the presence of the Internuncio in Brussels to receive the Pope's decree. It was then that he discovered that what had been condemned was other than he had signed originally. Caraffa could only suggest that the Internuncio take up the matter with Rome. Meanwhile, the Roman machinery continued to grind. On 4 April 1648, the Pope personally acquainted Caraffa with the decision arrived at in January. Those who had erred were to be removed from England. More, at least, was no longer there. But in Ghent he was removed from his post of instructor for a time.

More's correspondence shows some signs of bitterness and frustration, but nothing excessive. He accepted the decision, and his own removal from office, retiring to Watten. This was far from being a haven of peace, if only because it was still in or near the front line of the concluding Thirty Years' War. By December, More and Ward had a long apologia ready at Caraffa's request, which they sent to him. Oddly enough, this document reached the General without seal or wrapper; and more significantly, without the declaration which Ward for his part said he had enclosed. Caraffa had the grace to admit that there was some difference in the two versions of the propositions. However, the Cardinals of the Holy Office had seen and examined both, as they claimed. There seemed little point in re-opening an issue which would most probably end in a new condemnation and make the Jesuits appear obstinate. Meanwhile, More and Ward, could take comfort from the fact that before the court of conscience they were unsullied. More's health suffered somewhat from all this, as was to be expected of a man of his sensitivity. However, he was far from broken—and not for long forgotten.

On 27 March 1649, Caraffa instructed the Provincial to appoint More Rector of St. Omer's. His *Vita et Doctrina Christi . . .* was published at Antwerp the same year. He continued as Rector until 1652 when he returned to England, taking up residence, it seems, in Essex. In 1655, he returned once more to Flanders, this time to Liège. Appointed spiritual father, a task which allowed some leisure, he settled down to work on the book which lies before us. In May 1656, the General told the Provincial, Richard Bradshaigh, that he would be glad to see the history when finished. Nevertheless, he did not long allow him to continue his task uninterrupted. More became Rector of St. Omer's once again in April 1657. He was now a man of sixty-nine. His health was described as weak. Nevertheless, and in spite of his own request to relinquish this onerous task in 1659, he continued until the following year. This year, 1660, his history was published at St. Omer's. Rather unexpectedly, it met with little response, whether from Jesuits or from anyone else. There is no mention of it in the Generals' letters, at any rate at the time of publication and during the years immediately following. The Jesuit censors had not been enthusiastic. Indeed, they recommended that the book be delayed indefinitely. Perhaps the new General, Nickel, felt that More would have done better to spend more time and energy in resolving present difficulties rather than in analysing those of the past. Certainly, he disapproved of More's régime at St. Omer's as too easy-going. Indeed the Provincial was exhorted not to allow a repetition of this sort of thing for the future. In the circumstances, More's history would have left Nickel unimpressed except as the reminder of a too great distraction.

In 1661, More moved to the noviceship at Watten to become spiritual director and confessor. All this time he was a consultor of the Province. At Watten, however, he died, apparently of apoplexy, on 8 December 1661. He had lived to seventy-five.

More was honest, devoted, painstaking, with a careful eye for detail. This would make his history a useful source even today. But he also based his work on documents, his own experience and the experience of others who had been in personal contact with events. George Oliver's dictum on his history seems just: 'in elegance of diction it may rank below the classic histories . . . by Orlandini', and others, but 'it yields to none in candour, fidelity and unction'. For 'unction' we should, perhaps, read sincerity.

BOOK THE FIRST

1.   The Society of Jesus was founded in Italy by Ignatius [Loyola] about the same time that Henry VIII of England began to set up his own church . . . While the authority of the Supreme Pontiff was bearded by a proud and undisciplined monarch, the seeds were planted of an Order which bound itself by special vow to obey the Pope. Its object was to retain the western world in obedience to the Holy See . . . King Henry went on to destroy churches, overthrow religious houses, and even bespatter himself with innocent blood. Meanwhile, the Society of Jesus was confirmed in existence by bulls from the Pope. Also at this time [on 25 January] 1540, Edmund Campion was born in London. He was destined to be the first of his Society in Britain to pay for this assertion of the Pope's authority with his own blood. The example proved an augury for the future that others would not be lacking to do likewise.

2.   Of all countries to the north, England was nearly the last to see the Society of Jesus for the first time. Admittedly not the worst of its misfortunes, it learned to hate the Society before it experienced any real reason for doing so. Having more or less accepted the schism, England saw the cause of the Holy See and those vowed to its obedience as one and the same thing . . . Some of the Protestants, while rejecting the Holy See and its supporters, established a new sort of law which branded as *lèse majesté* all they did out of their kind of religious duty. They strove by ruthless inquisition and torture to drive them out of the kingdom or destroy them. But the Society took shape on the anvil, deriving spirit and resource from its contact with iron.

3.   The shape of even the distant future was not hidden from Ignatius while he lived. He was once consulted by the Roman Provincial on the advisability of admitting

a certain Englishman to the Society. Ignatius ordered him to be admitted, for the Society would one day flourish in England as elsewhere . . . (Orlandini, Book 4, No. 66).

4.   Just how inimical England was from the very first to the recently founded and confirmed Society while Henry VIII lived is not difficult to estimate. But while Robert was still the learned and virtuous Archbishop of Armagh, John Codure, one of Ignatius's first 10 companions, was marked out, by the Pope's authority, for Ireland.* On his untimely death, Alphonsus Salmeron was destined to succeed Codure. Together with Paschase Bröet and Francis Zapata, he went to Ireland. But as it happened, he was unable to carry out the Pope's instruction to keep the people in their obedience to him, or to fulfil the other functions of his mission. Nor could they stay anywhere without constantly changing their hiding-place. Salmeron incurred maximum risk to himself and his hosts thanks to the royal ministers' hatred and the cunning of the officials. Nor was he able to return by way of England; and while in Scotland, owing to the new ideas spreading from England, he was unable to do anything effective. So rejected, as it were, by the heat of Pluto's rage, he returned to Italy . . . (Orlandini, Book 3, Nos. 45, 58).

5.* When Ignatius saw his efforts availed so little to improve the situation of the crumbling kingdoms of the north, he fervently pursued what remained to him. He and his companions strove to bring them assistance by prayer. Ignatius left it to God and time to ripen a richer harvest, and choose the right kind of labourer for the reaping. It was evident from Salmeron's visit to Ireland, mentioned above, and Peter Ribadeneira's stay in England (*History*, Chapter 22)—Figueroa was then the Catholic King's ambassador to Elizabeth—that little fruit was to be expected from these good people in existing circumstances. They would need to be cultivated by men who knew their own language well and their own race no less. Lainez, the next General after Ignatius,

saw clearly that after Queen Mary's death the reins had
fallen once again to Protestantism. He therefore very
willingly received a considerable number of Englishmen
into the Society, thus imitating, in a certain sense, Gregory
the Great. Lainez helped them with such studies as would
make their intentions and abilities better known. Thus he
was largely responsible for the fact that many who applied
to join in north and south Germany and in Italy were
actually admitted. How far this fell in with the mind of
Ignatius is easy to see—apart from what we have said—
from his letter to Cardinal Pole. Pole had been a most
competent guide of Catholic affairs in England . . . The
letter runs as follows:

'The grace and charity of Christ be with you . . .

'From your Most Reverend Lordship's letter dated at
Brussels, 11 November [1554]'—at this time Pole was
preparing for his journey to England—'I understand the
high hopes you have had from God of bringing that kingdom once again into the unity of Catholic faith . . . I am
aware of the charity with which [you] embrace this least
Society of ours; and that even in the middle of most
important business you do not forget us; and you remain
anxious to know how we are getting on. You will be
glad to hear that things are going better in the Roman and
German Colleges. Apart from sixty who live in the
professed house, in the college itself more than seventy are
in residence. All the sciences are taught, save law and
medicine, with great profit for our own members and for
the external students. These are numerous—more than
five hundred, in fact. Those in the German college make
most progress in learning and good life . . . There is one
Englishman among them, a man of high talent and good
disposition. In our own college there is an Irishman, a
man likewise of great promise. If in future you should see
fit to send from where you are men inclined by nature
and natural ability to study to either college, I am sure
they would return after a short while with great advantage for their learning and living, and with a profound
respect for this Holy See. It is carefully ensured that if

there is anything wholesome in this city they will be
imbued with it in our houses; and anything here to the
contrary will not harm them. Please be so good as to
examine the whole question more closely. We have made
it our business to offer to others what the divine love has
put in our own souls . . . Rome, 24 January 1555.'

7.   It will be clear, then, from the saint's own words
how great was his love for the England of that time so
deeply torn by schism. Lainez followed his footsteps.
So did succeeding generals, not a few of whom admitted
and helped Englishmen. Thus it came about that Polanco
wrote in Lainez's name from Trent on 21 September
1562, to Francis Borgia, then doing duty in Italy, 'George
Ware, a young Englishman anxious to join the Society,
carries this letter. He seems suited for life by our rule.
He has made his confession and Holy Communion here.
In the judgment of our Father he can be admitted to the
noviceship, and if, in the course of visiting the colleges,
he wishes to stay at any of them, it will be permissible to
receive him as a guest'. Again, Polanco wrote to Everard
Mercurian on 7 November 1564, 'You write that four or
five young Englishmen are coming from there to Rome.
We have been waiting for them, and for others of whom
the rector of Louvain wrote. They have not yet put in
an appearance. It is to be feared that they may not have
been able to get as far as Italy. This is something which
happens to many coming from Germany'. Further, on
20 December, 'At last the young Englishmen previously
written about have arrived in Rome. One was overcome
by fatigue, and had to stay in Milan. Another, Rogers
by name (Rogerius), is hardly cut out for the Society.
We have therefore asked for a place for him in the German
College. He wanted this himself. Rogers has only three
crowns, but he needs clothing, bedding and other necessities, and four crowns a month to be earmarked for food
and accommodation. We have come to an arrangement
until his mother provides. The Englishmen in Rome
have made no contribution, beyond persuading him not

to enter the Society for a time! Of the other three one
is rather old and of sketchy education. The remaining
two are young men, but likewise not very well educated.
We received them here since they were worn out, after
their long journey, and had nowhere else to go. We felt
sorry for their plight. Otherwise they would not have
been admitted. You must make sure in future that we
know what to expect before you think of sending anyone
here, so that reply may be received from us before they
set out: unless, that is, anyone of such excellent attainments offers himself that his case leaves no room for
doubt . . .'. But whatever the numbers of these and other
groups, the mature fruit of their labour was not yet to
be seen in England. There the Society was for all intents
and purposes unknown before 1580. In other countries,
however, were men whose work cannot allow them to be
passed over in silence.

8.   Among the most noteworthy was Father William
      Good (*alias* Gorde). Mercurian, then a Provincial,
witnessed his dexterity with the spiritual exercises, and
sent him to Tournai in Flanders (in 1562). He was then
35 years old. Born and brought up at Glastonbury (at
the hospice of St. Joseph of Arimathea for gentlemen),*
he afterwards studied philosophy and theology at Oxford,
proceeding M.A. He received as the reward of brilliant
studies two ecclesiastical benefices, apart from a canonry,
and with praise from those who conferred them. But
when the schism which arose in England became heresy,
he gave up all this and his country as well . . . He did his
years of noviceship, and then joined a certain Father David
as companion to go into Ireland with the Archbishop of
Armagh. This was a man most devoted to the Society who
left nothing undone to keep his country in the Catholic
faith and obedience to the Holy See. Good spent four
years in that island with no evident result. But his labours
were incessant; and we may take as example what
happened one day when he was going along with a bundle
of altar-equipment. He was attacked by a number of

Irishmen hiding in the woods who took his package. When they came to open it up, they saw he was a priest (*see* Polanco's letters for 27 July and 4 September 1564). They therefore hurried after him, and falling to their knees, stretched their arms to the sky. The good Father could not understand them nor they him, although they shouted all the time. But it was in a language of which he was ignorant. By their gestures, however, their meaning was sufficiently clear. One of them, seizing the Father's hand, made the sign of the cross with it over his companions as though to absolve them. He then tried to get himself absolved by the ceremony using the hand of someone else in the company. But it was a piece of ritual vain and empty; as they fled from the spot it occurred to none of them to restore Father Good's bag!

In 1570, Good returned to Flanders where, even in the middle of theological studies, he continued to wield the sword of the spirit. To his industry, after God, the English Province owes its well-known son Robert Persons. He met Persons when the latter was breaking his journey at Louvain. Good taught him how to use the spiritual exercises of St. Ignatius. As he worked through them, he roused in Persons a distaste for the mundane which eventually overcame every other feeling. From Louvain Good went to Rome in 1577, where he was called to solemn profession of the four vows. He was destined next for Sweden, and afterwards Poland, being Anthony Possevin's companion for a time. From that Province Good went with Father Adam Brook, another Englishman, to accompany the Provincial to the fourth General Congregation, and with a right to vote. Good took part in the election of . . . Claud Aquaviva as General in 1580. Two years later he was serving in the English hospice, Rome—not yet formed into a seminary from the hospice of the Holy Trinity—as confessor. He fulfilled the task admirably, as increasing demands by the students of that time for stricter discipline bear witness; and also the unwavering vows taken by very many to undergo every labour, and even death, in order to keep the cause of their faith alive.

From Rome, Good went to Naples: which proved for
him a city of no lasting habitation. He died there in
1586. During his 25 years in the Society, he gained a
reputation for conscientiousness and sound sense. For a
memorial of these qualities, he left behind him the story
of the saints of England painted in colour on the walls
of the English College chapel. They were published
anonymously in Rome in a set of copper engravings
under the title, *Ecclesiae Anglicanae Trophaea* (*see*
Alegambe, S. J.). There is also extant in the English
College, Rome, a manuscript codex of the saints of the
Christian era in Britain, and a digest of the history of the
Kings of Britain and England, which he is said to have
compiled, briefly relating their deeds and assessing their
merits.

9.   Edmund Bonner, Bishop of London . . . had a
      nephew, Thomas Darbishire, as chancellor of his
diocese, and later as companion of his adversity. Darbishire suffered imprisonment and deprivation of the ample
property which he had built up by his uncle's favour
and his own skill in civil and canon law, of which he
was doctor . . . While Philip and Mary ruled he had presided by royal warrant over a society called by the name
of Jesus whose business it was to distribute alms, and
that generously. Not long afterwards, being unanimously
elected to take the place of a dead London member, he
came to preside over another college; this time of priests,
which took its title from the Lord's table . . . Subsequently, he offered himself to Lainez while that worthy
man was present at the deliberations of the Council
of Trent (1536).

10.   Ordered to go to Rome, Darbishire entered the
      Society in his 45th year, being enrolled on 1 May
1563. He moved to Dillingen before taking first vows.
He was asked, as was usual, whether he would be willing
to teach in any of the schools, for as long as obedience
directed . . . After he had spent some years disseminating
the welcome perfume of his goodness in Dillingen, he

was called to France as master of novices at Billom (Toulouse province) . . . (*see* Catalogue for 1568). He was a good mixer, ready for any task to keep the peace, or calling for the exercise of kindness and goodwill. He was sent to Paris for some years to lecture in Latin to the young sodalists. After this, he gave public lectures on Christian doctrine to large audiences at Pont à Mousson. Darbishire spiced his talks with many a fine flourish and shaft of specialised knowledge, so that he was listened to very willingly by the young, and, indeed, to their great profit. Even theologians of merit went so far as to admit that his words deserved an ampler auditory. Lest they should perish with their own pronouncement, certain excerpts of his oratory were carefully committed to writing . . . In 1572, Father Thomas was professed of the four vows. He returned first to Rome, and then to Pont à Mousson. There he eventually died in 1604, at the ripe age of 86. He had been 41 years in the Society. . . .

11. Adam Brook (Brooche) was born in a respectable part of London, and early given a good education. He spent five years in higher studies at Oxford, but when the ideas of the Reformers came to prevail, he fled overseas. Such was his character and eminent ability that he was admitted at Rome as a Jesuit towards the close of 1564. He was then 22 years old. After the noviceship, he was sent to Lithuania to do philosophy once again. He stayed on there to fulfil with distinction the highest offices in the province. He was rector of the college at Vilna, master of novices for four years, and then spiritual father for many more. He did everything with such care and eye for detail that the annual letters of those places describe him, with a flourish of metaphorical eloquence, as having begotten in Christ all the outstanding Fathers of his province! Furthermore, among his labours was that of expounding for 20 years at Bransberg and Vilna the points at issue with the separated brethren in matters of conscience and doctrine. This he did to packed audiences, winning no less esteem for his doctrine than

his devotion. He was especially dear to the Bishop of Vilna and Samogitia, but was highly regarded by the whole body of his clergy. In 1580, Brook was present, as we have said above, with Father William Good at the General Congregation, and with the right to vote. He died in 1605; and his manner of leaving this life matched his way of living it. He was genuinely mourned by everybody when his death occurred on 5 July. He had been professed of the four vows since 1578.

12. Laurence Arthur Faunt, working in the same region, wrote up memorials of the Society. Ribedeneira and Alegambe diligently listed them so it will scarcely inconvenience the reader to omit further mention of them here. Faunt came from good Leicestershire stock, but withdrew comparatively early to Europe . . . He was not more than 16 years old when he began to study logic, along with the external students of Louvain, but he was admitted to the Society in 1570. He studied theology in Rome; was sent to Poland, and spent much time at Poznan in debating matters of religion. He managed to keep within the bounds the temerity of some admittedly not very significant preachers who strove against him. He also published books, and taught higher studies. Faunt gained a far from indifferent reputation throughout the land both for goodness of life and the forcefulness of his teaching. He died of disease at Vilna in 1591 after recently professing the four vows (*see* Pitzius, 1591).

13. Other shining examples of wisdom and goodness flourished throughout Germany and Flanders. The Ingolstadt catalogue calls to remembrance John Vick [or Wick], an Oxford man and professor of philosophy and moral theology. The Roman record witnesses that he also taught rhetoric, Greek literature and other subjects. After taking his four vows in August 1588 he was lost to the living in the September following, but only after 25 years of usefulness in the Society.

Thomas Williams, also of Oxford, after hearing philosophy at Rome, went to Vienna for his theology.

He then taught grammarians for about four months, and afterwards expounded mathematics for 22 years at Olmutz. Nor was he overlooked in the distribution of other offices, for he carried out successfully the function of minister, procurator, confessor and admonitor before spending 13 years in a boarding-school as vice-prefect. He lived until 1611, bringing learning and holiness to his status of spiritual coadjutor. [He died] when he had completed 47 years in the Society, having arrived at the good age of seventy . . .

14. Another spiritual coadjutor who did much in several provinces by his good qualities and unflagging exertions was Richard Storey of Salisbury. He joined the Society at Tournai in Flanders at the age of sixteen. He stayed at several colleges in Germany, and perspired through several years of teaching the elements to junior forms. Called away eventually to Loretto, and after that to Florence, he finally settled in Vienna, 'where his selflessness and modesty, and the solid qualities which the Society demands of us all, left behind discernible effects'; hence his name found its way into the annual letters from Vienna (1600). Storey subsequently became involved in the Hungarian wars with the Turks, and fully engaged as far as his natural human sympathy could go. While serving men he somehow managed to remember the man . . . After enormous toil and a love of neighbour which did not flag, he left this life for the better one on 18 September 1600 . . . It was discovered in a diary that in the last nine months of his life he had heard 3,288 confessions among the laity, not to mention numerous students of our own, and others outside the Society, who had made general confessions to him.

15. Likewise destined for expeditions into Transsylvania was John Howlett. Born in Rutland, he set out for Rome in 1568. Howlett was admitted to Louvain in 1571; at the very time when Leonard Lessius was doing his noviceship by way of preparation for the excellent things he did and wrote later. Howlett left an

unfriendly England behind him at the age of 22 to become a celebrated teacher of philosophy in exile. He then joined the Society, studied theology at Douai, and then spent the next 10 years, partly in Flanders and partly in Germany, teaching grammar, rhetoric, Greek and Hebrew, mathematics and ethics, and finally moral theology. He died the year after coming to Vilna in Lithuania [1587].

16. The two Rastalls, John and Edward, from Glouces-
     tershire, were admitted at Rome in 1568, and, since there was still no way open for us into England, were intended for Germany. What happened to Edward, however, after he did his theology at Ingolstadt, remains a mystery. But John became a priest before admission to the Society, and functioned as consultor and confessor at Halle prior to being sent to Augsburg. Finally, he died in memorable circumstances at Ingolstadt while still rector [in June 1577] . . .*

17. Thomas Stephenson must also be remembered in
     connection with these foreign provinces. We meet him as an exile in the neighbourhood of Watten. He laid his foundation in the Society at Brunn in Moravia. Subsequently, he spent 14 years at Olmutz and Prague teaching rhetoric, Greek and Hebrew. But we must push back further to find the beginnings of this man's labours. He was born at Windleston in the diocese of Durham, and afterwards studied philosophy and theology first at Rheims and then at Rome. After ordination, he was sent to the English harvest at the instance of Allen and Persons. In February 1584 a Protestant magistrate delivered up two priests of good life and doctrine, James Fen and George Haddock, to shameful death . . . The very next day, Stephenson was captured and put in the Tower of London. For 27 days his bed was the bare ground. For another 39 days he was loaded with irons; and then, at the turn of the year, on 22 January, he was sent into exile with 19 other priests who had been gaoled with him (Ribadeneira, Book 2, chapter 38: some give June for

January). After this, he went to Rome, and helped Persons for a time with embellishments to his history. He returned to England and worked there strenuously for many years. Finally, when he was over 70, he was laid to rest at Watten. In his spare time he wrote a life of Thomas Pounde (v. infra), which filled a substantial volume, drawn up from Pounde's own adversaries. He also translated many works of Persons into Latin out of the English. In addition, he wrote a history of the world, but this served rather as an exercise for himself, perhaps, than an aid to posterity.

18. John Gibbons, of Wells, also preferred poverty with his Christ to a good time in the world. He joined the Society at Trèves on 8 October 1578. He studied philosophy and theology in the German College, Rome, making such good progress that he acquired a doctorate in both. Showing equal mastery in Christian doctrine, handling of souls, and understanding of his fellow-men, he was invested by order of Gregory XIII with a canonry at Bonn, near Cologne.* But . . . he entered the Society instead. The number of offices which he filled—and with universal approval—could be taken as the measure of his success. With results no less happy, he wielded his pen . . . A certain George Schone of Heidelberg brought out a disputation sneering at the chief shepherd of the Catholics as none other than anti-Christ. John clean wiped away his mud, and snubbed his impertinence with learned quill. Gibbons also published his reflections on the cultus of saints, and on holy communion in one kind. He must also, with justice, be considered the author of the *Concertatio Ecclesiae Anglicanae,* set out in three volumes; even if John Bridgewater put the finishing touches thereto, and dedicated an enlarged edition to the Elector of Trèves in 1594. Eleven years before, Gibbons had already given it to the press, so that the inhuman barbarities practised on the Catholics by the Calvinists would be evident for all to see. The offices Gibbons filled in the Society were the result of his learning and good religious sense. For

he expounded theology and questions in sacred scripture,
and was prefect of studies into the bargain. Afterwards,
he was spiritual father to our own men as well as the
students; and later still rector, at the college of Trèves.
He died in 1589, not less renowned for his wisdom in
guiding souls than for his learning and religious spirit when
it came to teaching.

19.   Richard, younger brother of the above but before
      him in the Society, may conveniently be dealt with
here since he laboured to old age among the people of
Flanders, assisting the English there from time to time
and as he was called upon. He received his earlier education in England; did a year's philosophy at Louvain, and
another at Rome in the German College. Then, in 1572,
he was received into the Society, spending another three
years in philosophy. After the allotted course of theology,
he toiled away in Rome and France for another 13 years,
teaching mathematics and philosophy. He expounded
Scripture and Hebrew at Coimbra, and was professed of
the four vows in that famous college. In 1591 he was again
sent to Louvain to unravel mathematics for the students,
and carry out other duties and labours usual in the
Society. Although he sometimes preached in St. Omer's,
and performed other services there, Douai was virtually his
permanent *point d'appui.* He brought to the press the
Decachorda of Viguerius, the supplement to Toletus's
course for priests, the sermons of Amadeus, Harpsfield's
history, and various other works. He also had in preparation the pronouncements of the Fathers, arranged by
chapters in alphabetical order, a colossal work involving
untold labour, but offering material to hand immediately
for sermon subjects, whatever else might be said about
it. Death robbed the parent of all earthly light before this
foetus was sufficiently formed to reach its own light
of day. He was in his 80s when he died; but it was years
he still wanted, rather than understanding, to provide the
colophon for a work to crown those other works of the
years that lay behind him.

20. In the Flanders catalogue, I find four other Englishmen who spent their working lives in the same
praiseworthy manner at Douai. Roger Bolbet [or Bolbert]
of Staffordshire completed nearly 13 years in the Society
before he died after ministering to the sick, and of the
disease he caught from them . . . on 2 September 1572.
The citizens of Douai thought so highly of him that at
one time they contemplated erecting a monument to
his memory at public expense (Sacchino, *History,* part iii,
Book 8, No. 228). John Burstard [Bustard] of Oxford
was admitted to the Society in his 19th year; and after
the noviceship was immediately given the task of professing metaphysics. After successfully negotiating theology,
he transferred to Douai where he was set to teach the
whole course of philosophy. A premature death removed
his gifts to heaven before he had been at the work a year;
and before he had reached the age of 27 (*see* the Louvain
catalogue for 1570, and that of Douai for 1576). Thomas
Martial [Marshall], a priest, and doctor of philosophy,
and also of theology, entered the Society at Louvain.
He taught philosophy at Douai for nine years, being then
called away to Rome to act as confessor in the English
College (*see* St. Omer catalogue, 1584). There he did not
survive long. Being visited by some disease, they transferred him to the Roman College for a more effective cure.
He died: but not before being professed of the four vows,
breathing his last on 22 July 1589. Then there was John
Columb of Devonshire who entered the Society at Louvain
in his 26th year. He was subsequently appointed principal
confessor to the Douai seminary, and preached until he
was 82 . . . when he died, after completing 10 years in
the Society.

21. We see also among the names associated with Douai
that of Thomas Coniers, who, after receiving a doctorate of philosophy, was admitted to the Society at
Tournai in 1584. After humane studies, and teaching logic
at Douai, he laboured energetically at Landen (? Lendium)
and Bapaume on the borders of France. He carried out

various other tasks, going to Rome in 1600. Later, he
returned to Flanders. Making Dinant his headquarters,
he ranged the vast solitude of the Ardennes, visiting
villages and hamlets, bringing to the thirsty souls of the
poverty-stricken inhabitants the refreshing waters of
Christian doctrine. Hence the townspeople were always
extremely pleased to welcome his colleagues also. For
their labours might be expected to continue to bear the
fruit planted and tended by Father Thomas (Bartholomew
Fizen, *Flores,* 1647). Their reputation had already begun
to grow among them under Lainez. Henry Somalio also
put in some hard work. He had opened schools aspiring
to be colleges, although without consulting Lainez.
Indeed, he strove in this undertaking for more than 10
years against the difficulties of those most troubled times
until all was on the point of collapse. The driving energy
of Father Thomas then appeared on the scene to revive
flagging spirits, and call and encourage members of the
Society. Some were sent to Liège to hold the ground by
patrols, as it were, until a more secure redoubt was
established. By 1612 this had grown into a college.
Once the college was founded, Father Thomas travelled
the whole province, operating effectively from the borders
of Hainault to the confines of Germany and among all
kinds of men. He never jibbed at the hardships of a
journey, crossing mountains and forest, going through
snow, hail, heat and sun that burnt; for his delight was
to be with even the less polished children of men. Preaching, confessing, expounding the catechism, he even
snatched extra time for such things before dawn and
after sunset.

Coniers worked with the same kind of zeal and the same
kind of fruit at Bastogne, a town almost in the middle of
the Ardennes, which had once been as miserable for the
neglect of its people's souls as for the poverty of the soil.
Indeed, so great became the veneration of the folk there
for him that, when the sign was given, at any hour of any
day, they would leave their occupations and flock to hear
him preach. Since the times were such that he could not

get the Society to put a college in the place, although he did his best, he made himself instrumental in getting the members of another religious Order to come in and fan the enthusiasm so happily kindled. Similarly, nuns well-versed in the spiritual life were brought from Dinant, and began classes for the girls . . . Nothing seemed difficult for a man who combined innate integrity, zeal for the faith, and dislike of the limelight, with decent reticence. He dressed like a poor man, ate sparingly, and prayed always . . . Busied with all this, he reached his 77th year, his 53rd in the Society. Returning from the country one Christmastide, he contracted an illness which proved fatal. When he had first entered the noviceship at Tournai he began to suffer sharp pains in the kidneys and bladder, so that the doctors decided he could not continue in the Society without being a burden to it. He was therefore told to leave. After praying to our Lady, however, he felt all his pain leave him, and after this cure, by her intervention as he piously believed, he sought for admission to the Society once again. The disease caught up with him now in old age, when he was worn out with work. In this also he saw proof that it was by our Lady's special benefit that he had lived and laboured to any good effect in the Society . . . He died on 24 January 1639. He was professed of three vows about 1600; for out of humility he refused, being then at Rome, to take the fourth.

22.   Of the rest whom time bore away in upper and lower Germany, their life was so brief that we can only guess from their beginnings how much praise they would have earned at an end longer delayed. We can hardly laud them for actual achievement. Giles Fesard, admitted at Rome, went to Prague after his studies, and became socius to Paul Campani, master of novices. He lasted one year. Hugh Scrivener of Hereford was teaching grammar at Brunn in 1590. Otherwise nothing is recorded of him. William Powell, from the diocese of St. Asaph, after 10 years in the Society and teaching the humanities, went to Cologne in 1597. What happened to him afterwards

does not appear. Elizeus Haywood, a Londoner, and graduate in civil law, spent some useful time at Halle teaching the catechism to unlettered persons—he derived extraordinary satisfaction from this—and then went to Flanders, doing service as preacher and spiritual director at Antwerp. He saw his last day at Louvain after 12 years in the Society. With what peace of mind he surrendered his possessions when he joined the same becomes abundantly clear from a letter to him from the General Everard Mercurian written on 15 January 1574. 'Concerning the distribution of your goods', he says, 'I cannot but heartily approve what Father Francis Borgia, of holy memory, laid down. His Reverence considered that equal portions should be made over to the colleges at Louvain, Cologne and Munich. Of the other income, 500 florins, which, as you write, you leave entirely to my judgment, I do not see what college would better profit by the bequest than Louvain'. So Mercurian. Elizeus, indeed, did not consider as goods at all what most men regard as goods par excellence. Philip Harrison of Oxford completed his studies at Pont à Mousson; took a doctorate in philosophy, and professed it at Würzburg; and later, ethics and mathematics. Eventually, he was summoned to Rome to St. Peter's, and after being professed of four vows set out for England. He died the year after [1578].

William Eaton, a Derbyshire man, lectured on philosophy and mathematics together at Cologne, Trèves and Mayence; and then on moral theology at Molsheim, where he subsequently filled almost all the remaining offices and dignities until 1606. Adam Higgins, Londoner, expounded the philosophers for nine years at Dillingen and Ingolstadt. He also taught secular and church history, and lectured on disputed questions in ethics. He came to Louvain as a man of ripe years, and for that reason was transferred first to Lisbon and then to Seville, where he was the confessor to the English students and later to the English merchants and factors there. He grew old in that place, where he ended his life and labours some time after 1615.* Robert Arden of Chichester was admitted at Louvain on 7 April 1565. He proved himself a competent worker in practically every ministry of the Society. He is on record as having taught the humanities and mathematics, and functioned as minister, procurator, spiritual father, preacher, penitentiary at Loretto and in St. Peter's. I cannot ascertain where he finally took wing for his eternal reward. These were the men who worked in northern Europe.

23. How much England owes to Spain and Italy in the way of hospitality and education is so obvious to every nation in Europe, and so widely known in England, that it would be indecent to pass over the fact in silence lest we seem ungrateful. Nor can we be too ready with our acknowledgment lest we appear too little vocal for so signal a benefit. Although the change from native food and air brought death to many, both countries gave most of them back to England again, and supported them in their labours. Humphrey Woodward's memory is cherished at Milan where he expounded Sacred Scripture for many years, winning an extraordinary appreciation for his deep learning; Possevin made a note of his commentaries in his own *Apparatus* . . . A manuscript of Woodward's is still extant in that province, as John Stephen Menocchi bears ample witness, who was provincial there and in the Roman Province. He himself ranked with the writers most admired.* Humphrey died on 30 November 1587. A letter of one of the Breras honours him with the following, 'The English priest Humphrey has died. He was a man of wonderful erudition, and deeply versed in the things of God'.

Edmund Harewood took a degree in philosophy before he joined the Society. He did the theology course at Rome, where he took up a residence that was to be permanent. We find that he spent 19 years there altogether as penitentiary at St. Peter's, or as minister at the English College. Afterwards, he was moved to the noviceship on the Quirinal to recover his health. He is reported to have died a holy death on 21 September 1597. Simon Hunt was

admitted before Edmund on 27 April 1578, also while
discharging the office of penitentiary. He died on 11 June
1585. Richard Tancred, however, a young man of 22,
did his studies at Olmutz and Prague, and then taught
Greek for two years at Vienna. He was summoned to
Italy, and died at Padua on 13 September 1596.

24. Sicily received Thomas Warcop, though he did not
      live long. . . . He reached his 23rd year as a young
man more than ordinarily well-read, and quick-witted
enough in expounding the questions put forward by
Reformers in debate—or so it seemed to him. . . .! He
came to Rheims where the English Seminary had recently
arrived from Douai. The particular citizen with whom
he found lodging was a Catholic. . . . Warcop came back
to the Church, and, indeed, became a priest at Rome
after some years of study there. He was subsequently
sent to Sicily in order to beg alms for his friends at
Rheims. In Sicily he sought admittance to the Society.
This was in 1587, and on Easter Day he was admitted at
Messina. Before he had finished his noviceship he was
called away to Spain to a new seminary which the Catholic
King had founded. He died on the journey at Alicante on
19 October 1589.

25. William Brunsley (or Brunsbey) [vere Brookesby]
      also came to the Society. . . . But although his zeal
for the good life and running the race set before him
reached the equivalent of a life much longer, he did not,
in fact, complete his novitiate. He was English. It will
not be out of place to put here the unusual story of
his struggle to remain celibate, which is told at length in
the annual letters for 1585, albeit the name was somewhat
changed there out of error. 'William Brusbey', they run,
'was an Englishman who died in the Roman College after
joining the Society. He was born into a distinguished
family, and at the age of 14 was sent to Douai for his
schooling. There he first came to know the Society, and
conceived a desire to join it. However, this good intention

had not yet sent down roots, and on his return to England was thrust aside, albeit by forgetfulness rather than deliberate intention. He was 22 when he struck up a close friendship with a good Catholic girl. Natural instincts now began to urge, as is normal, its own more pressing necessity, and the bond of marriage. His friend assured him of his approval if he wished to take his sister to wife. Indeed, he began to persuade him that he should. It seemed to be against friendship to repudiate such a match; nor was the idea of marriage by any means irksome to the young man. He loved the girl, and the girl loved him: and once they got to know one another they passed many a pleasant hour together. However, Providence saw to it that no thought entered the young man's head that was inconsistent with chastity. All the same, lest any should snatch this blossom from him, the Lord took pity on inexperience adolescence, and rekindled in his mind that former interest in the Society which now seemed moribund.

Such became the flame of this other desire that, putting aside all thought of marriage, he not only gave up all he actually possessed of wealth and fortune, but even the prospect of his father's inheritance. He began to prepare his escape. When the girl's mother and brothers got wind thereof they fairly rounded on William. By rebuking this sudden whim of his, and the alleged breach of promise involved, they tried to make him change his mind. The ladies besieged him with tears and entreaties. The brothers threatened him with all kinds of terrible things. 'You must keep your word once given', they raged. 'You cannot get a marriage on foot with all your incessant talk of love, and then with any decency throw it over!' William tried to point out that he had not made any promise; that he had not said a word to support their argument. After tossing it backwards and forwards, they finally told the girl to wait in her room with the door open; and then to jump out at the right moment. What right and reason could not do might be done by a little of the right kind of feminine persuasion. The girl did as planned. With the

aid of nature and the paint-pot, not to mention the honey
of her approaches and the gentle sweetness of her rebukes,
she drove the young man hard. She begged him with all
that was in her not to turn her away. She assured him
there was nothing in her birth, natural gifts or fortune
for him to look down on. Could he treat thus brotherly
love and her own? Was this how he solemnised a marriage
so ardently implored and practically concluded? If she
were thus cast off, he would be seared in his person and
honour with a mark of shame that would never fade. All
this somehow failed to move him. Indeed, he found
himself thinking more of the good life than of a good
wife in the life he was offered. He did not say anything
more, even by way of farewell. He simply left the house.
Soon he made his way to France; and not long afterwards
to Rome. He had not completed his two years' noviceship
when it became evident that a short and concentrated
life was to accomplish for him what normally took much
longer. With little more delay he left this confining existence for eternity. . . . He may well be the young fellow
described in Bridgewater's *Concertatio* as coming from an
ancient and well-to-do-family with lands in Somerset,
and tutored by James Fen, subsequently a martyr. He
was described as so firm in faith and goodness that no
enticement could shake him. He left his country of his
own freewill . . . and made it his chief concern to join
the Society. He died a holy death a few months after
admission. . . . Not long before he died, Bridgewater's
book was first published—in 1588.*

26. William Hart, a youth of 18 and among the first to
     be accepted at the English College, Rome, joined
the Society before he had finished two years there. He
passed from the college only to be numbered with the
angels. . . . George Gilbert may here be considered with
the others. He was the host of our Fathers and other
priests in England during most turbulent times. A nobleman (comes), and most generous benefactor of priests,
he died about this time [6 October 1583] in the English

College, Rome. Before he died, however, he was able to make his vows in the Society by order of the General. It will be more in place to sing his praises when we come to deal with the work of Persons . . .*

27. Although many were moved at this opening stage by a well-considered desire to join the Society, it is evident that not all remained firm. Some collapsed through weak foundations; others were carried away by the evil tendencies of the times. Sacchini tells in his *Borgia* how Edward Thorne, a young Englishman of 24, tried to join the Society, not because he was moved by the good life, or inspired by faith, but simply to escape poverty. Before he had completed the two years' noviceship he was applying himself to rhetoric at Dillingen. The flaw in his intention was discovered in the following way. Some doubt was felt at that time about the Jesuit philosophers Klessel and Simon regarding the orthodoxy of their religious views. In the beginning of the year, new preceptors were appointed. This was made the occasion for carrying out Pius IV's decree concerning the profession of faith which had to be made. It was proposed to everybody. Conscience, as he claimed, prevented Edward from taking it; and he said he would give his reasons in another place. The unexpected hesitancy on the part of the young man somewhat perplexed the bystanders, but he behaved so discreetly that no one suspected anything. When there was no one else present, he was asked the cause. He replied that he did not feel certain enough to commit himself concerning the cult of saints, purgatorial fire, the Real Presence, and many other matters. He was reminded that many aspects of these things are by their nature obscure, but in the last resort, the judgment of the Church Universal must be accepted as a true rule and guide. Many days were spent in disputation. In the end, he thought more of his own inspiration than of all the decrees of Supreme Pontiffs and Councils, and while on his way to the provincial at Ingolstadt, being loosely guarded, he escaped to a town in the hands of the Protestants near

Dillingen. About the same time, Klessel and Simon, without giving any open sign of dissent, suddenly ran to cover. Not long afterwards, they abandoned both the Society and Catholic faith, though with a different sequel in each case. Klessel, after wandering for a time amid uncertainties, returned to his original way of thinking, and fought to defend the ancient faith in speech and writing. Simon, while sharpening a quill at Louvain with which to jab the Society, came to blows with an enemy who suddenly crossed his path. He was killed.

Not unlike Edward in his line of action, but coming to a heavier fall, Thomas Longdall (Langdale), a priest, brought dishonour to himself and his brethren after nearly 20 years in the Society. It is established that he was admitted to the Society on 21 May 1562. His departure in 1582 is narrated in these words: 'Thomas Langdale was a priest of mature age and experience who performed the function of penitentiary at Loretto and Rome. This calls for a man of serious demeanour. But being summoned to Rome by the General, he took an English boat from Genoa. For some unknown reason he went to England where he ignobly apostatized'. Perhaps this is the Doctor Langdale noted by Persons in his memoirs as having disseminated at that time a treatise on [not] approaching the sacraments of the sectaries, notwithstanding the royal edict and fines inflicted on those who disobeyed. Many of the less convinced brethren [later] followed him into schism until works published by Persons and others against these rites taught them that the absence of a law is one thing, quite another the passing of a law designed to impose conformity. I would prefer to ascribe this commotion to Thomas rather than to Alan Langdale whose goodness, learning and enthusiasm for God's glory made quite a name for him, as Pits bears witness. Alan also flourished in the days of Queen Elizabeth.*

28. Christopher Perkins, likewise, did rather less than the best he might have done with the gifts of God. In fact, he was expelled from the Society, and eventually

lost his faith not only in that institution but in Catholicism as well. He was admitted at Rome on 21 October 1566, as a youth of nineteen. After passing the years of his noviceship and philosophy in Rome, he heard theology at Dillingen with sufficient profit to get himself employed on occasion as assistant lecturer to James of Valentia at Ingolstadt. He perservered until about 1580. Then he went to Cologne and elsewhere in Germany, making no little noise, and giving full rein to his talents of which he was very well aware. He made trouble inside and outside the Society; nor did warnings make any difference, until the Society decided it was better to forego his genius rather than the peace which could not be enjoyed while he was around. In England he found favour, thanks to his good appearance, and compliance with the doctrine of Elizabeth. He came to be counted among the pillars of her ecclesiastical discipline; was advanced to the rank of knight, and sent on embassy to Denmark, Switzerland and Venice. In the reign of James, he was considered to be the man who devised the oath which confused the due obedience of the subject to his monarch and that which was owing to the Pope's authority. It taxed the knowledge and conscience of a great many people, and was eventually condemned by the breves of Paul V and Urban VIII. Finally, at a good old age but at the end of a life far from good, Perkins finished his course as he had come to run it . . .*

29. Although perseverance was lacking in others who were admitted, they still managed to live good lives. Among these were Hugh Griffith, John and Thomas Wright, and one of the best-known writers of his day, Thomas Stapleton, whom the Flemish catalogues place among the novices of 1584. He had written to Rome about the happy lot in which his youth would be renewed like that of the eagle. What was it that altered him from a man with a vocation to the religious life, turned his eyes away from his own country, and brought him to reject the life of a priest living among his own people to carry

on the faith? They say that he was wont to remark that his weak will was unequal to the obedience demanded by the Society. At all events, as he became more renowned, so his opinion of the Society grew more appreciative. Pits describes him as follows: 'He was a man of piercing intelligence, sound judgment, deep erudition, astonishing industry and capacity for work, to say nothing of zeal. An accomplished and convincing orator, he was well-grounded in apologetics; had holy scripture at his finger-tips. Finally, he had arrived at such a pitch of mastery in his own field that he was considered, not unjustly, as one of the most learned men of his age. His reputation was so high, even with Pope Clement, that he was rated next after Allen as deserving the cardinal's scarlet. But death cut him off prematurely'. How much he attributed to the Society at his departure may be learnt from what he wrote to the General, Claud Aquaviva, from Douai, on 5 May 1587: 'I think this academy is sufficient witness of the fact that the foundations of my spiritual life laid down in the noviceship of your Society have not completely decayed. For it has now heard me give forth God's truth for several months. I do not think I would have taken on such a task for any other reason than the love of human beings which I imbibed in the well-ordered life of your schools. Humbly, I ask your Fatherhood that you will consider me, whether here in this place or in England: if, that is, it should seem good to Providence that I finished with exile, although I am well past middle-age. In any case, I will always show myself in word and deed a genuine admirer and respectful friend of your Society'.

30.   Now to return to other Englishmen working abroad.
   . . . Some of them aspired to give their lives to the Indian mission. Among these were Edmund Harewood, already mentioned, and Thomas Cottam. While they were still novices they applied for that mission, but did not get leave. John Yate and Thomas Stephens did. Yate entered the Society on 4 December 1574. He was recorded

as still alive in Brazil in 1601. Three years later, in his 54th year, and 29th as a Jesuit, whether from home-sickness or some other cause, he managed to get back to England. He was put in irons, though continuing to live a holy life and very close to the Society; but as some say, he was released from his vows before he set out, so as to be free for so hazardous a journey. When he observed any of our men behaving not quite according to the book he would say, 'Brother, you did not pick that up in the Society!' Some consider him to have been a Jesuit at his death. In the annals for 1624 we find, 'John Yate, Priest, was over 70 when, at the point of death, he was received into the Society. All speak of his good example whether as a man at liberty or in chains'.

Thomas Stephens, of the Salisbury diocese, was admitted a year later. He made an urgent plea to be sent to the Indian mission, and, indeed, arrived at Goa on 24 October 1579. He not only got to know the Malabar tongue but to know it well. He was rector of Salsete College, Goa, for five years, and is reported to have looked after 19 parishes in the island. He not only did much, but wrote much, that proved of great value to his people. He filled many rôles in the Society such as minister in the professed house in Goa, *socius* to the Visitor, and other tasks, and was active in that vineyard to the very end. He survived until 1609, being a formed co-adjutor from 1589. All the same, his distant wanderings and that of others seem to have put it into Allen's head about this time to complain to Gregory XIII, and the Jesuits themselves, about the poor distribution of labour involved in sending people who could do good work in their own country to the other ends of the earth. The outcome of this complaint we shall see in due course.

31. That many lay-brothers also came from England to join the Society at this time could doubtless be deduced merely from the holiness of brothers of this epoch! It could be concluded also from the readiness of Generals to admit them, and also from the overall

disposition and giftedness of so many men from our shores
for the duties of such. Nevertheless, in all these years I
can only find record of three, namely John Pellison,
William Lambert and Ralph Emerson; unless one also
wishes to include the names of those written down as of
uncertain allocation either for study or for physical
labour. Such was Thomas Lith, a Londoner, coming to
the Society at 19 in June 1555; 13 months before the
death of our founder. There was another, Thomas Christmas (? Natalis) [Noel?] who joined the professed house
of Rome on 2 October 1556. Perhaps also William Roussell
[Russell?] admitted at Rome in 1563. Certainly, Oliver
Manares, rector there from 1557, mentions in his Loretto
catalogue Thomas major and minor. He says of them,
'Thomas Major, Englishman, will be a great servant of
God. Thomas Minor is in every respect a good man'. Then
in 1561, 'Thomas the Englishman, although poor in
worldly goods, knows how to read and write, and will
be useful as a secretary'. Perhaps he was admitted among
the unclassified. Of Brothers Robert and William, both
English, who died in Flanders in 1564, one can hardly,
perhaps, make more certain conjecture; for the temporal
co-adjutors, usually referred to as 'brothers', were at that
time more frequently in the Low Countries called 'masters'
(magistri) when their work was clerical, either because
they had already obtained their degree in philosophy, or
else because they taught what they had formerly learnt.
William Lambert was received in the professed house in
Rome at 23 years old on 21 July 1557. He was cook there
for some years, and then went to Poland and Lithuania
doing various jobs in the colleges, especially as infirmarian.
He did well enough to make himself very acceptable to
Cardinal Hosius, and was commonly understood to be his
doctor. The year of his death is not recorded. Of John
Pellison I can only find the following written by Polanco
at Trent in the name of the General, Lainez, to Mercurian,
the German provincial on 20 October 1562. 'A brother is
also being sent by name of John Pellison, a tailor, such as
your Reverence asked for in your last letter'.

Ralph Emerson was travelling companion to Campion both in Rome and England; then to Crichton and Holt in Scotland, later to Persons in France, and then in England with Weston. He was a prisoner for many years in the Clink, and there are numerous stories of his endurance and steadfastness. Transferred to Wisbech, he suffered much from ill-health, and was affected by paralysis. However, he survived to go into exile at the beginning of James's reign with many other defenders of the faith. He crossed to Flanders, and, as Weston relates in the little life which Father General ordered him to write, completed his term of residence at St. Omers as one well-regarded for first-rate qualities. When they sailed together for England, Ralph carried a rather hefty trunk of books for distribution among the Catholics. They got this safely to Norwich, and then to London. While Ralph was out and about in London, his box was seized and taken to the officials. What could be done? It seemed unworthy in his eyes to abandon the books and charge committed to him, but to do anything about it involved considerable danger. However, he chose danger rather than the appearance of dereliction of duty. He went to the officials and asked about his trunk. They had already been into it and seen the books, and so he was dragged before the magistrate. They bundled him into jail and kept him so completely incommunicado that it was more than a year before anyone could find out where he was. Nor can we suppose that nothing was said about the books. For when Weston visited Haywood, another of our men, and then shut up in the Tower, the latter said to him, 'Well, Weston, you think you and Ralph came into England unnoticed; but in fact word of it got through to the Queen's Council'. Indeed, the royal ministers at that time had so many eyes about them that nothing went unobserved. With these other worthies we may number Nicholas Owen, commonly known as Little John from the slightness of his build. To us this was a term of affection for his constant readiness to help and oblige. He was extraordinarily skilled in the construction of hiding-places. When he fell into

the hands of his pursuers a second time he still refused to
reveal a thing. They tortured him with such inhuman
ferocity that his stomach burst open and his intestines
gushed out.*

32. So in all the provinces of the Society there were
     good men of all ages and degrees of learning, who
so far had had nothing to do with the spiritual welfare of
England, although they seemed to be pre-eminently
suited for precisely this task. Their virtue and learning
brought them renown abroad. From the year of Ignatius's
death (1556), until 1580, there were 69 Englishmen in
the Society, though not one was in England . . . Nor did
the memory of all survive. Some are only remembered by
their Christian name and their country. Such was Thomas
the Englishman at Loretto, David the Englishman at
Florence, and the other Thomas—'minor'—also English,
at Loretto. A certain Richard the Englishman died there
on 15 November 1574; Vincent Powell at Ingolstadt;
George Ware, of the Rochester diocese, at Prague in 1582.
A George Morbed of Sussex was at Toulouse. Father
Thomas, 'the Englishman', died at Paris on 27 September
1583, and Father Richard, 'the Englishman', in the same
place in May 1587. Of most of the others, their age,
studies, and grade in the Society are given, but on anything else there is only silence. They did not then write
up individuals in the Society as they do now. More often
than not it was because districts or colleges changed,
and it was not always possible to collect all the records
of one person among many. Again, a succeeding age might
be impeded by the difficulties of the times either in
making records or in saving the longer narratives from
destruction . . .

34. The charity which the Society freely poured out on
     individual Englishmen during the 25 years from the
death of St. Ignatius may be said to have served the
British Isles in General. If the Society had not opened
its doors to so many Englishmen, when the gates of entry

into England remained barred, where would we have found our Campions, Personses, Garnets, Walpoles and all the other belaurelled martyrs? . . . What they were capable of as ornaments to all kinds of learning clearly showed already on the open stage of many countries abroad. Although not yet present in person to help their own country, they adhered to its cause throughout the world. They were ready to assist it wherever they could, awaiting always the call of obedience.

END OF BOOK THE FIRST

BOOK THE SECOND

1.   Activities abroad described above were carried out
by men who lacked neither love of country, capacity
to express it, nor ardour equal to the toil demanded.
Already they were putting forth a mighty effort in every
clime from Tartary to India. They would have done no
less for England had circumstances allowed. It is now
time to consider the Jesuits who blazed the English trail,
braving the fury of the Reformers to become accepted
in that island as indomitable defenders of the ancient
faith. In order of merit and time we must begin with
Campion and Persons. Much more obscure and uncertain
is our knowledge of Thomas Woodhouse and John Nelson,
who were also enrolled among the martyrs of the Society.
Of these Thomas Stephenson writes in his life of
[Thomas] Pounde. Sacchini mentions Father Thomas
King as having been sent in 1565 to his own country,
where he died . . .

2.   Edmund Campion was born at London [on 25
January] in 1540. . . . How soon ability and hard
work began to bear fruit in the boy is clearly shown by
the fact that when he was no more than 12 years old he
read a speech of welcome to Queen Mary who was then
about to ascend the throne (1553). Mary died, however,
before the boy's gifts matured sufficiently to reap their
proper reward. Meanwhile, Thomas White, a man at once
noble, wise, and fervently Catholic, had recently founded
a college at Oxford dedicated to St. John the Baptist.
He wished Campion to become one of its first students;
which augured well for the light which would one day be
thrown by the quick intelligence of this young man on
the whole university. Nor did the omens deceive. In a
few year's time such was the brightness of his genius,

41

force of eloquence and attractiveness of manner that, not only was he employed as orator and proctor—very important functions of the university—but Elizabeth herself, who succeeded Mary . . . took it upon her to provide for and advance the youth (1566). She put her intentions to Leicester, telling him that it was the royal will that Campion should ask for anything he wanted. Perhaps Campion feared that by accepting the royal bounty he would be less able to enter unhindered on the search for religious truth, after which he was already an avid seeker. Perhaps he thought he would be more restricted in his enquiry and opportunity for following what he found. Or perhaps he was only too aware of the emptiness of courtly promises which were very much more liberal with words than deeds. At all events, he had to admit that in the end he received nothing more than the royal favour.

3.   Elizabeth . . . decided to follow in the footsteps of her father and brother in matters of religion. . . . She gradually introduced new forms of prayer and hammered out a new sacramental system. It was not difficult to persuade the less exacting that there was not much difference between what had been conveyed before in Latin, and what was now given in the mother-tongue. In fact, there was the great difference that what was now expounded in the vernacular was instituted as a slight to Rome. And those who, either from their own understanding or from careful comparison of book and book arrived at a deeper appreciation of the situation, could not easily bring themselves to exchange the use of long centuries for these novelties. Among such was Campion. The more trouble he took to compare the commentaries of ancient authors with the glosses of the new, the more he found himself drawn to approval of the cause he had already begun to love. Meanwhile, hope of honour and patronage, and the esteem of his friends, kept him oscillating between them so that he could not settle openly to be known as a Catholic. In particular, Richard Cheney's kindness to him was outstanding. He had gained the

Queen's favour and with it the see of Gloucester. His learning, instinctive goodness and courtesy, his manifest veneration for the tradition of the Fathers, and his dislike of rigid Calvinists whom he called puritans, well became the gentleman's name and authority. Having seen Campion, he never ceased to encourage him. All he could do to foster his growing interest in religious matters he did; and tried to follow up his well-meaning intentions with practical assistance no less than promises. Indeed, he brought it about that Campion received the Anglican diaconate. Nor could Campion, by reason of recent Elizabethan statutes, have exercised his easy eloquence on the people unless he had first accepted the laying-on of hands from Elizabeth's bishop.

4.   However, it was not long before Campion began to see a dawning light more clearly, . . . He began to feel more keenly the internal goad of what he could now see only as a fault. There was no remedy for it save in the one fold of the universal Church. After setting his conscience at rest through a Catholic priest, in order to escape the imminent danger in which such men usually found themselves, he made a discreet withdrawal to Ireland in the company of Richard Stanihurst. To him Campion was bound by earlier ties of family and now by shared studies. They found first what they needed most, refuge with a good Catholic (1569). Here amid a daily round of work and prayer, lest he should appear to have abandoned his studies entirely, Campion wrote in Latin *The Young Student,* * and in his own tongue, *The History of Ireland.* Of this he himself writes in one of his letters, 'I rather think *The History of Ireland* has perished. It was an impartial book (justum), and I had it finished. The Protestant magistrates (inquisitores) got hold of it'. Indeed, in 1570 a furious storm broke upon the Catholics for a double reason. Pope Pius V, brimming over with zeal, thought it high time for the Church militant to display her weaponry so that by this last resort Elizabeth might be deterred from following the path she had

entered. On 25 February 1570, the Pope declared the Queen a heretic *latae sententiae,* and absolved her subjects from their obedience. The sentence was put up in the following June [*vere* on 25 May] on the doors of the Bishop of London's palace. There was uproar in the whole island. About the same time, certain nobles in the North of England dared to take up arms for the liberation of Mary Stuart, Queen of Scots, then held prisoner by Elizabeth. They also intended to avenge the wrongs of Catholic believers. It resulted in bloody war being declared on all Catholics. The rashness of a few was taken to be the intention of all. As Catholics generally were supposed to be involved in the peers' rising, or in taking up arms for the Pope, there was no safety for them whether they remained at home or went outdoors. Campion was sought after even in Ireland. Although they could have nothing against him except his reconciliation to the mother-church, he knew very well a man cannot defend his house by innocence alone once fanaticism has crossed the threshold. He thought it better to fly than stay to hear the verdict of a dubious justice. Hence, disguised in dress and name, he left Dublin, first of all for England; and then, as soon as he could, he crossed to Flanders.

5.   From the very beginning of Elizabeth's reign, the former bishops and clergy were rejected, and a form of worship and discipline introduced which seemed to be directed particularly against the papacy. This new authority she had reassumed but a short time before, and it seemed a prime necessity to bolster and maintain it by associating it with that primary source of power and effectiveness in the state which derived from, and depended solely on, the Queen herself. The new politicians had also insinuated themselves into this power. Since Catholics rejected this [spiritual] power as growing from the wrong kind of root, not a few of them preferred voluntary exile to a substitute spiritual government. Turning on their heel, they went overseas, seeking refuge with Catholic princes. Not to mention many outstanding

for birth or possessions, women as well as men, noteworthy were Sander, or Sanders, Bristow, Harding, Smith,
Stapleton, and Allen. These and other learned and distinguished men with them worked in every field of letters.
They brought renown to themselves, their country and
their faith by their writings. . . . Nor did they easily give
up hope of seeing their country return to normal conditions since they had seen it so ready to adopt different
counsels under Mary.* Allen was primarily responsible
for co-ordinating the studies of these who taught in such
a way that experts in a particular field could help to
combat schism by publishing controversy; also gather
in one academy men less advanced in age and learning.
The former would not only teach and inspire them to
aim their javelins from afar, but also prepare them for
hand-to-hand combat in the heart of the arena. These
men first assembled at Douai in Flanders in 1566. They
were filled with an enthusiasm that promised great things
for the future, and a rich harvest after a sowing in ground
so fertile. But they also inspired the Protestants with
fear, and sharpened their fury against them. For they
realised that prison, exile, deprivation of opportunity,
even slander and threats, would be uselessly employed
in wiping out the veteran priests while others grew to
maturity to succeed them. A new crop was ripening
for the sickle, and a fresh reinforcement to whom the
difficult and dangerous appeared only as desirable. The
ears had ripened when Edmund Campion hastened to
England seeking a haven of peace amid the storm raging
all around. Hers was the earth he kissed; and warm as his
own was the welcome given him by those whom we could
call the salt of this earth.

6. When he considered at leisure his past way of life,
two things tormented the mind of the man now
dedicated to religion. The first was that so often in the
intermittent light of truth there were dark shadows of
inordinate ambition, the human respect usual with
younger men, and an exaggerated regard for the affection

and good opinion of his contemporaries. He had not
avoided these snares with proper nimbleness, nor done
anything to warn others whom he might have helped. The
other matter was that, since he had lived by the patronage
and human kindness of Cheney, he was now tainted with
a certain lack of decency. Campion tried to make amends
by sending Cheney a letter which is still extant.* In it
he thrust every veil aside, and earnestly exhorted the man,
to whom he felt he owed everything, on the subject of
the counsel he himself had followed. He besought him
not to allow himself to be dashed against the rocks and
shivered to fragments. Unless the writer himself had
steered clear of them, and sought the anchorage of the
ancient faith, he, too, would have perished utterly. While
he had striven to put things right by repentance, as far
as he could, and prayed by night and day together, he had
heard, as it were, God telling him to go to Rome; to
learn in that city what remedy he should use to eradicate
so deep a blight. . . . But he was careful not to let his
decision be affected by any sudden brainstorm. Nor
after making up his mind did he allow resolution to falter.

In Rome, the microcosm of all mankind, wherever
he turned, Campion could not but notice exemplary
goodness in every order. This awoke in a mind naturally
prone to devotion and easily roused to affection something like awed wonder. Perhaps it was the name of Jesus
which eventually seized his imagination; or a certain kind
of organisation which attracted him more especially;
one not only founded to save souls—and how many he
saw as lost in England!—but to carry out the Pope's
will with greater alacrity, and with a vow to that end . . .
Or perhaps it was the very newness of this Order, and the
sheer spectacle of its labours, to say nothing of its fresh
zeal, which struck him. At all events, it took ever stronger
hold of his imagination: and that at the very time when,
owing to the death of the General, Francis Borgia, all
the key-Jesuits from every Province were gathered together
to elect his successor. Perhaps there was also some more
hidden cause to spur him on ever more relentlessly to give

himself to the Society. It was not difficult for a man with motives so unmixed, and with more than common knowledge of the faith, allied with modesty, to ask for, and gain, admittance. Mercurian, recently called from ruling the German Province to govern the whole Society, gave him the satisfaction he wanted. With a recommendation to the Austrian Provincial, Laurence Mayer, Campion eventually arrived at Brunn. Here there was a noviceship.

7.   While Campion was laying the foundations of four-square and stable goodness through an even holier way of life, Providence was erecting yet another bastion of Catholic faith in England itself. Robert Persons, also of Oxford University, was a Fellow of Balliol College; a man of much ability, industry, and sheer wisdom. Older than most, he was also worthier and better-endowed than any of them. He had a corresponding following of students . . . as many, in fact, as normally fell to any three others. Whatever the rest might think or do in matters of faith, Persons made little secret of his sympathy for the Catholics. However, good gifts are rarely without rivals. Persons rendered his own implacable, because while jealousy preceded his own assault on Protestantism, this attack gave spur to hatred. The lady who was the oracle of her age and court pronounced it a crying shame that a man who thought and spoke his mind in matters of religion otherwise than the laws laid down should be the leader of so many young people. Moreover, these were the thriving and affluent, and all tended to the end of beguiling them with the silly ideas of the papists. Jealousy alienated at least one person* from Persons who did not differ from him very much, perhaps, in religious beliefs. He was particularly affected by the consideration that the youths Persons was detaching from Protestantism might be added to his own tutorial charge. That this person should lead the opposition was all too welcome to Protestant rivals.

One evening, the rival took one of the young men to the theatre, Persons being absent for the Christmas holiday.

Since that kind of excursion was forbidden to the youth,
he was bound to know all about it when his tutor came
home. So when he returned, he kept out of his way.
Influential friends were not lacking to make sure that
nothing unpleasant befell him. Hence when Persons on
his return sought out the young man the latter was
defended on every side by the united voice of Persons's
colleagues, not only in private but publicly. The right of
the tutor was called in question: for the greater part of
the university was now Protestant. The more extreme
protested that it was not to be endured that the youth in
question, or any other, should longer remain Persons's
student. He could not, or would not, conform with the
views of his country. Let him leave it, therefore, and go
somewhere else. It could not be denied that at one time
it had been agreed that he should go abroad. There he
could put into open practice what he inwardly believed
in his heart. Let him go now. With all willingness, they
would give him time to prepare for his journey; also see
that his duties and functions were carried out for him.
At that time he was dean of the college. He must conform
at once to their vote. The situation was difficult but had
to be accepted; unless he wished to be thrown out by
brute force one stormy night, he and his companions
with him. They threatened no less than this. Not so
much bro ken by the opposition of his enemies as persuaded by the advice of his friends, Persons signed his
resignation . . . on 13 February 1 573/4. By special concession, he was allowed to retain his room and students
for as long as he wished . . . but not later than the following Easter.

8.   Persons thus divested himself, by written deed, of
        his office and rights in the college, although his
tenure had been precarious enough during the previous
few months. The traditional Lenten laws of abstinence
were still supposed to be observed in the university.
Persons realised that the law was violated, and not only
in secret. Not a few offered open affront to the more

observing. While he was investigating the matter, the Protestants took it as a clarion-call to arms. They rose in fury, stormed up and down, and virtually rioted. They rang the bells in reverse peal as if the place were on fire, crying out, 'Stop the papist fire-raiser of Balliol College! Stop him! Water! Fire! . . .'

9. . . . Persons began his journey into exile in the beginning of June (1575). He reached Antwerp by way of Calais, sailing along the Flemish coast. The company of merchants which he was with was accustomed to visit the Frankfurt fair, and if they followed their usual custom would not set off before August. Persons intended to go to Italy so he turned aside now to Louvain. His intention was to put the cares of Oxford behind him amid the congenial surroundings of this university. Father William Good, mentioned above (pp. 14-16, 18), was then living in Louvain. He made it his business to look after exiles, and so discovered Persons. Good was delighted with his mature mind united with outward dignity of bearing. He was convinced that Persons was destined for great things. Good hoped that he would send down deep roots into goodness, and offered him sound advice to that end . . . He should recoup his forces; not only stay away from gatherings of people he knew, but put every other thought aside save that of getting nearer to God. He should think over what he ought to do now, and come to his decision in calm and tranquility. Most important, he must make up his mind in God's interior light. . . . He should do an eight-day retreat. . . . With this end in view, Persons set out for Padua with a few like-minded companions, but he first sent on a bill of exchange to Venice to cover the expenses of the journey. He had now set his mind on a more spiritual life, and in his fresh awareness of the transitoriness of things took a new and strange delight . . .

10. Persons stayed for a time at Padua. Subsequently, he went sight-seeing in Rome. Indeed, the Holy Year ceremonies, the renown of the city and the insistence of

certain friends made it almost inevitable. Meanwhile, Campion, who was not yet bound by vows, went to Prague. There he was to enlighten the rhetoricians with great credit; no smaller, in fact, than his ardour shown at Brunn when he was imbibing the deeper principles of spiritual life. There was a public school at Prague for the sons of noblemen. The Society accepted them on certain conditions. Their moral training was in the hands of the prefect, who also taught the 'rhetoric' class, and acted as director of our Lady's Sodality. The latter was dedicated to the Immaculate Conception. (The Sodality changed its title under General Claud Aquiviva.) With eloquent testimony to hand of his scholarship, Campion reached the close of 1578. He then presented a tragedy, in the presence of the Emperor Maximilian, which did equal credit to his skill and eloquence. [John] Pits, a reliable author, mentions it by the title of 'Nectar and Ambrosia'. Campion also gave a funeral oration in which he poured lavish praise on Maria Cardona Requesens, first Lady of the Chamber to Maria Augusta. He describes her as the very crown of the nobility. Campion was called to Rome in 1580 to lecture on philosophy. He took no little pleasure in these studies, for he was a man of keen intellect. But he also had to witness a Germany infected and overrun by grotesque ideas which no exertions could check, and no power suppress. He also reflected on the deplorable state of his own unhappy land, afflicted as it was by errors as gross if not worse. . . . Sorrow only intensified the flame of his yearning. . . . He had heard of Woodhouse's remarkable perseverance, who not long before had sealed with blood and life his assertion of the Pope's authority. He had heard now, on the very same day and even at the hour, many a gentleman's family had been raked over. Priests had been dragged from the altar as the sacred vessels were snatched from them. Even members of the nobility, including ladies with their children and servants, had been distributed among the various prisons. With mingled pride and sadness, he witnessed also the arrival in Rome of many fellow countrymen, among them friends from Oxford. These also, putting behind them secular concerns, elected to join the Society which he himself now loved so much. Among them were Robert Persons, William Weston, Henry Garnet, John Lane, and Giles Wallop.* This event somewhat cheered his depression. Campion thanked God that now some remedy for England's woes seemed to be at hand. He did not doubt that they and their example would, in God's Providence, be the cause of bringing many more yet to work for the spiritual rehabilitation of their island by faith and goodness. . . . Campion vented his joy in letters which show his great satisfaction at the benefit which the exiles brought with them.

11. Robert Persons, on returning to Padua from Rome, got together a good collection of books. He spent little time on the learning of the medicos. He felt a wound in his soul which needed to be healed by another kind of medicine. . . . From time to time, his thoughts ran on what he had considered privately at Louvain, and openly at Rome. . . . There among the marbles, domes, columns, circuses and amphitheatres, he had feasted his eyes, but his soul had found little nourishment. . . . He now appeared to himself not a little guilty for having thrust the religious issue into the background. He spent his day in study, conversation and business, but even at night while he slept, he could not find peace. He would see himself leaving the company of men to live among Alpine peaks. He would find some community with which to dwell apart. Indeed, he lived every kind of life in his imagination that might bring God and himself into closer union. Nowhere could he bring his mind to rest. He decided to go back to Rome, so that where he had neglected what was most important, God and himself, he might now be moved to know himself and God. There he would decide what to do with the rest of his life.

12.* Persons lived with his friends Luke Astlow and John Lane. Without difficulty, he persuaded them to look after business of his that needed immediate settlement at Rome and Parma. After journeying to Venice, and taking ship for Piave without mishap, he came to Ferrara. There he left his ship and went the rest of the way on foot to Rome. . . . A fellow shrouded in a riding-cloak became his companion on the road. His mien, dress and voice were calculated to rouse pity. Our pilgrim made no difficulty in admitting him to his company. Persons, in fact, helped him generously with money, food, and companionship. The sorry state and appealing air of the man suggested nothing to be afraid of . . . 'I was', he said, 'bound for many years by the vows of a religious Order; and then, making the most of better advice, I freed myself from that harsh slavery and took my liberty. People do not know what they are doing when, from earliest youth, without ever having tasted the sweetness of an easier life, they shut themselves up in the prison-houses. I did not look carefully where I was going, and I made the same mistake. However, I got out of it at last, and I would not let myself get caught again easily in those nets' . . . That the head was empty which had spoken thus was sufficiently proved by this gentleman on the run when they came to Florence. Rushing into a shop at the first opportunity, he bought himself a new silk hat—certainly an elegant and decorative item—and strutted proudly through the streets, although the rest of his costume was rough and ragged enough. He greeted his host with the words, 'Well, at any rate, it's good to have one decent thing to put on!'

13. Persons arrived in Rome towards the end of May. He now put second best behind him. After subjecting himself to his own closer scrutiny for a few weeks, he decided there was no time to be lost. He offered himself to Father Mercurian, the General of the Society. At first, Persons felt rather awkward, but when he was taken to his room and left to himself, he fell on his knees and made the total offering to God. He so overflowed with inner joy that then and there he made away all he possessed. With no hesitant afterthought, he adopted the Society's

way of life. In it he lived henceforth in complete peace of mind.

14. The 4 July was the day on which Persons was
    received into the Society, although he himself else-
where records it as the 25th, the Feast of St. James.*
On this day, possibly, he was admitted to common life
with the rest. Carried on the swift wings of his reputation, Persons was transferred to Padua to join the novices.
In the first place, this prompted his friends' surprise;
but soon the thought of following his example. Lane,
especially, his familiar friend at Oxford with whom he had
shared his first thoughts of leaving the schism, followed
him six months later. After his novitiate, he was sent to
Alcala but did not long survive. . . . On 6 May 1579, he
died as he had lived, generally esteemed for his good life.
Astlow was reported to be on the point of joining them
when death untimely snatched him away at Padua. Giles
Wallop made his vows in the following September, but
he also died shortly afterwards.*

15. While Campion teaches at Prague, and Persons studies
    at Rome, we would do well to cross once again to
England to observe a hero unconquered; the example
of a man who, persecuted for 30 years on end did not
weaken in his resistance, although the fury of his enemies
remained undiminished. Thomas Pounde . . . was the kind
of man we do not encounter by chance nor at other times
than these. It is recorded for this year (1575) by Thomas
Stephens whom he formerly kept as a servant, and who
was then bound for Rome, that Pounde tried to enter
the Society. He further reported that after some years
he had his wish fulfilled. Indeed, from Goa . . . where
Thomas Stephens arrived towards the end of 1579, the
latter expresses his thanks for this favour granted them
both. A letter of General Mercurian to the same Thomas
Pounde also bears witness to the fact that he was received
at the close of 1578. It seemed worthwhile to give the
letter here as testimony to an excellent man. It runs as

follows: 'Thomas Stephens . . . has told us much concerning your Reverence's unfailing constancy and devotion
to duty. This has pleased us very much especially because
for many years now you have aspired to our Society.
Therefore, although it is laid down in our institute that
none should be admitted to our number before being
well tried, moved by the glowing testimony of Stephens
and others, and accepting your trials and labours of so
many years as a lengthy testing, we will fall in with your
Reverence's worthy desires. . . . We now receive and
admit you into our Society as a true member of our body.
. . . We hope, however, that the infinite mercy and goodness of God will make it possible for us some day, when
you have got over your present trials, to enjoy your
presence and company. . . . However, we trust that all
this will be taken by your Reverence in such a way that
you will not expose yourself to peril without cause, or
hope of result. This would be rashness not courage. Nor
should you put your health in jeopardy through immoderate fasting and abstinence, to which we hear you are
prone. As the prophet says, "Keep up your strength for
God!" . . . One thing I would ask you: this advice touching
our Society should be kept to yourself. Let no one know
it, not merely by your dress and habit, but even from your
words and conversation, until better times arrive. Then
those desires of yours can be fully implemented with
God's help. . . . From Rome, 1 December 1578'. The man
whose strength of character we describe in his maturity
will also repay study in his beginning.*

16. The parents of Thomas Pounde were William Pounde
       and Anne Wriothesley, sister of Thomas, Earl of
Southampton. While still in the womb, Thomas thrust
out his right hand; which was taken to be the omen of
a fighter! His earliest years were spent in studies at the
College of our Lady, Winchester, where youngsters were
trained in Latin. At 23 he went to London to acquire a
reputation in law, and prepared to practise at the bar.*
He was not less conspicuous for physique, presence, and

physical strength than for alertness and intelligence. Consequently, he not only cultivated his mind but also took up sports; and those in which the very noblest sought to shine. He excelled at dancing. When his father died, angling for a career at Court, he uselessly poured out a considerable part of his inheritance on unrewarding hopes and pleasures. No one will be surprised that this should happen while Elizabeth reigned, for she drew all after her into a whirl of exgravagant living in which she herself was fully absorbed. Christmas Day 1564 was celebrated with customary splendour. Thomas Pounde was the Court Master of Revels. While they were dancing, the Queen took his own ungloved hand in hers, and covered his head with a cap she took from the Earl of Leicester in case, overheated by the vigour of the dance, he should take a chill. It seemed to him like the victor's laurels. The Queen asked for the same dance again, but pirouetting as usual, Pounde suddenly fell flat on his face. Admiration turned to ridicule. Said the Queen, 'Arise, Sir Ox!'. Stung to the quick by her words, he got up, went down again on one knee, and said in Latin for the assembly to hear, 'Sic transit gloria mundi'. He then made for the door, and not long afterwards finally turned his back on the Court and all its false hopes . . .

17. Pounde was 30 before he was reconciled to the Church. Before this, he sought to make reparation by cultivating all the good qualities. He spent a year in prayer. He was assiduous in his efforts at self-knowledge, taking no notice of what others thought or said of his adopted way of life. He put up with a good deal from his friends, and indeed, much from himself while he strove to love chastity, indifference to food and dress, and even hardship and hard living. Next year, he bound himself by vow to become a priest, after a self-appointed trial-period of seven years spent in doing good. At the end of that time he would enter the Society of Jesus, mainly because this would mean foregoing all honourable advancement. To this time those things are to be assigned which

Thomas Stephens, his former servant, relates of them both when in 1578 they sought admission to the Society.* He says, 'For much of the time I was with him—I will only speak of what I actually saw—he used to practise great austerity. He slept on a poor mattress on the ground, spending in prayer one hour at midnight, two, three, or even four hours at dawn, and a good deal of time in the evening; and with deep spiritual enjoyment. Protestants put it abroad that he was mad, or at least soft in the head and sunk in superstition. Even the family servants and some of his friends considered all this a failing in him. He steadily ignored it, as is the wont of souls privileged to be great. When a priest was available, he took Holy Communion on Sundays and feast-days, and sometimes more than once during the week. But first he made his confession, and urged others to do likewise. Very often he complained to his friends of the Catholics who, with so little risk to themselves—as it seemed to him—and amid such dangers to their souls, approached the divine mysteries so rarely.

Winchester, the seat of a bishop, was not far from his own house. Pounde heard that many poor, Catholic recusants—as people are called who have nothing liturgically to do with those who have given up the faith— were in hiding there; and that there was also an old priest who rarely celebrated, let alone distributed Holy Communion. Pounde put in a timely appearance among them. He investigated their living conditions, and made arrangements for a meal to be served to them after Mass and Holy Communion. He also distributed alms, and exhorted the priest to celebrate Mass, and the Catholics to communicate, more often. Furthermore, he bought up not long afterwards, and at considerable expense, a great number of cheeses at the annual fair. These he distributed to them two or three at a time, letting them understand that unless they responded with greater alacrity to their divine privilege and the grace of God, they could expect his friendship to cease! He was always put in singularly good humour whenever he saw anything from a dozen

to 16 young gentlemen in his chapel, and receiving Holy
Communion. Pounde was so keen on almsgiving that,
apart from the day-to-day benefactions which he bestowed
with extraordinary liberality, he was always pleased to
hear of some Catholic in need. He kept always before his
mind's eye the saying of Saint Paul, *maxime erga domes-
ticos fidei*. At the same time, he made little of these efforts
of his, and was prepared to beg insistently from the richer
members of his circle on behalf of afflicted or imprisoned
Catholics. I remember how on one occasion he composed
a veritable treatise on behalf of a certain papist, and sent
it to Henry, Earl of Southampton, to read. The Earl was
a relative of his and a very good Catholic. Pounde often
showed his beneficence even to non-Catholics to soften
their bitterness and render them more amenable to hearing
Catholic truth'.* In these words, then, Thomas Stephens
pleaded Pounde's cause and his own to Mercurian.

18. The fifth year had now come and gone. To bring
     nearer the fulfilment of his vow, Pounde sold part
of his lands. He then made arrangements for a certain
day when together with some friends he would pass into
France. While he was settling his affairs in London, and
doing his best to convert his host, he was unexpectedly
called upon by a pursuivant to give an account of himself
to the Protestant Bishop Sandys [or Sandes], and declare
how he obeyed the Queen's laws. No charge was brought
against him, no accusation made, and there was no evidence that he had broken the law. He was allowed bail
for his reappearance on a certain day. The suggestion was
made to him that a certain merchant living in St. Mark's
parish, and possessed by the devil, should be secretly
exorcised by the prayers of the Church. To the appointed
place, Pounde, duly armed with the relics of the saints,
made his way. He discoursed long and fervently on the
power of the Church against evil spirits, and on remaining
constant in the faith: but not secretly enough to prevent
his being seized on his return to London, and thrown into
prison on a charge of some kind. After four months,

Pounde signed another recognizance, and was left free to go to his father's house on the outskirts of London. Here he gave himself up to private prayer, and dispensed spiritual advice to his friends when he was with them. But once again our pilgrim was brought before a bishop, this time Horn of Winchester. Together with Pounde were not a few other Catholics of known reputation and good life. Hope of milder judgment was craftily held out to them provided that, in the course of the prelate's irksome questionings and speeches, they all held their tongues. However, their silence was put down to weakness and ignorance. The Catholics were insultingly and petulantly referred to before the assembly as dumb dogs. Thomas took it bitterly. Therefore, next day, when Horn proudly took up his place before the tribunal, and, praising Vincent of Lerins, showed that he set forth reliably the marks of the true faith, Pounde took up the argument. He contended that Vincent was a support for the Catholics against the heretics. He argued penetratingly that what a heretic cannot gain by force of argument he will attempt by shouting, verbosity and sheer denigration. Thomas was ordered to be led away while he was still arguing. The price which had to be paid for this demonstration will shortly appear from his own letter to those who were his fellow-captives.

19. It will be useful to recount the number and nature of the principal London prisons. There were three at the three gates of the city named respectively, 'New', another after Lud—a traditional founder of the city itself—and a third, the Gatehouse. This had once been the gateway of a monastery in the western part of the town. There were five more on the other side of the river: King's Bench, the Marshalsea—originally the principal military court, 'mariscalli sedes', the Clink—prison of the Winchester liberty, the White Lion, and the Counter. Scattered through the city were three more: the Fleet, so-called from the river-mouth there, another Counter, and the Bridewell. In these, for the most part,

they throw the more heavily-burdened debtors, and also wandering vagabonds. Lastly, in the eastern part of the city is the Tower of London. Here they imprison those involved in treason and crimes of a more serious kind. Thieves, cut-throats and criminals are sent, for the most part, to Newgate. Every one of these prisons had to be listed since Catholics were sent to all of them according to the mood of their captors. Individual prisoners will frequently be mentioned as their turn comes up. After two months' incarceration at Winchester, Pounde was put in the Marshalsea. Lest he be challenged again on the opinions of [Vincent] Lerins, Horn had the case transferred to the ordinary magistrates. These were uncertain of the Queen's wishes on the subject of Catholics generally, and sent them all to London. From thence Pounde wrote to the others: 'I have several times been questioned before Mr. Young; twice before five or six commissioners, while I was once brought out in public before a very large assembly, loaded with irons, Not surprisingly, I was thought to have stood up too freely for the truth in the presence of men who did not want to listen. While I was being dragged away to Newgate, the gaoler snatched up my cap together with my cloak as though I were already condemned. He left me my head; for which I as well as he am sorry enough! Bare-headed, I went loaded with a heavy iron, while the mob shouted, "Crucify!". From the "widow of Newgate"—a form of torture*—they got me a liberal alms. I waited about until four o'clock in the afternoon for the judges to pronounce sentence. I was then called for suddenly. My hand- and leg-irons were taken off, and my cloak restored to me together with my hat. I was taken to Lincoln's Inn, which was formerly my abode when I studied law. There five commissioners waited for me, among them Topcliffe, who was in charge of examinations. Orders had come from the Queen that by threats and flattery I should be moved from my purpose. All in vain, They urged upon me that if I wished to show myself faithful to the Queen, and a loving subject, I must disclose the names of those with whom, and in what places, I had usually consorted. I replied, "I am prepared to testify to the loyalty of them all, even with an oath. For the rest, a good man and a Catholic, born in the position I hold and well brought up, and finally, having my kind of conscience, must not create difficulties for innocent men, and well-meaning". Seeing they could get nothing out of me, they sent me back to my prison—with the kindest words. Two days later, Topcliffe called on me with the head gaoler. In a friendly way, they tested my firmness of purpose. There was much debate: but no progress. They commiserated on my condition. What most grieves them is my chiefest boast, my fidelity, and that my captivity should be because of my faith. After these came Young. He called me before him once again, and asked what Topcliffe had told me. Smooth and urbane, he expressed his fear that a man as hard and grim as Topcliffe might have left me with a rough experience. Young tried, in a most friendly way, to smoothe the path to the betrayal of my friends, so that I should give away some secret useful to him and his nefarious proceedings. He got nothing. Finally, he urged me to send a letter to the Lord Keeper of the Great Seal begging for mercy. This I did; with the result that from that time they have treated me with less consideration, as an obstinate character, in fact, and of all my kind the furthest removed from the good of the State: that is, from their heresy. So here I am, shut off from contact with everybody, and with no hope of milder custody, unless I come up before the next sessions at Newgate. I would appear as one guilty of obeying God and holding fast to the Catholic faith. This I had to tell you, fellow-prisoners, in order to counteract sinister rumours at my expense. At all costs, I exhort you to remain as loyal to the faith as I could wish. Farewell!'

20.   The many things which he said freely in the presence of lawyers, especially concerning the usurped power of the Queen in ecclesiastical matters, gave Pounde not so much a prospect as a hope that, at the next assizes, he would be called up on a capital charge. Seeing himself,

therefore, already on the way to public execution, he got down to his prayers in good earnest in order to prepare fittingly for the end. He hoped to fill his mind with a desire for it by praying, reading and writing. Many things were noted at this time, and duly recorded by the diligent hand of the same Thomas Stephens whom we met at Watten . . .* But the swift death to which Pounde aspired was commuted to prolonged imprisonment, of which I will speak briefly lest by relating one life too profusely we tangle the thread of our history. Since he did not cease with voice or pen to impugn the Queen's authority in the Church, or brace the resolution of the Catholic faithful, he was transferred, at the instance of Bishop Elmer of London, to Storford Castle [Bishop's Stortford] on the borders of Hertfordshire and Essex. There was a further order that none should be allowed to see him. As the smith attached his leg-iron, Pounde tried to kiss it. Another smith who fastened his iron collar drew blood. But Thomas, quite unruffled, merely remarked, 'I only wish this blood had flowed from the depths of my heart to help the cause for which I suffer'. The smith, intrigued by the man's patience, wanted to know the why and wherefore of it. Years later, he became a Catholic. He was arrested and died faithfully in prison . . .

After a year, Pounde was sent back to the Marshalsea. He was next confined in the Tower, being subsequently transferred to the Counter in Southwark; later still to Wisbech in the Isle of Ely where he spent many years with the numerous priests and laymen shut there. He lived on most friendly terms with Father William Weston, of whom more elsewhere. In 1597, Pounde was again brought to the Tower of London; then to the Counter in the City, and afterwards to the White Lion, to the Gatehouse at Westminster, the Fleet, and finally Framlingham in Suffolk until the reign of James I. At the same time that he sent the priests into exile [1604], James granted Pounde his liberty on bail. So after the distinction of living in 11 most important prisons he at length died in his ancestral home [Belmont] in 1615 at the age of seventy-six. Stephens, who collected his memoirs, affirms that he spent seven years in the Tower, four in the Marshalsea, six at Storford Castle, 10 in Wisbech, and three at Framlingham. The rest of his time, making 30 years in all, he spent in other places.

21.   Pounde was by no means the only sufferer, nor alone in being persecuted . . . Catholics as a body bore painful witness to their cause, and endured like vexation. It may be admitted, perhaps, that Pounde seems to have been more zealous than many another in professing the faith, and readier to speak his mind. It happened once, for example, that a priest before the magistrates got bogged down in the question as to whose power over the Church of England was supreme, the Pope's or the Queen's. Joining in the fray, Pounde counselled for all to hear, 'Say the Pope! Who else has a better right?' However, all the dispositions of authority were directed to the ruin of Catholics . . . The Queen's Councillors fully approved of independence in their own way of life, but were determined to keep it for themselves alone. They devised and put into execution everything which force, pressure and denigration could achieve to tread down the Catholics, and prevent them from growing in size or influence. Nor were the latter to be allowed to initiate anything at home or contrive anything abroad . . .

Men who arrived at episcopal and clerical dignity and wealth maintained, after accepting it, the power of princes in matters spiritual . . . They turned the meaning of Holy Scripture and the Fathers into another sense to defend their own persuasion. If any learned priests put anything in writing to rebut their falsehood, these same opponents tried to discredit such efforts in studied atempts to confuse the issue. They would carry out searches in Catholic households to seek out and suppress such books, overcoming their kind of argument with this kind of zeal. Some of them would commit men to prison, mulct them with huge fines, and commit to the flames as if guilty of murder, books they could not deal with by knowledge. Finally, there were the crafty members of government who worked as much through spies abroad as informers at home. They twisted the truth to serve their own trouble-making, even if foreign princes did nothing more than promote their own affairs, send a soldier to the frontier, enlist men, or even decide on peace with their neighbours. They threatened out of hand priests and all Catholics as if they were a mob of conspirators. Those who had lived in London for some time were handed over to be shut up by the town jailer, or else they were commanded by edict to go not more than five miles from their homes without written leave of the magistrates in whose districts they resided. Persons recalls these times in his letter to the Rector of the English College at Rome, dated 17 November 1580.

'The violence of the persecution is now extreme, and of a kind unheard of since England first became Christian. Everywhere noblemen and commoners, men, women and even children are being dragged off to prison. They are bound with iron chains, despoiled of their goods, deprived of light. In public edicts and in sermons and speeches they are defamed before the populace as traitors and rebels.' And again, 'Many gentlemen of quality, respected, rich and influential in their own districts have been shut up in these last few months . . . In this way, not only the existing prisons of England but many new ones added are still unable to cope with all Catholics they receive. All the same, pursuivants are daily sent out to search for more, and round them up. Yet their number, by God's mercy, grows every day so that their very pursuers almost grow tired'.*

It was claimed for the benefit of the multitude, who knew no better, that all this was taking place for political reasons; in fact it was for religion. [The persecutors] . . . were far from ignorant of the power of truth. This always prevails and reveals itself, unless it be consistently obscured by cloud. They were also alive to interests of their own to be provided for on the side. They therefore decided that on all counts the wings of the Catholics must

be clipped. To this end, they stirred up continual trouble
for them in their domestic life so that however much they
wished they could not raise themselves again . . . Thomas
Pounde . . . by no means a rich man, obeying the summons
of [the Bishop of Winchester] on the religious charge,
said that he had been stripped of 16,000 crowns for
refusing to abandon his faith. The issue was not simply
one of religion: the profit motive also entered. They held
back many from embracing the faith because they seized
family possessions in this way. But if they came across
any who wavered, they liked them least of all, since then
the source and origin of the money with which they
enriched themselves dried up; unless things fell out so that
somehow they could strip an individual of his entire
property . . .*

23. Allen was passing his 10th year [1578] in the semin-
      ary which he had founded at Douai when the
Protestant rebels in Flanders obliged him to transfer
elsewhere . . . He established a new seat, thanks to the
benevolence of the principal members of the Guise family,
at Rheims in Champagne. Such was the access of students,
men also of high quality that they far surpassed the Douai
men in numbers. They included many doughty warriors
for the cause of the faith in England, and some who were
to shed their blood for it . . . News of all this crossed the
Alps to cheer the hearts of those living at Rome. They
decided that the pilgrims' hospice, originally founded for
the convenience of private travellers, should be adapted
to serve the common and higher interest of the whole
island. What was begun at Rheims should be completed
at a seminary in Rome developed from that house. For
the English nation, like Christians from most parts of
the world, had a hostel in the city from earliest times, set
up by the generosity of their leading men, so that those
who went to Rome for the purposes of devotion would
have somewhere to stay. The first hospice, dedicated to
St. Edmund, King and Martyr, was set up in Trastevere
not far from the river, possibly with the intention that the

sailors, who had more need of such than most, would not have to go too far from their ships; or perhaps because in those days when overland journeys were not yet frequent or safe, the majority of visitors was ship-borne. Or it may have been, as one would expect in an unknown and distant land, that the earliest arrivals simply occupied the first place they could. When the visitors grew in number, and in later years devotion increased to that most doughty martyr Thomas, Archbishop of Canterbury, the hospice was established in a more convenient place inside the city on the . . . [Via di Monserrato]. Its annual income was increased to 2,000 crowns, with which the pilgrims were entertained, a number of priests was maintained to look after them, and other services were provided connected with the church. The needier visitors were lodged there for eight days; others for three.

In the years which we are considering, when Protestants were making life for Catholics impossible in England, France and the Low Countries, Rome was filled with refugees. A great number of younger men, drawn by flourishing schools, sought there a place for their studies. The worthy Owen Lewis, *referendarius* of the Apostolic Camera, and Archdeacon of the Church of Cambrai, suggested to Gregory XIII the first premises which he should allocate for this. It would also be for the good of religion if some of the younger men could be mingled with the veteran priests of the hospice, who looked no further than serving the one house: the youths who came from Douai and Rheims embraced by their institute the entire English cause. Based on the firm foundations of faith instilled in that school, they would go out from thence to re-establish the faith originally derived from that other Gregory. Their proposals pleased the Pontiff. He ordered seven to be summoned from Rheims, for it was reported that the income of the house would support this many, apart from the priests and pilgrims. Subsequently, the number of these generous souls seemed too small to the Pontiff, and he wished more to be added at his own expense. Then soon after, since these beginnings enjoyed no little success, he turned the entire hospice into seminary with all its rights and income intact, the chaplains being moved elsewhere: all this by his own authority. Its rule and administration were put in the hands of Father Maurice Clenock who was responsible for the discipline of the students and the general running of the establishment. He was also personally responsible for looking after the pilgrims.*

24. The opposing powers . . . hoped that with temples broken, altars overthrown, monasteries made empty, and priests expelled and exterminated, what was left would in time decay. And with decay all would be forgotten. But now they saw that the crumbling ruins would be peopled anew; that not even the severity of the law, cruelty of persecution, perils innumerable, and most cruel death, would suffice to intimidate men from attempting the reconversion of the new gentiles. They then decided that to naked force, which had achieved so little, must be added hidden fraud. It was thought that much would be accomplished if the elderly Marian priests could be set at loggerheads with the new priests coming from the seminaries. The flames of jealousy might be ignited. The former now grew weary from their length of years. The latter were young and vigorous, freshly sent into the field to do battle. The older priests had learning, but the younger were quicker and readier of wit. The Marian priests clung on to deep-rooted custom, while the new priests were better instructed in more recent procedures and church discipline. Each party urged the Catholics to follow itself rather than the other. The Protestant magistracy, anxious to pour oil on the flames, sought to establish an understanding with the Marian priests while doing their utmost to destroy their rivals. With pretended decency, they gave to the first exemption, or refused to notice what they did. The others they pursued with method and the rigour of the law, inquisition, penalties and tortures. Thus they drove them from the land, and even from the land of the living. Even in

the midst of prisons and torments endured for the love of God, the quarrel managed to creep in, as though the new priests were conceived and fashioned not to restore and preserve the puny flock, but rather to destroy the peace of the Church. After this they attacked the citadel itself, the recently-created Roman seminary. A dissension was set on foot among the students which threatened to raze it to its foundations. Thanks to the benevolence and liberality of the Pope, its students now numbered forty. Clenock, whom we mentioned above, was superior. He was a good man, of a learning far from superficial, and had been marked out during Mary's reign for the burdens of the episcopate. But whether because of old age, or because he was unable to rule over youth, or because one man was not enough for them all, he drew upon himself numerous complaints to the effect that his regime was neither just nor firm, nor measured in unweighted scales. As a Welshman . . . he was believed to favour his seven fellow countrymen much more than those who came from the rest of Britain. A small spark will light a large fire. Soon the whole house was in flames. The Cardinal-Protector Morone was approached. By means of petitions the way was opened to the Pope himself, through Lewis Blanchetti, prefect of the papal privy chamber.

They beseeched, implored and pleaded. Let them be given another Rector; another set of rules for running the house. They were afraid of leaving behind them any impression of vagueness in their thought. So they praised the Jesuits for their skill and experience of government, the number and worth of their teachers, their identity of purpose and rule, and finally the prestige they enjoyed with princes. These were the men to increase and strengthen the work begun. They therefore asked that the Fathers of the Society before all others should become their guides, philosophers and friends. The struggle went on for a long time with much ardour against the arguments on the other side. The Protector, however, upheld the cause of Clenock, and tried to subdue trouble-makers by threats and reprimands as well as persuasion. If only for this reason, the Jesuits themselves were reluctant enough. They were against any assumption of responsibility for the new seminary since they were already saddled with a number in the city. They would find themselves considerably distracted from more universal commitments by these relatively domestic tasks. For this reason, in their second general congregation, it was decreed that for the future they should not take upon themselves the government of seminaries in this way where it could conveniently be avoided.*

25. The situation grew so tense that when the cardinal offered the choice between remaining under Clenock and leaving the city, 33 Englishmen put the Welsh behind them and forthwith left the house. They were even ready to quit the city if other remedy were not provided. It was difficult to know if they were moved by a spirit of restlessness or genuinely worthy zeal. Outwardly, it had all the semblance of a riot. However, they claimed, in joint letters to the Pope, the cardinal and other officials, and not by this channel alone, that they were only moved by their desire to progress in learning and goodness. Their wish was simply to observe ecclesiastical discipline more exactly. For the future, they intended to work for the restoration of their country . . . To re-establish the Catholic faith, they were ready to pledge even life and blood. For this reason, by common consent, they asked for the Fathers of the Society to be their mentors in discipline and religious life, and to be governors of the whole seminary. Eventually, it was ordered that each individual should declare his opinion, and put it in writing under oath. The first wrote thus: 'I, Ralph Sherwin, testify to God . . . that I have in mind only the increase of my country's honour and its succour. I believe that the government of this seminary should be made over to the Fathers of the Society. This I humbly crave'. And later, in the sixth or seventh place, Mr. Mush: 'I John Mush, following my own conscience and initiative, humbly beg that the government of this institution be

made over to the Fathers of the Society etc.' [*sic.*]. All
without exception took this view. Thomas Goldwell,
Bishop of Saint Asaph, Richard Shelley, Grand Prior of
England, and any other Englishman in the city who
enjoyed influence were all summoned to the Campo dei
Fiori, that is, the English College. On Mercurian, General
of the Society, was imposed a precept of obedience to
consider how he might take over at once the government
of the college on behalf of his subjects (1579). The first
Jesuit Rector was Father Alfonso Agazzari of Siena, an
energetic man and extremely devoted to our people. In
his seven years' rule, he did much for interior discipline
and spirituality. He also extended the house itself, adding
to its revenue. Pope Gregory during his lifetime paid over
300 crowns a month from his own purse. He also gave
it the abbey of Saint Sabine at Piacenza which was worth
nearly 3,000 crowns a year . . .

26. Persons, meanwhile, having finished his studies, was
     transferred to the residence of the papal peniten-
tiaries. Here he was occupied with private studies, eluci-
dating the main points of questions called into dispute by
Protestants, and with questions that might be of practical
use to priests sent to England. Still he found time to deal
with religious matters of popular interest. By his advice
and exhortation to the young men, and to the Pope
through Fathers Benedict Palmio and Francis Toledo
[Toletus], he contributed no little to the calming of
the storm in the new seminary. To consolidate and extend
the whole enterprise, he suggested two things as supremely
opportune. First, Allen should be fetched from Rheims
to Rome to put both seminaries on a better footing. The
man whose renown was becoming world-wide could cast
his beams even more brightly from Rome. For he was
outstanding in mental capacity, scholarship, zeal for
spreading the Word, and authentic wisdom. Allen had
placed all these qualities at the disposal of his country's
good . . . He had already achieved much, even in his
absence from the scene, in France. It was believed he

would achieve most at Rome . . . This was fully recognised
by leading Christian princes. Indeed, he was to become
of their number, as will be related. The benefit of the
seminaries begun in these two places was soon felt since
the emulation of minds bent on the same goal meant that
each helped the other. In one place men were instructed
in higher studies. From the other they were sent forth as
masters to instruct others. The income of Rheims was
also increased out of papal resources.

It was fitting that those who were maintained by the
liberality of the Pope and by alms flowing into the sacred
shrines of Rome should not look elsewhere than to him.
To the Pope they owed their whole mode of life and
opportunity of advancing in knowledge. A certain firmness of purpose could be looked for, and constancy in
the way begun. Minds might falter midway which were
not tied by precise obligations, and then the outlay would
be wasted for its purpose by men departing to their private
studies. After all, they had come to be trained for the
public good. And so finally, at Persons's persuasion, an
oath in the following form was proposed to all who
wished to be enrolled among the students of the college:
'I, N.N., considering all the benefits God has bestowed
on me . . . promise, in due course, divine grace assisting,
to receive Holy Order, and to return to England to convert
the souls of my non-Catholic countrymen whenever it
shall seem good to the superior of this college to order
me in the Lord to do so'. From this oath, which was taken
after some months of prior deliberation, two things
followed. They sublimated all their actions and studies
as an expression of divine love towards neighbour. It was
open to everyone to enjoy, if they so wished, many years
of growth in personal integrity and knowledge. Under
the direction of anyone they chose, they could achieve
a morally excellent discipline whereby they would become
more capable of serving the country which was most dear
to them. They really set their minds to pleasing God;
and full of enthusiasm and determination to show themselves faithful to their promises, they adhered in remarkable

degree to studies in religion and letters. Seeking spiritual weapons from every quarter, the students armed themselves for future conflict. It might be by combatting with arguments those who believed they could defend heresy by spoken or written word. It could also come about by descending into the arena with the leaders and champions of those who offered them death, and the pains and torments far worse than death. For it was with these their foes thought to break them when they despaired of forcing them to yield. The fruit of their labour was to nourish not one county but the whole of England. Not a few who submitted to this discipline were outstanding in ability. They missed no opportunity to do their neighbour good. Which consideration moved Allen to look for a substitute for Persons whom he had destined to leave Rome behind him for England. He fully recognised that Persons had been the cause of his own coming to Rome.

27. It seemed wrong to Allen that while the pupils strove side by side in the arena and on the field of battle, their masters and instructors should not likewise be called thither . . .*

28. Allen excogitated on these lines to himself, to the Pope and cardinals, and to Persons and others in Rome on this subject of sending Jesuit Fathers to England. Finally, a day was appointed for debate. The Pope referred the matter to Mercurian. On this occasion, although the views of those opposing were supported by sound reasons, the opinion of those in favour prevailed. This result was due especially to Oliver Manare, the Assistant for Germany. He had charge of all the Society's affairs in northern Europe. Manare pleaded ardently for it. Claud Aquaviva then the Provincial of the Roman Province, supported him with his own vote. He also promised, if his superiors would permit it, to devote his own labours to this mighty work. There was no great difficulty in choosing the men to be sent. Persons in Rome was in their eye: a man well regarded, and equal to the distinction required in carrying

out such a task. Campion was at Prague, but his renown
never allowed him to leave Rome for very long wherever
he went. All were agreed in their estimate of these men.
The remaining Englishmen who had entered the Society
had either not yet completed their course of study, or else
had gone to more distant places in the north to teach a
variety of subjects. Thus they could not conveniently
come to Rome. To Persons in his presence, and to
Campion by letter, Allen offered congratulations on their
new opportunity for exercising holy obedience and charity
in service of their neighbour . . . A fragment of the letter
came to my hand, and it seems well to transcribe it . . . It
begins thus:

'Father, brother, and son of mine, Edmund Campion!
These different forms of address, all of highest affection,
I use deliberately. Although the supreme Father and head
of your Order, our Lord, as I understand it, calls you from
Prague to Rome, and after that to England, your brothers
according to the flesh also urge you. Even if you cannot
hear their voices, God himself has heard their prayers . . .
Make haste, then, dearest friend, and come to Rome as
soon as possible so as to meet me, at all events, by the end
of February. I would prefer you to come before the
middle of the month. Certainly, this would be best. Therefore, as your health allows—I permit no exception for
business or other impediment—make haste to get here
as soon as you can . . . I have no doubt of your own mind
and goodwill in the matter since you live most happily
not by your own will but by another's. Nor would you
shrink from going to furthest India, or from the worst
kind of peril at the command of your superiors. Our
harvest now is great in England, dearest brother, and
cannot be gathered in by ordinary labourers. It calls for
men of greater capacity, and for you especially, together
with other selected men from your Order. Reverend
Father General has acceded to the prayers of many people.
The Pope has approved—he is the true father of our
country. God Himself, doubtless, in Whose hands is your
destiny, has at last permitted that our Campion should be

restored to us: he who is better endowed than all with the riches of knowledge and grace . . . From the English College, Rome, December 5th, 1579'.*

. . . Allen himself returned to Rheims, while Campion was called to Rome by letter from Everard Mercurian. These young athletes had committed themselves to a way which Allen, too, must embrace in accordance with the demands of honour and charity.

END OF BOOK THE SECOND

BOOK THE THIRD

1.   (1580): Two letters from Mercurian to Prague followed up the decision to send Campion and Persons into England. One written in March was to John Paul Campanus, Rector of the college; the other to Campion telling him to come quickly to Rome. He had hitherto worked admirably for the Catholic cause in Bohemia. He was now to go to the assistance of his own country in so much need. He would work among a similar kind of people to enjoy, as it was hoped, a like kind of success. The feelings roused by this message in so generous a heart are not difficult to imagine. Campion derived strength of soul from the very cruelty of the recent persecution levelled at Catholic priests up and down England, and a constancy like their against whatever the future should hold in store. His genuine modesty made him believe that the situation called for much more than he found in himself, but faith reassured him that with God's added strength nothing would be toilsome. Since this journey did not spring from his own whim but from the will of his superiors, that is to say, as he believed, from God, he complied. Considering only the divine will, he hastened to fulfil with the utmost care all that was commanded of him. On 2 April he arrived in Rome; all the happier for learning that Persons would be his companion, and almost certainly his superior, in the great enterprise. He did not stay in the city more than eight days. They got their orders from Everard as to how the Catholic cause could be best served by the works of our institute. They must take no less care to avoid anything to do with the political affairs of the kingdom whether in spoken word or writing.

On Low Sunday, having first asked for the Pope's blessing, they set out. Ralph Emerson was added to their

party. As a lay-brother he would act as general factotum.
There is no more powerful weapon than living example.
The courage of such spirits in the teeth of all adversity
spurred on not only the energies of youth, but even the
flagging efforts of men growing old, to like labours and the
rewards which followed them. Four of them had once
been chaplains at the hospice; three more, student-priests
out of the new seminary, now advanced in the same line
of battle. Two lay-gentlemen made the number up to the
12 who set out that day from Rome.* The road into
Italy from the Low Countries was controlled at that time
by Spanish soldiers. To avoid them, and not in any case
unwillingly, they proceeded by way of Geneva, once
dominated by Calvin and now by Beza, to see the home
of this most tenacious form of Protestantism. They wished
also to test the strength of Beza's arguments, and even
more to try the defences whereby his paradoxes were
maintained. Admitted to an interview with Beza one
evening, they began to sound him out. The shrewd
veteran saw himself hard-pressed by the evident conflict
among the doctrines and authors of the breakaway movements; not merely in certain details and glosses, but in
matters which touched the fundamentals of faith, the
efficacy and necessity of sacraments, and forms of worship. Beza made excuse of pressure of business and the
lateness of the hour to cover his ignorance [of the
answers]. He sent his guests on their way, though with
all courtesy. Every stranger was allowed to spend three
days in that city. However, seeing they could accomplish
nothing but a useless war of words—or so it seemed—they
set out next day once more on the road to France. When
they got to Rheims, it was well into June. It is easier to
imagine than relate the kind of wonder with which
Rheims eyed this fresh team of Christian athletes; the
compliments with which the English seminary in the city
—and particularly Allen, the author and interpreter of the
plan—received these comrades; and with what joy. The
company which was to strike fear into the enemy could
only be a source of pride to the generals in the campaign,

and a spur to imitate them as companions of their perils.

2.   . . . The Protestant authorities had observed all the movements and intentions of Allen and Persons from the very beginning of the seminaries. They tried continually to overturn and bring to nought by every means available whatever was put on foot for the advancement of Catholicism and the consolation of Catholics . . . Everything about the present expedition was revealed, expounded, and described to the Queen's Council by messengers even from Rome itself. Secretary Walsingham had agents at his command everywhere, and obtained information by a varied correspondence from Geneva, and through spies stationed at Rheims. Watch was kept at all the ports. A register of names was drawn up. Even the pictures of Campion and Persons were posted. In order to avoid one noose hanging all, therefore, the nine priests entered at different places. The two of special interest in this context took the road to St. Omer with Ralph Emerson. Even here, it was not thought safe for three to travel together. Persons was the first to attempt entry. Campion expounds his plan and his frame of mind on this journey in a letter to Mercurian:

'Father Robert, accompanied by his brother George, left Calais with a very favourable wind after midnight the day before I started writing this. We hope, therefore, that he made Dover yesterday morning, June 16th. He went disguised as a soldier. He was so well made up and showed such a choleric disposition that he would have had eyes, indeed, who could discern beneath that costume, face and gait the goodness and modesty that lay in hiding. We are worried all the same, I will not say by mere rumours but by something positively like a clamour that heralds our approach. Only divine Providence can counteract this kind of publicity, and we fully acquiesce in its dispositions. Following orders, I have stayed on for a while, so that, if possible, I can find out from the captains and certain merchants who are due here how Father

[Robert] got on before I set sail myself. If I hear anything
I may make fresh plans. I have decided to make the
attempt whatever happens so that I can strike a blow for
the cause even if it means death. It often happens that a
conquering army's first troops in take a thrashing. Certainly, if our Society pushes on with this campaign, it
will be necessary to overcome much ignorance and sheer
wickedness. For which cause, in any case, the war was
declared. I am thinking of the 20th of the month for
going to Calais.

'Meanwhile, at St. Omer's College, I am getting myself
fitted out, with Ralph as my companion. What do you
think all this will cost? Especially since things are not
available as once they were. As we wish to disguise ourselves, and imitate the vain fashions of life around us,
many trifles which we think altogether silly had to be
bought for us. The money for the journey, these clothes,
and four horses which we shall have to buy on the spot
in England, will account for our funds. These must come
from the same kind of providence whereby loaves were
multiplied in the wilderness. But this is the least of our
difficulties. We will keep in touch with you. I won't
close up this letter yet so that if I think of anything else
I can add it in the next three days. Everything may be
decided one way or the other before this is read, but I
thought it worthwhile to put down, while I am still here,
all that concerns this weighty undertaking, and the latest
information on which all that is not yet written will
depend. A certain English gentleman comes to me often
who understands the political situation. He tells me that
the Bishop of St. Asaph's coming is noised abroad in
letters and conversation. This has stirred up a good deal
of speculation since the majority feel he is the kind of
man who would not take on such a troublesome burden
at this time unless something big were moving. I gave him
to understand the true cause of his coming and in the
simplest terms. All the same, he does not cease to wonder.
Among the English, the title and way of life of bishops
is honourable indeed. Today the wind is dropping so I

shall move off quickly for the sea. I have been most kindly entertained here at St. Omer's College, and helped in all things needful. Indeed, along the whole route we have received extraordinarily good teatment in all our houses. To this was added ths hospitality of the illustrious Cardinals Paleotto and Borromeo, and of the Arch-priest Collensis. We deliberately avoided Paris and Douai. We seem safe enough, provided we are not betrayed in these coastal regions. I have waited a further day, but since there is still no news either way of Father Robert, I persuade myself he got through safely. I pray God to watch over your Reverence, your Assistants, and the whole Society. Farewell! June 20th, 1580.'*

3.   Persons passed safely from St. Omer to Calais, and
     from Calais to Dover. In the latter port, he was providentially favoured beyond all his hopes. Face and dress were as changed as skill could make them, and his talk was affable and self-assured. Thus he presented to the port officials an appearance quite different from what they saw in their picture. So he and his companions asked for, and got, the proper permission to proceed inland. The unexpected mildness of the port officials provided an opportunity for sending quickly to Campion under the assumed name of Patrick, a travelling-salesman from Dublin. Persons commended him at the same to the officials whom he had found so easy to deal with. When he got the news, Campion crossed over at once with Ralph. Although, thanks to orders from the Privy Council, he found the port-watchers too alert to allow him through with the same ease as Persons, by dint of ardent prayer to God and St. John the Baptist, he got by. He had been devoted to St. John since he was very young, and it was the day after his feast-day. The petty officials were all ready to lead him away in bonds when, as the result of an unlooked-for change of mind, and contrary to what the bystanders expected, a messenger from the mayor of the town gave orders that Patrick should be released together with Ralph his servant. The astonishing casualness

of the mayor encouraged Campion's wondering heart to hope for no less help from God when he arrived at London than he had enjoyed at Dover. He was due to arrive there the second day after leaving Dover.

Persons had foreseen that the great city, with its teeming houses and population, would give the enemy a more perplexing problem as to where, with whom, and when, any new and sought-after visitor would take lodging than was the case in the port itself—provided he could leave it! Although it was to be hoped that Campion had got through, in the absence of news to the contrary, Persons asked young gentlemen of his own persuasion to watch that part of the town which lay towards Dover, and keep an eye on all the approaches. If they should come across anyone by the name of Edmund—this was pre-arranged with a servant—they should give him a friendly greeting, and guide him to Thomas Jay who was keeping watch on the shore. Jay, who used to pass up and down every in a small boat on either side of Gravesend, where he usually landed, recognised among the crowd of incoming voyagers a man who corresponded with Persons's description. He held out his right hand to him in a friendly way: 'Give me your hand Master Edmund!' The voice was unfamiliar, but the expression of his face, way of gesturing, talking and offering the right hand to Edmund as he got into his boat, were enough to dispel immediately all fear of deception. Then followed familiar greetings. They made their way to a house decided on long before, the one well content at finding his guest, the other overflowing with relief and gratitude for God's mercy. Persons's absence from the city was the only thing lacking to the day's perfection. But such was their readiness to accept anything in a spirit of acquiescence, that each did everything he could to intensify the other's contentment.

4. People attracted by like things are stimulated by their common interest. The inborn idealism of many young gentlemen had been fired by Campion's renown.

They now burned with curiosity to have first-hand contact
with him. Disregarding expense, and caring little for
danger, they were most in need of the reassurance which
is the special gift of an onward-looking Christian soldier.
They would certainly not allow this great leader of theirs
to go short of anything he needed. He in turn would distribute the Sacraments in a way that was impressive as
well as decorous. The times hardly allowed it but devotion
still called for it. They took him along to the fine house
of Baron Paget with an invitation in his name. Here on the
feast of SS. Peter and Paul, Campion gave his first sermon.
He preached on the unshakeable firmness of the Catholic
Church, and the cruelty of those who raged against her.
But he declared that they would never prevail against
her gates, nor destroy her liberty to proclaim her faith.
In this house Campion performed the other functions of
priesthood. He was all the more fervent for being called
to it by the enthusiasm, nay the importunity, of the young
gentlemen. Their gratitude, and the crowds of listeners
spurred him to his best. He refused to be restrained by the
ordinary bounds of duty . . . His efforts were unstinted
as long as the urgent promises and prayers of his devotees
were there to keep his zeal at fever heat . . . When the
Sacraments were celebrated, and Campion moved about
and preached every day, it was impossible that the Privy
Council should long remain in ignorance of what was
already common news throughout the town. Campion's
exact location was unknown, or could be borne with for
a time in view of the privileged position and authority of
the nobleman-organiser. But it seemed a mark of folly,
to those not altogether unwise, to hope that this could
go on for long amid so many suspicious and watchful eyes.
Persons, on his return to London, concluded that the
danger must be eliminated, and promptly. At first, he
decided to limit access to him. That proved difficult;
for Campion was now the one man in town who attracted
the attention and interest of all. Persons therefore decided
that he must leave. One danger, however, is born from
another.

5.   From the recently-founded seminaries at Rome and
     Rheims, not a few new priests had flocked in to
rebuild the slipping foundations of Catholic faith in
England. These men were altogether used to customs
prevailing in Europe. They knew, however, that this island
had more feast-days and fast-days, once universal, than
almost any other part of the Christian world. A day was
therefore fixed for a general consultation lest there should
come about among the Catholics, or on the part of the old
priests who still survived from Mary's reign, a quarrel over
the fact that the latter held to older English custom while
the former wanted conformity with the practice of other
places. A great' many priests were in attendance. Persons
and Campion were among them. It was decided that as
soon as anyone entered a district, he should make diligent
enquiry into its customs; then observe them without
change. For usage was by no means uniform throughout
England. However, since no one had authority over all,
it was difficult to oblige everybody unless all were agreed.
The Protestant rites were also discussed. People were
ordered by law to be present at these for the sake of
uniformity in worship. Was it permissible to be present
for any other cause? The view of those Catholics who
denied it now prevailed. Among other reasons, because
not only would it be against Catholic usage—these latest
rites were instituted to condemn and abolish such—but
also because the will of law and legislator was that attendance indicated conformity. This necessarily prevailed
over private reasons, and Catholics, if present, would
commonly be regarded as taking part. All Catholics were
therefore urged to take this counsel to heart. In this way,
they would also protect themselves from error and schism
which would be practised by such conformity, and gradually work its way more deeply in. Although a handful,
perhaps, would be sufficiently tough to resist the frequent
darts coming down on them from the superior position
of ministers' unorthodox preaching, ordinary people
would in time readily succumb. They would be tempted,
it was thought, by the prospect of immunity from fines,

easy-going moral behaviour, and some kind of imitation of conforming truth. That view had, indeed, already gained strength from the preponderating vote of the Fathers met together at the Council of Trent. To this was added the later declaration of Cardinal Toledo.

'Since such a decree is aimed at the Catholic Church, and in favour of heretical error, confirming it, and, in a sense, proclaiming it, there is no sort of reason for obeying it. To be present at heretical conventicles, and to frequent their churches indiscriminately like one of themselves, is not only to obscure true faith and religion, but also to profess the worship of a false sect through a certain exterior cult designed to that end. This is forbidden by the divine law, and cannot be made lawful by any dispensation. Nor can it be justified by any loss of temporal goods. That protestation, however, which is made by many Catholics, does not excuse from sin since it is contrary to the deed. If the fact is as it is described, namely, attendance at heretical churches, and being present like one of them in one of their conventicles when their purposes are religious, any protestation remains exterior to their sect; and to this end the decree was issued'. (14 June 1581.)

This is how Toledo replied when he was questioned round about this time. After his adliminal visit, Pope Paul V confirmed this in a Brief (literis suis).*

11. Spies and public informers were a repulsive breed of men who made it their whole business day and night to keep watch on Catholic houses throughout the city. If they noticed anyone making a visit for the second or third time, or saw a number of people calling, they would lay siege to the doors; even call on neighbours to help them, while they burst in, to lay hold on their man. Having seized him, they would bring him before the magistrate. If he showed the slightest hesitation in answering their questions, they led him away forthwith as a suspected priest to be heavily fined or subjected to prolonged imprisonment, or even killed. At this time, Sledd

was the worst of such characters. While the debate I
mentioned ran its several hours' course, and the priests
came together by groups, Sledd stopped Henry Orton
on his way there. Then he noticed Robert Johnson on
the same route, hastening to cross the river. Sledd followed
him stealthily, and laid hold of him at the entrance to the
lane over by the river-bank. Certain of his prey, he warned
him at whatever house Robert stopped off, he would go
to it at once. Perhaps he wanted to make some money.
Maybe his writ did not run on the other bank, where the
Fathers were in session. Possibly, he even wished to get
the upper hand of some other officious pursuivant. At all
events, he now clapped his hand on Robert, drawing him
back just as he was getting into the boat. Immediately the
cry went through the whole neighbourhood, as custom is,
'Papist! Priest!.' In the event Johnson, who had been
secretary to Mr. Talbot of Grafton, crowned his perseverance in faith with a glorious death. Meanwhile, the
tumult now borne across to the opposite bank of the
Thames warned the men in conference of their danger.
They hastened their departure.

Persons was by this time convinced that they could
do their work with more effect, liberty, and hope of
result, by going through the country county by county.
That was where he decided to go himself. This would be
more effective than to concentrate on teaching the people
of one city, however populous. Again not only Catholics,
but most gentlemen, lived much of the time in the
country, although for the necessities of legal business
many went up to London four times a year. Among the
Londoners, and others dedicated to the contentious ways
of law—these practically made up two halves of the city,
both of which were engrossed in making money—it was
more difficult and less rewarding to bring up the subject
of religion. Indeed, it would soon be a question not
whether Catholicism was to increase but be lost altogether.
Finally, in the country there were fewer eyes to spy on
papist houses. There one's neighbours were not so steeped
in malice that they could not bear even the name of

Catholic. In fact, for the most part, Catholics were well regarded by their country neighbours. In the towns their reputation was put in doubt by daily slander, alleged crimes, and the infliction of undeserved punishments. Their beliefs and professed way of life were treated likewise with contempt. For these reasons, Campion and Persons divided up the counties between them. So as to get Campion away quickly, they put London behind them that very evening. July [1580] was now running out.

Their plan was to return to the city at intervals as opportunity offered. At the meeting of the priests, they enlarged on the orders they had received from General Everard. These made it clear that they had come to help the common cause of faith and religion by tactics mutually agreed by all. There was nothing special about themselves except the stricter obligation imposed by formal vows, and the hope of greater help from God by reason of this obligation undertaken for Him. From any other sort of business they had strict command to hold aloof. However, the ministers of the Crown never ceased to denigrate whatever attempts were made on behalf of Catholicism. On pretext of treason, they slandered all priests coming from the seminaries, and particularly those termed Jesuits. Campion at Hoxton, where they met together at night, therefore drew up a reasoned apologia for the coming campaign.* He gave this little work to his friends to be presented to the Privy Council as opportunity arose.

In this work Campion admits first of all that he has taken Holy Order, and given his allegiance to the Society of Jesus. But this is only so that he can fight under the standard of Christ with all hope of money and fame set aside. He came from Rome to England at the General's command. With the same eagerness he would have gone to any other part of the globe had the General seen fit. The sole object of Campion's journey is the preservation and propagation of the Catholic faith by such means as are everywhere common to priests, and known to all, namely through the ministry of the Sacraments and preaching. Any other kind of business is alien to his institute, far from his own mind, and forbidden by the solemn command of superiors. He therefore asks that, putting aside all fear and suspicion that he is raising rebellion, he may have permission to expound his religious beliefs in the presence of the Queen and her Council; and also before university men and leading lights from the legal profession. The strength of the cause is not in doubt. Based on very plain and solid arguments drawn from every appropriate source, it must prevail. On the other hand, the form of belief and code of morals lately introduced can be proved shamelessly repugnant to the law's authority, the conclusions of the Fathers and theologians, and finally to the dignity of monarchs and nobility. In contrast, Catholicism will be demonstrated as most evidently agreeing with all these. Campion is not afraid to commit himself to discussion with the most learned individually on these matters, or as one man in an assembly. He is not being boastfully confident in the power of his own intellect, or the extent of his erudition, but comes as one provided with the firmest protection of truth unconquered. If none of this is allowed, he will at least pray daily to the same God common to them all to bring them to a better frame of mind. Nor will he cease to do all he can to promote the well-being of his most beloved country; winning over as many souls as possible until his life should end either by his own labours or else by the swords and torments of his opponents. This is the mind of the whole Society of Jesus; this the intention of all those who have been trained in the seminaries overseas. Their dedicated labours no subterfuge can undermine, and no force break.

12. After this, Campion and Persons one early dawn set off in different directions. It fell to Persons to look after Northampton, Gloucester, Hereford, Derby and the surrounding districts. As the man responsible for directing the whole mission, he stayed nearer London, the centre of commerce and affairs of every sort. Campion went with Ralph to undertake work in the remoter districts in the

North. George Gilbert followed Persons, the sharer of his journey, dangers and much of his expense. Not infrequently, he took on the duties of servant, although he was of good family, and as a youth possessed a proud spirit. Gardiner, the well-known tenant of Hoxton, was the first to offer his help to Persons whose discourses on the Catholic faith he had heard himself. Once he had been an enthusiastic follower of John Foxe, the man who compiled a huge volume on the Waldensians, the Poor of Lyons, the Hussites, and Wycliffites, and other Protestants before and after them who had suffered anything from Catholic rulers for desertion and profanation of the Catholic faith . . . Foxe hoped to persuade his audience . . . that the men of these persuasions were in no wise inferior in number, constancy or depth of conviction to the Catholics. Only in cruelty, indeed, if that could please the gods, did the latter excel . . . But when he began to reflect in the light of orthodox faith, Gardiner quickly saw that one could scarcely speak of agreement among people who never agreed except in one thing, namely, that they were opposed to the authority of a single head over the whole Church . . .

Gardiner not only persevered with unshakeable firmness, but endured many trials courageously for his faith. From all this, Persons learned much which proved useful to him later in producing a refutation of [Foxe's] martyrology . . . Baron Compton, Thomas Tresham and William Catesby, both knights, were all reconciled to the Church; also Catesby's uncle, and one Dimock, a fine gentleman, together with many other heads of important families. Catesby's uncle is worthy of special mention. He had spent many years at court, and indulged in every kind of vice, as custom is, until led by curiosity or the persuasion of friends, he conceived a desire to meet Persons. The latter talked to him about God and his eternal salvation. However, Catesby pointed out, 'The first thing is to convince me of God's existence. Then I will easily concede the rest'. Persons offered arguments ready to mind, but did not seen to make much headway. Then Campion arrived on the scene. He so overwhelmed the man with the force of his reasoning that Catesby, convinced at length, returned to the Church . . . Not long afterwards, Campion assisted him in dying a holy death. There was also Dimock's sister, a lady of acute mind and great ability, one of the Queen's ladies-in-waiting. She had accepted the most extreme teachings of the Protestants so enthusiastically that she had come to believe that the pains of hell, as we refer to them, were simply the prickings of every man's conscience. There was no pain from fire; certainly, no other kind of torment. At her brother's peruasion, she admitted Persons to talk with her. Hearing matters from him, she not only embraced the Catholic faith, but not long afterwards, surrendered all else, and retired to a convent in France. The remainder of her life she passed under vows . . .

Conversations like the above with people outside the Catholic Church gave Persons the idea, when he came to write his 'Christian Directory', of beginning with proofs for the existence of God. Of which more later. The way Persons and his companion lived, and what they did at this time, and the result of their labour, cannot be seen more clearly than in Campion's letter to Everard Mercurian, General of the Society. Although the letter appears in full in his [published] writings, it will not be useless to give it again here.*

13. 'Now we have been over here, existing by the grace of God, for five months, Reverend Father, I thought it would be good to describe the general state of things . . . The last news I wrote to you came from St. Omer. What has happened since then I will put down for you briefly . . . We waited four days for a favourable wind. Then on the fifth day, I set sail in the evening. It was the feast of my patron, St. John the Baptist, to whom I had often recommended my cause and journey. Early next day, my man and I got to Dover. There we were within an ace of being taken prisoner. We appeared, as ordered, before the Mayor. He had a very good idea of what we

were; opponents of the Protestant party, and fervent
lovers of our own faith who had concealed our true
names . . . One thing he insisted on, that I was Allen.
This I undertook to repudiate, if necessary, with an oath.
At length he reached a decision and repeated it frequently.
I would be sent up under guard to the Privy Council.
Nor can I think of anything apart from divine influence
that made him change his mind . . . Suddenly the old man
broke out that he was content to let us go, and added a
farewell. Thank God! We almost flew off . . . I got to
London. My good angel brought me—I did not know it
myself—to the same house which had formerly sheltered
Robert. Some young gentlemen hurried to see me. They
greeted me, dressed me, giving me the right appearance,
and sent me out of the city. I ride over some part of the
country where I am now nearly every day. The harvest,
indeed, is great. While on horseback, I think out my short
addresses, which I polish on arriving at a house. Then if
any come to me I talk with them or hear their confessions.
In the morning, after Mass, I give a talk. Their ears strain
eagerly for what is said. The Sacraments they receive
very frequently. In administering them, we are helped
here and there by priests whom we find everywhere.
In this way we meet the people's needs, and the work
of the district becomes more manageable for us.

'Our own priests, outstanding for learning and holiness
of life, inspire such a high opinion of our Order that the
awe in which the Catholics hold us is something I hesitate
to describe. Hence it seems all the more important that
the helpers of whom we now stand in utmost need should
be of a kind to maintain all this. Above all, let them be
practised in preaching. We cannot hope to escape the
hands of the Protestants in the long run; so many eyes,
so many mouths, so many traps at the service of the
enemy. My dress is very simple, and I change it often;
likewise our names. I am reading a letter on the first page
of which is written, "Campion has been captured". This
re-echoes again and again in my ears wherever I go, so that
fear itself has come to drive out fear. I carry my life in

my hands always. Let those who are coming to help us think about this. Certainly, the consolations arising from this work make up not only for the fear of the consequences but would compensate for any sort of pain with infinite satisfaction . . . Here among the very Protestants, at least when they are more impartial than the rest, the saying has gone abroad that Catholics are people who pay their debts; and in the same way, if a Catholic treats someone unfairly, they protest because from such a man this sort of thing is not expected . . . Nor is there any race of men less worthy or more unsound than their own ministers. Not unreasonably, we get angry that in this lost cause men so unlearned, so reprehensible, so divided among themselves, and so little worthy of esteem, should be in a position to lord it over the minds and spirits of the very flower of the nation.

'Threatening proclamations accompany us on all sides. Nevertheless, through caution, the prayers of good people, and most important, by God's help, we have safely covered a good portion of the island. I see that most people forget themselves while looking after us. Something happened at that time which I had not looked for . . . I had put in writing in the form of propositions some very reasonable postulates and demands. I admitted that I was a priest of the Society who had come with the purpose of spreading Catholic faith, teaching the Gospel and administering the Sacraments. I begged audience with the Queen and the principal men of the kingdom, and I challenged my adversaries to a contest. I decided to keep one copy by me for when I should be taken before the magistrates. The other I gave to a friend, so that if they should lay hold of me and my possessions, the other might be passed round indefinitely. My friend, far from concealing it, had it printed and published. Our adversaries were furious. They replied that they were willing to accept the suggestion, but the Queen did not want further disputation on matters which had been settled. They lash at us with insults saying we are seditious, hypocritical, even heretical —which causes us most amusement. In a remarkable way, this mistake has served our cause. If we are so commanded by public authority, we will declare what we have to say elsewhere than at the royal court. But nothing is farther from their minds.

'All the jails have been crammed with Catholics, and new ones are being set up. Now at last they admit openly that it would be more effective to deliver up a few traitors to execution than to betray so many souls. They say nothing now of their martyrs. We prevail as regards our cause, our number, our prestige, and the good opinion of all. Instead of a few apostates and worn-out tailors, we can offer bishops, local magnates, knights and gentlemen of most ancient lineage; as a demonstration of learning, probity and wisdom, well-instructed men in their prime and gentlewomen of renown. Others of more modest position are too numerous to count. But all of them are being destroyed, some in final holocaust, and others by suffering daily renewed. While I write this a most cruel persecution rages. Our household is sad; for their tale is either of death come upon members of the family, or of cramping cells and chains, or robbery of their belongings. All the same, they go on bravely. Even now, very many come back to the Church; new recruits are enrolled while veterans shed their blood. By this blood, which is sacred, and through these hostages, the way will be won to God, and in a short time, doubtless, we shall prevail . . . I am prevented by a warning of immediate danger from writing more at this time. Let God arise, and may His enemies be scattered . . .'.

14. Campion's memory has remained green in the North even down to our own day. They remembered his sermons on the Angelic Salutation, on the 10 lepers, on the king setting out for a far country, on the last judgment, and on many other subjects. They flocked to them with such enthusiasm that men in numbers and of notable family would pass whole nights in neighbouring barns in order to be present at the appointed time. They were not merely captivated by his eloquence or elocution, although

in both respects he was admirable. Rather was it the
warmth with which he spoke, and some hidden force in
his way of speaking which, as it was believed, proceeded
from nothing less than the Holy Spirit. He preached every
day, except when he had to withdraw from the throng
of besiegers in order to write. His friends' eagerness to
disseminate letters addressed to the Privy Council imposed
on him this obligation of writing. So much confidence on
the part of one individual, as much as anything he actually
wrote, was interpreted as rash folly and brazen impudence
by men who flattered themselves for a doctrine and learning they could scarcely sustain. Those responsible for the
peace of the realm, or more correctly . . . for cherishing
lowered standards of life, claimed that his writings aimed
at stirring up the mob and causing discontent. Every
entrenched authority protested against Campion's
insolence, and claimed that, however open and frank on
the exterior the Jesuits appeared, in fact they advocated
hidden trickery. Without doubt, they were preparing the
way for the Pope and foreign princes to invade the country
by force of arms. Hanmer and Charke also took up pen,
and issued books strong less in argument than in smell
of slander. The founder, origin, and teaching of the
Society they overwhelmed with ridicule, snapping their
fingers at everything suggested, and not only the sought-
for meeting.

Campion ignored this abuse, for his words were directed
to the leaders of the realm and the universities, not to one
or two petty functionaries in the market-place. He did not
speak his words to the wind, nor did he intend to indulge
in empty boasting. He set down the considerations on
which his conviction was based in a brief commentary—
the Ten Reasons. They were dedicated to the universities,
and contained the principal foundations of Catholic
belief. They were written in a style at once elegant,
succinct, forceful and dignified. The teaching of the
Catholic Church stands vividly portrayed . . . The argument begins from the sovereign authority and teaching of
Scripture, and from single or collated texts. This is

compared with the interpretation of antiquity, which must also give the meaning for us. The work begins with the nature of the Church. Others deny this as accessible to the senses, making it discernible only to the inner scrutiny of a very few. They play down its presence, although this is clearly visible in every part of Holy Writ. The book deals with the oecumenical Councils as Catholic first, last and in between; and with the Fathers who condemn these latest conjectures with singular unanimity . . . From the foundation of the Fathers, and equipped with all the apparatus of biblical learning with which the best authors set out, Campion's book resorts much to the authority of the past, the practice of the Church, and the Apostolic tradition. Mostly, however, and for preference, it is the frequent attestations of Scripture that coalesce, and drive home the arguments. Another point of departure is that more remote history which tells of our triumphs, progress, changing fortunes and hostilities . . . Finally, Campion deals with every kind of witness, and the arena of the university. Anything we discover anywhere provided new arguments for Catholic faith. Heaven, hell and the utmost parts of the earth; gentiles, Turks, Christian princes, flourishing universities, codes of law, the establishment of dynasties, the beginnings of royal houses, orders of knights, and even their liveries, windows, coins, doors, public buildings, all these objects and items testify that, of all the religions in the world, ours has the deepest roots . . .

15. Persons was not behindhand in his zeal for winning souls nor in writing. In these months, he published reasons why Protestant services should not be attended; this to brace up the hearts of Catholics against the spiteful edicts and fines which were imposed on them unless they were reverently present. He then issued a brief critique of Hanmer and Charke which infuriated both. They had fallen to rending Ignatius, the founder of the Jesuits, and what was taught by men of the greatest learning. Persons portrayed the Protestant leaders at this time—Luther and

Calvin—taking his colours from their own commentaries
. . . This little book, received with applause by Catholics,
was slight in bulk but distinguished for its service to truth.
It sharpened Protestant hatred against the author, and
stung them to the utmost effort to capture him and his
friends. However, he escaped the snares of his enemies,
and brought very many back to the Catholic Church . . .
To understand the state of the times, and the loyalty
of the Catholics amid the fury of their persecutors, let
us hear what Persons himself has to say in his letter to the
Fathers living at Rome written on 17 November 1580.*

'The entire kingdom rages most cruelly against the
Catholics . . . Their number, however, is more than the
energy of the pursuivants can cope with. I understand that
in one month alone 50,000 names were put down of
those who refuse to go to Protestant churches. Hence
they are commonly called recusants. You will gather from
this how great is the number of Catholics everywhere if
so many are prepared to go as far as to offer openly life
and fortune to the greedy will and arbitrary judgment of
their persecutors . . . It is noteworthy with how much
feeling and persistence these new rites are detested by the
majority, so that they will not go willingly even to the
doors of the churches. The request was put recently to
certain gentlemen that at least they should put in a
respectful appearance once a year. They could even make
a protest against the rites for which they came, provided
they showed themselves obedient to the Queen. They
preferred, however, to have their religious conscience
unaffronted rather than the liberty promised them. They
persuaded a small boy of 10 years that he could precede,
for the sake of courtesy, a new bride on her way to the
church. Afterwards, when he was looked on as a schismatic by his companions, he expiated his fault with so
many tears that he would let no one comfort him, until,
meeting me a few days afterwards, he fell on his knees
to ask pardon for the fault. He fervently promised that
for the future no kind of torment would move him to
compromise himself by the like lapse. There are examples

innumerable of this kind of thing which I will pass over. Such are the conditions in which we live that, although by public edict no one is allowed to come near us, everyone wants to see us notwithstanding. Wherever we go we are most eagerly received. Many people make long journeys in order to have our conversation for a few hours. They profess themselves wholly at our disposal. Everywhere they give us what we need. They even ask us to make free of what they have for ourselves. We find priests everywhere in sympathy with us. In sympathy with us? I should rather say in most things obeying us with the kind of obedience that springs from affection. To tell the truth, such is the reputation of the Society with everybody that we are not a little troubled to know how we can sustain it. Especially since we know how far we are from that perfection which they admire in us. Hence we need your prayers all the more.

'Not long ago, while they were pursuing someone else, they chanced upon Sherwin. He gave excellent witness to his faith as he stood before the Protestant Bishop of London. They weighed him down with plenty of iron. He carries it cheerfully; and, as he writes to me, seeing himself in chains for Christ, he can hardly repress a smile. It torments our tormentors much to know that by no sort of cruelty can they tear one Catholic from his convictions; not even girls. A young lady of good family was asked something about the Pope by the Bishop of London. When she insisted on replying as the truth was, she was ordered by the man, as he put all humanity aside, to be led away to the prison where prostitutes are punished. She went of crying out joyfully that she was not being dragged away for a crime but for faith and conscience. From morning until far into the night, after I have performed what belongs to God's service, and sometimes after having preached twice in the same day, my attention is taken up with never-ending business. My chief concern is to reply to questions of conscience; to send priests where they are needed; to receive people returning to the Church; to strengthen by letter those wavering in the faith; to get alms conveyed to those in prison. Every day, I beg and am begged from. So many things remain to be done that I could despair, but for the clear thought that anything at all that we do is for the glory of God. The consolation of seeing with what contentment they everywhere welcome our coming to these regions is greater than any effort of mind or body could be. I beg you to help us with your prayers so that we can live up to the great things everybody expects of us. Farewell!'

Nor will it be irrelevant to corroborate Persons's great faith from the testimony of a priest writing about this time. He wrote thus to the rector of a seminary, 'Our business is making marvellous progress. Although the majority despise the goods we offer, and are even repelled, there are still many who wish to buy; and a great many also who come to look at them. All the talk in England now is of the Fathers of the Society, whom here they call Jesuits. Many tales are made up about them as formerly by the poets about their monsters. On their origin, institute, way of life, customs and teachings, doings and intentions, many things are said; much that is contradictory, so that anyone can see they are the wild ravings of weak heads rather than plain narrations resting on fact. These are the sort of things, however, which are put about publicly and privately, retailed in sermons and written books. The main point is, they and all of us have come from the Pope as spies, traitors and disturbers of the public peace. Some of the Calvinists wrote against Campion, and against the whole set-up of the Jesuits, touching also the life of the founder himself, Ignatius. They did not get away with it unscathed. Within 10 days, a reply came out which put a permanent blush on their cheeks. I would never stop if I went on to describe all the fervour and zeal of the Catholics in detail'.

16. The more the zeal of the Jesuits and the priests strove to protect their faith from the daily attacks of the enemy the more ruthlessly did the latter dedicate his efforts to the task of undermining the determination

of all classes of Catholics. At the latest session of parliament* on 16 January 1581, it was enacted that all persons who had completed their 16th year should be fined 20 English pounds a month . . . if they did not attend the Protestant churches. February apart, all the months had more than 28 days, but they numbered 13 months in the year. Whosoever persuaded anyone to accept absolution from heresy or sin, or accepted such from a Catholic priest, was declared guilty of treason. They interpreted these things as departure from obedience due to the Queen. To be present at Mass made one liable to a fine of 266 crowns and a year's imprisonment. Anyone who celebrated Mass was liable to twice this amount. In this connection, something quite ridiculous happened not long ago, and altogether suited to the mentality of our magistrates when they are dealing with such matters. A secular priest was accused of receiving Holy Order overseas, but it could not be sufficiently proved to the satisfaction of the 12 men of the jury. They judged him, therefore, not guilty. However, because some apostate unknown swore that he had heard him celebrating Mass some 30 years before, although he was absolved of his priesthood, he was convicted of what he could not have done unless he had been a priest. Since he could not pay so great a fine, he was condemned to life-imprisonment. But what more nearly concerns us is that, on the excuse of these laws, the Earl of Southampton, Baron Paget, Lords Compton and Vaux, and Thomas Tresham, William Catesby, John Arundel and Nicholas Poyntz, all knights, were imprisoned at this time, as were also the distinguished gentlemen and men of substance, Ralph Sheldon, Thomas Throckmorton and many others.

Among the remaining Catholics who were also the most outstanding disseminators and protectors of the faith was George Gilbert. Some of the worst creatures of the night pursued him with the utmost rigour, either because he was a fine type of young man who easily outshone his fellows, or else because they smelt him out as one who had been recently in Persons's company. They took away all his powers and possessions, and intercepted by fraud a considerable sum of money which he had put together from the sale of lands. Since he could not stay safely in any one place, thanks to the pursuivants, Persons persuaded him to make his way first to France, and then to Italy and Rome. This man had been brought up to another belief from childhood, and he first went to Rome out of open-minded curiosity; but thanks to conversation and confidential exchanges with Persons, he changed his mind and embraced the Catholic faith: also a holy way of life to follow in his own country. He returned to England fully matured, the only representative of his line, and heir to an ample estate. He began to think of marriage, although it was probably about the time that contract was due to be drawn up that the news of Persons's coming to England got about. Putting off his marriage, therefore, Gilbert hastened to seek out Persons. Once again, he was captivated by his company and easy conversation on religious matters. Indeed, he decided to abandon all thought of marriage, and to live a life with and for God alone. Fired with zeal for the Catholic cause, he provided Persons with all things necessary for his altar, lodging, journeyings, and indeed all that was required for his ministry, Gilbert also won for himself by earnest entreaty the exclusive right to do as much for Campion and the rest of his companions. He was altogether as good as his word, and inspired many other young men of equal loftiness of soul by his example and exhortation. Eventually, he attached himself exclusively to Persons. Not that the well-doing of this excellent young man confined itself to Jesuits. He laid up treasure in heaven for himself with many other priests and Catholics. Eventually, he was compelled by continual harassing and pursuit on the part of the enemies of his faith to decamp. He went to the English College in Rome. Let us hear the shining testimony of Allen, at that time President of Rheims, and later Cardinal, in a certain letter of his written at this time: 'I have with me at this time an outstanding supporter and companion of the Jesuits and priests in

England. He is George Gilbert. For their sake, he has
suffered the robbery of practically all his goods and
possessions. Since the Protestants have pursued him
before all others—they know his work in upholding and
assisting the Fathers of the Society—he has come to
France on the advice of Father Robert and others to
preserve himself for another time. He will come to Rome,
God willing, in the autumn, to place himself at the disposal
of Reverend Father General and yourself. At his departure,
he left Father Robert seven horses for the necessary
journeys of the priests and Fathers in their work and
conduct of affairs. He has also left them a considerable
sum for essential equipment; paper, printing-press, type-
founts, ink and the like. Big things can only be done with
large help. There must be men who are complete despisers
of wealth: but they must be rich as well, so that they can
make a notable contribution to such work. June 13th,
1582'. Thus Allen.*

When he returned to Rome, Gilbert did not put on the
ordinary seminary uniform so that he would be freer to
attend up and down the city to the common business
for which he was so invaluable. All the same, he put on a
life that was truly religious: fasting, watching, corporal
austerities, and above all, a tireless zeal in prayer . . . Five
hours daily he spent in this; even more when he did not
have to go out on business . . . He used to say there were
two things that drew him to the Society in love and
reverence. The first was that this kind of life represented
most nearly the kind of life which Christ Himself chose to
adopt on earth. The other was that the Society excelled all
others where obedience was concerned. His great respect,
and even desire, for martyrdom was sufficiently obvious
to those who witnessed, not without being much moved,
the sudden and premature last illness of this promising
young man . . . He received permission from Reverend
Father General to pronounce his vows in the Society, and
to be buried at Sant' Andrea [the noviceship of the
Roman Province] . . . He closed his eyes for the last time,
as if in sleep, on 6 October 1583. Gilbert left a legacy of

200 pounds English to the novitiate, but Father General had it all sent to Allen for the use of the college at Rheims, saying that he also would like to help with the expenses of his colleges if it could be allowed . . . It was thanks to Gilbert's beneficence, among other things, according to Bombino (Vita Campiani, Chapter 22), that the chapel of the English College was decorated with pictures of the illustrious martyrs of England, and may still be seen today. He, in fact, found the money for it; but the idea itself, concept and working out, must be referred to Father William Good, who was at that time confessor to the college.*

18.   Among the priests, apart from Sherwin . . . Rishton, his companion, was taken together with some well-known Catholics from Lancashire at the hostelry of the *Red Rose* on the old hill, as they call it, at Holborn (or the *Red Lion*; so Persons qualifies this in his notes). When Persons went there to talk to them, he suddenly forgot the precise location of the streets and houses, and lost his way. He thus disappointed the satellites of Walsingham who went to open up the inn. Going elsewhere, Persons learned for the first time of the peril he had providentially escaped when he wandered off so aimlessly. Such dangers occurred continually. By night or day, in any house he entered, there could be an ambush. He usually hid himself in the hayloft, and left before daybreak, taking various precautions according to the needs of the moment. Even when the prisons were full, they set new searches on foot to winkle out priests. They usually began by loading them with irons. Then they tormented them with most exquisite tortures. In the end, they were disposed of by death or exile. One wonders how they had the hypocrisy to rage at the Spanish Inquisitors . . .

At last the printing press fell into the searchers' hands. Through Persons's efforts, it had been acquired some months before to print the books they came over to write. It was now lost, together with all accessories and equipment. Campion could not be safe much longer.

Although his capture and death have been accurately recounted by Bombino, the nature of this history demands that we summarise it in some few words. It cannot but be welcome to the reader especially since we shall insert certain facts which escaped Bombino.

19. Parliament had been prorogued [18 March 1581].
Campion's *Ten Reasons* had come off the press successfully before the seizure, and had been published and distributed among the learned. They pounced on it eagerly. Everyone dispersed to his own home when the usual law sessions came to a close in London. Meanwhile, reproaches were heaped on Campion by the Protestants because a mere individual had challenged all the learned men in England to a religious disputation. Of the day, and the preparedness of such men to listen and discuss, there was never a word among any of them. The one aim of all their decrees was to waylay Campion by any means they could. Although they had no hope of overcoming him by argument, they expected to bring him to heel with their fetters. In order that he might be removed as far as possible from danger, Persons prescribed for Campion the journey to the northern regions first indicated the year before. The further he was from London, the more difficult it would be for the wiles of Campion's enemies to work mischief. The latter grew quieter proportionately as Campion's renown decreased with distance. Campion was to go into Norfolk. He first made his journey from neighbouring Oxford, whence Persons departed at the beginning of August, to the Yates' house at Lyford. (Persons notes the date [of arrival] as 15 July.) During Campion's few days' stay there, a snare was laid for the unwary man from which he would not escape except by a glorious death . . .

George Eliot, up to the present a Catholic, was goaded to a considerable crime by his consciousness of past misdeeds. He had undertaken to deliver to Walsingham, the Queen's secretary, a number of priests who were well-known from having been long with the Catholics.

They would be put in prison. Nothing could have been more acceptable to Walsingham. He was, as Camden bears witness, a puritan (Annals: Annus 33, Elizabeth), that is, of the Calvinist persuasion, and one of its most fervent protagonists. In this way, he won the favour of William Cecil—who had the chief influence with the Queen—and of the other members of his party among the courtiers. Eliot's first prey, and an indication of his soul-sickness to come, was John Paine. Paine had denied that an unmarried girl, recently abducted by Eliot from the house of Mr. Roper, could be legitimately joined to him in wedlock unless she were first restored to home and liberty. Eliot took Paine unawares, and gave him up to the authorities to be tortured on a trumped-up charge of compassing the Queen's death. Eliot was goaded to ever greater fury; for now he had the reputation of a turncoat, and had contracted a mark which time itself could not erase. Furthermore, he was wondering how he could wipe out with new 'services rendered' a suspicion from the mind of authority that he had committed a robbery with murder. He asked Walsingham for letters under the royal seal by which he could have power to seek out and arrest Massing papists. He was sure he would have a Jesuit to show before long. Walsingham not only employed his powers of mind, but even consumed his patrimony, in fostering, provoking and rewarding this kind of pest. Praising his zeal in the Queen's service, Walsingham got signed letters for Eliot giving him hope of impunity, and also the widest powers.

Joined with an old fox not less greedy or daring than himself, Eliot, conscious of his recent perfidy, put London behind him, and went ranging through the countryside. Perhaps he received the commission from Walsingham—a most astute searcher—out of things hidden —or perhaps, following his own inspiration, Eliot imagined that Campion and Persons would be hiding out not far from Oxford. Possibly he thought that at Lyford he had a man well-known, but one who did not know Eliot's own treachery; through him he might be able to squirm

safely into the bosom of some Catholic family. At all
events, Eliot got to Lyford—not more than eight miles
from Oxford—on the morning of 13 August 1581, the
ninth Sunday after Pentecost. He called the cook to him,
who had come from one Roper's house where they had
been on the staff together. Eliot said he had a necessary
journey to undertake; and that quickly. He had come there
so that, if possible, he could fulfil his obligation of hearing
Mass, seeing it was Sunday. The cook, with some difficulty,
got leave of the mistress of the house—the owner was in
London, and in prison. The cook told the overjoyed Eliot
that it would not be just anyone, but Campion himself
he would hear that day.

At the name of Campion, Eliot showed a pleasure that
was not feigned. Artfully concealing the real cause of his
joy, he was admitted to the innermost parts of the house,
and was present at all the day's services, a competent
simulator of deep devotion. After the services, he carefully thought out the next step. Although the cook urged
him not to leave without a meal, his own impatience, and
that of his assistant whom he had ordered to stand by, got
the better of every effort to hold him back. He rushed
off to call his helpers in the intended outrage. The lady
of the house, who from the first had only been persuaded
with difficulty to allow a stranger to enter, and produced
one argument after another for her fear, saw no good omen
now in so much hurry on the part of her recent guest.
She hid her troubled thoughts behind a tranquil face, but
ordered the roads to be watched from a tower so that no
one should take them suddenly unawares. A few hours
later, someone arrived to announce that all the approaches
were besieged by a disorderly mob. It was obvious from
the direction they were facing, and from their manner and
attitude, that they were coming to the house. Too late, it
was understood that 'the mother of peril is too easy
credulity': a bad thing, easy to condemn quickly, but not
to avoid promptly. It was a company of the Berkshire
militia with their officer whom Eliot had ordered to come up
by virtue of his royal warrant. Before they were admitted,

Campion pointed out that it was himself in particular they were after, and begged the household to let him depart. With God as his guide, he would either escape the watchfulness of his pursuers, or if, to his peril, he fell into their hands, he would at least spare an entire family from the grave molestation and even cruel barbarity of men whose blood was up. His prayers were vain. Their reverence for him and his priest companions, and their desire to put fortune to the test for all of them, gave edge to the hopes they set in hiding-places scattered throughout the spacious house.

20.   From the earliest days of the persecution, when to be without a priest was considered by the Catholics among the worst misfortunes, the spitefulness of a ruthless foe left them free neither night nor day from the fear of raids. To provide for themselves against so much watchfulness on the part of their persecutors, they used every device they could think of. Necessity, the handmaid of their devotion, was also the mother of the invention which taught them to make hiding-holes to meet sudden surprise. They were to be found in almost every house. They would set them in walls, or spaces beneath the eaves, in dark corners under stairs, and in the thickness of cellar foundations. They were constructed at night by men who could be trusted so that scarcely the servants knew of their existence. They were provided with altar-equipment, and, for the most part, they were relied on with ample justification for the safety of the priests. In a large house, wherever they went, and whatever means they used for their search, the shrewdest inquisitors were left baffled. In this way, since there was no chance of escape, Campion was forced to take refuge together with two other priests he had found at the house. When Eliot and the soldiers were admitted, they over-ran the house. They tried the walls; they measured up the rooms; they overturned the beds. If any of the panelling fitted badly, or there was any unusual feature in the roof, they tore it apart. Every corner was searched until evening came on, but in vain.

By now the soldiers were tired of running up and down, and their officer was even more tired of the loutishness of Eliot, the ringleader. He began to curse his own zeal that had made him so easily accessible to a man raw and unknown, even if he was furnished with a royal warrant. The officer also offered his excuses to the mistress of the house for the intrusion, begged her pardon, and gave orders for departure. Eliot, on the other hand, fell to rebuking the slackness of the soldiers by whose indolence or nonchalance the papist priests whom he had seen with his own eyes, and touched with his own hands, were to be allowed to escape. He decided that he must pull the place apart himself. He must either reveal the man in hiding or else leave the house a ruin. He read his commission again, exhorted, and even threatened, the officer that if he did not add night to day in searching, the Privy Council would by no means interpret the episode in his favour when the story of the affair came to be narrated in London. It often happened that the silence of the night betrayed what daytime noise covered up. The light of a candle would sometimes shine before the sun. No need to go on. The fury of a man beside himself conquered the humanity of the officer. The ruthlessness of the betrayer deprived the lady of the house of any chance of respite. The soldiers went back to their vigil.

The lady's hope was that the men left on guard would prove fonder of sleeping than watching. But she did not get her wish. Still, the night passed safely. In the morning, however, when the officer again gave orders to leave, Eliot, once more worked up into a high state of excitement, ran up and down like one out of his mind, poking the wall here, there, and everywhere. At one point, he happened to fall backwards. His hammer struck the wall with the whole weight of his body behind it, thus breaking open the hiding-place where the three priests quietly awaited the will of God. Uproar broke out immediately. All were amazed at the unexpected and unhoped-for turn events had taken. Everyone interpreted according to his own philosophy. The matter was reported to the Sheriff of

Berkshire, where Lyford was situated. He sent the prisoners to London under a suitable guard of militiamen in accordance with instructions from the Privy Council. Thanks to the decency of the sheriff, and of the people of many sorts who ran to see and speak with them, their journey began pleasantly enough. But when they reached Colebrook, 15 miles from London, he got new orders from the Privy Council to the effect that their hands should be tied behind their backs, and their feet under the horses' bellies. In this manner they should be brought to town. Campion, moreover, had a label fixed to his hat, 'Edmund Campion, seditious Jesuit'. By this device the Queen's Councillors made it clear in advance that they would discuss religion not with argument but with provocation. London . . . stretches about two miles along the Berkshire road from the Tower . . . To this citadal the three were led bound through the main streets of the city. They bore witness to their inner contentment and serenity by the expression on their faces—they could make no other gesture—for the benefit of the crowd which turned out to see them. They were subsequently distributed among different prisons.*

21. At first, Owen Hopton, Lieutenant of the Tower, treated Campion kindly. He tried to win him by pleasant words and promises . . . to the beliefs and ethics of his own sect. He expounded at length, and gave generous reassurances concerning the Queen's good nature, the many honours that would follow by way of reward, ample possessions, and even the hope of obtaining an archbishopric. Hopton set so much store by the force of his courtier-like eloquence, and the abundance of his tempting propositions that among members of his own circle he falsely put it about that Campion was practically won over by his confidence tricks. All the sermons through land and city re-echoed with the idea, not as the vain hope of one individual, but as fact already accomplished, that Campion had forsaken his own people for their adversaries. How idle was the tale, his severe sufferings, endured

with the utmost courage not long afterwards, amply
demonstrated. For he was laid three times on the rack
with his hands and feet pulled tightly apart, the joints of
his whole body being dislocated by the tearing force of
the pulleys. It seemed to him that he would die from this
barbarous tearing and twisting of every limb and sinew.
Sometimes it was relaxed, less from the compassion of
his torturers than the inability of the sufferer to endure
more. Monstrous as it is, there were men whose effrontery
was such that, when the Queen complained about it, and
wished to forbid such inhumanly cruel torture as reflecting on her honour, they told her Campion was by no
means grievously tormented. He was able to get up at
once and walk, and sign his interrogations. They might
have got away with this but for the fact that even after
the torture had stopped for many days, it was evident
to the eyes of all who flocked to the court for the trial
of his life that he appeared quite broken. He was in so
much pain that he was unable to raise his hand in the
usual way without the help of a nearby priest. The latter
reverently kissed it before holding it up with his own.

The mercy of the torturers was so evident to the Queen
herself that the further comment which they gave her in
reply made no mention of religion but dealt only with
questions of politics, and the wicked purposes abroad
against prince and country. Nor did she ever suppose
priests to be capable of such a sub-human crime as that of
wickedly conspiring for the destruction of their prince.
Overcome, however, by the insistent persuasions of her
Councillors, she granted to their importunity what her
own prudence would have denied. Their refrain was that
these men should be killed for the good of the State;
indeed, lest the people should take it badly that through
the private machinations of these men, and the public
negotiations of Catholic princes, change should be made
in religion. At that time, it is true, Alençon, the French
king's brother, was staying in England with a view to
negotiating his marriage with the Queen. While the
Councillors thus had a chance of uprooting men who were

outstanding for doctrine and way of life, they advisedly decided that to make it a matter of religion would be a wrong and hazardous procedure. They concluded that the proper path to their unworthy goal, and the way to please the people for whom they had concocted their fables, as Alençon declared, would be to make up crimes and catch their victims in the toils of their interrogations.

22. Lest they should appear to shun a meeting with Campion, now in their hands, all those learned and erudite men, whom he had first challenged by letter and then in the published *Ten Reasons,* fixed a day for a dispute. They laid down conditions which no one else would accept as fair or even tolerable to the side in disagreement. They decided to enter the arena only after they felt sure of finding their adversary weakened in body by lack of food, and almost at his extremity through torture. They thought there would be more suffering to break their opponents' mind than strength to contest in debate. They were as careful as they could be to prevent any previous word of the debate decided on from reaching Campion and his friends. Thus the latter would come unprepared not only by books but by any thought for the contest to come. The judges and recorders, moreover, were all to be members of the sect opposing. In the debate itself, when points brought up had to be proved or disproved by the authority of authors, they offered their adapted texts.

For this reason, Campion refused to make use of the Greek New Testament. He professed to expound at length for his hearers an entire passage from St. Basil. He showed that it was not from ignorance of Greek, as they took it, that he rejected the first passage, but because he was afraid the text was imperfect; possibly corrupted by Beza. He demonstrated with equal felicity that the works of Luther which they produced were baked from no better paste . . . Three whole days they debated for three hours in the morning and as long again in the evening; with such success for the Protestants that from the second day the

the assembly preferred it to be in secret rather than witnessed again by the people who had flocked there. On 31 August they met in the chapel in the Tower, a roomy place where the audience was large. On the other days [18, 23 and 27 September] they were crowded into Owen Hopton's parlour, where the hearers were few since the place allowed access to no more.

The fact that Campion's opponents were changed gave more than a slight indication of wavering confidence. [William] Fulke and [Roger] Goode succeeded Nowell and Day—some add Whitaker and Beale. They had no better fortune than the first two. In accordance with the liberty those who are conquered always assume of dissumulating their defeat, it was soon put about among the populace that things had gone badly with the Catholic champions. The fact is, there is no trace among the writers of that time of any triumph; and it is said they decided by common consent not to challenge the Jesuits in any future debate. If so, this was a very clear sign that far from winning they lost the disputation* . . . Philip, Earl of Arundel, was present at this debate. King Philip of Spain, subsequently of England, had received him from the baptismal font in 1557. The Earl was now a grown man and of great ability. He readily grasped the conclusion to which Campion's audience was drawn like himself by sheer force of reasoning and weight of authorities. Although he was more pre-occupied with the Court than religion, and had scarcely given a thought to spiritual matters or salvation in a long time, he left that scene with the seeds of faith and devotion deeply sown. A year or two later it would grow into a stout sapling of Catholic conviction.

23. Campion's unconquered spirit could not be softened by flattery, broken by torture, or worsted in debate. His defeated adversaries came away with weariness of mind and a sense of reproach after this triple contest. The only remedy they could look for to erase the memory or reduce the smart was Campion's blood. The machinery used before was put in operation once again to bring the

hatred of Parliament and cruelty of magistrates in such causes to grind the Catholics between its wheels. But they only succeeded in making more obvious the innocence of those they found guilty, so that one could doubt whether they drew more odium on themselves or honour to their victims. The 20 November (1581) was chosen as the day for the matter to be submitted to a last judgment. There in Westminster Hall were assembled before the judge, Sir Christopher Wray, the lawyers, witnesses and 12 jurymen. The arraigned were led in: Campion and six other priests to be tried for their lives. They were accused that at Rheims in Champagne in France, and at Rome, they had plotted to kill the Queen, and to extirpate the religion now professed in England. They determined to overthrow the kingdom with help bought from foreign rulers. For this reason they had crossed to England. Their intention was to draw away the allegiance of as many as they could from the Queen to the Roman Pontiff. After the indictment was read to the assembly, each raised his right hand as custom demanded. Both denied that any thought of conspiracy had crossed his mind, least of all to destroy the Queen, or plot to disturb the peace of the realm. Campion called on God, angels, heaven and earth itself . . . to bear witness to his innocence. How they did, indeed, bear witness will appear subsequently. Now to show how the three Crown attorneys, Anderson, Popham and Egerton, tried to prove the arguments on which the indictment rested. With what little justification innocent blood was sought by men filled with error or hatred will appear more clearly than the light of midday.

24.   I find there were six heads of charges produced to maintain the indictment—Campion was primarily involved—which were couched in most vehement and biting terms even if they could prove nothing; or even give a semblance of plausibility to the accusations.* The first charge was that of plotting against the Queen's life. There had been a conversation 10 years before with the Cardinal of Santa Cecilia on the subject of Pius V's Bull

excommunicating the Queen, and absolving her subjects
from their allegiance. Thus there could be no other reason
for Campion's coming than to bring about what the Pope
had decreed in his own writing, namely the ruin of the
Queen and her realm. 'Subsequently, when the same Pope
premeditated destruction with military assistance from the
King of Spain and the Grand Duke of Tuscany, how could
it be unknown to you, Campion? For while you were at
Prague, you were called to Rome, and sent here immediately at the Pope's expense. What did you intend, except
to be the standard-bearer of an army, the Pope's interpreter, and the instigator of rebellion among these
Catholics of yours? In the course of your journey you
consulted with Allen, the man who lauded the Irish rabble,
and to what other end but to stir up similar strife here at
home once you had come over? So that you could start
your fire more easily and secretly, you entered under a
false name and in disguise; as a gentleman, or a soldier,
or a merchant intent on profit. What should a priest do
with a sword? What should a messenger of Christ, as you
like to think yourself, be doing with feathers and silken
doublets? What has the light of the Gospel to do with
the things you pursued in the shadows?

'If you love your country or any good purpose had
brought you back to England, there was no need to hide.
Wrongdoers hate and flee from the light, as you do, but
not those who think only of good and holy things. As I
can accuse you out of your letters to Thomas Pounde,
you not only sought permanent hiding-places among the
papists known to you, but the secret things learned from
them you wrote that you would never declare, however
much force of racking or stretching with the rope you
had to endure. True? What secret things would you wish
to hide which cannot be disclosed under any kind of
pressure? Surely they are the very things which should
especially be known by those concerned with the
country's welfare? Since no question of religion was
involved, what had to be kept so secret that when you
came to mention the person implicated you remained

silent? What of the fact that in the houses you visited, papers were found on which there was writing about an oath whereby the supreme power of the Queen is repudiated, and obedience denied? Who can doubt that you proposed this oath? Do you not admit that you were sent to establish the authority of the Pope? What more apt could be devised to prepare men for rebellion, or to estrange more completely the minds of subjects? Nor is your objection valid that the papers were left by someone else. Just as in a house which a rich and a poor man enter, if a treasure is found, there can be no doubt it was left by the rich man rather than the poor, so it must altogether be assumed that these papers were scattered about by you as one of the Pope's disciples. You do not wish to swear to the Queen's supreme authority. You are now asked, what is the present force of Pius V's Bull? Would the excommunication apply? You have maintained an equivocal silence. Likewise, you compared those who presided at your examination with the pharisees who tried to bring about the death of Christ when they asked whether it was lawful to give tribute to Caesar or no. Truth does not skulk in corners. Unless your conscience pronounced you guilty, you would certainly not have hidden your inmost convictions in silence.

'You have heard Cradock say that he was present when the conversation ran on the holy pact concluded between the Pope and the English priests to restore religion in England. To which pact 200 priests gave their names. Richard Shelley, whom they call Prior of England, was chosen to lead the army; although at first, like Demosthenes, he said he would take poison before he lifted a weapon against his own country. But there is no doubt about the pact. The number of priests is mentioned; that you would be among them none could doubt. Finally, you have heard Eliot solemnly declaring that with sorrow you spoke of the crimes—heresy in particular—which now hold sway in England, but that you hoped that before long a day would dawn which Catholics could hope for and heretics fear: all this while he was present at your sermon at Yates's place. What sort of day could that be except the kind the northern earls hoped for? The same men who desired to overturn our religion in order to establish yours, and took up arms against the Queen. They intended to throw down from its foundations the peace of the realm. Which peace and happiness, by God's mercy, is greater than ever it was in living memory, and thoughts of gratitude for it should have been roused in the hearts of all subjects. But there were Felton and Storey, and many others I have mentioned of some standing, who made a bid to get a name and notoriety by trying to overthrow the kingdom rather than serve it. Who will not consider Campion of their number? Those nobles did not take up arms without the instigation of the Pope; nor did Felton, save from a desire to please the Pope, stick up his bloody Bull on the gates. Nor did Storey make himself the humble servant of the Spaniard save to assist the wretched counsels of the Pope and that king for this country.

'How could it be that Campion, the same Pope's disciple, sent by him to this kingdom, furnished by him with the widest powers, and well-provided with money, would be without all thought of trouble-making of this kind? That Pope was always the enemy of this Crown, the enemy of religion, impatient of our prosperity, envying our peace. What stone do you suppose he would leave unturned to put obstruction in the path of our country and our faith? Nor could he have found anyone more fitted for his purposes than this man whom he singled out to corrupt others. If he had sent Spaniards they would not have been able to hide; if Frenchmen, they would have aroused suspicion; if Italians, we would have spurned them as crafty contrivers of evil things. The task was entrusted to our fellow-countrymen, those born among us, and brought up with us. They have been nourished with the milk of our own universities, and given skill in our own tongue. They were equipped to work our own destruction. And by what means? Secretly, they were to creep about the land, in disguise and known by false names, so that they could hide the kind of life

they professed, and wander about unrecognised. To what
end? To turn the people from their due obedience to the
prince; so that they could establish their own religion,
that is, the Roman, and render, or at least try to represent,
our own way of life as based on inadequate foundations.
By what means? By celebrating Mass, by administering
the Sacraments, by hearing confessions. Which is as may
be. But more especially by praising the fervour of the
northern earls, and proclaiming the constancy of Storey
and Felton; by holding up for admiration the kind of
reasoning Sander favoured in Ireland. In a word, what
mercy could this kingdom expect, I ask you, at any time
from a Pope so hostile to our affairs? What fidelity could
we look for from those who have vowed themselves to this
Pontiff in complete obedience? What security could one
accept from exiles who, by flying away, put off all love
of their country?

'Lastly, how could their return be without danger
whose departure was occasioned by great wrongdoing?
I beg you, concentrate your attention on these circumstances. Reflect on the arguments. There is nothing to
exonerate men of this stamp from the charge of shameless murder. Since this is the case, and reason demands
that those guilty of the crime of *lèse majesté* be punished
according to the law, this we demand in the name of her
most serene Highness, so that in accordance with what
we have said you 12 men may arrive at a verdict. And
you, my good Lords, agreeably with your outstanding
prudence, pass sentence.'

25. The Attorney pronounced these words with great
     vehemence, his face sternly set, and with gestures
calculated to convey severity. This duly roused the
audience. Campion, affirming his loyalty and obedience
to the Queen, and an affection for his country from
which he had never swerved, spoke his defence in these
words.

'Our laws, as I understood them, have been passed with
so much foresight and caution that they do not intend to

rob any man of his life on the mere conjectures of any orator whatsoever. Nor do they intend to put him at the mercy of anyone who can make a violent speech. The matter should be decided either on irrefutable evidence or on most certain testimony of men beyond reproach. Hence I fail to see the purpose of so much bitterness on the part of the Crown prosecution. What if the Pope is opposed to the religion now established in England; if the King of Spain and the Grand Duke of Tuscany intended something to the prejudice of England; if the northern earls began a rising on their own initiative; or if Felton, Storey, and even Sander and Allen intended some offence against her Majesty? Let them stand or fall by their own consciences. Am I to be considered a traitor because like them I am a Catholic, or even because I am a priest? No more than if I had to do with sheep, or had relations or friends suspected at any time of sheep-stealing, and on that score alone were considered a robber of the flock or sheep-pen. These are darts prepared to arouse hatred and supicion, and certainly wound no one until they are directly aimed at someone. We are supposed to have withdrawn subjects from the Queen's allegiance. Where is the proof? We have reconciled men to the Pope; men have been put at peace with their God and brought back to the bosom of the Church. But they are not thereby taken away from the Queen's obedience. We worked for the disturbance and overthrow of the realm, as it is said. On whose witness? What is the proof?

'The objection based on the conversation with the Cardinal of Santa Cecilia, I must say, is about something that took place more than 10 years ago, not long after I first came to Rome. Who the witnesses were, I do not know; but certainly, it was not for my own merits that I was admitted to his presence, and received with the greatest courtesy. He promised to do his utmost to help me if I desired to enter anyone's service. I thanked him in terms of the least presumption that I could find that it was not my intention to enter anyone's service, but I had decided to give my obedience to the Society of

Jesus. He asked me what I thought of the Bull of Pius V. I said that it had caused the Queen to lay her hand heavily on the Catholics, and had provoked much harshness. The cardinal did not say much else except that its effect should be mitigated so that Catholics could recognise the Queen without danger of censure, and obey her. How such a conversation can be turned into a charge against me, I cannot understand. More especially since that Bull was published some years before I came to Rome, and was already well-known through the whole land. As for the armies of the Pope, the king, and the Grand Duke of Tuscany, since I was living at Prague, I was very far away from every contrivance of this kind. Fully occupied in the academic pursuits laid down for me, I was called away to Rome. After eight days in the city, I received the confidential orders of my superiors: but these had nothing to do with any army. They were simply my personal marching orders for England.

'I obeyed at once. I set out, no traitor or party to my country's overthrow, but simply as a priest sent to administer the Sacraments. Had it seemed good to my superiors, I would have accepted this kind of embassy—God be my witness!—just as readily and speedily if it had been for the furthest Indies, and to teach the gentile nations the identical faith held by Catholics everywhere. Provided with generous faculties, I hastened here at the Pope's expense. What were these faculties? None other, indeed, than you yourselves have mentioned, namely to administer the Sacraments. If the Pope paid the expenses, it must be attributed to his liberality. It was for no other purpose than to assist generously this journey undertaken for religion. I do not deny that I had supper with Allen on the way. Some of the time was given to recalling old memories. Of the affairs of the Queen and her realm there was never a word; nor of the troubled state of Ireland. On what pretext, then, can I be called the Pope's interpreter in all that concerns the destruction of this kingdom; or the right-hand man of Allen since, by the papal authority, which is supreme, I was strictly forbidden to deal in this kind of business? Has he, do you suppose, no authority over me? Allen I admire for the soundness of his doctrine and faith; but by my profession I would not allow myself to be moved by his authority over me—which is nil—nor even by his persuasion. My dress which you object to, and my change of name, were not to cover treasonable activities but simply to imitate the first missionaries of Christ. For Saul, afterwards Paul, the apostle of the gentiles, had himself let down in a basket secretly, and so escaped the watch of his pursuers. Such devices were always considered not merely licit but positively advantageous. He did not run away from the light but simply looked for suitable times and places for spreading the Gospel. It was not that he lacked any desire to shed his blood for Christ. All the same, he appealed to Caesar lest he be killed by the hostile Jews. And why should I not be allowed to do what was permitted him? If I have sinned by putting on silken doublets, you can see that I make up for it now by wearing an Irish coat and a worn-out suit.

26. 'I wrote to Pounde that I would never reveal any secrets; under no pressure would I be forced to expose hidden matters of the sort he had in mind. What sort of hidden matters? Simply those things which are revealed to a priest in sacramental confession by his penitents for his shriving. (Yepes, lib. 4, chapter 8). Since I am a priest, I hold myself bound by all the obligations which have belonged to that office since its original foundation. Among them is the inviolable duty of never revealing to anyone the things uncovered while conscience is relieved in confession. The divine law commands this. Whoever breaks it, makes himself guilty of very grave sin, and liable to eternal punishment. I have been falsely accused of this crime by the malevolence of spiteful people, and I have purged myself by what I have written, as far as I can. To call these principles in question is not religion but the hallmark of men who know nothing about the meaning of the word.

'The third objection about written papers concerning an oath may be easily explained. I never had any power at any time to demand an oath from anyone. If I had, it could not be proved that any of the papers were mine, or that anything was written in my hand, or marked with any sign that was recognisably my own. What has the idea about a rich man and a poor man both entering the same house to do with this issue? What he had to prove was that no one except myself, the "rich man"—that is to say, a man of my calling—entered the house when I did.

'I was unwilling to swear to the supreme power of the Queen. I kept silence when asked about the Bull of Pius V, and I think I had the human right to do so. Not many days ago, the Queen consistently with her exceptional spirit of mercy wished to see me. She asked me if I recognised her regal dignity and authority. I replied that I did, and honoured and revered her as my Queen and lawful sovereign. "Has the Pope power to cut me off from communion with the faithful?" "I am not", I said, "a suitable judge between yourself and the Pope, or an arbiter sufficiently learned for a cause as great as this. Even if he did so, it could be doubted whether it applied. In matters purely spiritual, as the theologians admit, the Pope cannot err when he is publicly teaching the Church in matters pertaining to faith, but he can err in judging practical situations". Those who presided at my examination asked the same questions. But their words and sentences were so involved that I gave no definitive answer. Therefore not without reason, I have described such questions as bloody and pharisaical. I recognised in the Queen royal dignity and true power. I still do. I acknowledged that obedience was due to her from me and all her subjects. I still believe this. I willingly give to Caesar the things that are Caesar's. But also to God the things that are God's. The commissioners questioned more searchingly. What if the Pope by his lawful power should cut off the Queen from the allegiance of her subjects? I replied that those who ask that kind of question are not looking for a man's religion but his blood. From admissions and concessions on those lines what would not follow? Therefore what must be admitted or refused in such a case, I decline to say. They cannot fairly ask me such things. These are questions for the schools not courts of law. They do not deal with anything actually done. This alone, according to law, comes within the competence of a jury. Now to deal with the witnesses.

'Cradock talks of a holy pact, of 200 priests, and of an army. What can he really claim? He was present at a conversation. Whose? I should guess that of the idle sort of people who are likely to say anything. He heard something about an agreement to restore religion. Where was the treason in this? And about an army: what was this army which the soldier Richard Shelley did not want to lead, and which was planned by the 200 priests? Was I one of the 200 who were to plot in this way? The witness, whoever he was, does not say this. One question must be obvious to everybody. How did this great light, I ask you, which the man who says he was present at the conversation did not see, come to spread its rays as far as England? As for what Eliot says in his last reference about a day to bring fear to heretics, I call God to witness all I had in mind was the day of the last judgment which will bring fear to us all, even if not to all of us to the same extent. No state is so holy that there are not glaring evils in it. There is no minister of any persuasion who does not sometimes preach on the day of divine retribution for the transgressors. In this way, I reminded my listeners of that day; not a day on which any earthly prince would take up arms to destroy the peace of this realm, but when the Supreme Judge of all mankind . . . would punish or reward according to every man's deserts. This was the great day which I pronounced to be for the good and comfort of believers and a cause for fear in those who had rejected the faith.

27. 'If my memory is correct, I have now gone over everything with which I have been charged. It remains for the jury to decide whether we had any evident intention to kill the Queen or disturb her kingdom. I especially

ask you to bear in mind that day I mentioned which all must fear. On that day you will also be called to account for the judgment of this day. You all know how dear to God is the blood of an innocent man. Our blood is now sought after. Our life or death is in your hands. We appeal to your conscience. We ask that nothing determine your judgment except the God-given reason within you. Keep to the point, I beg you. Do not let the insignia of office turn you aside from truth. Do not allow the elaboration of flowery speech to put you off. We must trust now to your integrity and good understanding.

'A conviction rests on three foundations: interpretation, witnesses, and the facts themselves. In our case, everything turns on the exercise of our religion. You can easily see how much weight should be given to interpretation, especially when it is a matter of life or death. In a case of this kind the law demands certainty as to the fact. As for interpretation, nearly the whole day has been spent on this. Everyone must realise the slight grounds on which it rests. You have heard the witnesses. What kind of men are they? How far can you trust them? It must be obvious to everyone that they are men of no religion. Sometimes they pretend to be Catholics; at other times something very different, all depending on where hatred or love of money leads them. How surreptitiously they have proceeded! How hesitantly they took the oath! Could they say anything for certain about anything? Did any of them swear he saw me or any of the others actually doing something to harm the Queen or subvert the kingdom? Or even saying anything in this sense? They swore to no such thing. True, we have celebrated Mass. We have heard confessions. We have absolved. But they harm no one. They are merely concerned with what everyone desires, namely peace of soul. So that you can clearly understand that what has been done against us concerns religion, not affairs of state, you certainly ought to know that liberty has been offered us more than once on condition we foreswore our own rites, and no longer refused to be present at those you regard as sacred. Far be it from us to abandon those things which you yourselves cannot but approve when you think about them calmly. Far be it that we should adhere instead to what the rest of the Christian world rejects. As for the questions abour papal power, the Bull of Pius V, and how we would react to any invasion brought about by the Pope's command, we replied not at all, because although the subject has been proposed to the most learned men we find no certain answer. These questions are for the schools, as we have said, and do not come within the scope of what you jurymen have to know. As men learned, wise and circumspect you are constituted to recognise an act, not to indulge in vague speculation. If you are aware of any word or deed issuing from us in prejudice of her Majesty, then condemn us. We will not repudiate your verdict. If you find no such act, spare our lives. Spare with them your own reputations and consciences'.

28. When Campion had delivered all this, still calm in mind and countenance, one of those near the judge warned the jury that the entire question turned on whether the accused were to be believed when they gave evidence about themselves; for they were men fighting for their lives. Or should the jury not rather believe the witnesses who, quite freely and under no one's pressure, had also spoken on oath. It was clearly indicated to the jury which side of the balance should be tipped. Although they deliberated for an hour in a place apart, they pronounced everyone guilty who had been up on the capital charge that day. The Queen's attorneys asked that the judge should pronounce sentence according to the findings of the jury. The judge made it clear that no mercy would be shown to the guilty. He asked them if they could produce any reason why the death sentence should not be pronounced. Campion replied, 'If we had any fear of death, we would never have taken on a life in which we must see death before us every day. However, we thought it our duty to preserve our lives—although we have no real control over them—as long as possible by avoiding danger

as far as we could. How successful we were, you can see.
But I imagine it is obvious to everyone that we have been
found guilty not for any offence against the throne, but
simply for our religion. No reliable witnesses said anything
that did not pertain to religion. No sound conjectures
against us have been put forward even if the matter had to
be finally settled in this way. And if all the things alleged
against us were true, the crime would be so enormous
that it could not be expiated simply by a visit to one of
your churches. We die, therefore, for religion. There can
be no more honourable cause in the eyes of God or man,
and so I cannot see any of us shying at death. As for
myself, may you judge me according to your own consciences. I do not think there is anything else to add for
my defence'. The judge passed sentence in these solemn
words: 'Let these men convicted of treason be led back
to the prison whence they came, and from thence be
drawn to the gallows to be hanged, and disembowelled
while still living . . .'.

Campion thanked God by reciting a Te Deum . . . He
accepted the sentence of death eagerly, and word and
face showed it. He also made it clear that it came easily
to him to despise honour and comfort, and those transient
hopes which Owen Hopton had offered him on the very
first day he entered prison. In the same way, he showed
his small concern for this present life which fades so
quickly, and that there was nothing he was not prepared
to endure for spreading the Christian faith. Ten days
they debated the day and the number, and, indeed,
whether any of them, should be killed at all. It was evident
that the sentence was iniquitous. They were well-educated
men, students from their earliest years, who had entertained no thought of bloodshed but only of upholding
their religion. It was visible from far off that the charges
were based on mere interpretations intended to deceive.
They were not produced on the evidence of reliable
witnesses, and were further coloured with the meretricious
persuasiveness of corruped eloquence. The more violently
they were pressed home, the less force they could exert

to sustain the argument. The unaccustomed delay of the punishment destroyed hope that it was near. But there those who refused to await the conclusion of calmer and more prudent spirits who were in any case not numerous. The rest were rather concerned to concoct something for the ignorant multitude that would help spread hatred of Catholicism. They seemed to think that if their own reputation had suffered from a trial that had been manifestly unjust, this result could be reversed by the execution of an equally unjust sentence. From six priests who had been condemned with Campion, and from seven more who were humiliated by a similar sentence two days later, they chose two to add to Campion's company. They were Ralph Sherwin, alumnus of the Roman seminary, and Alexander Bryant from the seminary at Rheims. The authorities decided that 1 December would be the day of their last public appearance. As for their smallness of number, the aim was not to spare their companions but to present them for torture a few at a time on other occasions and in different parts of the city, so that the minds and ears of the people would have the constant reminder of their treasons drummed into them. In this way, they might be induced, together with their bishops, to root out the alien religion entirely.

29. The day was not more welcome to the bloodthirsty than to those whose blood would slake their thirst. Brought together from different prisons, they hugged one another and showed their spiritual joy. They congratulated one another by gesture as well as word for what they had looked forward to as a happy outcome. Campion was tied full-length on a hurdle of osiers. Sherwin and Bryant had another like it. All three were dragged along with their feet towards the horses's hooves. As they bumped along the cobble-paved streets, they were splashed with filth from the puddles, assailed by the shouts of an abusive mob, harassed further by the importunity of Protestant ministers who tried to make them change their minds. But ever in the midst of all this, they did not lack genuine

consolation which came not only from God but from the
devotion of the Catholics who followed them on their
way . . . Nor did the Catholics fear to make their devotion
plain . . . They ran to them. They spoke to them. They
begged their help and advice, and took turns to help them
as far as they could in their extreme necessity. They
ignored the angry looks of the guards. They were not put
off by threats or held back by embarrassment. Nor were
they afraid of being considered connivers, associates, or
approvers of treason. The slander which their enemies
desired to fasten on the victims more securely by bringing
them this kind of death was now, even while they lived,
entirely dispersed. Those who were witnesses of the
applause they drew, and did not rebuke it, acknowledged
in their way that the victims had not in fact been traitors
whatever the accusation.

From the Tower to Tyburn, the place of execution, the
distance is two miles. When they arrived, Campion was
the first to mount the cart beneath the triangular scaffold.
With the noose round his neck he began to speak as if
from a pulpit to a crowd which stretched away on every
side. He took for his text the words of St. Paul, *Spectacu-
lum facti sumus Deo angelis et hominibus*. When he was
some way into his sermon he was told to confine himself
to matters which fitted the occasion, and to leave out
the rest. He should acknowledge the crime with which he
was charged, and humbly ask the Queen's pardon. He
replied, 'I am guilty of no crime agains the Queen, unless
the religion I profess be a crime! As a priest I undertook
to spread this faith. For this cause I came to England. To
it I have given myself wholly. Seeing that I must die for
it, I do it willingly. I beg you to believe me in this last
hour of my life; before the God who sees me and to
whom I must render an account of my most inward
thoughts . . . I have never revealed anyone's secrets given
me in confession, as some spread about who wished me
and my religion no good. I humbly pray God to protect
the Queen and the ministers of the Crown. I forgive
from the heart the injury done me by the jury and others

who have wronged me. I die a Cathloic; and I ask those who are of my persuasion to recite with me, if they will, the Apostles' Creed'. After this, while he prayed silently for a few moments, the cart on which he stood was driven away. Cut short by the strangling halter, he gave himself to God and immortality. His body was cut in pieces according to custom, and distributed among specified parts of the city.

30. With this triumph, Campion finished his life on earth at the age of 41, with nearly nine years spent in the Society, but leaving a memory that would live for ever among men. He was by nature gentle, and inclined to all those good qualities that make a man of unblemished life, reticent, unassuming and tranquil.* His intellect was decidedly keen, and since he had cultivated the humanities from his earliest years, he was an accomplished orator, an acute thinker, and a theologian of weight. Of the great treasure of learning he had amassed, especially with regard to controversies with the Protestants of the time, his *Ten Reasons,* mentioned above, addressed to the university dons, give eloquent witness. But when he wrote them he had no fixed abode. He hid with the Catholics anywhere he could. He was far from London, books, and all other aids of a writer. He not only composed his 'reasons' with finished perfection of language and argumentation, but filled all the margins of the paper with annotated references from most of his authors. When, at Persons's suggestion, the sources and originals were checked, every single reference was found to correspond exactly with the book, chapter, and page referred to. It was extraordinary that a man immersed in other preoccupations should have been able to retain in his memory so many different and widely separated sayings of the Fathers and the Protestants, and quote them without mistake. How profoundly he cultivated the good life, and with how much enthusiasm he tried to keep goodness in himself, increase it, and communicate it to others, his whole existence bears witness. His few letters which came to

light abundantly corroborate this. He speaks thus to the
novices of Brunn, where he himself had done his noviceship a few years before (Letter 6):

'I know how much freedom there is in obedience, how
much pleasure in work, what delight in speaking, how
great the dignity of self-effacement, the depth of peace
in the midst of conflict, the sheer nobility of endurance,
and how much is made perfect in infirmity. But to put
these qualities in practice and reduce them to action,
this is so necessary; and this is your task as here on earth
in a few turns of the track you already run the wider
course of Paradise . . .'

Again, he appeals to Gregory Martin, an old friend
(Letter 7): 'Make the most of Rome! Do you see the
cadavers of that city? What can be glorious in this world
when so much wealth and honour have vanished? Who
have lasted out the squalid changes wrought by time?
And what? Only the relics of the saints and the fisherman's chair . . .'

And in the eighth letter, also to Martin, 'Truly, I love
you for the martyrdom of Cuthbert;* or rather we love
you. For in many ways that narrative stirred up joy in
divine things. Unhappy man that I am! He who left me so
far behind even as a novice! Be kind to your old friend
and mentor. I am now more desirous than ever to bask
in the aura of these names'.

How was it that Campion received Eliot with so much
kindness when the latter met him in the Tower after his
death sentence? Eliot asked pardon for the wicked deed,
saying that it had never occurred to him that he would
be accused of murder or involvement in a capital charge.
He would never had done as he did had he forseen that
they would proceed to stronger measures than making
Campion wear chains. Campion reassured him most
kindly, 'I beg you, Eliot, be deeply sorry in the presence
of God's goodness for the crime you have committed. If
you do that, whatever happened before, or will happen
afterwards, will only serve God's glory'. When the
betrayer replied that he was afraid lest the Catholics plot

harm to him . . . Campion replied, 'You have nothing to fear on that score. I know well enough that Catholics do not think that way; and if you listen to me I will shield you from danger. With my letters you can go to a man of great renown and integrity in Germany. Under his patronage you can, if you wish, live safely'. Eliot, burned even more deeply by this flame of charity, could only show confusion. He was content, like Judas, with an outward show of repentance. The head-keeper's permission had allowed Campion's betrayer to come to him. But this same jailer also allowed the light which shone from Campion's example of charity to convert him. God must be with those who revenged their worst injuries with such magnanimous retribution . . . Perhaps this was the keeper of Campion's prison in the Tower of London who is on record as having come to the English College, Rome, in 1583, to study better things.

31. These fires, laid, kindled and fed with the object of inflaming betrayals and seditions, were not derived from different fuel than that which similar enemies scattered through Germany and France . . . Let the heterodox shrill as much as they like about conspiracies. That they might be brought into disrepute, Catholic priests were cried aloud as the instigators of plots and the people who carried them out . . . Their adversaries were not so constant in the calumny which they wanted all to accept that they did not sometimes admit that it was calumny which they were peddling instead of truth. 'Certainly', writes Camden when he speaks of the conspiracies fathered on the Catholics in Elizabeth's reign, 'to find out what was in their minds, crafty devices were adopted; forged letters under the name of the Queen of Scots and the exiles were left about and deposited in the houses of the papists. There were spies everywhere to pick up rumours and fasten on words. Others were admitted who passed on gossip &c. [*sic*]'. (Camden, *Annals* . . ., 1635 edition, p. 261* . . .).

Campion justly objected, being accused in connection with papers found in houses where he had stayed, that if they wished to prove anything against him they must first prove the papers had been left behind by him. He likewise rightly repudiated any conversation about a 'holy pact', and 200 priests—at which Cradock claimed to be present— and all the rumours put together by men of this stamp. By wiles of this sort, heretics and politiques played a game among themselves involving the blood and life of innocent men. The man who suborned Eliot was Walsingham, the most assiduous deviser of tricks of this sort. As Camden bore witness (An. 33 Elizabeth: 1590/1), he was 'a most fierce upholder of the puritan faith, a most ingenious investigator of hidden causes, who well understood how to win over men's minds and exploit them for his own purposes'. In this matter he spared no expense in order to satisfy his most bitter hatred of Catholics. He cultivated the favour of the Queen and more powerful courtiers. 'Indeed, he exhausted his own fortune by great sums of money laid out in this way so that he died in debt, and was buried at St. Paul's in darkness and without solemn funeral rites . . .'.

32. Nor can we decently pass over in silence Sherwin and Bryant, the men who shared Campions's immortality. Especially since Sherwin was not only his companion in martyrdom but also of his journey into England, and of his dispute in the Tower with the Protestants. Sherwin also sustained the latter with invincible firmness of mind, the best of weighty reasons, and with full freedom of speech. Two years before he crowned an exemplary life with a most blessed death, Bryant elected to join the Society, and in the event bound himself by a vow to enter it. Sherwin took a degree in philosophy at Oxford, and was elected to a fellowship. The more he examined the foundations of heresy and schism, the more he was convinced how insecure and badly knit together was the edifice . . . He went first to Douai, and then to Rome, to begin a building on rock. Already outstanding for his knowledge of Latin, Greek and Hebrew literature, he would add to it the strength

of the philosophers and theologians. He accompanied Campion and Persons on their journey in 1580, and stopped for a time at Rheims at the suggestion of Thomas Goldwell, Bishop of St. Asaph. He also was thinking of crossing into England. In the event, the Bishop was forced to abandon the idea on account of ill-health and old age. Sherwin, however, got to England. But he was unable to excape for long the watchfulness of angry Protestants. He was captured after a few months, and put to a year's test in the harshness of various prisons. But I cannot say he was much grieved or put out. Reading his letters shows that he so overflowed with consolation that he could scarcely restrain a smile when he heard the rattling of his chains . . . Writing to his friends not many days before his death, he said, 'Certainly, I had hoped to put off this mortal body a long time ago, and to kiss the holy and glorious wounds of Christ . . . This desire of mine has so strengthened and guided my soul that the sentence of death passed on me not long ago has not much awed me; nor the prospect that my life would be short caused me pain'.* Later, when Sherwin was as close as could be to death himself, he pressed a kiss on the executioner's hand all bloody from the butchery of Campion. Most fervently repeating, 'Jesus, Saviour!' he surrendered his own soul . . .

33. Alexander Bryant was a Somerset man. After completing more elementary studies at home, he applied himself to philosophy at Hart Hall (so called from its rebus), Oxford. Richard Holtby was a professor at that time. He persuaded his students to accept the Catholic faith which he himself accepted in his heart. Holtby sent Bryant on to Rheims. After completing his studies, Bryant returned to England in 1579. He subsequently became Persons's intimate friend as the man who reconciled his father to the Church.

Caught in April 1581, Bryant was first put in the Counter to be reduced by starvation. For it was included in the jailer's orders that he should withhold food and drink from him. He also seized anyone who came from

elsewhere to greet the prisoner. After he had suffered
many days' hunger, the jailer allowed him a piece of
mouldy bread and a little cheese. He quenched his thirst
with the water dripping from the roof, or from cider gone
sour with standing. In fact, it was the intention of those
who carried out these extremely cruel measures not only
to break his spirit but also, if they could, to disfigure his
face and appearance by hardship. His features were those
of a young man of 28, exceptionally handsome, and
revealing a mind that was unspoilt. His also was a winning
gentleness allied with good humour. When they realised
that breaking him was more than they could do, he was
transferred to the Tower. There they tortured him not
only with hunger and thirst, but with needles driven under
the nails of fingers and toes. He was not shaken even by
this torment . . . With eager expression, he recited the
50th psalm. Nor would he give any information about
himself, whom he had stayed with, at whose expense,
whose confessions he had heard; where he had celebrated
Mass. What of Persons? They assumed that he knew all
about this from the place where he was captured. Where
was the press? And the books? What had been sold?
How many remained to be sold?

They applied such a degree of tension when they
stretched him on the rack that all his joints were dislocated. At the end he lay as one dead, without feeling
and without movement. The following day, notwithstanding, he was obliged to repeat the experience. Again
they dragged him apart with torture even more cruel.
Concerning this notable outrage, Norton who presided
over the questioning, boasted in the court that he made
Bryant a foot longer than God created him. They took
Bryant down from the rack with hardly a sinew entire,
and then threw him into a pit, leaving him in solitary
confinement for 15 days without light, and lying on the
bare ground. Even his tormentors were amazed by the
endurance he showed in the midst of atrocious suffering.
Even they were moved by the unbroken calm of soul
reflected in his face. But they preferred to attribute it

to the devil's artifice rather than to fortitude given by God. In this they resembled the pagans of antiquity.

34. The source of all Bryant's nimbleness and strength of soul may best be judged from what he has to say himself in the letters which he sent from prison, shortly before his death, to the Fathers of the Society. He explained by what chains we are all bound in order to seek God, and how we must offer ourselves to Him in holocaust . . . 'For these reasons', he says, 'I made a most firm decision two years ago to adopt [your] way of life if this should seem good to God. After putting this proposal to my confessor, a prudent and learned man, I feel moved all the more strongly thereto. Frequently, I have reaffirmed this decision of mine. However, I have put it off until now, hoping that I was offering God a labour not entirely useless in this harvest of souls . . . I have now ratified it with a vow. Nor have I done this rashly or without advice. On the first day of my torture, I found my mind ready and even willing to undergo the suffering which I expected. The intention, in which I had persevered, of joining the Society came back to me . . . I made a vow in these words: "When it pleases God to grant me liberty—if it ever pleases Him, indeed—then within a year I will place myself entirely in the hands of the Fathers of the Society of Jesus; and if, God inspiring them, they admit me, willingly and with the greatest joy, I will dedicate my whole will to the divine obedience for ever"'.

'That vow was a source of great comfort to me amid my worst trials and sufferings . . . God revealed immediately, in my view, that this was acceptable to Him. For by His infinite goodness he was present to me in all my pains and torturings, strengthening me when I most stood in need; freeing me from spiteful snare, crafty tongue, and from the roaring lions all ready to rend me. For at my last racking, when my enemies raged their worst, and my arms and legs were dragged apart with terrible violence—perhaps I do not speak wonders but certainly, as God is my witness, I speak truth—I felt practically no

pain at the end, but rather did I seem to be relieved from
the ache of the torments to which I submitted before. I
felt myself at peace and tranquil. When the commissioners
saw this they gave orders as they went away that I should
be reserved for the like torture next day. I heard them;
but I was full of hope that with God's help I would bear
all with constancy. I called to mind as far as I could the
appalling sufferings of the patient Christ. I had the sensa-
tion of something like a wound in the palm of the left
hand, and a copious flow of blood from it. No wound
appeared in it subsequently, but at the time I felt no other
pain.

'To return to my proposal: since not the slightest hope
is left to me of meeting you again, good Fathers, in the
liberty which we formerly enjoyed, I leave my cause with
you. In the meantime, I humbly ask you to decide my case
according to whatever seems good to you in the Lord. If
it is the done thing to admit anyone in his absence, I
would beg to be admitted with all the insistence I can
muster . . . I promise by this letter obedience before God,
the tribunal of my own conscience, and all of those placed
in authority or already constituted my superiors, or so
to be constituted for the future; and to obey all the rules
and regulations in force in the Society as far as I can and
God gives me grace . . . If it is a question of bodily health,
there seems no cause for hesitation. My original strength
has almost returned to me, and I am getting stronger
every day. I commend myself to your prayers, expectantly
awaiting your decision about me. Farewell!'*

Before he was brought out to answer the capital charge,
Bryant took care to have his tonsure uncovered to show
openly how much store he set by his ordination, and how
far were the indications of his state from something to
be ashamed of. He also made a little cross out of wood,
with an image of Christ modelled in charcoal affixed to it.
This he kept in his hand . . . When a bigot tried to snatch
it away he said, 'You may succeed in tearing this from
my hand, but you will never tear from my heart what this
cross symbolises . . .'. With this unshakeable steadiness of

purpose he died . . . the third after Campion and Sherwin. Justly, he is to be numbered with the Fathers of the Society to whose company and institute he had bound himself by solemn vow. Persons himself described the triumph of these men in his letter to Father Alphonsus Agazzari, Rector of the Roman seminary, on 23 December 1581. It is worthwhile reproducing here the testimony of so great a man to illustrate an episode well attested in itself. It runs as follows:

35.   'Most Reverend Father,
        'Since I have this opportunity, which I have most eagerly sought after, of sending you a letter—for some days my channel of communications was closed—I could not forbear to write you a few lines about our affairs of which, doubtless, you will before long have a longer narrative. After all our disputations in the controversies, which you heard about, on 20 and 21 November, 13 priests were brought to trial and condemned for treason. They were Edmund Campion, S.J., Ralph Sherwin, James Bosgrave, Thomas Ford, Thomas Cottam, Edward Rishton, Robert Johnson, Luke Kirby, Alexander Bryant, John Hart, George Shirt, William Filby, Laurence Richardson, and the 14th, a student of law, Henry Orton. I think that of these about eight were at one time or another in the Roman seminary. Many things were objected against them as they stood at the bar, but principally that they had plotted with the Pope, the Catholic King, and the Duke of Florence to invade England; which never entered their heads even as a dream. They defended themselves well on every count. Their principal accusers were three young men who had at one time been in Rome, namely Munday, Sledd, and Caddy. If only on account of their youth and insignificance, they could never have known anything of such a matter even if it had been mooted; still less when it became abundantly clear from their answers, actions and the way things fell out that nothing of the kind had ever been projected. Indeed, they showed themselves to be the merest sycophants. They objected only matters of

common knowledge, and, in fact, demonstrated that the accused could have had no sort of connection with a crime of this sort: the accusers claimed, for example, that the Pope had favoured them; that some of them had spoken with the Cardinals, and things of that sort. All of which showed plainly enough that they were brought to make the accusation either from fear or hope of reward. It seemed that all had been settled beforehand so that the accused should be condemned. Their defence, therefore, could not prevent the sentence of death being passed on all of them after exchanges lasting a few hours. They all accepted it very cheerfully. Indeed, when each had made his protestation with regard to his innocence of the crimes with which they were charged, every one of them showed very real contentment at the sentence. Campion testified to it by quoting aloud from Holy Writ. "Te Deum laudamus!", he cried. Father Sherwin exclaimed, "This is the day which the Lord hath made. Let us exult and rejoice in it!". The rest gave further most ample proof of their spiritual happiness to the wonder of all present—a vast crowd—who were much moved.*

36. 'There can be no doubt, Father, it was a wonderful experience. Nearly everyone was overcome with astonishment at the sight of so many young men, after very frequent and extreme torture . . . accepting the sentence of a most cruel death so constantly and readily. And from all this they could have freed themselves with the smallest kind of concession. Father Campion referred in the same place, for all to hear, not only to the life and liberty promised them, but also to the highest favour of the Queen, and promotion for all of them, if they would go to the Protestant churches. This they altogether refused. Father Campion mentioned by name the present Lieutenant of the Tower, who had been among those who had offered all this to them. He added further that, if they did not comply, apart from other tortures, they would have their finger-nails prised off by the insertion of extremely sharp needles. How wretchedly they had harrowed

Campion with various well-chosen tortures was sufficiently evident on the day when he came forth with his whole body broken, and his hands done up in bandages on account of wounds inflicted during his torment. He could not move them to his face, although his mind remained firm and unbroken. Indeed, he replied in a voice that was ready and firm, showing a serene countenance for something like three hours on end during the time he stood before the tribunal. Certainly, his very enemies praised his endurance, wisdom, and moderation with more than ordinary tokens of appreciation. No one, however, dared to call him innocent on account of the ferocious edicts by which all were ordered to regard him as a traitor to his country.

'On the first of this month of December [1581], Fathers Campion, Sherwin and Bryant were drawn on their backs from the Tower of London to the place of execution nearly three miles away. While they were dragged through the streets of London, many of the Protestant ministers hurled insults at them. They made no reply, but sang hymns and psalms. Eventually, they arrived at Tyburn where a vast crowd awaited them. Father Campion went up the ladder first, and began to address the crowd on the words, "We are made a spectacle to God, to angels and to men". But the Sheriff of London, who presided at the execution, rudely interrupted him, and forbade him to speak further.* He ordered him to prepare for death and ask pardon of the Queen and people for his crimes against the State. He replied that he was unaware that he was guilty of any, and had never contemplated anything against the realm, as was sufficiently well-known to men as well as to God. He died for Catholic faith alone.

'At once, one of the heralds burst on to the scene—he had been ready for this—and began to read aloud a writing in the Queen's name whereby she wished it to be made known to all that these men had been delivered up to death not for religion but for treason. The crowd, however, seemed little impressed by this, and rather suspected a trick in this new and unusual artifice. Campion repudiated the claim briefly, adding a few but very effective words for the bystanders on the truth and worth of his Catholic faith, and that he was happy to die for it. They then threw him down from the ladder, and when he was hanged, cut him in four pieces, his two companions being forced to look on to make them afraid. But they were quite unshaken. When he had dispatched Father Campion, the executioner came with his hands and arms all bloody to Father Sherwin. To frighten him, he seized hold of him saying, 'Come on, Sherwin! Time to get yours!' With a face all happiness, Sherwin embraced the executioner, and kissed the gore on his hands. The crowd was very much moved by this, and there was a general murmur which dragged from the official in charge permission for this next victim to say what he wanted. He therefore went up the ladder and gave a most effective exhortation. When it was finished, he put his neck in the noose amid the cheers of the throng. 'Well done, Sherwin! God receive your soul!' The noise lasted quite some time. Nor could it be induced to die down even when he was dead.

'Bryant, the third to die, said little apart from a short confession of faith, and a protestation of innocence not only of any deed but even of any thought against the Queen. Truly, his innocence showed in his face—like that of an angel, for he was a very handsome young man not more than 28 years old. He deeply touched all those who looked on, especially when he said he was filled with great joy that God had chosen him and made him worthy to suffer death for the Catholic faith; and this in the Society which was also Father Campion's, whom he revered in every corner of his soul. It was true enough that his enemies hated this young man with special fervour on account of his intimacy with the Fathers of the Society, and about whom he refused to confess anything even at the height of his torture. He sent a letter secretly from his prison asking to be received into the Society [see above], relating the extraordinary experience whereby he had known the presence of God in the midst of his sufferings. I think you have already received a copy of his letter.

37. 'While these martyrs were being torn asunder, the
      Catholics did their best to retrieve at least a few of
their remains. But their enemies exercised great care to
prevent this. One young gentleman, however, pushing
through the people round him, let his handkerchief fall
in order to get it soaked in Campion's blood, or at least
that it might collect a few drops. But his attempt was
instantly noticed, and he was seized and put in gaol. All
the same, while he was being arrested, another took the
opportunity in the general confusion to cut off Campion's
finger and make off with it. That, too, was observed, but
although a rigorous enquiry was set on foot, it proved
impossible to find the man who did it. Another young
man, when he saw that nothing could be taken surreptitiously, secretly offered £20 of our money to the
executioner for a single joint of Father Campion's
finger, but he did not dare to give it. Their clothes were
much sought after by Catholics, who tried to buy them,
but so far they have not been able to get anything. It
is thought that their enemies tried to burn everything
so that nothing should fall into the hands of the
Catholics.

'As soon as they were dead, another edict was printed
and published to prevent anyone thinking they had
perished for their religion. This had never happened before
in England to men condemned in public trial. The other
11 were not yet punished but were kept, as we have said,
in various places, more particularly in the university towns
and seaports, to strike greater fear into the rest. Father
Persons was strenuously pursued by the enemy, and there
was a persistent rumour that he had been captured: for
which great thanksgivings were offered up by the Protestant clergy. Four gentlemen in whose house Campion had
stayed, as it was believed—admittedly, it could not be
proved—were fined 9,000 crowns. Other suspects were
subjected to questioning. They also scrutinised those who
refused attendance at the Protestant churches. Such
were obliged by the recent law to pay a fine of £20 a
month. Many were stripped of nearly all their possessions.

The situation now approaches something like extreme crisis. However, the Catholics have remained most constant . . .

'From all this it can be seen how much previous preparation is needed before our brethren can join us here. They must be completely self-effacing, long-suffering, resolute, and above all, intent only on serving God, their neighbour, and one another according to the law of brotherly love . . . Let them come, then, joyfully and cheerfully; anyone, that is, who particularly wants to bear the martyr's distinctive palm. God will see to it that they get their desire.

'There does not seem to be much else to write about. Gaspar, William and Robert are well,* although William has been rather seriously ill just lately. Their creditors cling to their heels, but God has so far protected them . . . Remember us, dear brothers and most dear friends of all mankind. Farewell . . . 23 December 1581. Yours Eusebius.'

38. Of the wonders that Bombino describes at length I will say nothing here lest I do again what is already done . . .

The greatest marvel of all, without any doubt, was Campion's invincible endurance. Perhaps we may be permitted to corroborate the fact out of the mouths of his foes. Baron Hunsdon, who was present at his torturing, exclaimed, 'You can pluck out his heart more easily than we can find words to express what religion meant to this man. Here is the essence of Christian fortitude: a virtue which cannot be turned aside from the right path by extremity of pain or fear of death. This is what the martyrs, by God's grace, clung to constantly. So they inspired the Church militant here below, and gave encouragement by an example lived among us . . .'.*

BOOK THE FOURTH

1. (1582). Persons was responsible for the English Mission. When there was no further hope of liberty for the imprisoned Campion, he thought it best that leading priests should consult one another on the most effective way of carrying on the work begun. James Bosgrave and Thomas Cottam had been condemned for high treason along with Campion, but their story enjoyed a different sequel as will be related in its own place. Gaspar Haywood and William Holt had also come in to assist Persons. The latter had a great many books in hand intended to buttress faith and devotion. No one wished to publish them in England itself. Nor did anyone wish to publish abroad unless Persons himself was present. Persons was anxious to consult Allen on many things designed to meet the needs of the seminaries, which could hardly be dealt with, as it seemed, except in Allen's presence. Persons also wished to set on foot the production of commentaries on the New Testament, to be called after Rheims from their place of origin. For this work he had collected £300 in English money from friends. Furthermore, he had observed many things in the way of life of priests and Catholics which seemed to call for intervention by learned opinion. It was also necessary to consider measures needed to keep Scotland for the faith. Thither Persons had sent a secular priest and later Father Holt. Finally, there were many Catholics of name and position who had pointed out that, while means had been provided for studying philosophy and theology at Rome and Rheims, there were no facilities in England for giving ordinary education to the young without grave risk of disturbing their faith. Could not Persons investigate the situation, and establish something suitable for them abroad? Everybody regarded these items as of maximum importance for the Catholic cause.

They prevailed on Persons, now that Campion was removed from the scene, to go to neighbouring France; though not to make a stay of long duration, as it was said. As soon as he had reached Rouen, he had his 'letter of consolation' to the Catholics printed. It was written in English on the subject of the persecution.* Persons also produced a defence of the censure against Charke, and a book entitled *The Christian Directory* or *De Resolutione*. This book dealt with the principles of Christian faith, with God, with Christ as man, and on the rewards and punishments of good and evil deeds after this life. All was clearly set out. What made for goodness, and how the obstacles thereto might be removed, was clearly demonstrated in an appropriate style calculated to persuade. It is not easy to describe the eagerness with which it was received, the spiritual profit with which it was devoured, and even to this day how much it has been read by every sort of person of both sexes . . . Although it is only here and there that he touches on a very few questions that are controversial, he shows in the clearest possible light what Christian life ought to be . . . He urges the minds of reflecting men with a most compelling array of reasons to do what is right . . . Indeed, if Persons had done nothing else in his whole life, by this one work he would have earned immortality from his countrymen, and the reputation of a man who did more by his single-handed labour than a whole company. Father William Bathe, an Irishman, wrote a most glowing testimonial to him . . .

[Bathe's testimonial is written in very general terms. He mentions a traveller from England to Belgium, 'a very important Councillor of the Queen in Ireland', and a nobleman and others who were won over by Persons's book. Indeed,] 'the Protestants themselves were so stirred at reading this book that, making a few changes, they had it printed for themselves at London' . . .

The theme of Persons's *Letter of Consolation* is as follows. Two laws were passed against the Catholics early in 1581. The first imposed the monthly fine to which they were liable for refusing attendance at the Protestant churches. The second inflicted the death penalty on those who used the sacrament of penance, and another fine on any who attended Mass. In the first place, the *Letter* showed how lofty was the cause for which they suffered those fines. These were intended, quite simply, to prevent them from following their consciences . . . Nor should Catholics give scandal to their neighbour or help his downfall by bad example. They could not violate their own allegiance to God once given, nor countenance schism or dissimulate their religion. They should not share in the sinning of others any more than they should set themselves in opposition to the Catholic practice of universal Christendom. It demolished what appeared to be the objections of paying the fine, showing the deceptive dangers of wealth, the difficulty of using it properly, subject as it is to uncertainty and linked with empty pomp . . .

2.   Persons's letters to the General show how great was his industry and enthusiasm in his efforts on behalf of the Catholic faith in England. They also reveal that, as far as the times allowed, he devoted himself to the spiritual profit of Scotland. A letter to the General makes his purpose clear.*

'Pax Christi,

'Very Reverend Father,

'Last month, I wrote your Paternity a long letter about our affairs. Now events of much greater importance have taken place, which I thought I should relate without delay. Father Campion, after being twice tortured, went through four disputations in prison with his adversaries, to the great advantage of the common cause, and the gain of many souls, as later, perhaps, you will hear in more detail. As I told you before, I took advantage of an opportunity to cross to France so that I could expedite certain necessary business which I could not do by letter and in absence. It was a matter of prime urgency to confer with

Monsignor Allen on a number of projects. There are many things pertaining to our work, and the scene of our labours, which I certainly could not put down in writing. In the second place, I wanted to set up a printing press in some place close at hand to print books written by our men in English as occasion demands. Nothing has helped, helps, or will help to preserve our cause for the future so much as the printing of Catholic books both of controversy and devotion. Thirdly, I needed to see the Archbishop of Glasgow, the Queen of Scots' ambassador at Paris, about help for Scotland. On this the conversion of England very much depends. I particularly wanted to rouse him with reasons and encouragement to burning zeal so that suitable men may be sent to Scotland; especially at this time when, as a result of Morton's death and the prince's present frame of mind, there is no small glimmering of hope. I also wanted to tell him some of the heretics' secret counsels which are designed to overthrow Scotland completely, and suggest how they might be foiled. Fourthly, I wanted to find some means whereby the King of France may be induced to intercede for the Catholics with the Queen, at any rate to get some alleviation of the crushing monetary fines imposed by a certain recent law on all who refuse to attend Protestant churches; and this concerns all Catholics. These were the principal heads of business which obliged me to come over.

'By God's help, the first three points have already been dealt with, to the great profit, as I hope, of the entire cause. The last item, to tell the truth, is thoroughly bogged down. When the King was asked by the Apostolic Nuncio, in the name of His Holiness, to write to the Queen on behalf of the afflicted Catholics of England, he replied that he could not do so in view of certain secret factors which had to be taken into account. However, we do not give up. In our rebuff we try to stand firm, like Moses, and go on hoping against hope. Just now I am fully occupied at Rouen, where I await the return of my assistant from England. I sent many letters by him to console the Catholics, written as if they had come from the north.

No one in England knew of my departure; nor am I known to any here except to Monsignor Allen at Rheims, the Archbishop of Glasgow at Paris, and here at Rouen to Monsignor Michael de Monsi, nephew of the illustrious cardinal, and Archdeacon of Sens. He is also a counsellor of the national Parlement. Furthermore, he is most enthusiastic in God's cause and that of the Catholic Church. It is understatement to say he is a most ardent lover of out Society. I have recourse to his good offices and influence in everything; for out of his goodness of heart he has most readily put himself and all he possesses at my disposal. Today I received two great bundles of letters from England by my assistant. I learn from these, apart from what I have said above, that I am much sought after by the Catholics there. Hence I must speed up my return; especially because Fathers Gaspar and William, who were the most recent to enter, are a long way from London. They are going through other districts where they are said to be gathering many souls. Pressure is gradually increasing on the Catholics from new and determined persecution, but thanks to the courage and inward peace they derive from God, they were never more light-hearted. However,the more our enemies fear for themselves, the more they grow cruel. The outcome of all this will be of crucial importance.

'When I first came to England I tried to weigh up, as far as I could, what parts of the country most needed our help, and what could most serve our enterprise at this time. I learnt that there were three regions into which priests had not yet penetrated. First, there was Wales, a wideflung region, nor yet so hostile to the Catholic faith. But thanks to shortage of men to work there it has fallen into considerable ignorance. Prostestantism has come to win no little approbation by its familiar use. For this reason, I have sent some priests there with an introduction to some of the gentry to receive them. In this way, a wide door has certainly been opened, and many are daily reconciled to the Church. A second area is Cambridgeshire, which has been totally under the influence of Cambridge university, an entirely Protestant institution. On this count, many remedies were sought out in vain until at length, with God's help, I managed to introduce a priest into the university itself as a student or gentleman-scholar. I got him a place with a family not far from the city. To this project, Providence granted so much success that in a few months he won over seven youths of excellent prospects and ability. Already they are to be sent to the Rheims seminary. I got to know this today from one of them who has just arrived here. An even greater harvest is daily expected in that place.

'The third district is the largest of all; that on the borders of Scotland and England covering four or five counties, though whether as dioceses or counties they must not be understood as large individually. To these counties practically none of the priests had penetrated. This area, however, is of the utmost significance for our cause both on account of its proximity to Scotland and because its inhabitants are of an open and generous disposition. I have therefore directed a number of priests to work there, one especially who seemed to stand out above the rest for common sense, single-mindedness and as a man well-informed. He spent about 10 months in those parts, and returned to me at the beginning of this last summer. He reported that much was to be hoped for from those regions, even allowing for the fact that the persecution was then becoming so fierce that it was extremely difficult for anyone to survive. He also reported—this I particularly recommended him to find out—that a passage from those parts into Scotland was not difficult. When we understood this, and took the advice of certain of the more discreet Catholics, we sent him back into Scotland to try out the route. Our greatest hope is in Scotland, from which not only England's conversion depends, but that of other regions to the north. The right of succession to the English throne belongs to the Queen of Scots and her son since the line now reigning is at an end. Of the son himself some hope has been conceived, especially after the murder of the Earl of

Morton. It is important to cultivate him sufficiently while
he still shows a considerable spirit of obedience to his
mother, and before he becomes confirmed in Protestantism; also while he remains offended by the Protestants,
as he has been recently. We thought we should not neglect
such opportunities. So we were extremely sorry that the
business had not been more energetically pursued by those
whom it chiefly concerned, that is to say, by the Scots
themselves. For many reasons, our cause is equally theirs.
With this in mind I collected alms from the Catholics,
bought things necessary for the priest's journey, and sent
him with a companion into Scotland. I wrote out for him
beforehand the main headings of subjects he should put
to the King if opportunity presented itself of getting
into his presence. If he could not reach the King, then he
might put them to some of the nobles.

'The first of these headings was that he should undertake to protect Catholics in their affliction, especially
those who withdrew into Scotland. For it was only
Catholics who would favour his hereditary right to the
throne of England. Secondly, he must explain the
numerous and weighty reasons which should move the
King to favour the Catholics and their religion, and to set
the Protestants aside. Such reasons included security in
his own kingdom, the succession to England—this he could
only obtain throuh Catholics—the friendship of neighbouring Catholic princes, and regard for his mother. She had
been kept from him and held in prison in spite of innocence. His father had been killed by the Protestants, and
they had often laid ambushes against his own life. These
had been discovered and avoided by God's mercy, also
through the Catholics. Finally, the priest should offer the
King the support of both Scottish and English Catholics
in bringing Scotland back again to Catholic faith. Support
of this kind would come particularly from those of us who
were priests, even if it cost life itself.

'After receiving these instructions, he departed. He got
into Scotland and, by God's grace, enjoyed considerable
success. This will be evident from his letter which follows.

He did not dare to commit top secret matters to paper, but told his assistant to recount them to me verbally—and to no other mortal besides. This man got to London, but when he could not find me, he did not dare to narrate what had been committed to him to my deputies. All the same, he left his master's letter, and this was at once sent on to me. He further added—this also is evident from the following letter—that his master had been favourably received by the Scots. My deputies promised to send on everything to me, and also to send any replies of mine back. A day was agreed, namely 26 September this year [1581], when I would hold conversation with a number of Scottish gentlemen. But today is the day, and this I cannot manage at all. However, here is a copy of the letter in which it is to be noted that where the name of Mr. Redman occurs I am understood':

3.   'When I first arrived in Scotland,* I was obliged by my necessity, and to avoid falling into greater dangers, to go to the dwelling place of the Warden of the Middle Marches. He is a Calvinist. He lives at a place called Seiford. It was here that I was asked why I came. I replied, as a refugee expelled for conscience's sake from my own country. Asylum was not denied even to wrongdoers, and still less should it be denied to men expelled for their religion. The Warden replied that there was no worse offence, or greater crime possible, than to be of the wrong religion, and thus an enemy of Christ's Church. "This is very true", I replied, "but the whole controversy centres in who are the enemies of the Church". "That", he said, "is beyond controversy. Papists!" Hearing this I smiled, and said that if he pleased we would see about that after supper. When supper was over, a chapter was held, as they call it. This meant that one of the ministers —three were present—read a psalm and gave a short address. While this proceeded, the Warden, his wife, and many other nobles and gentlemen listened with heads reverently uncovered. Alone among them, I sat with my hat on: which surprised many. After the sermon, I

showed all due respect to the noblemen present, and then explained why I was unwilling to uncover during the minister's address. "But at least", said the Warden, "you ought to show reverence for the Word of God!" I replied, "I must say that Scripture poorly expounded is not the Word of God, since it contains an element of the erroneous. This is very far from being the Word of God". Hearing this, they called on the minister to defend himself. He had also heard it, but refused from the beginning to take any part in the conversation. But the Warden insisted. At length we came to the controversy about whether it belonged to the Church alone to decide the meaning of the Scriptures. We spent a great deal of time discussing this. Finally, the Warden said that the opinion and reasoning of the ministers pleased him little: so little that in future he would not be so ready to condemn the papists. He added that a certain famous preacher would be coming next day, a Sunday, 27 August. He would be able to satisfy me on all points. I said that I was already satisfied by my own people; and I desired to satisfy others about the truth of the Catholic faith, especially his Illustrious Lordship. For this purpose I would willingly talk with him. So on the day following, but at a late hour in the morning, the minister came. I had not yet finished saying my office. Some of the servants told me that the Warden and the rest of the assembly—more than a hundred—were waiting for me. I hurried into the hall, and after an obeisance to those present, I asked the minister to propose what he wished, or else give me leave to offer a suggestion.

'As the event proved, he was a preacher not a debater. Nor did he wish to condescend to quarrels and hairsplitting with me. "But I have no intention", I pointed out, "of behaving in any contentious or sophistical way. I simply want to set out the truth peacefully and quietly in the course of discussion. This can be either in Latin or the vernacular". "Let us have it in the vernacular", said the Warden, "so that we can all understand it!" But no consideration, and no amount of persuasion—or even rebuke—from the Warden would induce the minister to agree to rules of debate. The Warden grew angry at this. "I see, indeed", he cried, "that we may be deceived and dealing out error; even a certain good Scotchman! Thank God there are still a few left who know enough about it to defend our old religion". After saying this, he promised before all present to give me a safe-conduct for the whole of Scotland. This he ordered to be immediately put in writing for my servant as well as myself, and added that he would like a longer talk himself some other time about these matters, either with me or with anyone else I sent to him. He promised him all courtesy and complete security.

'I left this place to go to the Lord Baron of Grencknols. In his heart he favours the Catholic faith, though in the cold fashion to which they are accustomed here. I explained my views to him, and the desire of English priests to run any risk—even that of losing their lives— for the salvation of the Scots, and for their return to the unity of the Catholic Church. I also told him that some already intended to join resources and efforts with those of Scottish priests to the same end . . . Genuinely pleased, he thanked God for such lofty ideals. When I asked him afterwards to look to his own soul, and return to the unity of the Church, he said that he would be readier to comply than I to ask. At the beginning—I forgot to mention—he begged me insistently to give him some kind of recommendation to the Queen of Scotland. From all this, Mr. Redman will be able to guess how much help he will get if he comes to these parts. From here I went on further, calling at another Baron of the Seton clan on the way. He is a confirmed heretic, and at his table I heard unceasing and appalling blasphemies. However, I said nothing until after supper when I had about an hour and a half's conversation with him against this vicious habit of blasphemy. After much argument on both sides, at the end of it all he thanked me very graciously and promised for the future to declaim less vehemently against the Catholics. He assured me that his house would always be most ready to offer me hospitality. And this applied to any other English Catholics.

'At long last I got to Edinburgh where the King's court was. I spoke with various noblemen; with Lord Seton, senior, the Lord Prior, his son, and with others to whom I made clear the cause of my coming, and our interest in their well-being. They treated me kindly, and took me to the King himself. What I said or did with him I must not put in writing here. From the court I went to the country-seat of Baron Geron, where not a few of the Scottish nobles had assembled. They assured me unanimously, and through me Mr. Redman, that they wished to make it clear that whenever we were pleased to come—they urged me to make it soon—they would guarantee the maximum safety, for we were Englishmen and not subject to their laws. They promised many other things concerning the King which I omit here. Nor did they promise protection to ourselves alone but also to any others sent by us. These were to be recognised by secret signs which I will reveal in another letter. The names follow of those who favour the Catholic faith, and who could easily become good men with the help of God's grace, and by dint of some persistence—I admit that at the moment they are far from the state of grace: the Sieur d'Aubigny, the Earls of Huntley, Eglinton, Caithness, the Barons Seton, Oglevy, Grey, Ferniehurst, and certain others, on whom our labour would not be bestowed without fruit or welcome. But we must not be a burden to them. This above all must be made clear to Mr. Redman so that he may have the wherewithal to support those he sends here, at least for a time. Otherwise, it will be very difficult to effect anything. Indeed, I think he would achieve nothing. He must also make provision that only the élite are sent here, whether from the point of view of good life or learning. If he has no such available, let him wait until he has. Better to send none at all than men unsuitable. The latter could greatly hinder, especially in the beginning, when the whole authority and prestige of the Catholic cause must depend on the knowledge of those who profess it. Mr. Redman must get many prayers for this work. It is of the utmost importance here, and indeed,

not negligible for the advantage of all Europe, as you see.
If ever there was a time that called for prayer and work,
it is now! Farewell!'

4.   [Persons continues] * 'I got these letters on 15 Sep-
      tember. The necessity of that time, and the pressure
of other business, prevented me from satisfying them by
being in Scotland the day prescribed. But I did all I could
in the circumstances. I wrote to Lord Seton explaining
the cause of my delay, and urged him with all the reasons
I could muster to adhere to a resolution which concerned
his own salvation and that of others. I added that before
long he would hear much from me about further negotiation. I also wrote into England to the effect that, by
whatever ways he could, he should deal with the Queen of
Scots about the matters mentioned above. I promised
that I would be with them shortly to deal with the rest,
as I understood that I was very much in demand. I also
instructed this priest to stay in the neighbourhood of
Scotland for the time being until he should hear otherwise
from me. I sent him what I could for his maintenance.
So now I depend entirely in all this on your reply. First,
should I pursue it or not? All the English Catholics urge me
most vehemently—in unmeasured terms, indeed!—to carry
on with it. From the conversion of Scotland depends all
our hope, humanly speaking, for the conversion of
England. If that king were once confirmed in Protestantism—and there is no doubt that he is most dangerously
imbued with it—no kind of help or refuge would be left
for the unhappy English. While Scotland lies open to them
as a refuge to which they can flee, they have a source of
boundless comfort. For the present, access to the King
is easy enough, and he himself sufficiently flexible. Later
it may not be so. Furthermore, it would be an excellent
thing for ourselves if we could spend a month or so in
Scotland to avoid something of the worst in any storm
that might arise. The Scots themselves have a few men
available who are completely suitable for the task, and
we would like to send them all there. They are, however,

few. They will not, indeed, be at all sufficient for so great a vineyard, especially at this time when the need is greatest.

'The next two years seem to be the ideal time for winning Scotland. Men hold sway in many places, especially the outlying parts, who will hardly offer any resistance. No laws have been passed against us, and we share our language with the Scots. I saw to it also that printed Catholic books should in future be introduced into Scotland as assiduously as into England. By this I mean books in the common tongue on controversial and devotional subjects. Up to now these have only been seen in Scotland in very small quantity or not at all. Scotland has no printing press, and the Protestants print their books in England. Lack of such books has left Scotland more in the grip of heresy than England.

'If the idea appeals to your Reverence that I should pursue this enterprise, then apart from your own directions, I would also ask you to get His Holiness to consider our needs, at least for a time. For this endeavour cannot be furthered without money, as can be inferred from my letter above. The Scots themselves are poor, and stand in great need. Nor have they shown up to now so much zeal for the Catholic cause that they are prepared to spend money on it. They think that they are doing a great deal for us when they make horses available, and offer some protection. The Catholics of England are everywhere bled so white that they are unable to provide for themselves and their own people in prison. These are very numerous and suffering much. But I have already laid out on the business more than a thousand crowns which they donated. At the same time, I am not unaware that His Holiness is weighed down by the burdens of even greater expense. I am therefore decidedly reluctant to ask him for anything. But if from the depths of his generosity, he could see his way to giving us 400 crowns a year for two or three years, we do not doubt that much could be done to advance the cause to his own satisfaction and the advantage of all Christendom. With this money

I could at least buy clothing, horses, and equipment needed for priests to be sent into Scotland. Admittedly, it would barely suffice for a journey of about 300 miles. However, I would certainly make it go as far as I could. I therefore beg your Reverence especially, and all the Catholics here likewise earnestly beg you, to do what you can to promote this business with His Holiness, and to reply as soon as you can on what is decided.

'Your Reverence can see the straits we are in. If we manage to win over this young prince of Scotland it would help us greatly. If His Holiness is pleased to show us favour, as we certainly hope he will, then his money should be sent to the Apostolic Nuncio in Paris to be paid to us·four times a year, that is, once a quarter. He should pay 100 crowns to a man going by the name of Eusebius Eugenius. This will probably be the Archdeacon of Rouen. We hope for your decisive reply some time before Christmas; and for the first payment in the year following; that is, 100 crowns. Furthermore, if His Holiness should see fit on this first occasion to let us have 200 crowns— there are many things to be bought—it would be extremely welcome. After that we would not expect more than 100 crowns every three months. Too much here on money! But how necessary a topic! Time and again it causes us great sorrow to think we can accomplish nothing here in the spiritual sphere without the aid of filthy lucre.

'Concerning the Italian they are looking for, your Reverence will know what to decide. A mediocrity would never do in these conditions. But I know that the best are so indispensable to you and your own purposes that they cannot be spared for us. What is to be done we must leave to you to think out. Certainly, it would be better not send at all rather than send someone unsuitable. Such a man could do extreme damage to the whole venture, and particularly to the reputation of the Society. They will expect a great deal more from them than from us who are English. If Father Achilles* could come I think he would be most suitable. I do not dare to ask for Father Bellarmine. Father Ferdinand I find acceptable for his good qualities, but not for learning. The Spaniard mentioned among those who might be sent was considered unsuitable by everybody. Even if his character were altogether fitted for it, he is not particularly adept in the humanities and languages. These are highly thought of here. Nor in theology and controversy is he notably skilled. Don Bernardino de Mendoza, the Spanish ambassador, found this and reported it to me before I knew the man was to be sent.

'Mendoza is very devoted to our affairs and to the Society. He promised to receive the Spanish Jesuit very willingly into his house if he were a man of some standing, and likely to uphold the reputation of our cause. Otherwise he was quite unwilling to consent to his coming. "It is difficult for you to conceive", he said, "how much offence and scandal could be given to the prejudice of the whole venture by even the least deficiences in your men if they became public". In fact, to stir up greater dislike, they are now beginning to oppose the whole movement as one coming simply from us. They are calling the Catholic religion the religion of the Jesuits. Hence some edicts were lately promulgated at Oxford and Cambridge Universities to find out who was in favour of the Jesuits' religion. They carefully obliged everyone to declare under oath whether he knew or suspected anyone to be in favour of the Jesuits or the Jesuit system of belief. I must, therefore, insist strongly with your Reverence that none be sent here except men who are really capable of the task. If Father Peter Ximenes or Father Emmanuel Vega were sent in the place of Father Diego, given that more learned men are not available, it would be vastly preferable because they are better acquainted with humanistic studies. Canon Law, on the other hand, of which Father Diego was a professor, is of no use among Protestants.

'I have tried to set these matters down simply and clearly for your Reverence. I leave everything to be determined by your judgment. I have appointed two merchants for the better assistance of our affairs and the advantage of both kingdoms. They are young but knowledgeable.

Their cover will be that they are delegates of important business-men. One will go to England, the other to Scotland. They should be able to return to these parts with the utmost freedom and safety. They will take with them certain wares which we hope will be bought up immediately by the Catholics. In this way, their expenses will, in large measure, be looked after. Besides this, they will concern themselves with our business, especially the question of importing books, letters, and other essentials. At the same time, they will have wares of some other kind to afford them better cover.

'Today I received another letter from England by which I understand that I am much in demand, especially among those in prison who want me to provide alms. Wiser men of greater influence insist that I get something done in the Scottish business before I commit myself again to the perils of England. They add that they can help me with the rest of the enterprise by correspondence, and also through Father Gaspar at least for a time. I will not overlook this possibility. Father Gaspar came to London last week from the county where he is concerned to get substantial alms to help those in prison. He wrote to me at this time to tell me that he enjoyed the greatest possible favour among the leading men of that county. Father William felt rather ill after his arrival, but got over it. He is now working hard. They write further about the Italian whom they would like to see placed with the King of Scots as his tutor in that language. If someone is sent, he should come to the house of the above-mentioned Archdeacon of Rouen where he will find everything ready, and detailed instructions from me. He should stay away from Rheims and Paris so as not to arouse suspicion. I should be written to under the name of Mr. Roland Cabel, merchant. Monsignor Allen wrote on the subject of authority to dispense in day-to-day cases arising. These should be given to the Apostolic Nuncio in Paris. Approach him also about printing the Hours of the Blessed Virgin in English, translated from the Latin. I beg your Reverence to promote all this with his Holiness, for it will be to the advantage of an enormous number of people. Farewell.'

5. Edmund Hay and William Crichton, both Scots, were successfully sought for to go to the assistance of Scotland. Persons ordered Crichton, together with Ralph Emerson, formerly the companion of Campion's journeys, to attempt an entry.* Crichton completed the journey successfully, and returned [to Europe] in April 1582. He went on to Rome to get more advice about the mission. While Persons remained in France, Crichton prepared a house to receive young Englishmen and instruct them in Latin. This was possible owing to the generosity of the Duke of Guise. The house was situated at Eu in the region of Normandy nearest England. The youngsters could be taken there on a far from difficult crossing lasting only a few hours. The Duke undertook to pay from his own income £100 in our money every year; that is, 400 Italian crowns. This was duly paid as long as he lived; which was until 1588. After founding this house, Persons went to Spain. He set before Philip the unhappy state of the Catholic cause with so much persuasiveness and authority that the King decided to pay 2,000 ducats a year to the seminary at Rheims. He also ordered 24,000 ducats to be paid to James, King of Scotland, so that the youthful prince might be won over, and his mother, imprisoned in England by order of Elizabeth, receive assistance. How much energy Persons put into all this is evident from the letter he sent to Crichton:

'From 1580, when I first went to England at the command of my superiors, I began to promote the interests of the King of Scotland in every way I could. Without delay, I sent William Waytes, a priest, at my own expense from England into Scotland. Later on, I sent in Father Holt. Since these beginnings did not go badly, I wrote to Very Reverend Father General to see if some Jesuits of your own nationality could be sent there. When it was decided to send your Reverence to reconnoitre, you will quickly remember how eagerly I reacted to the news.

I was then at Rouen. Indeed, I gave up my own companion, the only one I had, so that he would follow
[you] into Scotland. When your Reverence returned, I
was never behindhand in advising or helping you. I
embarked on an arduous and most difficult journey into
Spain. Even getting as far as Lisbon involved great risk.
With no less peril, I went on to Flanders, and subsequently
undertook a third journey to Rome. All this I did for
God in the first place, but also for the King of Scotland
and his mother. Even if my labour was unavailing for the
end in view, on two occasions at all events, I managed
to obtain from the King of Spain for their use 24,000
crowns, and from Pope Gregory XIII, four thousand. I
do not know if others have performed offices of this kind.
I feel obliged to mention these things to answer those who
make out that I am an adversary of the King of Scots.
To refute them, none could be a witness better stored
with facts than yourself. You know and can call to mind
all these things.' Thus Persons.

By praising him to the Catholic King, Persons also
prepared the way for Allen's promotion to cardinal. After
Allen's advancement, Persons made it clear that this was
very acceptable to the Society, and especially to himself.
This was indicated when Allen wrote the following to
[Dr. Richard Barret], whom he had appointed in his
place as president of the seminary at Rheims [from
31 October 1588]. 'My promotion is a welcome thing
and a matter of joy to you. But the cause you find in it
for rejoicing is all the greater because it leaves all of you,
by whom I am so much loved, bound by a fresh bond of
affection and gratitude towards the Society as a whole:
and in particular, towards our old and singularly good
friend and principal colleague. For next under heaven, it
was Father Persons who made me a cardinal.'*

At that time, an illness overtook Persons in Biscay
as he was returning from Portugal. It caused him some
delay. He wintered at Bilbao, and then went back to
France where he lived for most of the time at Rouen.
Founding his college at Eu, publishing books, and dealing

with all the other business of spreading the Catholic faith, he was as immersed as he could be in work and study. Indeed, how essential and useful was his protracted stay in France, the well-disposed reader may see from a letter written from Paris, which he visited from time to time, to the Rector of the English College, Rome. It runs as follows:

6. '. . . By order of my superiors I am here for the time being to expedite certain business with more commodity. It is also to prevent my presence, which is extremely hateful to our adversaries, from being a cause of increasing pressure on our friends. The majority of Catholics thought I should yield a little to the present time . . . For the situation in England has been lately much disturbed. A mad kind of violence on the part of the Protestants has hitherto prevailed so that some of our connections and principal instruments . . . have been cut off . . . But our enemies dropped everything else to seek me out. Apart from the trouble this caused everyone, it was also dangerous for my brethren and fellow-priests. They were very often captured when I was the one actually sought for . . . I look for nothing more certain; certainly, I long for nothing more ardently, than to return to England as soon as possible with the approval of those by whose desire, judgment or command I am kept here. Meanwhile, we run our course from this place; and at this time nothing is more remarkable than our success. It is hard to believe what our people say about the increase of Catholics this last year after they read certain books written on spiritual topics, and Holy Scripture, translated into our own tongue and interpreted in a Catholic sense. I am always hearing men who know and understand the situation affirm that they think there are twice the number of Catholics in England this year than last. That this is possible could be gauged from one fact. Of two priests recently sent here from England on business, one testified that he knew of four priests who, in one county alone, Hampshire, have brought back more than 400 to the bosom of the Church since last Easter.

'So it is that, although many priests from the seminaries are gradually coming into England, they are still much in demand, especially in certain counties where priests are in short supply. They call especially for more priests of the Society. For which reason Monsignor Allen and myself have written to our . . . Father General. And now we ask your Reverence to help us with this request. The six most recent martyrs, namely Kirkham [Kirkeman], Lacy, Hart, Johnson, Thirkill and Leyburn, who suffered at York during the last few months [1582-3], brought about a wonderful accession to the faith. After their most glorious death, our enemies have not only raged against bodies and lives, but also against the goods, estates and possessions of Catholics. This they do more ruthlessly than ever. Captured priests are not tortured on the rack or killed as before. They are simply imprisoned. Hence the number of those shut has markedly increased in many prisons. There are 30, for example, in Hull. Twenty-six priests are held at the Marshalsea in London. Here, by God's mercy, nearly all celebrate Mass every day. Certainly, by God's Providence, those imprisoned priests are quite often of greater service to us where they are than if they were still at large. Many people can come to them. They in turn have a safe and enduring lodging, and people visit who cannot find priests elsewhere. Even if they are nearly always in London or other big towns, they are in a better position to deal with business, at least in those places, than other people who do not have so many friends there; or if they have, they do not dare to make use of them as openly as men can who are already in prison. Evidently, men at large fear to fall into dangers which those already in prison need fear no more.

'Furthermore, when the youth of England falls into misbehaviour and vice . . . and the judges throw them into prison, it is remarkable how much good they derive from the company and conversation of priests. They often learn more about decency, self-control and orderly life after a month in that school than they learned in may years of liberty. For these reasons and others, our enemies do not

now seize hold of priests quite so eagerly. Indeed, it is
believed that some would like them all to go free, if they
could release them with propriety from the prisons
without losing face. For this cause also the Protestants
are apt to get angry when some admit too readily that
they are priests. So it was that just recently your friend
Lomax was rebuked on the side by the magistrate because,
after being arrested at the port, he admitted he was a priest
without more ado at the magistrate's very first question.
On account of this quite unnecessary confession they were
obliged to send him to prison.

'Of the crowd of young men who daily flock to us from
the English universities and other good schools, there is
no need to enter into a long disquisition. I know you have
heard already from the letters of Monsignor Allen about
this, and you will realise it more effectively from the great
number of most gifted students who have come to you
from this mission; of whom not a few came recently from
England after taking their degrees in the universities.
They will tell you in detail, and with all eloquence, the
state of English affairs. I have only this to say: the number
of those coming to us is very great. Although it is matter
for rejoicing, and affords us great hope, that God should
send forth by His grace so many men of such high quality
out of Sodom, at the same time, they overwhelm Monsignor Allen with their expenses—both those who stay
at Rheims and those who set forth on the road towards
you. Unless God helps us by a miracle, such an enormous
burden of expenditure cannot be borne. Add to this the
fact that there is a gradual stream of gentlemen flying from
England with their wives and children to avoid the most
spiteful thrusts of persecution. All of them come to Allen
as to a common father. From this your Reverence will
realise how large must be his heart and treasury to stand
the strain of an outlay so varied and considerable.

'The rage of the puritans has now begun to storm as
furiously against the more moderate Calvinists, so that
they in turn sometimes feel obliged to behave more
moderately towards us. It looks as if the matter will be

settled by force of arms, but we are in some fear lest the total force of the Calvinists be suddenly transferred to the puritan faction. These are far more inhuman enemies of ours than the Calvinists. I imagine that you have heard of three books recently published by the puritans against the Queen and Calvinists generally. We have the books here. The third is entitled *Postulatio Reformationis sine Dilatione,* and threatens radical and open rebellion. It was on account of this book that they recently hanged two puritans publicly in Suffolk amid a great rumble of protest from the rest of the sect. The Catholics, on the other hand, strive valiantly for their own faith. They are pursued by printed books as well as speech, and they alone are harried and fined, although they are good and faithful subjects. Indeed, the puritans, who openly reveal themselves to be the Queen's enemies, are free of all vexation.

'The State Councillors hear of these things, and pretend not to, because the greater part of them are puritans themselves. Notwithstanding, they would like to free a number of Catholics if it could be done on a good pretext, and leaving their honour intact. This would be easier if the Catholics were prepared to conform in some respect, even the most trifling. So it was that most recently they offered this condition to a certain important nobleman of learning and discretion whom they had previously ill-treated for a considerable time. They said that they would free him from prison immediately, and from all money fines—which were very heavy—if he would promise them just one thing. When he asked what it was, they replied, "It is not that you should renounce the Pope or come to our church. We know you will not do these things. But the Queen asks no more than that you promise not to receive in your house any Jesuit, or any of the more recently-ordained priests whom those traitorous seminaries of the Pope send over here". He replied to them, "If you will show me any member of the Society, or of any of the seminaries, who has perpetrated some treasonable act against our country, or committed some crime for which he should be judged and called an enemy of the

State, I will not receive him in my home. But to promise in a general way that I will shut out from my house all those men whom my religion represents to me as special servants of God, that I cannot do. Nor would I dare to do it even if the extreme penalty of death were to hang over me, lest I bring down on myself the heavy anger of God's judgment". Although at first they were angered by this answer, afterwards they were so affected by it that they allowed this nobleman far more agreeable conditions of imprisonment even if they did not set him free.

'I pass over the numerous answers of other Catholics on the same lines . . . This, then, must be the end. Your Reverence sees how much we need your prayers and help to persevere in this great work. Pray to God: intercede also with His Holiness, our illustrious Protector, and all other lords and patrons of ours so that they may be kind in our behalf. Finally, send us suitable labourers who will push forward strenuously under the yoke of Christ. Ultimate victory will assuredly be ours, though it may be delayed, and getting it a business burdensome and bloody. Your friend Birkhead greets you all. He was here with me recently. Please, your Reverence, greet all our friends for us, especially the Reverend Lord Bishop of St. Asaph, and all of our Society, and your College, the which may God preserve and increase by His Grace. Farewell! . . . Paris, 24 August 1583.'*

7.   Meanwhile, in England the contest was not waged without shedding of blood, ours included. Thomas Cottam, among the six priests declared guilty with Campion in 1581, was kept in chains until 30 May the year following. He was then brought forth to torment along with William Filby, Luke Kirby and Lawrence Richardson, secular priests. Cottam, a Lancashire man by origin, was brought up to study from boyhood. He left his parents as an adolescent and went to London, attaching himself to Thomas Pounde. By this man's efforts he became a convinced Catholic, crossed over to Douai, and there dedicated himself for many busy years to

philosophy and theology. For those early beginnings he
wrote thanking our brother, Thomas Pounde [on the
Sunday after Ascension Day, 1575], . . . Wishing for a
more stringent way of life, Cottam set out for Rome, and
was enrolled among the novices of the Society on 8 April
1579.* Not many months later, he was seized with a
violent illness, and on the advice of the doctors, sent back
to his own country. On the journey he fell in with Sledd, a
spy of the worst kind, at Lyons. While in his company,
this man sniffed out the fact that the other was bound
for England. He took careful note of his name, features
and everything else by which he could be identified, and
handed over the dossier to Elizabeth's ambassador in Paris.
The ambassador sent it to the Council, and the Council
passed it on to the port authorities to keep for the proper
time. Cottam got to Rheims. The deacon was ordained
priest. In company with John Hart and Edward Rishton
he crossed to England. From the previous information he
was arrested at the port, and handed over to one Haward—
who had disembarked with him—after his bond had been
taken up. He was duly consigned to Baron Cobham,
Warden of the Cinque Ports. When Haward first left the
port for the open road he addressed Cottam in this way:
'Sir, since I am a Catholic I cannot with a good conscience
hand you, a priest, over to the magistrate. Let us go up
to London together, then. Afterwards, I will fend for
myself as best I may, and you can do what you like with
yourself'.

When they arrived in London, Cottam went straight
to the prisons to consult men of learning whether it was
permissible for him to slip off in this way at the risk of
the man who had thus taken care of him. Some said he
could, and some that he could not. When the matter was
taken to Persons, he gathered up the opinions of a great
many persons before deciding that it would be better, even
at Cottam's own peril, to shield the man from danger;
such kindness ought not to redound to the disadvantage
of his guarantor. It was not long before the situation
obliged him to do just this. The man who had given a

bond for Haward saw him again in London. He complained that he had not kept faith; that he would be
ruined, and his entire family laid low. He himself was
threatened with punishment and torture on account of
the priest-prisoner. 'Therefore, as matters have fallen out,
you, Haward, must answer for the captive this very day to
the Vice-Warden of the Ports'. Haward was beaten down
by the insistence of the man, who became threatening.
'Suppose I stand in for your prisoner', he said, 'Will you
let me go free?' 'Certainly, provided that in the meantime
someone else will stand guarantor for you.' Haward found
a sponsor, and made a friendly call on Cottam. 'You know
the conditions and the laws under which I live, and how
much danger I shall run into if I fall into the hands of
these men. You know your position, and how much risk
you run. I will not force the issue either way. Do what
you think best. Even if they try every kind of torture
on me, I will never bring myself to betray you, or persuade
you to give yourself up.' Cottam raised his hands and eyes
upwards. 'God be praised!' he said, 'My mind would never
have been at rest if I had escaped from disaster prepared
for you'. He therefore set his affairs in order and a few
hours later returned to custody while the other took his
freedom.

8. Now we must look at the crafty and unreasoning
    cruelty of the enemies of the Catholics. No capital
charge was made. There was no pretext for holding Cottam
apart from his priesthood. They had heard that he had
fallen under suspicion of some crime or other. They interrogated him, as if he himself had actually committed the
crime, about punishment inflicted on him in the interval
since he had confessed, which was some time before.
In order to escape the full force of the tortures prepared
for him, he now admitted certain things without really
meaning them. They asked him for what delinquencies
his punishment had been imposed. Sensing a trick, he
replied that he was used to confess what was sin to God,
and to the priest, God's vicar, but to no one else. They

immediately submitted him to the torture of the rack,
but he breathed never a word. At last he cried out that
their proceeding was inhuman and barbarous. They only
dragged him further apart. He refused, even if he were
killed by torture, to say anything about himself or anyone
else. Goaded to fury, they stretched him with the utmost
cruelty. When later he came to vindicate himself before
the tribunal from any taint of wrongdoing, he made a
public protest at his treatment. Owen Hopton, with his
usual facility for lying, tried to deny everything. Cottam
called on God and the rest of the commissioners to bear
witness to the truth. In the first place, he called on George
Carey, who, while present, had himself asked a few
questions of the usual kind. He well knew that these mean-
ingless questions had been put many times to priests who
witnessed to their faith.

They then fell back on the usual questions which
Campion rightly described as bloody: 'What about the
Bull of Pius V? Is everybody in England bound to observe
its sentence as lawful? That, or any other such judgment
notwithstanding, is the Queen to be considered as lawfully
reigning? Are not all Englishmen bound to obey the
Queen? Could the Pope give the northern nobles, or
Sander in Ireland, leave to take up arms against the Queen,
invade the kingdom, and raise rebellion? Has the Pope
power, whatever the cause, to absolve the Queen's subjects, or those of any other princes from the obedience
and fealty they have once sworn? Does Sander in his
Visible Monarchy, and Bristow in his *Motives,* state true
or false doctrine when they deal with this Bull? Finally,
if the Pope were to declare the Queen unlawfully reigning, and her subjects truly absolved from their obedience,
or if any prince were to take up arms against England by
the authority of the Pope, which side would you take?
Or what would you deem to be the duty of a good
citizen?' Cottam tried to avoid all these questions with
one reply: 'I think in all these things as the entire Catholic
Church thinks.' Nor could they wring anything more
from him.

By way of last resort, they devised a third way of causing confusion to induce, if they could, Catholic priests to adopt their views. From 5 February until Pentecost, they ordered all, willy-nilly, to be dragged to the Protestant sermons which were held in the Tower. Here not only arguments, but untruths and plain abuse were freely resorted to in most bold and cunning fashion by carefully-chosen preachers. They achieved nothing. A soldier jammed the listeners close together, but they kept their minds intent on the real subject . . . And so they were able to accuse these masters of their mistakes even while they were still speaking, as well as when they left the pulpit. Owen Hopton did nothing to restrain the preachers. Indeed, he himself had his mind full of the usual barbarities and tortures. Cottam made a special point of approaching John Nichols, the apostate, reminding him and all present of their duty . . . This freedom of his was thought to have hastened Cottam along his road to martyrdom.

9. Cottam was accused of having agreed with Campion at Rome and Rheims to do away with the Queen. One frivolous and empty item was alone forthcoming to sustain so serious a charge, namely that he had come into England at the same time as the other. He refused to answer what was asked about Pius V's Bull. When he was taken, he had in his travelling bag, as was claimed, Aspilquete of Navarre's book of cases of conscience. Cottam had jotted some notes in it of certain considerations which weakened the supreme power of the Queen in ecclesiastical matters. Cottam said he knew nothing about the book. If such had been found, he had no idea who had planted it on him. It had nothing to do with him. On the subject of the Bull, he replied as was fitting for a Catholic, namely that he thought in this matter with the universal Church. The cause of his journey into his own country had been none other than to restore his health shattered by the Roman heat. If that had continued good, he would have gone as far away from

England as India. He had given his name for that enterprise not long before, and with no thought, moreover
of ever seeing his own land again. But in the presence of
prejudice one cannot shake off calumny, however false.
Cottam had to die because he was a Catholic priest after
the heart of Catholics.

On 30 May 1582, Father Cottam was led forth with
the three other priests mentioned above to execution.
He was the last to die. With extraordinary craft, they
tried to turn the man's mind aside from its straight course,
pointing out the cruelty of the killing with a hope of
saving his life. Two or three times he was commanded
to look at his companions, to see them as they hung from
the gallows; also when their bellies were ripped open with
the knife, and the internal organs of stomach and chest
laid bare. He had to see them as their hands were cut off,
and their limbs hacked from their trunks. Cottam merely
looked upwards while he commended himself, and the
martyrs undergoing their passion, to God. 'Good Jesus',
he cried, 'what kind of display is this? Lord, forgive them.
Lord, give your servant grace to persevere to the end!' At
that point, they undid the rope and let him down from
the cart. They dangled the prospect of a pardon before
his eyes. 'We know you crossed over for health reasons',
they said. 'You will easily save your life by pleading with
our merciful Queen. You have only to admit here in public
that you did not come to England for the same cause as
the rest. You do not approve of the Pope's reasons for
sending priests here. Acknowledge the Queen as the
supreme head of the Church, to whom alone the affairs
of England are committed, and to none beside. What
are you waiting for? Why don't you prefer life to a
horrible death? After undertaking such a long journey for
your health's sake, do you now want to throw away life
itself?'

The gladiator undaunted was convinced that they were
opening up a pit beneath his feet, and not a path to mercy.
Raising his voice, he cried out that he would not swerve
the width of a finger-nail from his Catholic faith. If he

had a thousand lives, he would prefer to throw them all
away. He was grateful for the Queen's mercy, and prayed
she would live safely and happily. But he could not
acknowledge in her more power than was recognised by
the Church universal. When they saw that they were
making no progress with him, they pushed him up again
on to the cart, and told him to beg pardon for the crime
committed against the Queen. He rejoined, 'I have not
harmed the Queen by any crime. I only hope most fervently that she will enjoy health of body and soul. Further,
I would willingly suffer this death, and many more tortures besides, if I could thereby ensure her eternal
happiness. I pray God to pardon me in whatever way I
have sinned; and if anything remains to be declared in His
honour, that He will put it into my mind. I ask everyone
else to forgive me as I from my heart forgive all men.
Although the iniquities of this land may call down severe
retribution from God, I pray that He may turn aside His
just anger, and inspire all men with better ideas in matters
of religion'. He then took the executioner's hand. 'God
forgive you', he said, 'and make you his servant . . .'. At
length, at the sheriff's order to destroy this traitor, the
cart was drawn away to leave him hanging . . . When they
came to hack open his chest, it was seen that he had
supplied his own punishment in the hair-shirt pressed
against his flesh. Although the Protestants received this,
for the most part, with a smile, they could not prevent
themselves from wondering at this priest who died so
well. The Catholics looked on with plain veneration.

10. This cruel and barbarous procedure of the justices,
by which priests were harrowed with unheard-of
forms of torture, was fully approved of by the more
powerful members of the Privy Council. They were
content that after being condemned on slight and even
false evidence, the victims were dragged to the gallows
to be torn apart half-alive according to the ritual reserved
for traitors. To them it seemed both good and useful . . .
To the Queen, however, it seemed morbid and cruel.

Indeed, she thought it infamous. She therefore rejected the reasons given for past excesses which those who presided at the torture-sessions offered her.

She desired them to desist from cruelties of this kind, and the judges likewise from passing the death sentence. Perhaps this was due not so much to prudence or to compassion, as Camden suggests,* but rather to a certain fear of causing enmity with Henry III, King of France. For when he was solicited to take the place of his dead brother, the Duke of Alençon, as the protector of the rebels in Flanders, he replied that, according to the Pope and Canon Law, it was not permissible to make treaties with heretics; especially with those who killed innocent priests by means of unjust decrees and savage punishments. Whether from enlightment or fear, although extreme measures were not everywhere done away with, they were changed for the present (1585) to exile. However, they were strengthened subsequently by laws hardly less severe. Catholics were also to be wrung out of their rights by twisting the laws themselves, with however much injustice, as will be described in its place.

In 1585, 70 priests were expelled to taste the hardships which must always be the lot of exiles. Nor was that all. Their adversaries tried to destroy their good name, as far as they could, by every wile and hardihood. The first 20 were chosen from the various prisons in the city. Henry, Earl of Derby, was then setting out on embassy to France. These would be an argument on his tongue, in the presence of the King, to praise this latest kind of gentleness and mercy. Among the first exiled were Gaspar Haywood, James Bosgrave, John Hart and Edward Rishton, who subsequently wrote the history of the schism . . . Warned of their imminent exile, they were allowed no other liberty save that, in the presence of the gaoler who heard all, they could arrange with their friends about paying their expenses. How small was this concession in their straitened circumstances! But they had to go. While they were being put on board ship, Haywood, who was older than the rest, offered protest for himself and his companions. They were being punished with exile as innocent men. They had come to England to spread the faith. They would rather stay to protect it; and they were ready to exchange danger of their lives for the chance to bring cheer to the Catholics and the hope of mutual advantage . . . They therefore asked to be shown the letters commanding their exile.

Their pleas were in vain. They weighed anchor and set sail. After two days, having covered a great part of the sea between, they again asked about the letters which they wanted to read or hear read. These were now produced. At once there was seen by way of heading, 'These men are all guilty of various treasons and conspiracies against the Queen and her realm; and this is proved either by their own testimony or that of others. They have been condemned after judgment in open court, or kept in prison awaiting it. Although they have merited the extreme penalty, yet by the Queen's clemency they are now ordered merely to depart the realm &c [*sic*] '. What were their feelings as this was read out? . . . They cried out that they were themselves betrayed, and burdened thus with the grossest calumnies and slander. No witnesses and no confession could be produced to brand them convincingly with their grave stigma of conspiracy, or plotting against the Queen and her realm. They demanded that the sails be set for the way they had come, for England: there they would stand up in the courts and proclaim their innocence to the world; or else bring their lives to a glorious end among their own people. They achieved nothing. Their enemies had put it about that they had crossed over, all of them, from fear of punishment and death. Or what was worse, it was also rumoured that, having come to terms with the Protestants on certain points, they were considered worthy of mercy. However, it was easy to dispel this idea. It was immediately evident that they were all of them only too willing to go back to England whenever their superiors saw fit. They made no account of torture and cruel death. In the meantime, they comforted one another with the thought of the apostle, that they were found worthy to suffer insult for the name of Christ.

11. These events overtook all alike. Now to look at some particulars which touched our own Society. Gaspar Haywood, the younger brother of Eliseus, mentioned above, was the son of John Haywood, gentleman, poet, the contemporary of Thomas More. Haywood was now in his 27th year, Master of Arts and priest. He joined the Society at the professed house in Rome on 21 May 1562. After two years' theology, he was sent to Dillingen, and expounded moral theology and apologetics for 17 years, in the course of which he became a doctor of theology and was promoted to the four vows. He was well-versed in Hebrew, and succeeded in devising a short and easy method for learning the language by means of cards. The letters of Pope Gregory XIII, then reigning, to Duke William of Bavaria testify to the zeal of Haywood's work in the English harvest-field whither he was sent by the Pontiff. The Duke was also Haywood's patron in these years. These are Gregory's words:

'Beloved son, and noble Sire, greeting . . . The harvest is great, the labourers few. Pray, therefore, the Lord of the harvest to send workers into his harvest. We do, indeed, pray. But we must also, according to Our office and solicitude for all the Churches . . . send men; and only those whom we know to be altogether fitted for the task. We must also ensure that in this enterprise we have the Catholic princes for our helpers, among whom we consider your Grace of first importance. The priests of the Society of Jesus in England ask us to send them helpers for the work zealous in their cause and anxious for Christ's glory and the good of souls. They mention especially Our beloved son Gaspar Haywood, an Englishman, and priest of the same Society. they hope that his authority, which is not slight there, will stand him in good stead. We wished to tell your Grace this, as it is of the utmost importance for God's glory. This alone we seek. And for the safety of those we send, they should make their departure as secretly as possible. We are confident that your Grace will fully approve of the cause and of our zeal in it; also that you will readily allow Haywood to depart in view of the pressing urgency of the situation. Given at Rome, at Saint Peter's under the fisherman's ring, 27 May 1581; in the ninth year of our Pontificate.'

Haywood came to England with William Holt in 1581. During Persons's absence in France, Haywood acted as superior [in England] of the Jesuits. When the question of fasts and feast-days came up at the meeting of the priests, he disagreed with Persons, desiring that the old customs of England should be brought into conformity with more recent canons. Hence word went round among the enemies of the Society that Haywood disagreed with Persons on most things. Persons denies it in his *Apology*. Indeed, on this precise question he came round to Haywood's view. Nor were they afterwards at variance.* Frequently laid low with the agony of gout, Haywood could not rival Campion and the rest in his labours. Because of his complaint, he was dispensed from the fasting laws. Not everybody, however, interpreted his privilege alike when they saw him eating meat. He once happened to be enjoying the hospitality of a schismatic—a man who did not much differ from the Catholic way of thinking, and who, for his wife's sake, a Catholic, was very kind to priests. During Rogation-tide, the table was provided with two kinds of food for the members of the household, including Haywood. Some, like Haywood and his host, took meat; others, with the lady of the house, only fish. Some argument arose at the table about this distinction. Haywood gave them the several-pronged argument which the theologians produce. Mine host, however, was very much against the distinction and, indeed, gave the impression of being not a little annoyed. Not long afterwards, he went to the shops and bought a copy of the edict which sent priests into exile. He returned with it to Haywood, and asked him if he were affected by it. 'Certainly', said Haywood, 'but I'm safe with you, am I not?' 'But I never promised you this kind

of immunity. Nor do I find your way of living and thinking so much to my taste that I would want to put my head
and goods in jeopardy on your account. Therefore, as from
now, I consider you my prisoner!' His wife's tears and
promise of money were enough to secure Haywood's
release that same night. We need to be careful where we
are, and who is watching, when we make use even of a
permitted liberty!

Times got gradually worse; and bringing with them as
they did continual searches, they forced Haywood for
the most part to lie low. However, he fell into a snare
from which he derived as much security as he could wish.
He was summoned to France, and when he was almost
on the coast of Normandy he was driven back to England
by an adverse wind, captured, and put in irons. He was
then brought forth with other priests to answer the capital
charge; nor in this was he immune from trickery. For at
his entrance into Westminster Hall, before the very seats
of the judges, he was taken apart from the rest and put
in a neighbouring room under guard. They did not want a
learned and eloquent man to give the lead to his companions. They also thought that the views of the rest
would be affected if he could be brought to waver in any
degree in his own faith, even if the rest might well wonder
about the cause. Perhaps he had shown himself more
obedient to the Queen than was fitting, for he had served
her as a boy. This was what Hopton quietly insinuated,
and it was open to suspicion. But when he was taken back
to prison Haywood could not be drawn by any kind of
promise, or cowed by any sort of fear. He was sent into
exile alone, going to Dôle in Burgundy . . .

Four years later, Haywood went to Rome, and then
settled at Naples . . . He wanted no special treatment in
his extreme old age, but was content with routine arrangements. He was very prompt to obey the sound of the
bell, whether it rang for recreation or for some spiritual
duty. But it was clear from his ready response of visage
and gesture that this was due less to the prospect of
relaxation than to the spirit of obedience . . . [He died]

on 9 January 1598, having lived 63 years, 36 of them in the Society, including 28 from his profession.

12. James Bosgrave of Godmanstone was born in Dorset. He studied rhetoric and philosophy at Rome; was admitted to the Society on 17 November 1564. Afterwards he went to Germany and Poland, being ordained priest at Olmutz in 1572. He spent the next 12 years teaching rhetoric, philosophy, mathematics, apologetics, Greek and Hebrew. In 1580, he went back to his own country, among other things to recover his health. He was soon obliged to know England as a prison. Such was the medicine it provided for his sickness. Bosgrave was captured after a short interval of liberty, and put in the Marshalsea. There his courage showed in endurance, and knowledge in his conversation, even if bodily weakness was equally plain to see. Walker and Fulke were at that time going their rounds, and a great many more of their kidney; men thirsty of fame while they taught terror. When they could not overcome in arguments priests already bowed in chains, they overwhelmed them with shouting, putting words about of victories won only in their own imagination. For this reason, Bosgrave, Sherwin, Hart and others asked for a public disputation to circumvent loss to faith by the mendacity of these men. They asked for conditions which, if observed, would allow of no deception by false rumour, but which would have permitted them to teach the truth to those who listened. Nor did their adversaries seem to refuse it.

In September (1581), George Carey, who was in charge, gave orders to the head gaoler [of the Marshalsea] that if there were any papists—at that time they used this term derisively to describe Catholics—who wished to defend their beliefs in disputation, they should write down the heads of their arguments. The names should be attached of those who would defend them, and they should prepare themselves for the fray.* They would shortly be told in what place, at what time, and under what conditions the disputation would take place. The heads were duly written down, names added, and the signed papers handed over. All was sent to Carey and the Protestant ministers. The subjects for dispute collected by the priests did not please them. They put forward others which our men did not refuse. The day decided on was 29 December, feast of St. Thomas of Canterbury. There was great expectation before the day, and the zest of battle.

Their enemies, however, did not await the appointed day. They dragged off Bosgrave and Hart to the Tower to be tried not by discussion but torture. They had previously transferred Sherwin on 5 December to that place, and on the 15th and 19th tortured him most cruelly so that he would be less able to stand up to the debate. This was how they later treated Campion, as we have seen. Bosgrave was present with the rest, although none of them except Campion and Sherwin was allowed to speak. When Bosgrave was on trial for his life, three charges were maintained against him: he denied the supreme power of the Queen in spirituals: asked about the Bull of Pius V, he had made no definite reply; hearing report that the Pope, the King of Spain and the Grand Duke of Tuscany had conspired against the Queen, he had not revealed it to the English administration. As if, indeed, anything heard of this nature should at once be taken by any individual to authority however uncertain the foundation on which it rested!

There were many more reliable ways for those things to come to magistrates when such stories first began to go round. And so Bosgrave had also agreed with Campion and the rest, to do away with the Queen! This was the cause of the ferocious sentence. How could he have done this, being cut off by vast distances for many years, and so unknown to his own people as to forget even his mother tongue! In fact, he had seen none of those with whom he was accused of conspiracy before he had come to the prison! . . . However, his adversaries punished him not with death, although he was found guilty with the others, but with exile. Perhaps it was because King Stephen of

Poland had begged his life from Queen Elizabeth, praising him lavishly in these terms:

'Stephen, by the Grace of God, King of Poland, and Grand Duke of Lithuania, to the most Serene and Sovereign Lady Elizabeth . . .

'James Bosgrave, theologian of the Society of Jesus and professor in our Academy at Vilna, has now been detained in prison for some time in your Majesty's kingdom. Many have been captivated by his holiness and learning; and we hear that his imprisonment is for no other cause than professing the Roman Catholic faith which he imbibed with his mother's milk and stoutly persists in. Notwithstanding, we do not doubt that your Serenity understands how much it means that a man of outstanding holiness and erudition should be long absent from an academy which he himself is so anxious to develop. We certainly can easily perceive that his absence has greatly hindered the cause of learning. This is why We earnestly beg your Serenity to do Us the favour of sending Our theologian back to Us a free man. Thus he can continue in his former office to instruct our subjects in the religion and letters which will be so great an adornment and source of profit for Church and State. We do not doubt that your Serenity, in accordance with your goodwill towards Us, will grant Us this man; nor that you will insist that, since Our kingdom is open to all of your good subjects whatever their religion, religion should be a matter of capital offence in our subjects. For the rest, We hope that your Serenity, in accordance with your royal benignity and clemency, will shortly command that the remaining Catholics likewise be set free. [You] will then have done something in full accord with your own humanity, and truly most pleasing to Us . . . Given at Niepolomice, 29 January 1583; in the seventh year of Our reign.'

Elizabeth had not yet put on quite so much humanity. All the same, she allowed this particular case to be examined to see if there were reason for not sparing the condemned man. Nothing was found against him and he was released as a royal favour. So he set off once more for Poland by way of the coast of France, and spent the rest of the summer in that country. He was professed of the three vows at Calisz on 25 April 1604. He died on 27 October 1623, when he was well over 70 years old . . .

13. John Hart tasted tribulation before he was admitted to the Society. He first fell into enemy hands after being sent to Oxford; in which university he distinguished himself in the bachelor's degree in theology. To soundness of knowledge—Camden said that of all the priests at the time he was the most learned (Annals, Eliz. 27)—he could add pleasing appearance and impressive bearing. Hence they hoped that, if not by reasons, he would at least be won over by flattery, promises and the prospect of a great name in his old university. They stalked him for two or three months. When they saw that they were wasting their butter and time, he was sent back to prison in London to become the companion of Bosgrave and Sherwin, first of all in the Marshalsea. They were still together when Hart was dragged off to the Tower. He was condemned on the capital charge along with Briant and his associates. After sentence was passed, they again put Hart to the trial of persuasion and torture on four occasions, using every instrument at their disposal: but he remained firm. They threw him into a dungeon 20 feet deep in the ground where the air was damp and repellent with filth and darkness. After nine days he was taken out; and in this way better prepared, they put him to debate with Reynald, a man who enjoyed a great reputation among the Protestants as a savant. In this way, what their bad treatment had lacked to convince Hart might be supplied by this man's reasoning. But finding greater strength in his infirmity, Hart routed his adversary, and showed clearly the superior force of truth as opposed to a false claim to it. They loaded him with irons for his persistence, and then put him back in his dungeon for more than 44 days. Two years went by while the above events unfolded. Not unjustly, one of his fellow-prisoners

wrote: 'John Hart has endured hard and daily conflict
but his mind remains steady and settled'.*

These things were thought up, proposed and carried
out without reference to the judge's sentence, over and
above the ordinary law; all at the whim of private individuals to change and break the mind of man. But a man
under sentence should not be subjected to more punishment than the law demands. It is only too evident how
abominable were the conditions in which the priests were
held, and in the hands of men who were quite devoid of
humanity. Anyone was allowed to inflict what torment
he pleased on them. Their shame was the greater in so far
as they were unable to shake even one of our men in his
convictions by these devices . . . Hart was driven into
exile with the first to go. He entered the Society at
Verdun, trying so hard for this while still in chains that
even then he could be considered already a member.
From Verdun he was sent to Rome, and afterwards to
Poland, dying at Jaroslav on 19 July in the year following
(Jaroslave Annals for 1594/5). Seven years later his grave
was opened with a view to transferring his corpse to a
more fitting site. It was found to be preserved intact.

Exile as a punishment was taken to be an act of the
Queen's mercy, but how much mercy there really was,
the laws of the same year 1585 passed against priests and
refugees sufficiently demonstrate. The 20 whom I mentioned were deported on 21 January. In the following
March, all priests were proscribed who had been ordained
in the first year of Elizabeth's reign and subsequently.
They were ordered to leave the kingdom within 40 days.
Any of them who returned, and people who offered them
hospitality, were to be indicted, the former for treason
and the latter for felony. Both charges involved the death
penalty. The goods of all alike were declared liable to
forfeiture by the state. If men in training in the seminaries
did not return within six months, they would be considered traitors. Anyone who sent a youth to the seminaries was to be fined 400 crowns. The one so sent would
lose his inheritance, unless he returned forthwith and

conformed to the law; that is, embraced Protestantism.
Whoever sent assistance to refugees abroad was liable
to loss of property and perpetual imprisonment. Such
was the celebrated clemency now proclaimed for the
time to come.

14. The authorities did these things openly in England
    so that, having struck the shepherds, they could
scatter and destroy the sheep . . .
    Meanwhile, after getting the general vote, the Society
appointed Alfonso Agazzari, a Sienese, Rector of the
Roman College. This was in 1579. Agazzari was a man
most fitted by capacity for work, enthusiasm and religious
spirit, to get things moving. Further, as is most necessary
when placing authority in the hands of a foreigner, he was
a great lover of our people and cause. He considerably
increased the property of the seminary, and inspired such
great fervour in the minds of his hearers that, in the nine
years he ruled them, nearly 100 labourers were sent into
the vineyard, and 19 added to the Society . . .
    That long-standing model of all politicians, the Privy
Council of England, fostered and encouraged spies everywhere. Wearing an air of piety and devotion, they slithered
in among the faithful and into the very seminaries. Mixing
truth and falsehood, they reported back to the Council
by letter, or men like themselves, whatever was done at
Rheims or Rome, with anything else their spiteful imagination felt like stirring in. Some of them were motivated by
jealousy. They did not approve of the designs of Allen and
Persons, or else were not always consulted. They tried to
destroy the peace of the seminaries, and whatever the rest
did to promote the Catholic faith, they did their best
to ruin.*
    Among such a certain Vaux whom the Inquisition put
in chains when they found him out. There was also
Solomon Aldred, later quite openly the servant of
Walsingham; and Fisher, eventually convicted of fraud.
Among them were Charles Paget, Thomas Morgan, Thomas
and Francis Throckmorton, Parry, Griffith and Bateson

who, placing themselves under the protection of the great, nourished a hope in Popes Gregory and Sixtus that things would go better with the Catholics in England if Allen and Persons abstained from writing, and from any other dealing in English affairs. It would be best of all if any Jesuits still in England were recalled, and no longer sent there in future. Next—a thing hard to believe as coming from Catholics—they used every endeavour to persuade authority that it was cruel to send innocent priests to most certain slaughter in England with only very slight prospect of achieving anything. Papal money would be better spent on helping liberally certain private individuals than by giving it to theological colleges, which were weak and insecure helps to the faith. Finally, pouring slander over the discipline of the Roman College, they said that it was more adapted to boys than to form men; especially those men who had passed their youth at the universities, and were obviously adequate to exercise discipline over themselves.

Since the Catholics of our nation in Rome were untried and inexperienced, all this seemed to them like reason; and it was a fairly easy matter to foster strife among the seminarists themselves, and between them and their superiors. For if they were refused anything they at once fell to complaining; and they found willing listeners among their countrymen before whom they aired their quarrels. Admittedly, the latter did not depart easily from the settled way of things. The devil himself put on piety to assail with more subtle devices those who showed more religious sense. The question was put to them, 'Which is the more perfect state: that of those who bind themselves by a vow not to do any work, even the most perfect, except by the will of the superior, or of those who, having taken the college oath on the priesthood, run fleetly to the perils, ambushes, prisons, tortures and crosses for the sake of spreading the faith?' Youthful ardour usually rushes to do daring things in a hurry while those more mature are content to go slowly. These men played much on this, and claimed that the free obligation undertaken by the priests was a far greater thing than all the vows of the Orders. Many days were wasted in that kind of debate. There were zealous minds on both sides. The enemy took care that it should not be as in the schools where the war-like word can come from a mind at peace. To contest of words was added bitterness of feeling. This split the distracted and divided seminary into parties.

The system ceased to be a means of whipping up religious zeal. Rather was religious zeal used to maintain division. Regard for the ideal of the religious life everywhere went down. Gradually, religious superiors lost their influence. And then, seeing that a limited range of tricks would not suffice to bring all to the ultimate stage of wickedness, the adversary showed himself no less versatile than perfidious. Since he could not persuade all to accept what he proposed, those whom he saw bent on taking religious vows he left to their own devices. Let them go to the Orders provided they do not enter the Society of Jesus! Almost at the same time, seven left for the most praiseworthy Order of Preachers. Would to God it had been after due consideration and with steady purpose! They went off without the knowledge of the superiors of the seminary, led by their own spirit to embark on this very considerable undertaking. With like inconsistency most of them not long afterwards threw aside the obligation thus assumed, and so fell from being either shining ornaments of the seminary, or adornments of their most distinguished Order. The leaders of the dissidents included especially the man who formerly envied Persons, as we have said, at Oxford University; and in the second place all those whom he had set on edge against the discipline imposed by the superiors.

The matter was carefully gone into by the Bishops of Piacenza and Cremona (?). At the instance of Sixtus V, the leaders were expelled. A number of others left; and the exit of most of them was inglorious. Tydder, Shawe, Bell and Major, priests, put from them faith and chastity. But Gifford and Gratley failed to cultivate their familiarity

and correspondence with Walsingham and other Protestants with sufficient caution so that they did not long
enjoy their advantage. At the order of the Pope, Gifford
was seized at Paris, Gratley at Padua. Gifford was condemned after trial, and died in prison at Paris at the end
of a good deal of suffering in expiation of past enterprises.
Gratley was taken to Rome, and detained by the Inquisition for a good many years. He survived to live in exile
in Apulia. Others went to England. Through tricks of the
same sort they stirred up much dislike throughout the
country against Allen and the Society among the priests
working there to preserve the faith.

Allen at this time took up residence at Rome. His
personal prestige and Persons's hard work did much to
settle the minds of the students. Among other remedies
tried to restore peace was that of providing the English
with an English rector. To him they could communicate
their complaints, as they conceived them, more intimately,
perhaps, and with greater trust. William Holt was the
first to hold that office, which he took up at the end of
1586. After Holt was sent to Flanders, Joseph Creswell
succeeded him. It was this year that Allen was made a
cardinal. In accordance with his greater dignity, he was
able more effectively to employ all the means available
to establish and preserve peace. While he was in Rome,
they respected and feared him. When they were out of
his presence in England, men were not lacking to pursue
him with slander inspired by envy. This was because he
seemed too friendly to the Spaniards and because he
worked too closely with the Society of Jesus. These were
the men to whom he referred before he received his
dignity in a certain letter written by the Rector of the
Roman College (1582): 'I only write this to the Illustrious
Protector so that he may refuse to listen to certain idle
and envious men who say that all priestly offices and
appointments in the colleges are at our disposal &c. [*sic*]'.
Which complaint, in fact, changing only the name, was
also levelled at the Society; as though all obeyed us, and
as if everything inside and outside England was done by

our advice. How widely that accusation was spread, and
with what bitter fruit, I thought it not out of place to
narrate in this summary. It seemed better to confine the
storm which raged throughout most of these years into
a few narrow pages rather than expose what remains of
this history to the perpetual tossing of waves which would
only make the reader seasick.

15. Before Haywood and the rest went into exile,
    Thomas Mettam, a priest honoured for age, learning
and goodness, was received into the Society after almost
10 years' imprisonment. Persons wrote of him to Ribadeneira on 15 September 1584,* 'With regard to the
members of our Society in England, two priests were
killed, Campion and Cottam. Four were kept in prison,
Haywood and Bosgrave in the Tower of London, Mettam
and Pound in Wisbech. The latter two are still there &c.
[*sic*]'. More definite information was contained in General
Mercurian's letter to Mettam himself: 'I was very consoled',
he said, 'by your Reverence's letter to our Father Darbishire on account of the good and salutary desire revealed
therein. That this comes from the Holy Spirit, we do not
doubt. Therefore we would fear to offer slight to the Giver
of all gifts and graces by not acquiescing for our part in
your Reverence's desire . . . Wherefore we take your
Reverence into our company . . . embracing you in the
spirit from this moment as a true and living member . . .
We likewise hope that . . . when your Reverence has been
freed from your present straits you will be ours not only
in mind and inclination but in fact and deed . . . It remains
for me to warn you that your Reverence should not reveal
your intention or this concession of ours to anyone rashly;
indeed, not at all, unless all danger is absent and some
appreciable benefit appears thereby . . . Rome, 4 May 1579'.
The Roman letter for 1592 garlands him with this eulogy.
'In England the holy confessor of Christ, Thomas Mettam,
died the death of the just, in prison where he had been
confined for the Catholic faith 19 years. His martyrdom
was all the more cruel for being of daily occurrence.'

William Weston came to England in 1583. For his honouring Edmund Campion, for the hardships he went through, and by goodness which shone particularly in deeds, he gained for himself and the Society a considerable reputation even among his enemies. In 1586 Henry Garnet and Robert Southwell came to swell the number and credit of the working-party here. William Weston was born at Maidstone in Kent. He was Campion's contemporary at Oxford University. After his conversion to Catholicism, he set out for Rome at the age of 25, and was duly enrolled in the Society on 5 November 1575. In the following year he was moved by the Andalusian Provincial to Montilla. After the noviceship there, he spent some time studying philosophy at Cordoba—he was already a bachelor of arts—and then theology. For a year or two afterwards, he was engaged in the Society's Apostolate. He enjoyed unusual success, first at Cadiz and later at San Lucar and Seville, giving help especially to the English in those centres of trade. He gave his labours to the Spaniards as well, and was not without a reputation for holiness even at that time. His indefatigable zeal in preaching, and austere usage of his own body, together with his unassuming nature, were then already noteworthy. He was by instinct a friendly man. Another who shared a room with him, found him very frequently on his knees. While he was praying he seemed to be studying, and while studying to be praying. He would sometimes be found curled up under the table so that his rest should not be entirely untroubled. He did a turn in the scullery almost every day, doing the most ordinary chores.

In 1582 he was called to England. He found a new shirt prepared for his journey, but he left it behind being satisfied with the old one. He sold his horse on the road out of hand, and completed the journey to France on foot. When he met Persons there, he received a letter from him to a well-known house not far from London. There he was received in kindly fashion; but as the times were full of fear and suspicion, the lady of the house did not dare extend to one unknown even so much hospitality as an overnight stay. Being sent away, even if courteously, he took a different road towards London. If he had taken the usual well-worn highway, he might have been observed by some rascal or other. The lady had not recognised the indications given by Persons. Indeed, the name of Persons himself seemed new to her. Weston, therefore, assumed that he had mistaken the house, or new people had rented it. A few days later, he chanced on a priest who was going to the same house. He recommended Weston to the lady. She was sorry for what had happened before, and put the blame on her own fear. She now looked after Weston and offered a means whereby he got to know many Catholics. The following year, he brought Philip, Earl of Arundel, back to the Church, and so grounded him in sound principles of living that his life became most praiseworthy for its religious sense and balance. The priest brought back many others to the right path, and confirmed practising Catholics in their convictions.

Weston enjoyed liberty for two years, travelling up and down the country. Eventually, he was taken by a low trick and imprisoned in the Clink in London. The excellent Countess of Arundel managed to get into the prison disguised, and offered to buy his freedom with a sum of money. Weston, however, replied, 'Not at all! My capture had nothing to do with money. For my part I will not be saved by money. If God wants it so, He will move the hearts of those who shut me up to restore me to liberty. I leave myself to His Providence'.

There was a certain sailor in the Clink whom some burglars had hired to get away secretly a certain amount of swag. This man came often to Weston in the course of his prison duties, and sometimes asked for a tip. In this way he hoped to save up to buy his liberty. 'I will give you something', said Weston, 'even if you will not get freedom from gaol by it. Look after your soul, and keep it out of harm's way!' At the same time, Weston told him what to do. The man listened eagerly and often, so that he became a Catholic, and received sentence for it. He was called upon, as custom was, to take part in the Lord's

Supper in the Calvinistic manner with other miscreants before their punishment. He refused, acknowledging himself a Catholic. Life and freedom were then offered him if, setting our usages aside, he agreed to take up their ways again. Instead, he continued unflinching in the faith he had so recently made his own, and exchanged this lugubrious existence for the certain hope of happiness in eternity . . .

17. At Wisbech, on the borders of Cambridgeshire and Norfolk, there is a castle built in an extremely damp site, and surrounded by marshes on every side. To this place, the Protestant authorities transferred a great many priests from London. Perhaps they intended that those whom they were ashamed to punish publicly might be dealt with by the sheer inhospitality of the place. Certainly, the prisoners were far from the teeming city. Their food was sparse enough, and there was also less opportunity for dealing with their neighbours in matters of religion. Weston, sent there after a few years, found more than 30 Catholic priests and laymen. With the utmost peaceableness and perfect harmony among them, they imitated paradise, arranging all their daytime—and indeed nighttime-activities with admirable order. There was frequent prayer, systematic reading, and commentary on the Scriptures, at stated hours. Nothing unwholesome came to their ears or eyes—or to those of the Protestants there! The priests were glad at Weston's coming. His reputation for goodness, learning, and numerous sufferings in Christ's cause, had preceded him. They took him as an ally, and almost as guide, in what they had set before themselves. They made him chairman in their debates on dogma and apologetics, and their interpreter in Greek and Hebrew. They came together most eagerly to hear him discourse on the rules of upright living. His way of life was such that they all promised themselves, and with reason, that what proceeded from him would be authentically holy. For he passed days and nights in prayer, so that a priest who was living with him averred

that he did not see him stretched on his bed for a whole year, save for a few days when he was ill. For the rest of the time he either stood or sat, or prayed on his knees, only getting a little sleep when he could keep awake no longer. He was unassuming with his fellows, quiet in conversation, hard on himself and indulgent to others. At the same time, he fulfilled all that was required of a man who was sensible as well as good.

After some years of the above, two men were imprisoned there for the faith who were of a bitter and quarrelsome turn of mind and hostile to our Society. One of them we have frequently pointed out as a jealous man. The other was a certain doctor of medicine. I prefer to suppress their names. Granted that they disagreed with the ways of the Society, and quite frequently attacked it in speech and writing, where their names should now be written is, I think, best left to God's judgment. The curious reader will be able to judge for himself out of the relations from which these things are taken. In any case, it is repugnant to the nature of things not to spare the good reputation of the dead as far as one can. But these two men, untameable by nature and impatient of any discipline, added to their company a third of like temperament from among the older hands. They then began to pour scorn on all existing arrangements. This was especially true after the death of Thomas Mettam who, by his prestige, had to some extent managed to constrain this particular man and those who felt with him. Now they no longer turned up at the Scripture readings. While Weston was talking to those who assembled, they heckled him. They would allow nothing to be prescribed for them, neither timetable, exercises, nor periods of prayer and study. Free of every rule, they took to an undisciplined and haphazard mode of existence. Liberty—in this instance it came close to licence—always offers a strong temptation to form cliques. Not a few gave themselves over to the friendship of these men, and so they split the whole house into factions. From this there arose drinking bouts, quarrels, noisy scenes and wordy exchanges. Not infrequently they came to blows, and no regard was had for clerical decorum. Idleness is invariably the gateway to all the vices. As when the dykes are broken nothing is safe from the flood waters so here nothing was secure from these men of heedless tongue and life. So it was that 18 of the more restrained priests, with Weston and Pound, kept to themselves, avoiding the company of the others lest the scandal whose coming to birth could not be prevented should involve everybody.

A superior had not yet been provided by the Popes for the priests working in England. Every individual pursued his own work with the kind of zeal he had brought back from the seminary. If any difficulty or something unusual presented itself, either they reached a decision by discussing it privately among themselves, or they crossed over to those whom they had come to regard almost as parents during their exile. Some went to Allen, some to the Society, as opportunity offered. Since the 18 whom I have mentioned felt Weston to be an adequate support in what concerned faith and doctrine, they wrote to Garnet—now in charge of the Jesuits in England—to ask him to allow Weston, however unwilling he himself might be, to preside over their affairs; not only their consciences but all they did the whole clock round. Garnet was a man who had a good grasp of what was going on, and could also look to the future. He so far acceded to their wishes as to allow them Weston for director; but he must abstain from the outward marks or title of superior. Nor was he to enjoy a more honourable place in the dining-room or elsewhere. He could not punish, or even reprehend, anyone who broke rules prescribed by himself. Nor if debatable points arose was he to take it on himself to decide the answer. Satisfied with any arrangement that came from him, Weston's party now called on the other 13 to live together with them at peace. They urged the others to curb what seemed to them an erratic mode of existence, prone as it was to engender many abuses. They would do better to accept a few simple rules. This met with point blank refusal.

Indeed, the other party branded the separation of the 18 as a schism. They laughed at their democratic regimen; interpreted Garnet's restrictions as a stealthy attempt to seize the reins of government. They said that the proposed rules resembled the customs of the Anabaptists, who claim that all are equal, rather than the usages of the Church Catholic. The ancient heresy of the Arians was being reintroduced, which included the saying, 'Let no greybeard deter you!' Lastly, it was not fitting for worthy priests to be restrained within limits prescribed by a power more than episcopal, but wielded by men no higher in rank than themselves. Most ways were tried to make them more amenable and keep their angry spirits within bounds. But no solution was found to last; not even the wrath of God poured out on the obstinate. For the doctor of medicine suddenly lost the power of speech, and died. The other priest, defaulting to the Protestants, had it in mind to join the strength of the Bishop of London's household.*

18. A number of stable and learned priests in England now began to see clearly how many evils could creep in with time if all were allowed to do as they liked, and if no superior were provided for the very numerous younger men who were coming out of the seminary every year. Besides, it was essential for the well-being of all the priests that there should be exchange of advice and help among them. They therefore began to work for an organisation which could include all priests in the country under moderators of some kind. One such could preside in the north; another in the south. This grouping they called the 'Association'. It may have been in imitation or emulation of the Society whose effectiveness and inner harmony they thought—not without reason—derived from the union of many individuals under one head. They gave a written form of rules already existing in concept, and set up a form of government through rectors, assistants, a secretary and other officers. They also discussed who were to be admitted, who expelled, the procedure at their meetings,

ways of appeal, and what was to be done in the matter of punishment. The assent and signature of the majority was required. Some, indeed, gave their names to it. Others approved the principle, but dissented as to means, and doubted the outcome. What was posited by no authority and depended only on common consent, they thought, could be as easily set at nought as set up at all. This would be evident when someone's opinion departed from the rest according to the nature or mind of the individual.

Even at Rome, Allen was aware of the opposition to himself and the Society. Morgan, Paget and Throckmorton had aroused and fostered it in France, and it had now crept into England itself drawing a great many (plures) of the priests to its side. No more potent remedy was to hand for the situation than to give the clergy a head from whom peace and calm might flow. This would bring union among the priests, and from them spread to the rest. The priests themselves, and all other Catholics of greater weight, wanted the same things. Two of them were sent to Rome to put the request. The question was laid on the anvil. A man was sought to bear such a great burden worthily. After soliciting many opinions in England and overseas, the majority was found to agree on George Blackwell. He was proposed to Clement VIII, the reigning Pope. Not long afterwards, by letters of Cardinal Cajetan, Protector of England, Blackwell was inaugurated as superior of the English clergy. He had the power and title of Archpriest of England, and was given 12 assistants to advise him.

What was conceived as a measure to establish peace and quiet, however, only served to infuriate the minds of many, and bring about dissension. Some took it badly that they were overlooked when it came to voting, or when the assistants came to be chosen. Others wanted two men to have authority, and to be bishops into the bargain, rather than that all power should go to one man. They claimed that the title and office of archpriest was something new; and for so great a number of priests as there were in England, unusual. Some claimed that the notion and very title of a régime of this sort had come from the Jesuits, because they aimed to rule the rest of the clergy through men leaning towards themselves.

Further, because the entire arrangement depended on the Protector's rescript, and not on a papal Brief, they alleged that authority of this kind was insufficient and not to be admitted. They ought to be allowed to choose their own superiors. This would be more in keeping with the canons and ecclesiastical custom. Some even went so far as to claim that, since his authority came from the Pope, it would be most dangerous to obey him! For the man who recognises any external authority over this land suffers the loss of all his goods and perpetual imprisonment by the statute of praemunire. But in the end they were few who hedged in Blackwell once he was chosen, and that they did cautiously. In the view of the majority he was a man worthy of authority and of the place he occupied by reason of his goodness, discretion, knowledge of doctrine and experience.

It was the Pope who thought that he should have the title of archpriest, and not the more sacred dignity of bishop. It was his idea and that of the cardinals who advised him. It was not due to the Society or to the mere suggestion of Persons that the other alternative was rejected. Persons, indeed, acted more than once, and far from sluggishly, in the matter of getting a bishop appointed for England. His letter of 17 November 1580, written to the rector of the Roman seminary from London, runs,* 'There is very great need of a bishop to consecrate the holy oils for baptism and the last rites &c. [sic]. For lack of one we are reduced to desperate straits, and unless his Holiness gives us timely assistance in this matter, we do not know what will happen before long. We hope His Holiness will shortly send someone to help us out. Certainly, it is in the common interest that we should have someone very soon'. At this precise moment, when the appointment of a superior was being openly demanded, nine reasons were drawn up in writing —still extant—which Persons presented to the Pope and the cardinals. In these he set out the utility and necessity of having two bishops in England. And because the question of meeting the expenses needed to maintain such a dignity was by no means trivial, he got into touch beforehand with excellent Don Francisco de Sarmiento, Bishop of Jaen, to help with the project. Generously enough, he promised to support two or three. A letter of Persons to Allen in 1592 bears witness to this. However, it seemed good to His Holiness to set up an archpriest.

The majority of the priests fell in with this decision most willingly, and demonstrated their pleasure and satisfaction in a joint letter . . . Some quite serious and learned men, however, allowed themselves to go astray. They not only saw fit to ignore, but even to condemn, and as far as they could, reject, this public authority set up, prescribed, recommended and ordered by legitimate superiors. Some of them had themselves been the first to desire the establishment of order among the priests, and had privately worked for it . . . In this contention and controversy of so many years standing huge damage has been done to the Catholic cause. Disgust has been aroused even among our most ardent supporters. Much has been written and spoken touching not only our Society but also the authority of the Holy See and its whole mode of governing. I therefore thought good to set down a few of the many points which could be made to wipe out the injury which appears to have been offered to the Apostolic See; also to cast some light on those aspects of the Society's proceedings which have not been properly understood.

19. Some regard it as a last straw added to a great bundle of impositions that, almost without their knowledge and without the least intimation of their consent, a superior should have been thrust upon them. First, we will say nothing of the fullness of power which His Holiness exercises over the univeral Church throughout the world; nothing likewise of differing customs in diverse places in the matter of presentation and election of prelates. But

if the question were necessarily one to be decided by the
vote of many men, whose votes should be asked for?
Should all the priests scattered through England have
given their voice? What was the precedent? All could not
come together in one rendezvous, nor could everybody's
vote be collected by letter. Indeed, it was not easy to say
even how many priests there were in England! In fact,
it is most certain that the views of a number of people
were solicited before the archpriest was chosen. Present
at Rome at the time were Richard Haddock, doctor of
theology, and Dr. Martin Array, both elderly priests, to
whom the worthiness and knowledge of the archpriest
were very well known. He was among those proposed by
the priests in England who wanted a head, and who were
put forward as fit to receive the episcopate. It was bewil-
dering, then, that his promotion to the archipresbyterate
should have caused displeasure. Rome also asked Henry
Garnet for the names of all the older priests in England,
so that from their number one to three might be selected
for episcopacy. This detail was debated and decided on
at the very beginning in Rome. Six others were to be
promoted to the rank of archpriest. In a list of 3 December
1597, there appear among the names that Garnet noted
down even some of his own adversaries. Of those mentioned some subsequently complained most bitterly of
being passed over. At all events, the Society's sincerity
and plain dealing is evident in this. Nor is there any doubt
that Persons's opinion in the matter was also sought.
But it was wholly a matter for the Pope or Cardinal
Protector to decide whose counsel they wish to adopt.

It was also wholly within the power of the archpriest
to choose his advisers and officials for himself, as is well-
known to be the case throughout the Church where other
prelates are concerned. Nor are His Eminence the Protector, or the Pope, as most devoted fathers of us all, to be
considered strangers to our affairs. That this particular
superior was chosen by the Society, and likewise his
assistants, is altogether at variance with the truth. Several
letters of the Cardinal Protector are extant in which he

makes it clear that the archpriest was his own favourite. Of the first 12 Assistants, six were chosen by the Protector and the rest by the Archpriest himself. Why is it so important to know when, how, and on whose information the Pope issued his commands? . . . Whatever the Pope did in this way, and whoever the consultor of whom he availed himself, it could well have been the disposition of Providence . . . Who could honestly affirm that the letters of institution were written by Persons without the Cardinal's knowledge . . .? Or that the Cardinal gave him permission to write what he thought fit, and then merely put his own hand and seal to what was written? Or perhaps everything came from the Cardinal without the Pope's knowledge! A man must be in love with his own imagination to dream up such things about men who, in fact, were far from lacking common sense when they came to deal with questions of such importance.

20. As for authority usurped by the Society over the rest of the clergy, or sought through those elevated to high office, this was very far from its intention. Jesuits regarded themselves not as prelates but as helpmates for all the clergy, sent like themselves to the English mission. Their priestly functions they exercised not as superiors but as equals. Jesuits take nothing to themselves except what is granted by the Apostolic See. So it is reasonable that they surrender nothing to other men's jealousy that is demanded by their work and enterprise for the help and guidance of souls. However, the genuine praise given us by others will never be drowned by praise of ourselves . . . People demand with good right that any Christian fulfil his obligation; and therefore, the innumerable good works which come from the Society. Perhaps it is not for me to mention that the learning and goodness of the majority of priests flowed from the Society. Certainly, it was the Society which obtained for Douai College from Gregory XIII at Rome its original monthly pension of 100 crowns. In which connection, the college thanked Everard Mercurian, the General at that time, in an open

letter. Gregory Martin mentioned the fact in a letter to his old friend, Edmund Campion, in these words: 'That most blessed father and pope, Gregory XIII, endowed our college at Douai with 100 crowns a month. It was mainly due, Edmund my friend, to the man who, although he is leader and ruler of your entire Order, desired to compete with us only in zeal and goodness on our own behalf. So he obtained for us as much as he could by his influence and authority. We had always regarded the Society with the same reverence as other bodies, although it deserved more. But for this benefit which we have now received we must hold it in special esteem; love and hold fast to it even more than others!'*

By the efforts of the Society, the income of the Roman College was much increased, and the college itself brought to its present size. It seems that it was due to the Society that Rheims seminary received an annual income of 2,000 crowns from the Catholic King. The Bridgettine nuns at Lisbon received the same amount. Three large seminaries at Valladolid, Seville and St. Omer attest the enthusiasm and affection of the Society for our own people. In nothing were they inferior to the Roman College, and from them came a great many priests destined for this mission. Thanks to Divine Providence, most of them were actually sent there.

Continual reminders of the Society's regard for the English nation are the various convents of nuns throughout the Low Countries. The English exiles were everywhere received by the Society with the utmost kindness and consideration. The Society's charity penetrated even to the very galleys from which, thanks to Persons's intervention, at least 300 slaves were rescued. Of these, 34 at Naples regained not only their liberty but also the ship which they had lost; and the goods of which they had been despoiled were made up to them. In England itself no one can be unaware how assiduously the Society formerly made its collections for priests coming into the kingdom for the first time. Nor did it pass over other necessary claims upon it. Not that all could receive help from it; and since the business of public collecting is more suitable for layfolk than Jesuits, they turned it over to them completely. However, the Society felt that the care of the new priests constituted such a claim upon it—as Garnet bears witness—that in one year it used up for this item alone £200 sterling . . .

21. George Blackwell himself we can produce as a most well-informed witness . . . After working for 20 years in England, he became angry at the pettiness of squabbles over such matters, and sent the following to the Cardinal Protector written in his own hand. So far are those Fathers from any lust for power that they have provided us everywhere with an outstanding example of self-forgetfulness, urbanity, patience, religious spirit and brotherly love. We would be most ungrateful if we did not respect them as fathers, embrace them affectionately as friends, and respect them dutifully as benefactors. We should take them as teachers to imitate for their zeal, and acknowledge them with filial honour.

They have been most sturdy fighters and our principal helpers in the cause of rescuing our country and Church at a time when she has been buffeted by tempests very diverse among ourselves. Those who belittle them know neither them nor themselves. Who on our side provided assistance for priests coming in from overseas, if not the Fathers of the Society? Those who were shut out from any other house were received by them. When their clothes were in rags, the Fathers dressed them decently and fittingly. When they had nothing to live on, and no money, the Fathers looked after them. When they did not know where to stay because they were unknown, they were completely equipped by the Jesuits with horses and other necessities for their journeying. Places were very carefully made available to them where they could reconcile the lapsed, strengthen the faithful, and do praiseworthy work for spreading the faith.

'Nor did the Jesuits' charity end there. We who have borne the heat and burden of the day these many years,

acknowledge that we have had from them something outstanding in the way of help and encouragement in our
needs. If your Lordship only knew how much money*
the Fathers have consumed in these and other works of
theirs for religion; and how ready they have been to
succour the saints held in prison, and others weighed
down by all kinds of difficulties of time and circumstance!
How these men have always run to their assistance! If
you knew all this, I do not doubt that the unbridled impertinence of men goaded by envy, who want to snatch away
the Jesuits' reputation and destroy good feeling towards
them, would be curbed forthwith. Jealousy dogs the footsteps of all good men. But just as mist covers all in the
beginning, and disappears as soon as light falls on the
things it tries to smother, so likewise I allow myself a
very large hope that the darkness of malevolence that
has obscured the view of the Fathers will be blown away
by truth, and all things appear as they really are. I hope
also that your Lordship will make provision against the
liberties of detractors who so readily fly to injure good
people to the detriment of Catholic faith. The strength
of the Jesuits has remained unmoved among us to this
hour . . .' So Blackwell. To whom, if it were necessary,
many more writers in the same vein could be added.
However, they may be seen in the relation of the visitation
made by Cardinal Sega and offered to Pope Clement.

No one can justly complain that Jesuits have tried to
remove so much as one person from his office. Such a
thing would be wholly repugnant to our purpose. For
good priests we try to find good places. When anyone
wishes to keep the restless characters by him we are most
grateful. For in this way, they will not be able to wander
about so freely so as to disturb the minds of others. They
will also be that much further removed themselves from
the danger of falling away and apostasy. To all else must
be added the incredible amount of work involved, and
anxiety, expense and danger, in what Jesuits do for young
men and women in getting their money overseas. In the
early days, almost uninterrupted hospitality was offered

in most Jesuit houses, especially to priests who had no fixed abode. Not a little attention was given to expediting business with Rome; and to an enormous number of other things which would be more fittingly commemorated by others than by themselves. For all these good offices, what the Cardinal Protector formerly wrote in a certain letter of his for their consolation is altogether appropriate. He declares that their lot seems to be a most happy one. All the more because, although they try to do good to everyone, they do not always, perhaps, get the thanks due to them. This only means that their reward in the next life will be all the greater.

22. Men were not lacking (v. supra, para. 14) whose intention it was to put narrow limits to the work of religious in England, and even to get the Society out of the island altogether. The following, I find, was a decision put down in writing by some of them. 'Although it would be asking too much to oblige any religious to go about in his habit in these dark days in England, nevertheless, in order to establish some kind of distinction between religious profession and ecclesiastical authority, we ought not to allow too many from any one of the religious Orders to enter this country until God shall see fit to effect its complete conversion; and only provided that any Congregation (Professio) will accept the place due to it. But if some should come in, shall we say for health's sake, or for other reasons, let it be so that neither they nor any others who are already here, of whatever Order they be, have any further authority in this kingdom of England and Scotland than to perform sacramental rites, and to catechise and preach to those among whom they move, giving good advice and good example to everyone. But they must not be allowed to interfere in any ecclesiastical affairs in which jurisdiction or the power of the keys might be usurped. The object is that, since the conversion of England first began with the preaching and martyrdom of the seminarists, long before any religious as such wished to take note of our miseries, so likewise the former, as of

right, may assume to themselves the credit, merit and
triumph of England's conversion.'

It would have been, indeed, a wretched state of affairs
and altogether deplorable if this kind of thinking had gone
on in the mind of any man of faith who was also wise . . .
Did it not mean that priests who were religious were not
to be considered part of the clergy? The fact that such are
bound to a religious observance by vows, and that some of
them are linked to the Apostolic See by a special bond,
does not mean that a pretext for contempt arises from
that! Nor are they to be considered less suitable on that
account for functions that do with the priesthood. Nor
should they for that reason be cut off from any association
of Catholic clergy . . . Concerning the Society, it is a
matter of general knowledge that apart from trying to
perfect themselves—this should be the chief concern of
everyone—Jesuits are obliged by their institute to devote
themselves sedulously to helping others to perfection.
As in the case of other mendicant orders, therefore,
Jesuits do not depart to the wilderness to give themselves
to God alone, and to perpetual contemplation, as with
the Carthusians and other monks. The Society has
embraced a way of life which combines the contemplative
and active. They are always available to the Pope for any
kind of ecclesiastical task or undertaking . . .

23. In this connection, attention must be drawn to
       another point of certain and established Catholic
teaching. No simple priest by force only of his ordination
has actual jurisdiction. A great many priests, indeed, live
as hermits, or else in the cloister, or occupy simple
benefices without any cure of souls attached. All jurisdiction, however, flows from the Holy See as from its
source, and like a perfume flowing down from the head,
is diffused through the whole Church. From this and
what will be said in the next chapter, it follows that it is
not unfitting or incongruous for religious qua religious
to look after the spiritual welfare of their neighbour. It
is not unfitting if actual jurisdiction is not given to other

priests simply because they are priests. Not simply on
that account do they have power over Christ's flock,
but only when they are sent out with legitimate authority
by the Pope or other prelates subject to him. How does
any gulf arise, then, between regular and other priests
so that all may not play an equal part in working for
the good of neighbour? Jesuits shun ecclesiastical dignities
as far as they can, short of the sin of disobedience. But
for the most part, no dignity has been conferred on
priests in England, nor any jurisdiction conceded for
exercise in the 'external forum' [outside confession].
All priests sent to England can assist souls, as far as divine
grace will allow, without any external jurisdiction. Nor
in this sphere is the work done perfunctory . . .

Jesuits received the ancient privileges of religious
Orders, and new ones adapted to this particular mission.
Perhaps more appropriately, or more conveniently—let
there be nothing invidious in the word used—missions
of this kind were committed to Jesuits rather than to
other priests. For it belongs to our Society, according
to its institute and various privileges, and also its special
vow approved by the Holy See, to be sent to different
missions throughout the world. Our men in those missions
are subject to obedience. They possess nothing of their
own, nor can they acquire anything for themselves. They
are obliged to the observances of religious life as far as
local circumstances allow. They must be known to one
another and be seen by one another. There must be
nothing harmful hidden in their teaching, nor anything,
as far as possible, indecorous in their behaviour. The above
considerations greatly further the services which must
be supplied in the mission so that least harm may come
to the man himself and the greatest benefit to others.
No one need envy the Lord of the Harvest for having too
many workers to send into His vineyard. The Jesuits did
not do so when from 1580 they crossed sea and land to
make proselytes, and sent from the seminaries, adequately
and most opportunely founded by them, workers of the
highest suitability. Therefore the Society, in order to be

of most use to the mission, does its utmost to get equipped
for the task in the best possible way. Nor does a Jesuit
take to himself any honour save that to which he is called
by a lawful superior. And concerning the appointment
of the Archpriest, the Society did nothing which it was
not open to anyone else to do, namely reveal its mind
on the subject when asked, clearly, sincerely, as if in the
presence of God.

24. These are the points which it seemed desirable to
     make in connection with complaints against the
Society with regard to pushing the cause of the Archpriest. We omit the various calumnies in spoken word and
books which have erupted from minds more disturbed
than the situation ever warranted. To dispose of such, it
seems more effective to pass them over rather than refute
them, since any sensible person can see that they rise from
no firm subsoil, and grow up without roots. In these first
beginnings, when scarcely five Jesuits were to be found
in the whole island, the rest of the priests numbered more
than three hundred.

Such was the jealousy of some roused against Jesuits
that you would think that if they were saved the rest could
not be. To no one should it seem beneath even human
frailty if, as Jesuits have increased and multiplied throughout the whole of England, the same kind of jealousy
should still creep in at times. Some men think to obscure
the reputation of the Society for goodness and learning,
spread far and wide as it is by its leading members, by
reason of certain individuals who keep in their sights
honour, dignities, personal advantage, or some temporal
gain which they have pursued alongside the most worthy
purpose of saving souls. This is altogether foreign to the
spirit of the institute . . . Let us now return to Weston.*

25. The undisciplined priests realised that in their
     counsels with their fellow-captives, whom they hoped
to corrupt, Weston's influence was most powerfully
opposed to them. They therefore saw to it that he was

transferred from Wisbech to the Tower of London. There his destiny was to have a poky cell and a short bed. Even so, assisted by a little light which came through a narrow slit, he spent his days and nights reading the Scriptures. At the commencement, he chanced upon the passage from Proverbs, 'as a door turns on its hinges, so the lazy man turns in his bed'. He at once determined to do without his own bed—this he had done at Wisbech—as far as superiors would allow it. He used to say that loneliness, darkness, filth, lack of space, and all the other discomforts of that prison, could easily drive a man mad unless he cultivated the closest kind of union with God. In that grave, if I may so describe it, he lived seven or eight years, and with so little sight left that he had to depend on what he remembered from books. He is said to have had by heart the complete text of the Bible. With the death of Elizabeth, and the hope of better things for England at the accession of James VI of Scotland, he was driven into exile, with most of the other priests, in 1603. The general opinion of his holiness was such that, like the weightiness of Persons's writing, and the fluency of Campion's speaking, the goodness of Weston's life passed into a proverb. Men of contrary religion, as well as of our own, reverenced his goodness. Thomas Garnet, subsequently renowned as a martyr, when he was doing his noviceship as an exile at Louvain, told how Weston's gaoler at Wisbech, while reading Watson's *Quodlibets*, noticed that some of them smeared Weston most unkindly. He threw the book away at once in indignation, and declared with an oath that all the things objected against Weston were false. He said that Weston led a good and innocent life at Wisbech, and this man attributed so much to his prayers that he could only wish most fervently to be commended in them to God. The man likewise by whom he was guarded in the Tower asserted that first he had a devil, and now a saint to look after. He referred to Weston since he would not have so described Norton, the pursuer of Catholics whom he held before.

In exile, Weston went first to Rome and then to Seville and other parts of Spain. When he got to Madrid, the Provincial and the oldest Fathers begged him on their knees to pray fervently for them. For most of them remembered from previous experience how even then he had gained the reputation of a saint. Weston was appointed rector of the English seminary at Valladolid as surpassing everyone else in wisdom and goodness. He died leaving behind him in everybody a deep nostalgia for his company. His death occurred in April 1615 . . . The last obsequies were performed not only in the English College, but also in the professed house of our Fathers, now the College of St. Ignatius. There was a great gathering of all the Orders. Francis Labata, a well-known preacher at that time, delivered an address. He told how, when Weston was asked by someone in England to exorcise an evil spirit, he was asked by the spirit for permission to enter into Queen Elizabeth. Weston refused. He wished her every grace of soul and body, and considered it a crime to do her any harm. For however much she might differ from him in faith, she was till his queen and sovereign . . .

Weston completed 17 years in prison. We learn from his own lips something of what he suffered in those years, although he was a very sparing commentator on what occurred himself. He claimed that whatever he suffered during the rest of his life in the way of pains and illness could not come up to the sufferings of even one day and night that he had had to endure in the Tower . . . His own modesty forbade him to allow most of his experiences to reach us, although at the command of his superiors he wrote down the story of the rest of his life. But he could never be persuaded to give a full account of his experiences in the Tower of London . . .

END OF BOOK THE FOURTH

BOOK THE FIFTH

1.   (1588). The thought occurred to Philip II, that most careful King of Spain, that it would be of advantage to the Christian cause if certain high-minded men were chosen from the Inquisitors to examine the way of life and customs of the Society of Jesus everywhere in his Kingdom. To the General Claud Aquaviva, this seemed unfitting, and at variance with the procedures used with other Orders. Therefore, to dissuade the King, he sent Persons to Spain, a man always acceptable to its monarch, and one whom the General had always found good at persuasion. Persons sent John Gerard and Edward Old-corne to England by way of reinforcement, and then set out on his own journey. His road lay through the cele-brated shrine of our Lady of Loretto . . . Leaving Loretto, Persons sailed for Spain from the port of Genoa, taking as his companion William Flack. The latter had just finished the course of moral theology at Loretto. After the King heard Persons, he accepted his point of view, so that the entire operation of inspecting the Society now devolved on two Jesuits. One of them was nominated by the King, and the other by Claud, the General. Claud wrote in reply to say that none seemed to him more suitable than the man who was then filling the office of Visitor in Spain, Giles Gonzales, the King's natural subject, and noteworthy for birth, faith and good life. The King gave him for companion Joseph Acosta, a man famous in Portugal, and rejoicing in a similar reputation for integrity. So the matter was settled by joint arrangement of King and General.

Providentially, the above solution proved beneficial not only to the Society at large but to England in par-ticular. Dr. Barret had now succeeded to the direction of the seminary at Rheims. It was named after Douai; and after the murder of the Duke of Guise [1588] it was transferred back from Rheims to Douai. Barret asked Persons to explain to the King the difficulties arising from the number of students and the expenses involved, and to ask him for an increase of the stipend. This the King, thanks to Persons's efforts, had hitherto allotted generously every year. Persons sounded the King, but had to report that it would be difficult to get him to increase the original allowance. He would more easily be attracted by the distinction of starting something new. Since Barret had more students than he could cope with, he would send Persons 10 or 12 promising young men. There was no reason to doubt that the latter could get them placed with prelates well-disposed to himself, and with other men in leading positions, who would meet their expenses in the interim until a more permanent solution suggested itself. Henry Floyd, deacon, and John Blackfan, sub-deacon, were sent from Rheims together with James Boswell. At that time war was raging in France between the League and the King of Navarre. Roads were very often blocked by the military. Nor was there any alternative to the route through France. Meeting with the forces now of one side, now of the other, by God's mercy, they contrived to get past both. It was extrenely difficult to persuade Duplessis-Mornay, who was content to be considered one of the principal pillars of the Calvinist persuasion, that Catholic Englishmen, and clerics into the bargain, could have any other purpose in going to Spain, England's enemy, than to work for the embarrassment of their prince and country. For the Spaniard had lately mounted against them the threat of a vast fleet. At this very time warships were being got ready by the English to invade Portugal. Duplessis said that on that account these men must either be traitors or spies. It would be better to have them sent to La Rochelle, and from thence into England; just as they had sent in some favoured souls on a previous occasion who subsequently suffered death for Christ. However, our travellers were provided with the letters of d'Epernon, Lord of Saumur, which Mornay then governed. Hence they spoke with more assurance about the studies they had to pursue. With these as their sole object, they had undertaken their journey. Thanks to a good word put in for them by Duplessis's wife, they were at length dismissed, agreeing only, on Duplessis's urging, not to become Spaniards.*

2.   Leaving Nantes behind them for Bilbao, at Burgos they had to struggle through a storm no less furious than the one they left behind them in France. The day after they arrived in the city, while coming from the principal church to their hospice, the officials of the Inquisition arrested them. Who denounced them, or gave the prompt to this, is uncertain. There was a hue and cry through the whole town. They were Lutherans, boon-companions of Drake. Drake had recently committed piracy on these shores, and afterwards led the fleet we mentioned against Portugal. As his friends they were dragged off to prison. Their luggage was searched, and their money taken away. But the tribunal of the Inquisition found nothing in their baggage to cause suspicion. They then went through the letters which they had brought from Rheims from the President, Dr. Barret. They read others which they had accepted in Paris from a certain Spanish Father, a reader in theology, addressed to the rector of the college at Burgos. Orders were eventually given that they should be suitably accommodated for the night. Next day, they were summoned to court. In a long speech, they explained the causes of their journey. They were set at liberty amid genuine praise. On the financial side, however—they held their money in common—their embarrassment was far from slight. The registrar most obstinately refused to admit that any money had been taken from them. Blackfan even declared by whom it had been taken. He detailed the amount and currency—17 Spanish crowns. There was no witness, and Blackfan's statement was unsupported.

At length, the credible and authoritative assertion of some third parties carried the day. Who could believe that men who had put hearth and home behind them, and had set forth on such long marches, with only high purpose before them, would be thus seized upon almost as soon as they set foot in a haven overseas?

When the registrar continued to be obstinate, the senate sent a man to sell his silver—unless he gave back the money forthwith. At last the money was produced. It was the very same that Blackfan had asked for. The next day, while they were getting ready for the road, an important official, at the senate's order, led them to the main *plaza* as they were leaving. He proclaimed to the people present that no taint of guilt hung over them. They were exiles for the true faith, and had come to this place to study. They had it in mind to return to their own country, the loftiness of their souls rising superior to all the cruelty of the heretics. The people should not, then, offer them abuse. Rather should they be honoured for their firmness of faith, integrity of life and courage in misfortune. The official conducted them to the city gate, showed them the way to Valladolid, whither they were bound, and with a friendly farewell bade them Godspeed.

3. At Valladolid, by the advice of the Spanish Fathers, they came to live at their house until Persons should have word of their coming and go to meet them. Here were added to their ranks, in the first instance, four from England, and then 10 more who had come from Douai. A college began to take shape on a road outside the town not far from St. Ambrose—the name of the Jesuit college— where they went twice a day for the purpose of academic exercises. So great an enterprise was not begun without enemies. The city had already opened its gates and homes to young men from Ireland, who were exiles for the same cause. It was therefore apprehensive of being burdened with new guests, and used its influence with the King to get these men either attached to the Irish or else altogether excluded. The King put the matter to the Benedictine abbot—as yet the city was not provided with a bishop. He wrote back to say that he thought that the young

Englishmen should be kept and looked after as showing high promise for the end they had in view. He left the question of amalgamation in the air; but amalgamation had to be accepted for a while.

In the event, Persons thought separation would be better for the purposes of a seminary. He made over to the Irish the whole of the site which the city had given them, and then bought another property, thanks to the generosity of certain noblemen, as I have mentioned. Roderic de Cabredo was assigned to the English as rector, another man as confessor, with a temporal co-adjutor as well. Their principal benefactors in these beginnings were Francis de Reynoso, Dean of the church at Palencia, and Alphonsus de Quinones of the family of the Counts of Luna. This gentleman had shut himself up in his house to give all his time to God and the things of eternity. He had been most generous to a great many people. He got to hear of these young English Catholics in exile, who had sought refuge in that city in order to complete their studies, and return to restore the faith in contempt of every danger. he made available 15 ducats a month to be distributed to each individual. He also donated a further 400 to cover the cost of buying a farm; and yet another 100 to purchase proper clothing for the community. Reynoso provided the house with the rest of its furniture, and every month while he lived, made a further contribution of 100 ducats.

In one way and another the enterprise was somehow kept going; and while the 1,600 crowns, which the King allotted annually out of the revenues of Leon, could be collected. The corporation of Palencia, a town not far from Valladolid, made over as alms a certain quantity of wheat from the people of Medina del Campo. However, it had to be asked for by one of the students from the seminary sent to the corporation every year to make the plea. When the King moved from Madrid, he took up residence at Valladolid, and asked to make a personal inspection of the daily life and régime of the seminary. He was delighted with the number of languages in which the young men gave their addresses of welcome, paid the money which was due, and increased the annual pension he had been thinking of giving. Finally, the nobility, men and women, since they frequented the house and the tiny chapel that had been built, adopted one or other of the young men practically as a son, and undertook to pay his expenses. The college flourished in the years that followed, and grew in reputation for genuine religious spirit and well-grounded faith. All the more so after an image of the . . . Madonna, which had been defaced by non-believers in the course of a piracy, was transferred there with all due solemnity, and placed on the high altar under the title of *Domina nostra Vulnerata*.

4.   Prior to this, there was Bartholomew Perez, after-
        wards Spanish assistant and then provincial of Anda-
lusia, a man on the best of terms with Persons. He also undertook to provide for the upkeep of some of these young Englishmen if they were admitted to Seville, a market town not far from Cadiz . . . Persons, one of those great-souled men who are always on the look-out for the chance of doing a good work, sent two on ahead without losing any time. He followed them himself in the company of four others also chosen for the task. The first of these were George Chamberlain, whom we subsequently observe at Ypres in Flanders gracing the house of the bishop, and John Worthington, a relative of Cardinal Allen. On the way, they devised a short speech in Latin, and the pair of them delivered it with all the grace of elocution they could command. After stating in this way the causes of their exile and the purpose of their studies, they drew to themselves a great deal of sympathy and encouragement from the bishops and abbots along their route.

They were graciously received at Seville by the Fathers and the Corporation. They enlarged on their way of life and their intellectual activities. Their clothes, following the customs of the colleges, were fashioned unpreten-tiously so that they deserved all the more to be spared from any want in the matter of domicile, furniture, or anything else essential to their common life. On the feast of St. Thomas of Canterbury (1589), during the Mass solemnly offered by the Bishop of Seville, Worthington asked for his blessing, and then mounted the pulpit to speak for an hour in Latin. After the ceremony, kneeling before the altar, all present bound themselves by an oath said aloud. This was according to the formula introduced, as we have said, at Rome in the beginnings of the college there. This also had been Persons's idea. When Chamberlain had shown them then and there the meaning of the oath, its value and usefulness, he went on to address the people in Spanish. He departed amid enthusiastic applause from his listeners, and with decidedly hearty congratulations from their new hosts. They then settled down to scholastic exercises and the serious effort required to meet their objective.

And so the city continues to this day [1660] to assist that house with a certain subsidy by way of alms. Francis Peralta made a praiseworthy rector for a good many years, and was altogether acceptable to the students. Nor did the young men flock to any other place with more enthusiasm than to Seville, both for this reason and also because, although the climate reached the limits of the possible where heat was concerned, they still preferred that and the studies at St. Hermenegild's to those of Valladolid and Rome. However, it would be difficult to determine which of the three places had the most learned men, or sent back to England the greatest number of steadfast defenders of the faith. How great was the growth of these seminaries in a few years, both in numbers and repute, may be seen from the letter addressed from the City of Seville to Pope Clement [VIII] on 23 December 1596. It ran as follows:

'*Beatissime Pater,* It has come to our knowledge that Father Robert Persons, an Englishman well-known in this city and throughout Spain, is going to Rome to inform your Holiness of the state of the seminaries and houses founded in this country for Englishmen under the favour and patronage of our Lord the King. This city is therefore pleased to write to your Holiness, as head of the Church, to give some brief account of the good which the Church as a whole, and England in particular, have derived from this work: and England is now in so much need of help and spiritual assistance! This enterprise is wholly excellent, and has been carried forward with much satisfaction and joy to us who profess ourselves true sons of the Church . . . We could bear our own witness to the considerable and genuine renown of the Valladolid seminary of which we have received word from reliable sources. There rather more than 60 people are provided for. As much could be said in praise of the other two hostels or residences in San Lucar and Lisbon set up for priests sent from the seminaries to England. But what concerns us more nearly is something in our field of vision, namely the seminary founded in this place, to which the whole city, whether out of the common funds, or through private charity, lends its very liberal and benevolent support. Certainly, it is all very little when we consider the deserts of those very holy men (Angeles). For such they are here considered and believed to be, since they have dedicated themselves to defend and propagate our faith at the cost of studies, labour and even life.

'Equal, however, to so noble and exalted an end, is their formation and discipline, their purposeful demeanour, religious sense, and unassumingness . . . Hence it is that people everywhere give the unanimous praise, and feel a thrill of pleasure whenever they see them. They understand that they have among them not only a new kind of house for a new kind of religious, but a very breeding-ground of martyrs . . . Which voice of the people we take to be also the voice of God. This community has plenty of good reasons for hatred and disgust of the English nation, from a human point of view, on account of exceedingly great harm suffered in its trade and business from the pirates of that race. Nevertheless, even in the midst of so many humiliations and losses, far from cooling on that account, the desire to help them and do them good grows daily more ardent. Etcetera [*sic*] .'*

5.　　When he had worked out his plan, Persons spent some years in getting the first foundations established. He then devoted himself to beginning new works, and managed to get the 2,000 crowns a year paid, which he first acquired by his begging in Rheims, although times were very difficult. In the port of . . . San Lucar he got possession of a house near the church of St. George which had formerly served the English merchants when they were still Catholic. Here he installed some of the priests of our own race, who collected alms for themselves and the College of Seville from the Spanish businessmen calling there from the Indies. They also explained to any Englishman who happened to sail there the fundamentals of religion, as opportunity offered. In addition they worked to better the lot of the prisoners. Persons got most of these restored to liberty for a price or a prayer, and in this way made himself very acceptable to seafarers. After a time, he went to Portugal, and secured a site at Lisbon for the same reasons which moved him when he set up the house at San Lucar. And so in a port which was nearer to England, priests setting out from the seminaries for their own country could have a place from which to look about at leisure for suitable shipping without incurring much expense. To maintain it, the Duke of Bragança and his wife were the first to donate 100 crowns. Henry Floyd was put in as superior; the same whom Persons had taken as his companion before he himself set out to join the Society.

Persons also devoted no little time to writing, and noted down a great deal of historic value. Since their enemies were pursuing the Catholics equally hard with writings, as well as with words and deeds, Persons put on record those things which would hearten the Catholics; also sear the others for ever with the mark of fanaticism and untruthfulness. Although some of the things he wrote appear rather harsh, the circumstances offer ready excuse. For the most part, they appeared so to non-believers, or to those who looked on the Society with a jaundiced eye, and found fault with everything it did.

What pundit ever erred even lightly in his writing, and yet was not angry with the man who gave him even the lightest of admonitions . . .? The man who cannot otherwise be cured calls for sharp remedy. But although Persons was a courteous man—indeed, courtesy itself—it may well be, he could offend people on occasion by a shaft of wit. But what kind of person did he offend? Only the kind of man who, when his error is uncovered, interprets it as defamation however great the gentleness with which his error is exposed. As for that book which came out on the law of the realm and the succession, whom did it offend but the heterodox? In fact, that same book is to be ascribed not so much to Persons as to Allen and Francis Englefield and others of their circle. This is very aptly pointed out by Persons in a letter to a friend (of 24 May 1603), and by Camden (Anno Elizabethae [1594].* Certainly, King James, whom it mainly concerned, gave no sign that he had been upset by the book. Perhaps it offended the man whose name was put to it, Robert Doleman. But that name simply means in English, he who divides and distributes to every man his share. This is why the work is so titled, and not because it is intended to call to mind any particular priest of that name.

6.   The extinction of the princes of the Guise family so prostrated Persons's plans for the establishment at Eu, that little enough remained to keep the enterprise going for much longer. Slight also seemed the hope of keeping up the numbers of the two seminaries in Spain, as well as the reputation of Douai, on the annual allowance, and at a time when not a few mature students also needed to be sent to Rome to study philosophy and theology. From England itself men reduced in numbers and suitability were now to be expected: fewer than in previous years when Protestantism was by no means so entrenched. It had also been learned from experience that men who left the universities with only a superficial education before becoming Catholics, and then passed quickly through a few years of study, went back to their country after

ordination only to return too easily to former habits as well. This in contrast to those who had nourished religion along with the sciences when their roots were tender, and by subsequent endeavours replaced them with stronger.

The adverse fortune of benefactors, then, destroyed what had been begun at Eu. Persons was convinced that it must be started up again elsewhere so that young men, as early in their lives as possible, could be transferred to a school of good life and learning . . . There they could absorb their religion along with *belles lettres,* and attain to a certain excellence in humanistic studies. Their minds now bring credit to the lecture halls of philosophy and theology, and prove an adornment to the schools of 'poetry' and 'rhetoric'. Nor was much time needed to decide in which countries an opening should be sought for such a work. France was torn by upheaval; and every passing day showed that the generosity of the Catholic King was greater than his power to perform. But they were especially roused by the recent decree from England that young children should be snatched from their families and handed over to Protestant instructors to be taught the official religion. The township of St. Omer had real attractions. It was distinguished for a faith and fidelity that had never yet been broken. It was also conveniently near the ports, being roughly equidistant from Calais, Gravelines, and Dunkirk, from which sailing to England was quite straightforward. Finally, St. Omer seemed most suited to English youngsters by reason of its similarity to England in weather, scenery and mode of life. Furthermore, it was as far removed as it could be from the peril of Dutch invasion. Ten ducats a month were accordingly begged from the Catholic King to pay for the upkeep of 16 youths at St. Omer. Letters were also granted whereby the execution of the project was entrusted to Mansfeld, at that time governing the Flemish Provinces for the King. To Richardot also, President of the Council, letters were sent, and to the bishop and civil administration and others, including William Flack. Persons sent for the latter to come from Italy to be his socius (1593).

When Persons arrived in Flanders, he communicated his plan to Oliver Manare, the Provincial, and to the Fathers of St. Omer. He also presented the King's letters, and generally tried to push the matter forward with all diligence. But not many were willing to help a new work at its beginning when the outcome was uncertain. Some condemned outright a place almost surrounded by water so that it could only engender ill-health. Some saw the project not merely as new, and one in which everything was therefore uncertain, but even as trivial, petty and scarcely worth so much trouble. Others again were opposed to receiving foreigners, especially Englishmen, with whom Spain was at war, into a township so near the frontier. Even if the young men were altogether above suspicion, who could trust the characters who would seize the occasion to come sneaking into town? Who would be responsible for the cost? Generosity can be fervent at the outset but very often cools as a work proceeds. Furthermore, the new house, almost under their very noses, wore no very agreeable aspect for Cardinal Allen and Dr. Barret, President of Douai. They feared lest their own youths be drawn away, and likewise their grants, so that their own seminary would be not so much relieved as emptied by the new project. In the event, the house set up was in its beginnings very small.

At the commencement, the young students were ordered to be seven in number, although later this was raised to eighteen. Flack himself acted as procurator, while Nicholas Smith was added as spiritual director. The King increased their allowance to 2,000 ducats a year to be raised from import licences for cloth. If for any reason the money fell short, it was to be taken from some other completely dependable source in the treasury returns. He left it to the Jesuits to determine the number of young men to be looked after, since he had founded the house under their discipline (King's letter to Ernest, 4 March 1594).* A larger residence was acquired—now occupied by the Capuchins—and eventually a third, which was purchased from Dean Bersac for £750 of our money.

The Jesuits had lived in it since 1560. It was a large house on a site in the town, but open and well-aired, and in a very good neighbourhood. It had quite extensive grounds, and was not too far from the Jesuit schools. The township had very recently been upset by French raids, and, in its own eyes at least, never seemed sufficiently secure from the outside world. In addition, it was accustomed to the burden of serving as winter-quarters for the military. Various objections were now put to the King, but the town could no longer hold out against him when, in accordance with his prerogative, he commanded that the youths be received at the house. In order to give it a certain immunity, the rector was made subject to the monarch. Preoccupied with cutting expenses, the town could by no means be persuaded, either by reason or entreaty, to allow the building now purchased, or any which might be purchased in future, to be free from liability to military requisition. John Foucart, a Walloon, was therefore appointed as rector, with the royal assent; but the obligation remains to this day, and the house was saddled with soldiery in the same way as before it was bought.

7.   The seminary gradually developed in numbers, endowment, and buildings bought or newly constructed, and, as had been envisaged from the beginning, in learning and religious atmosphere. From the start, it had to compete with the best wits from among the local population who frequented the school of the Belgian Fathers which flourished at that time. In the years that followed the erection of classrooms inside the walls of their own residence, a considerable body of youth worked so industriously and profitably at Greek and Latin that the fame of the establishment spread far and wide through the whole region . . . Giles Schondonck of Bruges, rector after Foucart,* was a man born and bred to the task of teaching youth by the soundest principles. He had his goal so clearly before him that those he accepted were altogether capable of the highest attainments. He either

sent them back to their own country, or on to the higher studies at Rome or in Spain.

These were no smatterers but outstanding scholars with every refinement of the humanities. From the very outset, Schondonck added Greek to Latin, cheerfully heard their first stammerings, and rewarded them with praise. When they had acquired a certain vocabulary, he taught them to deliver (interpretari), from a raised place above the table, excerpts from the Greek New Testament, Isocrates, Chrysostom, and similar works. Now they turned Greek into Latin, and then Latin into Greek. To those who had made some further progress, he gave certain themes or theses on which they had to debate, first with some preparation, and then extempore. One would defend, another attack, refuting the proofs of the other. The sentence was first pronounced in Greek and afterwards in Latin. So it was brought about that, because middle and senior 'Grammar' joined in for exercises of this kind, those who were eventually promoted to 'Poetry' and 'Rhetoric' could debate most readily on any subject put to them on the spur of the moment, and in either language. When people outside were invited to their monthly exercises, and witnessed this—they themselves suggested any topic they pleased—none of them failed to applaud their cleverness, application, spontaneity, and finally, style. Nor did anyone fail to be struck by so much familiarity with both languages on the part of young boys, and likewise by their store of knowledge and ideas, to say nothing of understanding.

Not less was the trouble which that admirable man, Schondonck, took to form his pupils in good living. He received the youths when they were at their best for absorbing the principles of sound life, being already remarkable for serious purpose. These could be led, for the most part, by gentle ways, and by the appeal of decency and a desire to stand well. As he himself excelled them all, so whatever he gave them in the way of precept was sprinkled lightly. He ordered the day from dawn until late at night with so much precision that this too caused admiration in those who saw it. In after years, it spurred the Belgians to emulate the kind of discipline found among the English. In order that they might be imbued in the pleasantest manner possible with sound religious principles, he wished the greatest number possible to be taught to sing, and play various instruments. He bought a neighbouring house, and turned it into a chapel where the sacred rites were very adequately performed, and embellished with variety of music. Finally, he established sodalities among the adolescents, under the patronage of the Blessed Virgin and the angels.

In this way, those who set out on the path of perfection with unequal steps were spurred on by the keenness of competition. The two adornments of goodness and learning flourished during the 17 years when he was rector, and had such a good effect on the house that the charity of the man and his praiseworthy qualities got back to the ears of the Protestants. They followed with admiration what they forbade by their laws. The Catholics, indeed, were convinced that they could put their children in no better place than under his roof and influence. When he received the boys, he used to claim that he had everything that was English apart from the language; and when it came to forming them, he seemed to have an outstanding gift that was only God-given. While he was in charge, the number of youngsters grew to more than a hundred. This continued down to our own day, thanks to the system laid down by Schondonck, so that in justice to this man may be attributed the growth and renown of so great a college . . .

8.   While a programme to supply and train novices was being carried through by Persons in Spain, the veterans on the English mission had descended into the arena bravely enough. Daring all things, they grasped undaunted towards the palm of victory. John Cornelius, who had led a life of singular goodness, graced the year 1594 with a death for Christ suffered with consistent fortitude. He was born at Bodmin in Cornwall of parents

in modest circumstances—they are said to have come from a line of chimney-sweeps! How true the saying, 'God looks upon the humble, and recognises high things from afar'. This truth Cornelius proved in his own person. Both English and Irish writers allocate the martyr to their own nation. I have seen for myself in the English College, Rome, that in 1580 he put himself down on paper as Cornish. Hence I call him English. There is also some dispute about his mother, whether she was English or from a good Irish family. Certainly, at the end of three years, after she had been living as a widow in England (in Insula), Cornelius got his mother placed with his hospitable patron, Lady Arundell, so that both were looked after in a manner befitting the generosity of their noble hostess.

Cornelius himself was so drawn to study, even from his boyhood, that while his companions were at play he would occupy himself with books. John Arundell once noticed him hedged behind his papers: the same Arundell who, uniting the renown of his household with ample possessions, came to be known in the West Country as 'Arundell the Great'. He asked Cornelius why he did not prefer to play in a nearby field. 'Because', said the boy, 'I get more satisfaction out of books!' Arundell, intrigued by this reply, gave him a gold coin for his ready answer, and advised him to continue as he had begun. In this way he would receive ample reward for the rest of his life. He subsequently encouraged the boy while he was still at home where he made no little progress. Afterwards, Arundell sent him to Oxford University for several years, and eventually to Rheims. This city he left for Rome in 1580 to apply himself to theology. Next year, he gave the Christmas sermon in the papal presence according to a College custom.

He was a great example to everyone in the house of every kind of good quality. Cornelius became so absorbed that although he frequented the Roman College for three years during his studies—it was not far away—he still did not know how one got there from the English College!*

Ordained priest, Cornelius returned to his old Maecenas, Arundell, who received him into his house and made much of him as long as he lived. On his death, he recommended him to the widow of Baron de Stourton, whom he had taken for his second wife. Arundell was outstanding no less for Catholic faith than for very considerable abilities. Giving back the advice he had himself received as a boy, namely to continue in the way he had begun, Cornelius enthusiastically encouraged him without ceasing to persevere in the religion he had first imbibed. He must allow no sort of difficulty to move him from it . . . Nor was his counsel without effect. Cornelius himself, thanks to the goodness of his life, and his winning enthusiasm in preaching, upheld and propagated the Catholic cause in those parts for some 10 years. . . .

John Cornelius allowed no atmosphere of corruption, and no fear of persecution, to turn him aside from the task of finding salutary remedies; and in season and out of season, applying them. Changing the place where he stayed, he would everywhere call the Catholics together to give them heart, and exhort them to perseverance. He would cheer them with his talks, and strengthen them with the sacraments of Penance and the Eucharist. They flocked to him with the utmost readiness even when the weather on the night was bad. Often, since it was unsafe to come together in private houses, he would search out a secure place for his talk in the heart of woods far from the main road. Anywhere and everywhere, he was heard by eager ears. He had a wonderfully animated way of talking, a kind of intensity that persuaded, if also a certain sharpness when it came to a dressing-down. With all this went sheer persistence. By the time that the third year since his coming into England was nearing its end, he had succeeded in reconciling completely more than 30 families . . .

An old man who happened to be a Protestant lay abandoned by everybody in a lice-infested cottage in the heart of the county. He suffered from a disease which barred all hope of cure, and the lice covered him. Indeed almost every part of his body was undergoing loathsome attack. He was repulsive both for the brutishness of his appearance and his nauseating stench. When John got to know of the unhappy man's state, he rushed to him at once. After finding him, he passed the whole night with him, cheering him and bringing him hope of a better life. He won him from mistaken beliefs, and eventually got him to make his confession, He then fortified him with the annointing, and promised to bring him Viaticum if he lasted another night. John returned to his own people from that vigil with his clothing so covered with filth and vermin that when he took it off it could never be used again . . .

His devotion to his God was prodigious; likewise his disregard of himself. He had definite times fixed for everything he needed to do, which he would never alter save for some extraneous cause. He used to say Mass at five o'clock in the morning lest any necessity arising subsequently prevent the celebration. He was wont to say that in that function alone his mind relaxed in a certain sense of the divine presence . . . He never failed to be moved to tears in some part of it; and also when he read over again the history of our Lord's passion during Holy Week. Sometimes during meditation he was so taken out of himself that when a gentleman called on him once for advice he found him kneeling on the ground with his arms folded across his chest, and his eyes quite still and apparently looking up at something. It was quite some time before he could be recalled to himself by any noise, and it was difficult to determine whether he was still in this life or not. Finally, the visitor roused him by a special effort. Cornelius begged and prayed him not to let anyone else know in what state he had found him.

In his physical austerities he was most severe. He wore coarse sacking made up in the form of a coat reaching to his knees, and harsh to the skin by reason of knots which were woven into it throughout. For many years he fasted four times a week, until he was forbidden by Henry Garnet, after he became his subject, to continue with

such drastic self-denial. Cornelius generously gave his all
to the needy, ignoring his own needs and relying on God.
He urged everyone to the same generosity, for they could
be certain they would never lack essentials if they pledged
themselves to Him. What others begged from him he
never asked for again, telling them to relieve the pressing
need of someone else while saying the Lord's prayer for
him . . .

The royal pursuivants cordoned off for search one day
the mansion of a certain gentleman at Mile End—the place
is named after a milestone one mile from London—while
Cornelius was staying there. They entered the house
unexpectedly, and burst into an inner room where John,
unmindful of danger, had taken off his cloak and coat,
as is usual in one's own room indoors. He was busy writing,
and happened to be holding his pen in his mouth, a habit
of his. Wondering at the noisy clamour for admission, he
looked up, and seeing the pursuivants remained motionless
in his chair. They stayed where they were, and looked
round as though disappointed of their prey. Then John
guessed what had happened. By a miracle their eyes
were prevented from seeing him. Quietly he made his
way out through their midst. No kind of greeting was
offered, and none returned. He did not even take the
pen from his mouth. Passing through the garden, two of
the Catholic servants met him, and noticing the decidedly
casual dress of a man of his gravity they asked him what
was up. When they learned what had happened, they
thanked God, and praised the holiness of the man whenever he was mentioned.

9.   In the judgment of the divine gardener, it was now
       time to gather the fruit. One of the less important
servants, a man whom the mistress of the house had taken
pity on, and admitted to the household to do the rougher
chores, conceived the quite crazy notion of taking a
gently-born girl out of the family circle to wife. Being
rebuked rather sharply for his audacity by John, he
betrayed him to the royal officials (1594). Sir George

Morton [High Sheriff of Dorset], administered the county
for the Queen . . . Among his officers were two justices of
peace, George Trencher [Trenchard] and Ralph Horsey.
To these the faithless busybody secretly gave an account
of all that had taken place at the house for some time
past. They decided to attack the house on Easter Day
[March 31]. John got wind of the danger—I have no idea
how—and made up his mind to escape. The lady of the
house made no difficulty. In the middle of the night, he
distributed Easter Communion to the household, which
had already been informed of its dastardly betrayer. They
grew calm. John then withdrew to cast about quietly in
search of souls in the neighbourhood. He grew more
careless about his own danger and, incidentally, that of
the others. Indeed, he was wondering whether to return.
However, when the lady began to urge his homecoming
he was unable to hold out longer against so much faith
and charity; even if it meant the end of his fortunes, or
if circumstances so determined, loss of life.

On the second Sunday after Easter, when the passage
in scripture on the Good Shepherd occurs, Cornelius
was making his thanksgiving for the Mass he had said at
five o'clock. It was then that the two justices of peace
with their retinue arrived. They crossed the surrounding
walls, and broke into the house with swords unsheathed.
Doors and anything else barring their way they either
overthrew or broke down. But John got himself into a
hiding-hole just in time, and the low cunning of the
pursuivants was frustrated for five or six hours. Despairing
of their quarry, they were getting ready to depart, loaded
down as they were with the religious books and sacred
vestments they had seized. But Trencher, one of the two
leaders, was annoyed by the complaints of several concerning the incommensurately small return for so
troublesome a search. 'I would have seen to it', he cried,
'that the takings corresponded with the work done, or
even went beyond it!' He called the servant to him who
had been the betrayer. 'Hey there! Open up the priest-
hole!' In the course of carrying out his household tasks,

he had sometimes got into the remoter corners of the house, and thanks perhaps to someone's carelessness, had seen it open. He now led Trencher directly to the place.

When the hiding-hole was opened, John appeared before them intent on his prayer. At the sight of him the pursuivant mob let out a great whoop of triumph and dragged him forth. Even after Trencher hauled him out, Cornelius remained unperturbed. When that official said how glad he was to have captured him, Cornelius replied simply that he was even gladder to be captured. He gave his surname and Christian name when asked, and admitted that he was a priest. Indeed, he showed very great concern to be known as a Jesuit. When they upbraided him for running away and taking to hiding-holes, he pointed out that the Apostle of the Gentiles had made his escape from Damascus in a basket let down from the wall by his brethren. Thomas Bosgrave was present, a relative of the lady of the house through her husband. Keeping his own head bare, he could not sufficiently bemoan the fact that John was not treated as his dignity demanded. Bosgrave put his fur cap on John's head. Reprehended for his zealous desire to look after a traitor, Bosgrave overcame his resentment on John's account at the latter's earnest plea. Because of all this, Bosgrave himself was taken into custody. Cornelius got on a horse in the cassock and cape he was accustomed to wear in the house. He made the sign of the cross, and then with Trencher at his side was led off. But he looked more like a companion than a captive. For even in his enemies, his dignity, unassumingness, long-suffering and courage in adhering to his faith, roused admiration . . . John was kept 14 days by Trencher while the decision of the Privy Council in London was being solicited. He was treated magnanimously and decently, being the daily guest of his captor's table, and having the run of the library whenever he wanted it. It was Trencher's wife who made herself primarily responsible for his comfort, being altogether won over by the good man's courtesy.

Cornelius met Protestant divines frequently, and clearly defended the worthiness and strength of his religion, but not without earning appreciation for a certain modesty. Charke, easily their leader and principal in the whole of that county, rashly asked him if he would care to debate with him in Latin, Greek or Hebrew. Cornelius replied briefly that he would follow up the invitation in whatever language was used. In the event, he exposed Charke to public shame, since he established the fact for all to see that he was comparatively ignorant of any of them. Two little wives of some preachers challenged him, with a certain feminine impudence, to discourse with them on the Sacred Scriptures, but he brushed them easily aside, and quite demolished their pretensions. Sir Walter Ralegh, knighted by the Queen's grace and further ennobled by his knowledge of mathematics, passed a whole night in discussion with Cornelius to remove his doubts on a number of topics. John pleased him by his gracious manner of proceeding, and by everything else in his discourse, although he seemed rather to displease him by something he put forward on the subject of atheism. However, Ralegh made a promise as he left to use his good offices with the Queen for him. On 14 [April], order from the Privy Council in London was carried down to the effect that John should be brought to alter his convictions by all means possible. If he proved obdurate, he should be brought to London immediately. Trencher, in order not to waste energy trying to convert John, ignored the first part of the order, and obeyed the second part forthwith.

10. On arrival in London, Cornelius was put into the Marshalsea. Soon after he was brought before the Privy Council. Among others present were the Archbishop of Canterbury, the Lord Treasurer, and the Lord Admiral. First they assailed him, completely innocent as he was, with insults. On his side, he insisted that he had done nothing unworthy or reprehensible at any time, or anything unbecoming one of his calling (Yepes, *op. cit.*,

p. 635). They examined him as to what other places he
had been in, and with whom he had stayed. This he
refused to answer as it was asked with a spiteful intention.
'Whatever else you refuse to reveal will be got from you
by torture!', they said. He was immediately taken back
to prison where by fasting, self-chastisement, going
without sleep, and generosity to the poor, he prepared
himself to undergo in fitting manner a worthy death for
his Christ. It was in this place also that Cornelius pronounced the vows of the Society. Afterwards, a copy of
them was made by Henry Garnet in the presence of three
witnesses, one a religious, and the other two lay-gentlemen.
This Cornelius did with so much joy of spirit that he
wrote home to say that nowhere else at any time could
he have found so much satisfaction in the things of God
as that prison had engendered. Morton, meanwhile, keeping before him zeal for the public good and obedience to
his Sovereign, wrote to the Council. He told them that he
could not see how people who had been so angered could
be pacified unless that priest were killed whom he had
recently sent on to them. The Council decided to send
back Cornelius forthwith. His own great comfort was to
take with him from London as many consecrated Hosts
as he needed, in the event, to make his Communion up
to the last two days of life. He was delivered into the
keeping of the High Sheriff of Dorset. His custody was
quite mild. Having three days to wait for the companions
of his torture, Cornelius practically went without food
and passed the whole time in prayer, almost without
sleep. Indeed, he treated himself with such harshness
that the High Sheriff was worried lest he end his own life
by his devotional austerities. The guards were indulgent
in allowing access of Catholics to him; and he was so
conscious of the fuss the latter made of him that he said
he greatly feared that these attentions would distract
in some measure from his own inner devotion.

On 2 July, Cornelius was led bound along the streets
to the assize court. After him came Thomas Bosgrave
and two servants, Patrick and John, of whose services

the Father had availed himself for a long time . . . The voice of a crier declared him guilty of *lèse majesté* because he had said the Masses forbidden by the Queen, heard confessions, and had with him a written attack on the royal edict against Catholics and priests. Not dissimilar was the accusation against his companions. They had treated a priest with respect and given him obedience. Asked according to custom by what judges he wished to be tried, Cornelius replied that his first preference was for men chosen from the Catholic clergy, men like himself.* Or if that could not be, then by men chosen from Oxford University. They ordered him to be content with time-honoured custom, and proceeded to accuse him and his associates of treason. Then Bosgrave and the two servants threw themslves at his feet to receive the blessing they begged of him. At that sight, neither the people nor even a thief with them, who also received the capital sentence, could remain unmoved. The Father cheered the thief with a few words, and in the end, just before execution, knew him for a fellow-Catholic.

Cornelius dealt in kindly and considerate fashion with the Protestant parson, so that if he had not been the herald of an unacceptable doctrine, Cornelius would certainly have accepted his ministrations. At 5 p.m., he was led back to prison, and seeing his executioner, said, 'Truly, I am very glad to see you'. The rest of the evening was passed in prayer, mutual encouragement, and in hearing the confessions of no less than 22 of his cell-mates. Walmesley the judge, in the midst of some emotion, and bowing as it were to necessity, had praised the learning and goodness of the priest, and put off passing the death sentence as long as he could. Now he delayed the execution, offering their lives if they would go to the Protestant churches. They all firmly refused, and the hour, 2 p.m. on the day following, was allotted for the bestial punishment. Leaving the prison, John cried out, 'From the cross to Christ is a glorious transit!' A hurdle stood ready. Cornelius laid himself down on it with complete composure of mind and outward mien. While he was being jolted along, every so often he exhorted his companions, who followed after him, to remain firm.

At the sight of him, one good man—and well-to-do—was so deeply moved that he went up to him and begged his blessing, promising he would join the Catholics, and leave off going to Protestant assemblies. When they got to the place of execution, the thief was the first to be hauled up on the beam. The Father had so heartened him that he said it was a joy and an honour to suffer death with heroes of this kind. Next, the second, John, went up. He kissed the rope, saying that he willingly gave his life's blood for his faith. After him came Patrick plainly admonishing the throng that the faith which he was sealing with his blood could alone bring salvation. He was strangled by the halter. Following these came Thomas Bosgrave. Since he excelled in breeding, knowledge and eloquence, he held a most attentive audience with a full discourse on the Catholic faith.

The last to enter the arena was John Cornelius. After a short speech, he kissed the ground under the first rung of the ladder. Next he kissed with great reverence the foot of his companions hanging from the beam. Then he embraced the gallows, crying with the Apostle, 'Oh, holy cross so long desired!' As he went up, he looked about at the people, and in doing so was especially struck by the words of the psalmist, 'They have exposed the mortal remains of Thy servants to be food for the birds'. He was forbidden to proceed to a discourse, but managed to say that what he had wanted to do for a long time he had done not long before in London, namely, gain admission to the Society of Jesus. He had not been able to do his noviceship in Belgium, although he would have made his way there very shortly. However, he now did it more gloriously by this last agony. He then prayed for those who had hounded him; and for the well-being of the Queen and of all the Protestants. Kissing the noose held out by the hangman, he put it round his neck, and was at once pushed off the ladder.

When the executioner cut him down, he was not yet dead, and as he fell on the ground he lay writhing and gasping. While the hangman ripped him up in front, the priest moved his hand as though to make the sign of the cross on his forehead. The divided body was stuck on four stakes, and hung up in the place of his torture until late in the day. Then with the bodies of the three others all was buried. His head, stuck on top of the gallows, marked the end of the triumph . . . Out of regard for the popular wish, the head was taken down on the sheriff's authority. They were afraid that the very heavy storms might fall on the crops which had taken place elsewhere on the previous occasion of such executions. The head passed into the possession of Catholics.

12. Cornelius by his life and death diffused a glow of religious conviction and constancy in the western parts of the island. Robert Southwell and Henry Walpole, from the beginning of the following year, became likewise sound pillars of strength in the south and north; Southwell in London, Walpole in York. Both tried to imitate the unbroken martyrs of the early Church. Burning with desire to spread Catholic faith, they were called on to endure corresponding hardships, and to win immortal glory by the end appropriate. Richard Southwell of Norfolk lived about four miles from Norwich in the parish of Horsham St. Faith's.* He was a gentleman of considerable means, and Robert was his third son. As a child Robert was extremely beautiful. One day a woman stole him while he was left in his cradle somewhat longer than usual by his nurse, and left her own child in his place. The theft did not long remain hidden. The abductress was caught while begging at a house not far away, and admitted that she had done it for money. The boy was brought back. Robert considered this amongst his greatest blessings, and often recalled this divine favour with a lively sense of gratitude . . . Eventually, when he became a priest, he would not rest until he found the woman who first discovered the abduction. Recognising

in her the instrument of God's mercy, he reconciled her to the Church . . .

Southwell was sent to Paris as a boy of fifteen. He spent two years as the guest of John Cotton, a man of breeding and of superlative character and faith. The boy had recourse to Thomas Darbishire, mentioned above, as his spiritual director, telling him anything which touched that most sensitive mind of his in the way of wrong-doing . . . Already he had conceived the idea of embracing a stricter way of life, and giving himself to God in the Society of Jesus. He did his utmost, through his enthusiastic insistence with those who could give him what he desired, to join the Jesuits as soon as possible. But although he was impelled by the best of intentions, he had to wait until age and due deliberation more strongly recommended the staying-power of his good resolutions . . .

13.　[This section, covering most of pages 173 to 175 in More, is devoted to a long and elegant complaint by Southwell against the delay imposed on him before he could become a Jesuit.]

14.　His desire to join the Society persisted, and enthusiasm grew with time . . . A letter is extant which suggests that he departed for Belgium to perfect what in intention he had already begun. But since Southwell's ardour could not find what it most desired to feed on in Belgium or France, he went to Rome. There he hoped to imbibe the truths of his faith more rapidly since he would be drinking with that much more avidity from the very fountain-head. He was not yet 17 years old, but he was admitted to the noviceship on the vigil of St. Luke, 17 October 1578. The new Jesuit reveals in another letter how much fruit came from his stay below the Alps. 'Remember', he says to himself, 'indeed, call often to mind that day when, all impatient to join the Society, you sought several times to be admitted and with so much insistence. Remember how you even gave way to tears . . .'.

15. On this awareness of his past, Southwell proceeded
    to lay the foundations of his future great qualities.
He strove with the utmost eagerness to reach the height
of perfection. The Wise Architect did not design a
structure flimsy and insecure, but an edifice already
firmly founded, and one which no future storms would
shake. It was established four-square on self-knowledge:
something essential for building up every kind of positive
quality, and praised by all the ancients. This kind of
thinking, and how it was put into words by Southwell
and fixed in his memory . . . is to be found in *The Way of
Life*, written by Anthony Sucquet,* a man made for
moulding souls in goodness, and one whose work is
worthy to be remembered for ever . . . [Southwell himself
wrote] 'In the last resort, I entered the Society fully
aware of considerations of this kind. So I must not expect
anything throughout my life . . . except to suffer and be
afflicted by continual tribulations, so as not to have peace
even for an hour. Indeed, to be afflicted, I must count
among the principal benefits of God, since this is the
only way to be like Christ . . .'.

16. Received into the Society in Rome, Southwell
    spent a great part of his noviceship at Tournai* in
Flanders. This was to ensure that a young man with all
the ardour of his aspirations, and not yet equal to the
immoderate sun of Italy, would not be overwhelmed
by the effect of two kinds of heat. Furthermore, being
gifted with such excellent endowments, and possessing
a keen and questing mind, he roused hopes that he would
rise to great things, and Rome should not be the only
beneficiary. How long he passed in each place, however,
I have not found in the records. His religious sense, which
the taking of first vows implanted deeply in his soul,
we can learn from the narrator himself, and from the
title of one of his own writings, 'Certain thoughts which
came to me on the feast of St. Luke after taking vows'
[18 October 1580] . . .

17. Southwell was recalled from Tournai to Rome to
hear philosophy and theology. He refused to lag
behind any in understanding, application, giving satisfaction in his life as a student, bringing profit to himself,
and living a life that was truly good. He shone especially
in ingenuity and application when he came to make his
defence of propositions drawn from the whole of philosophy (*Universa*). After finishing his theology course, he
was made Prefect of Studies in the English College. This
was at a time when the young men were very numerous,
varied in their gifts, and noted generally for brilliance.
It was not easy for anyone to lead them unless he himself was completely equipped and instructed in all the
branches of religious knowledge. Southwell did not lack
the capacity to understand a problem quickly. Neither
did his judgments limp for want of solid reasons. He could
explain things clearly, and there was a certain inborn
suavity in his manner. His natural dignity was linked with
a mien that was unostentatious; and even when immersed
in studies, he remained untiring in his striving after goodness. By administering and teaching with authority, and
encouraging souls towards perfection, he won for himself
the goodwill of all . . . [More spends the rest of section 17,
the whole of 18, and the first 20 lines or so of 19, on the
spiritual prowess and principles of Southwell which
belong rather to a spiritual treatise than to history. On
paper, they sound platitudinous at times. Put into effect
by Southwell, surely they explain, and alone explain, the
most important aspects of his greatness].

19. . . . While Southwell was at his studies in the Roman
College, and in the midst of preoccupations as prefect
at the English College, Allen and Persons again appealed
for the help of Jesuits in the English harvest. Southwell
was assigned to Henry Garnet as companion when he
set out for England on 24 March 1586. As Southwell
himself not inaptly described them when he bade farewell
to Persons on the Milvian Bridge, they were like two
arrows shot at the same target. This was borne out by

events. Each won laurels for himself in defending the
faith. How completely Southwell was filled with a desire
to win such laurels, he himself showed in his letters from
the English College, as Prefect of Studies, to the General,
Claud Aquaviva: 'I will only add one thing concerning
myself. I desire nothing more, nor could anything more
welcome in this life happen to me than that, if it seems
good to your Reverence, I should do my work for the
English nation in person among them. Furthermore, it
seems to be a divine inspiration that I should do this
work where the highest hope of martyrdom is held out,
namely in England itself. At all events, I will not cease
to beg God for this in my prayers . . . From Rome, 23
January 1585'. We derive the same impression from
another letter, written while he was travelling, to a Jesuit
who had once been his spiritual director at some time or
another. [There follows a letter of 25 July 1586, which
similarly expresses Southwell's desire for martyrdom.]

Southwell wrote further letters, perhaps to the same
man. In any case they were put on record for this time,
and were written to a priest of the Society. From early
boyhood, Southwell had been on intimate terms with
him, and by way of brotherly confidence told him that
up to that time he had never asked anything of God in
vain. However, there were still two items outstanding
for which from boyhood he had prayed for constantly.
First, he wished to give himself to Christ, life for life and
blood for blood; but before that, to get through a great
deal of hard work for the good of souls. As it happened,
Southwell achieved both. He spent nine years cultivating
and suffering in the Lord's vineyard. Finally, he shed his
blood in a good death . . . After some years of exertion
in the field, he came to write the following account from
which the wretched state of things at that time and the
steadfastness of the Catholics may be recognised . . .*

'So far we live and thrive, unworthy as we are to suffer
imprisonment. We get your letters more rarely than we
send them to you, but now we can scarcely send them
with any sort of safety. We know for certain that some

of them have disappeared *en route*. We have been writing to you once a month, and sometimes more often. Hence we are very much surprised that our friends reproach us with great negligence in writing. Would that it were as safe to send as it is agreeable to write. If it were, you would have bundles of letters every day!

'The situation for Catholics is, as always, wretched; full of fear and danger, especially after our enemies became subject to a war-scare. Our men in prison are happy and cheerful. Those who are free do not expect to remain so for long: but they do not worry much. They are all of them braced up to suffer whatever God's cause may bring. They are more anxious about His glory and the good of souls than any temporal misfortune . . . Two priests captured not long ago were given a harsh reception. They were obliged to undergo everything imaginable in the Bridewell where they were engulfed. In fact, it is scarcely credible what kinds of torture they had to put up with in that place of torment. Not only was the food poor in quality and meagre in quantity but in addition so bad—indeed, filthy—as to make those who ate it vomit. Work was without intermission and unreasonably arduous. Even the sick were driven to it by thrashings. Their bedding was straw already filthy before it collected more filth from the place where it was put. They were not allowed to buy food with the money given them unless it was the kind of stuff they would rather pay to have taken away than purchase for use. Sometimes they were hung up for whole days by their hands, with only the tips of their toes touching the ground. The finishing touch was that those who were kept there were left in a pool of filth and a mudbank of ordure. This is the one purgatory we all fear; the place where those two butchers of Catholics, Topcliffe and Young, enjoy complete licence in applying torture. But whatever happens to us, in the last resort we will be able to endure it thanks to Him Who gives us strength. Meanwhile, may all workers of iniquity be overthrown, and God speak peace to His people . . . 16/26 January 1590/1'.

In another letter of 8 March [old style] 1591, Southwell relates the following: 'We make progress amid tempestuous waves with no little peril, but in spite of all, our Lord has been pleased to preserve us until now. We met together to renew our vows as our custom is—matter of great consolation to us. Some days were spent in discourses and spiritual conferences . . . Indeed, it seems to me that I am witnessing the beginnings of religious life in this island, and albeit amidst tears, ourselves sowing the seed. Thus it may be that others coming after us will carry their sheaves with joy to heaven . . . All the same, our joy was turned to sorrow as sudden alarms sent us packing in all directions. As it turned out, the danger was greater than the harm done. We all survived the storm, although I with others among us, thinking to escape Scylla, fell upon Charybdis. But by God's mercy we all escaped wreck and we now ride at anchor in a safe haven. In another letter of mine I spoke of the most recent martyrs Bales and Horner, and the good example which the public had by their holy death. By such dew is the Church refreshed . . . Meanwhile, the rest of us wait until our own day shall dawn—always supposing we are not unworthy of so much glory—and this shall be our day of reward . . .'. The Lord did not long delay the much-desired fulfilment of his wish. Southwell was captured the following year . . . and after three years of prison and enduring most frightful torture on 10 occasions, he was freed [by death] from the chains which held him.

20. When Southwell was first sent over, the situation in England was most troubled. Seventy priests had been exiled the previous year, although this was something intended as an act of grace. Francis Throckmorton's treason, whether real or contrived to stir up hatred, was held up to general execration, as was William Parry's not long afterwards. Following this, there was a disturbance on the part of some gentlemen which was put down with the death and attainder of most of them. In the same year, 1586, after the lapse of a few months, bloody laws were

passed against priests who came back to their own country. The captive Queen of Scots was made ample occasion for general suspicion, and spies were everywhere. It can only be attributed to God's protection that anyone at all was able to get on to the island unharmed in view of universal watchfulness in the midst of so much fear. Slip through Southwell did, however, and passed some months at the home of Baron Vaux together with Garnet. Vaux, an outstanding character, used to bring his guests most amicably together in this way; this for the sake of the faith he so ardently followed, and also for Persons's sake, thanks to whom he had been restored to that faith.

The priest died whose services as spiritual director had been used by the Countess of Arundel. Southwell then transferred himself to her household. He did not move away from there until he was dragged off to prison six years later. He spent his remaining three years surviving torture, and in the end found his triumph in death. Nowhere in England was life more restricted than in the great houses of the Catholic gentry. In the large households which they maintained, the majority of the servants were usually Protestant, with very few Catholics, either because they were not always suitable for the more important offices, or because their masters thought to live in greater security from the law if they gave their confidence to fewer people. Therefore a priest, as far as possible, was kept out of sight, and cut off from the general bustle of the house as much as could be. Remote from everyday life, only one or two of the servants might know of his existence. He was shut up in his room like the proverbial sparrow sitting solitary on the housetop. In this way he passed his days and nights. He was obliged to get his fresh air cautiously through a window, moving about carefully lest he be noticed by those who were not supposed to be aware of his presence. He administered the sacraments to few, and was able to converse now and again with even fewer. From the well-furnished tables only a modest something would be carried to him, and that furtively by a servant. Natural hunger was satisfied, but with little temptation to gluttony! His own attitude of mind was the only seasoning for whatever was set before him. If in this he was deficient, then in the greatest houses he had to live in utmost want. This was the kind of lodging Southwell found with the Countess. It was a house, moreover, made sorrowful by the imprisonment of her husband, the Earl, in the Tower.*

The Earl's father, the Duke of Norfolk, guilty of an attempt to marry the captive Queen of Scots, and accused besides of plotting with other enemies of Elizabeth, namely the Pope and the King of Spain, had been executed in 1572.* Arundel's grandfather, on trivial grounds, as Camden says, had met the same end several years before. His great-grandfather likewise. Disturbed by the continual misfortunes of his line, Earl Philip, who also feared the severity of the laws against Catholics, and the power of their principal foes, thought to withdraw himself secretly from the kingdom. He had written out for Elizabeth the causes of his departure to be handed to her when he was safely away. But before he could leave, he was discovered through the infidelity of some of his own men, and detained. He was led off to the Tower.

A year passed. No charge was made. Then, lest they should seem to have shut away a completely innocent man, Howard was accused in the Star Chamber, before the leading men of the realm, of having entertained priests. This was forbidden by law. He was also charged with keeping up a correspondence with Allen and Persons, the Queen's enemies; and with slandering in written word the present way of running the country; finally, that he secretly intended to leave the country to fight for Spain. They sentenced him to a fine of £10,000 and imprisonment during the Queen's pleasure. Nor was this the end of his troubles. After three years in prison—the Queen did not see fit to free him—he was arraigned on a capital charge. The heads of the accusations scarcely differed, as Camden bears witness, from those brought against him in 1586. All the same, he was found guilty. There were those who were sorry enough that this choice bloom of the nobility should have withered so soon—he was then hardly 33 years old. But there were others who praised the Queen's wisdom to the skies, for by this example she had struck terror into the principal men among the Catholics. She subsequently spared his life, feeling that she had sufficiently broken the influence of even so great a man; but because he had enjoyed influence with the Pope—or so it was thought—he had thereby clogged the channel of royal grace. He endured 10 years of prison, during which time, day and night, he gave himself to prayer and penance. He lived his last day on earth in 1595.

21. It was Southwell's task meanwhile to soothe the other partner of the marriage with every healing balm he could think of. Through spoken word and written exhortation, he taught the Countess of Arundel not only to bear her bereavement, but also to accept it for the love of her sublimer spouse, Christ Himself; also by pouring out her prayer more frequently to God she could show that more abundant obedience which she could not give her husband while he was absent from her. For her assistance, Southwell drew up a rule of life which was subsequently printed, and so helped even more people. He also wrote her a more diffuse letter of consolation. In the event, that likewise proved most useful in easing the smart of Catholics generally. Southwell also brought solace to the Countess by his very understanding letters. Among them are those he sent after Arundel's condemnation to death. In this way, Southwell was able to strengthen a noble mind already braced to surrender the ultimate forfeit of life itself . . .*

22. . . . The Earl of Arundel, expecting to lose his life by another's hand, filled the interval of waiting with prayer. Six years after the sentence, he met his end while following a religious discipline not only tougher than anything the easygoing could approve of, but even think it possible to endure . . . (Camden, Anno 38° Elizabethae). His body was laid to rest without ceremony in the chapel

of the Tower where he had lived as a prisoner. Thirty years or so later, when King James somewhat relaxed the reins of rule, Arundel's truly noble Countess obtained permission for his remains, enclosed in an iron coffin, to be laid to rest in the family sepulchre. He lay, in a little chapel he himself had built at Arundel, under the following inscription: 'Here in this grave lie the venerable bones of Philip, formerly Earl of Arundel and Surrey, thanks to permission graciously given by King James at the instance of Anne, the Earl's most devoted wife; thanks also to an exceptional sense of filial duty in his son, Thomas. His remains were transferred to this place from the Tower of London in 1614. The Earl was first sent to prison for his profession of the Catholic faith under Elizabeth. He was subsequently fined £10,000, and in the end most unjustly condemned to death. After living like a saint for 10 years and six months in closest confinement in the same Tower, he fell asleep in the Lord on 19 October 1595, not without suspicion of poison . . .'

Southwell did not observe such complete seclusion in the house of the Countess that he could not slip away on occasion, with her approval, to bring assistance to others. Both could take credit for this work of spiritual usefulness, for while he bore the burden of toil and danger, she carried the entire expense. After being away for a time he would return to his accustomed solitude . . . How much he preferred this to the other uncertain, nomadic way of life, one can learn from his letter to another priest who in his wanderings had nowhere to stay. 'I am extremely sorry', he said, 'to hear of your unsettled mode of existence whereby you are the fleeting visitor of a great many people and the abiding guest of none. We are all pilgrims, I must admit, but not simply tramps! Our life, but not our way of life, is uncertain . . . Inconstancy is a form of mental illness when it drives a man to be always visiting new places with never one good thought to rest in. Constantly changing one'e environment is the mother of idleness and instability, better calculated to affect than perfect our nature however

good . . . Rare is the company from which you escape
more innocent . . . There is a middle way, moreover,
between wordless isolation or silent obscurity and continual change of companions never the same. The two
extremes are equally to be condemned. The best course
is something between them, namely, to go out to other
people with a purpose, and then to return to ourselves,
as it were, at well-defined times. Give due regard to the
nature of things; the seasons of the year; the alternation
of day and night are laws which are everyday proofs of
order of this kind. Some seasons call us forth; others
suggest that we stay indoors. When you are in a house,
learn how to get on with the company. Also train your
mind to hug to itself the thoughts which make for goodness in all its practical applications. This should be your
delight before all else. In this way you will live every day,
I sincerely hope, a life that is truly good. Farewell!*

23. As a Father in Christ, one of Southwell's first pre-
    occupations was to beget for his Master the man
who had been his own father. He was rich, and took to
wife a lady from the Queen's court who had once tutored
Elizabeth in Latin. His sympathies lay with the Catholics,
but he kept away from Catholic services to serve the
times instead. He enjoyed the protection of the law,
which was willing enough that all who conformed with
the Protestants at their prayers should be left otherwise
unmolested. Thus he retained wealth and favour. Son
Robert wrote him a very long letter which by way of
beginning asked pardon that one his junior should presume
to teach the older man, and appear to put a dunce's cap
on his father's head. However, he set out his reasons and
ideas with so much artifice that he not only won praise
as part of the first reaction, but actually achieved the
result he longed for. He expressed his pleasure on his own
and his father's account in another letter. This thanked
God because He had first given his father to him as an
initial pledge of what would become for Southwell's
utmost efforts their most acceptable reward.

Southwell realised that it was a common weakness of even the loftiest minds of that time that they would light on some contemporary triviality, and proceed to write up and elaborate the theme in books without value if not actually pernicious. To provide a remedy for this unhappy state of affairs, as far as he could and supply religious literature of a kind that made pleasant reading, he made it part of his apostolate to spend the hours of solitude in writing religious tracts. They were written in English, some in verse and some in a flowing prose which aimed at elegance of language and happiness of expression. Of this kind were the lament of Peter after his fall, and the sighs of the Magdalen for much-desired death. Southwell also produced a great many poems which were published with wide approval; these in addition to the letter of consolation to which I have referred. This letter he composed for his father, as also another little work, which are still read with much pleasure even today (Letter 37 to his family on the right use of time).* Whether lying hidden at home or emerging into the open, Southwell found no boredom in solitude and no harm in society. Among other things, experience taught him to put a proper value on time, and arrange his day in orderly fashion. As in everything else, the return was very small. Indeed, it occurred to him that even the man who worked very hard in this life lost a great part of it. How much then, he who did nothing? Or using it badly, sped through it all? . . .

24. Southwell prayed, studied and wrote. Thus he laid up a store to be generously given to his neighbour as opportunity offered . . . However, those were times when evil did its utmost to bring his best efforts to nothing. Whatever could be done by force or cunning was tried alongside every shift of trickery, and pursued with unbridled ferocity . . . Southwell remembered that in ancient times many suffered similar things. By patience they too had risen superior to most inhuman and appalling cruelties . . . Southwell pondered on these things and

wrote about them in order to stimulate himself and others to successful combat whereby, through a labour that lasts a little, a peace could be obtained that would endure for ever . . .*. Just as Eliot, the apostate, served Campion to this end, so now a woman of like kind prepared the way for Southwell.

25.   At Uxenden, nor far from Harrow, lived the Catholic Bellamy family. Campion and Persons had tilled this ground. It was now to be regularly watered by Southwell's assiduous attention. Whenever, that is, he could relax in a freer atmosphere from the rigour of his loneliness. Anne Bellamy, a daughter of the family, spent the early part of her life in lively attachment to Catholic faith and practice. For its sake she refused to be intimidated either by the effrontery of men without principle or by the stern experience of prison. Protestant zeal did not always stop short of molesting young girls who, in fact, were beyond all suspicion of doing harm by reason of the innocence to be expected of their age, sex and condition. And so Anne was imprisoned in the Gatehouse at Westminster. She gradually lost her virtue in that testing-place of virtue; the goodness which she had imbibed from the daily round at home she exchanged for sluttishness. Hoping for an easier kind of imprisonment, with the ultimate goal of liberty, she allowed herself to become too intimate with the head gaoler. From day-long idleness and mixing in bad company, she gradually became vicious. In the end, she put off her religion together with the chief ornament of her womanhood. After amusing herself for some time with surreptitious debauchery, she contracted an unworthy marriage . . . The way of iniquity slopes smoothly downwards, and he who is once ensnared can descend by leaps and bounds. Her base doings with the gaoler begot avarice; and when she could hope no longer, either by right or favour, to sustain her greed from her father's goods, she thought by a further wrong to exploit a new possibility.

Anyone who received a priest at his house was by the recent law liable to the capital charge, and also confiscation of his goods. Corrupted by acquisitiveness and lust, Anne turned her attention to Southwell. She told him by messenger that she wished to meet him in her father's house, and arranged a day. On that day Southwell was there. Perhaps he was ignorant of her recent fall. Perhaps he hoped to bring some healing to an ulcerated soul, and thought that such a meeting would help . . . The lady revealed all to the gaoler, the day, the place, and the man she had destined for his prey. As she was fully aware of all that was going on at home, she could describe the hiding-holes of the priests, and where and how they were to be found. The gaoler had a word with Topcliffe. It was Topcliffe who openly admitted that no one ever took greater pleasure in hunting wild beasts than he in searching out and harrying priests. He rushed at once to the house, and had it surrounded by a posse of his strong-arm men. He set a watch on every approach lest anyone escape his toils. Then he broke into the house, went through the rooms, and probed that part of the roof of which he had been told. There in hiding he seized Southwell together with his equipment, bound him, and led him away. He wallowed in his triumph at taking the longed-for victim in the broad light of day, and before a crowd which had collected in considerable number.

How much, or what in particular of her father's possessions came thus to the daughter who had betrayed him, remains unceratin. However, we saw in Flanders subsequently the old man Bellamy, fallen from what was a tidy fortune, and become an exile dragging out the little of life that could remain to him in a manner poor enough. Topcliffe, meanwhile, took Southwell to his own home, and inside a few weeks tortured him on 10 occasions so cruelly that he would have preferred death 10 times over. Next he sent him to the very prison where the head gaoler and Anne, with the memory of their squalid deeds still fresh, could pluck some further fruit of avarice from the new guest. What kind of welcome he got, how much severity, or what form of treatment he received, or how he was kept for the two months he stayed in that prison, and what was the cause of his removal to the Tower, has not come to my hand; nor yet what he had to endure in the Tower, nor what he did during the several years he was hidden away there, cut off as he was from all contact with the outside world.

From the first, he imposed a rigid silence on himself whenever he was brought to question. He adhered to it so tenaciously that the commissioners declared that he seemed to be a block of wood rather than a man. Cecil, at that time the head of the Queen's councillors, is said to have uttered the following publicly when the subject of Southwell's torturing came up: 'Antiquity may boast of the heroes of old Rome, and of the endurance of prisoners under torment, but our age is no wit inferior to it. Nor need the spirits of Englishmen yield in anything to the Romans. We now have in our hands a certain Southwell, Jesuit, who has been tortured with the utmost severity 13 times, but he could not be brought to confess anything, not even the colour of the horse on which he sat on a certain day. He was afraid lest from this clue his enemies might hazard a precise guess as to the house or the Catholics in whose company he had been that day'.*

Torture apart, Southwell was examined by the same men fairly often. He replied courteously. If Topcliffe tried to make any contribution, however, Southwell would not pay him the compliment of even a single word. When asked the cause of this, he averred, 'I know too well from experience that this fellow is not amenable to reason'. He had less than nine whole days or nights alone with himself or God, but no one could doubt as to what use he put his isolation . . . The order of his day, or how he managed to pass the time, must be left to the reader's imagination rather than my writing. Although his sister Mary, wife of a certain Bannister, was sometimes given access to him, nothing leaked out of the things which he reserved for God alone to remember, and to reward in eternity.

26. From 1580 until 1596 never a year passed without one or more priests or laymen, men and even some women, being numbered among the martyrs for the faith, the authority of the Pope, and the sacraments. In the course of 16 years, something like 200 were estimated to have been done away with. Only six or seven of the Society are found to have suffered in this way. This could be attributed to paucity of numbers. It could also have been due to a certain fear and jealousy on the part of our enemies. Those Catholics considered to be leaders of the rest might, by their constancy in dying, and their goodness and learning while they lived, make the others whom they left behind in the front line more ready to do and die. What other cause could there have been for keeping Robert Southwell 30 months in the Tower? Already his excellent endowments and merit were achieving renown in published books. Why else did they keep William Weston before him many years in the shadows, although his reputation for holiness cast its light over the whole of England? There was no question of doubting whether they were priests or not. For this cause they had made away with more than 100 secular priests. They liked it even less when they were members of the Society. If they could, they would have done away with them all. Jealousy restrained their ardour to destroy, except when they felt they would do more harm by sparing than by killing . . . The disinterested reader will discern, not without a certain curiosity, how the forms of English justice were observed in all this. Bombino has described them for us in his 'Campion'.

27. On 18 February [1595] Southwell was transferred from the Tower to Newgate. He was shut up in a subterranean dungeon called Limbo on account of its darkness and depth. Two days later, he was taken to Westminster to stand trial on the capital charge . . . He said the prospect made his heart leap for joy. The day before his transfer, the judges Popham, Owen, Evans, Daniel, and others, held session at Newgate. A jury of 24 was

empanelled for the trial. Popham addressed them thus: 'I sit here as judge for charges of every kind, but I do not intend to mention them all on this occasion. Bend your minds more particularly to a law passed in the 27th year of the Queen's reign. This law made those who received Holy Order at Rome after the feast of St. John the Baptist in the first year of her reign, guilty of *lèse majesté* if within 40 days they did not depart the kingdom but stayed on after that. Those who receive or maintain any such in their homes are guilty of the same crime; and they are liable to confiscation of their goods. How necessary these provisions were, is, I take it, evident to all. For her Majesty could never have known peace of mind while a place in her realm remained for these trouble-makers. None of her subjects could otherwise enjoy his possessions without living in considerable fear.

'Who were they who incited the gentlemen of Northumberland, and Throckmorton and Parry, Hacket, Yorke and Williams?* Who were they who got into line the Spanish fleet of '88, urged it on, and I would almost say built it, by their combined efforts? Was it not Allen and Persons and their assistant priests who were scattered about everywhere and eventually blown over to us? But when just retribution had been meted out to the guilty, the entire matter could have been consigned to the darkness of oblivion—if it had not been dragged forth by recent and continued crimes to start the whole affair going again, and to make it appear as if laws were passed not to inspire fear but contempt. Listen to what is summarily charged against a certain Robert Southwell. I prefer to leave it to you to provide a remedy'.

(The form of the indictment): 'The jury make presentment on behalf of the Queen that Robert Southwell, late of London, clerk, born in this kingdom, was ordained priest by the authority derived from, and pretended by, the Roman See, after the feast of St. John the Baptist in the first year of the Queen's reign, and before 1 May in the 32nd year of our said sovereign lady. Having not the fear of God before his eyes, he did not in the least regard the laws and statutes of the realm. Nor did he fear the penalties attached to the same. On 26 June, in the 34th year of the said Queen's reign, he behaved treacherously, and was a false traitor to our Lady the Queen, and so remained, contrary to the statute given and devised for such a case, and against the peace of the said sovereign lady, her crown and dignity.

'If, therefore, those who clip and debase the coin, and minters of false money, are punished with the most severe penalties for treason, how much more should men be severely punished who corrupt the minds of their fellows with a religion that is superstitious; who, thirsty for blood, trouble us with fears unceasing, and with plots and betrayals? What crime will he not be capable of, given the opportunity, who breaks the laws, and despises the punishment ordained for the guilty? You it is who must decide whether he who stands accused is guilty of this crime. This is your duty.'

Inflamed by this speech, the 24 men withdrew for a brief space to consider their verdict. The Attorney-General, Sir Edward Coke, followed them, to urge on, if it were needed, men already rushing well ahead. There followed also Anne Bellamy . . . now completely broken down, to add her own testimony on the priesthood. After a short interval, it was once again the turn of the judges. A 'true bill', or valid indictment, was issued. This was the preamble to the trial. Afterwards, Southwell was arraigned at Westminster. Raising his right hand after the indictment was read again, he was asked whether he would plead guilty or not guilty. 'I admit', he said, 'that I was born in England, and am the Queen's subject. Neither do I deny that I am an ordained priest; and for this status of mine I return the deepest possible thanks to Almighty God. That I was at Uxenden is plain for all to see since I was led here a captive from that place. I would not have been there, however, if I had not been enticed like a mouse into a trap. I call God to witness that I am innocent of all treason or conspiracy to the detriment of the Queen, her government or the state. My sole purpose was to administer the Sacraments according to the Catholic rite, and assist the consciences of those who desired it'.

'Say in one word, as custom is, whether you consider yourself guilty or not guilty.' 'I plead "not guilty", then. As defendant of my innocence I call upon no other than God; and I appeal to you, my judges!' 'Far be it from us', replied Popham: 'Our task is to pass sentence once the facts are established. Decision lies with the 12 jurymen.' These had been chosen from the 24, and Popham had seen to it that they had been announced by the crier. 'Is there any man among them, Southwell', he said, 'against whom you wish to object, as is your right? These represent your country; to whose and God's judgment, if you submit yourself, stand forward. If you refuse, that will be considered to convict you of the charge.' Southwell then said, 'Seeing that the law so stipulates, and that I must have either those men or you as my triers, I must obey this unfair condition. Indeed, I must forgive the 12 men; and since I do not know any of them, I am bound by Christian charity not to think unfavourably of any one of them. But after I commit myself to them, they will certainly demonstrate whether they be fair-minded or not when they come to give a verdict, according to your law, on an innocent man. I allow, then, since necessity obliges, that these men try my case'.

28. The 12 men heard the accusation recited a second time according to prescribed form. They then conferred on it and other charges in a place apart. Out of hatred of Campion's religion, as well as following custom, they were quite capable of destroying the accused. Indeed, they showed themselves prompt to do so. Lest they should lack enthusiasm for the deed, however, the Attorney-General got up and harangued these 12 jury men in a speech divided under three heads: 'The indictment you have heard is contained in three points: that he is the Queen's subject, that he received Holy Order by the Roman rite, and that, after receiving it, he was at

Uxenden. He will not admit that he is guilty of any of them. You have heard the blasphemy. What further need have we of witnesses? As the law ordains, a subject of the Queen who after receiving holy order by the Roman rite returns to England is guilty of *lèse majesté*. For the Queen knows no superior in her own country. Among her own people she alone can and should rule in all things. Who then could have the audacity to accept authority from a foreign prince, bring himself here, and exercise the same as over subjects? Especially if he accepts authority from a prince who is altogether hostile to our Queen, and the insatiable foe of our religion and tranquility.

'The law has taken care to provide for the security of our Queen and our religion. First, none must recognise the authority of a foreign prince over subjects of this realm. Secondly, no papal correspondence must be brought in. Entry is likewise forbidden to waxen images, and beads, which they call *Agnus Deis* and grains. Again, books are forbidden which, under cover of religion and learning, spread a pestilence which all must flee if they have any regard for their well-being. Finally, what vigilance or what harshness in the law could be held excessive to prevent the further evil, and culmination of all the others, whereby droves of priests and Jesuits have been sent into the kingdom. By their means throughout the world discord is set in motion for the benefit of the Spanish king and the Pope. Through them wars are stirred up, and the way is prepared for foreign occupation. Christ commanded us to render to Caesar the things that are Caesar's. The Apostle admonishes us to be subject to princes and powers, to obey their commands and be ready for every good work. These neither acknowledge authority nor wish to be subject to the Queen. Indeed, they call subjects away from their obedience. True, they obey orders—but the Pope's! They are ready for anything; but what kind of thing you can easily see for yourselves! They wound religion. They do not fear kingship. They take away mutual trust and good dealing from among men by their meretricious and contrived answers to questionings.

'You, Southwell, were among the first to teach that if a man were asked if he had seen you at someone's house, he could reply on oath that he had not, even when he most certainly had. If you deny that, there is someone here to affirm it. In truth, what is that if not lying, perjury, deception, and holding open the door to evil cunning, so that nothing in law or in justice, or anything else henceforth may be done according to the usage of our forebears? All must be liable to fraud and deception. How in the last resort will you deal with such men? It is altogether obvious what punishments, what condign penalties they merit who go about to confuse, pervert and overthrow the kingdom, its religion, peace, life and the customs of its people with their loathsome principles and practice'.

29. Before this onslaught, Southwell stood his ground like an athlete unwinded, his mind unbowed and alert. He often begged leave to reply to individual objections as they came up. Frequently, he tried to interpose relevant observations as they occurred to him. He claimed that his memory and powers of concentration had been weakened by torture, and it was difficult to remember all that was scattered through a very long speech. He called God to witness that he had been 10 times put to torture; each time worse than death. He gained no concession. They greeted his discourse with shouting, derisive laughter, mockery and interruptions. The following is the summary of what he said, either in sustained oration, or through the interruptions:
'I know by your laws that priests returning to any of the Queen's dominions may be charged with treason. It is not in your power, however, to prove by wit or learning that those laws are consonant with the precepts of Christ or the Word of God. What you say about giving to Caesar what is Caesar's, and obeying the authorities, we also acknowledge, and render to the Queen what is the Queen's namely her power over our bodies and all that pertains thereto. Our souls are something different. On this

spiritual plane lies all the power which we respect in the Pope; breves, medals, grains and everything else of his are connected with this; and also anything that priests do who are sent here for the sake of dispensing the Sacraments. That the kingdom may flourish mightily in peace, for this we pray. May it be holy in its religion! I say it for your peace that this will never come about through your beliefs. We respect kingship in all that touches kingship. But you doubtless recall, regarding the matter in hand, that it was said by the apostles, "Whether it is better in the sight of God to hear you rather than God, judge ye!" We serve the Spanish king in nothing against her Majesty. Nor can it be by any means proved that we had anything to do with the fleet of which you speak. Let the king have his own. That the Queen may enjoy hers, is also the devout wish of everyone. This loyalty our faith also teaches us.

'Perhaps you will be good enough to explain what you mean regarding the complicated reply which you say that I gave. You should find it less incomprehensible than the gentleman who has just spoken against me tried to make out. I ask you, Mr. Attorney, to consider the case of a King of France taking up arms against us, invading the kingdom, and seizing the realm. He then looks for the Queen, who has retreated to some hiding-place in the palace of which you are aware. Suppose you were taken in the court, and the king asked you where she was hiding, and refused to believe you until you were sworn. What would you do? To hesitate would be to reveal; not to swear, to betray. What would you reply? I suppose you would point out the place. But who of all people here present would declare you to be a good man and faithful subject of the Queen, and not rather a traitor? You would swear, therefore, even if you knew, that you did not know; or say that you had no idea where in the palace the Queen could be hidden so as not to use your knowledge for a frightful crime. In this way, Christ said in the Gospel, "of the day and the hour no one knows, neither the angels in heaven nor the Son", meaning so that He could reveal it to others. This is the constant interpretation of the Fathers. And this is precisely our predicament. Catholics are endangered as to their liberty, property and lives if they keep a priest in the house. Who would forbid them to avoid such a calamity by an equivocal reply? In these circumstances there are three factors to consider. First, the injury you do if you do not swear. Further, that you are not bound to reply on everything to everyone who asks you questions. Lastly, any kind of swearing is permissible if you swear truly, judiciously and justly. This is manifest in our case.'

Southwell was prepared to say more, but they shut him up with abuse and insults. They called him a boy, a Thraso,* an ignoramus who boasted the opinions of Fathers he had never seen. When asked his age, he replied that he had lived to the same age as Christ on earth, namely 33, and that his time, too, was running out. They also turned this against him, saying that he made himself equal to Christ. When he saw they refused to act according to reason or moderation, and turned everything to dissension and contumely, he addressed himself to the judge: 'As far as I am concerned', he said, 'I am ready to give an account of my words and deeds, if you will listen to me. If it is to be a matter of shouting and insult, we have no such usage. I have never said or done anything treasonable, contrary to peace or the Queen's dignity. I have submitted myself to be judged according to your usages. Pronounce judgment, then, as far as you can, according to any law that is just and consistent with fair play'.

The judge addressed a few words to the jury, and ordered them to retire once more to deliberate. They returned after a short interval, and declared Southwell guilty. He was asked, according to custom, if he had anything further to say in his defence. 'Only this', he replied, 'I ask God from my heart to forgive, in His great mercy, all those who have conspired in any way for my killing.' Sentence was then pronounced in the prescribed form. He was led away to execution two days later.

30. It was 3 March [1595] (new style). The day had
       scarcely dawned when the gaoler came to warn him,
after he had been awakened, that this was the day he must
die. Southwell embraced him warmly. 'Truly, you bring
me most welcome news', he said, 'I am sorry there is
nothing much left for me to give you. But take this
nightcap of mine as a token of gratitude.' The gaoler
treasured the cap as long as he lived, and refused to part
with it at any price. Southwell was now stretched on a
hurdle. His mind leapt for joy even more than his body
jumped about during the unusual horse-ride. Frequently
he cried out, 'Christ, my God, you give your unworthy
servant too much honour. You allow him too much
glory'. When he reached the death-dealing scaffold, he
raised himself up as far as he could. He greeted the final
cross which he had longed for even as a boy . . . As he was
led under the scaffold on the cart, he made the sign of
the cross, and addressed the crowd on a text of the
Apostle. They waited tense and silent for God. 'If we die,
we die in the Lord. Whether we live or die, therefore, we
are the Lord's . . .

'As for the Queen, I never wished or did her any harm.
I have prayed for her every day, and I now pray for her
again with all possible fervour . . . May she use and enjoy
the generous gifts God has given her to the undying
glory of His name, the happiness of the whole kingdom,
and the eternal welfare of her own soul and body. As
for the miserable state of my country, I think I could
weep in begging for it the light of truth . . . I see they are
urging me not to take up too much time, and so I surrender this soul of mine into the hands of my God and
Creator . . . I am not interested in what happens to my
body . . . I die because I am a Catholic priest, and because
I was received, while still a youth, into the Society of
Jesus. Nor was anything else ever brought up against me
during the three years I have been in chains. No one who
understands aright can possibly doubt that this death,
therefore, however unworthy and shameful it may seem
now, will achieve for me a share of eternal glory . . .*.

31. He made his speech, directed with much fervour to fervent spirits, in a way that moved his listeners to considerable sympathy. Even the Protestant divines, who interrupted from time to time, were eventually reduced to silence. Southwell, himself protesting, strove in a loud voice to cope with their importunity. 'Whatever these men say or do', said he, pointing at the ministers, 'I live and die a Catholic. All of you here who are Catholics bear witness to me in this; and pray for me!' Then recollecting himself, he got ready for imminent departure, praying in Latin with the utmost concentration of mind and body . . . After this, they drove the horses and cart away from the place, and once again he fortified himself with the sign of the cross . . . He hung still living for quite some time, beating his breast with his hand . . . In the end, the executioner, who had not adjusted the rope properly, clung to his feet and killed him. Some wanted him cut down still breathing, which would have been in strict accordance with the sentence. But the people prevented it. So did the magistrate who presided over the execution . . . Eternal happiness already seemed to shine in the dead man's face. Neither the pallor of death nor the bruising compression of the rope disfigured his countenance. His heart slipped from the hand of the blood-bespattered executioner; nor did it prove easy to burn . . .

Some considered it proper to mourn after his death the man whom living they tried to destroy. They even thought this a service of God. Baron Mountjoy certainly admired the steadfastness of the innocent victim. 'May my soul', he said, 'be with the soul of this man.' On two or three occasions, he forestalled some who tried to cut the rope while Southwell was still alive. And the bystanders admired Southwell as much as he did. No one smeared him after his death. None, contrary to usual custom, wronged him by word or deed. But the butchery now followed its normal course. His body was cut into four sections, and his head stuck on a pike. No one made a sound while it was done. So ended his drama. But there remained at least in Catholic minds the living memory of a man who seemed in all things perfect. His ability, judgment, and savoir-faire were certainly much above the ordinary. These qualities were further adorned by his carriage and physical aspect. Add to these his gift of oratory, while an intense desire to work and suffer for Christ animated and perfected all else in him. There was a wonderfully steady purpose in following out the principles of the good life he had made his own . . .

32. [An undated declaration is given here which illustrates, from his own hand, Southwell's extraordinary devotion to his spiritual vocation as a Jesuit.] *

33. In the same county of Norfolk lived the worthy and ancient family of the Walpoles. From it sprang Henry who added a martyr's glory to the lustre of his house. He was the first-born of a numerous progeny. Although he was born to parents whose ancestors included many of aristocratic descent, their chief pride was that none surpassed them in the sterling quality of their religious faith and Christian life. Henry was nurtured from childhood in Catholic tenets and principles of right living. When he was older, he gave such example of discretion and good sense that he could take the place of parents for his brothers. Three who left England when the time was ripe followed his example and joined the Society. He saw a fourth brother become a soldier under the Catholic King. After acquiring the elements of Latinity, Henry was sent to Cambridge to study philosophy, and spend four years in learning languages. After this, he moved to London to study civil law. As his wits were sharp, and he was an ardent devotee of Catholicism, he gave no less attention to the questions controverted by Protestants than to the study of law; and with such good results for his devoted efforts that, since he did not work for himself alone, in a short time he had added 20 adherents to the Catholic party. Some of them set out for the seminaries. Others began to live their lives according to rule of a kind. Or else they simply tried to persevere in living by faith in

their own homes. In any case, they spread the religion which they had embraced at his urging. Henry himself, meanwhile, did not influence them more by persuasion or book-learning than by the example of his own life . . .

Walpole was present when Campion had his dispute in the Tower with the Protestants on matters of faith. He was also present when Campion was tried for his life; and at the end, when he died for his priesthood. Henry was impressed by the firmness of a mind that was also humble. He noted Campion's modesty, although his victory over the Protestants was self-evident, at least to Walpole. He was impressed by the fact that Campion remained unmoved in the midst of insult and contumely: in fact, as dogged in suffering as he was invincible in dying. Admiring these strong points, Henry felt himself strongly drawn to follow his way of life. This gave him the first idea of leaving his own shores to seek out others where he understood that this kind of life still flourished. A Protestant magistrate's anger assisted this mood. The anger was roused initially by a hymn with which Walpole celebrated Campion's death. Rage was increased when the gentleman in question heard of Henry's sustained efforts for his faith: how he battled for the tenets of Catholicism and strove to make them known. There was also the special trouble he took with a near relative to win him over from the Calvinists.

This relative was Edward Walpole, whose father was a most diligent puritan. Edward absorbed the principles of this movement no less avidly than his parent. He was the eldest son, and the one his father loved most. Henry made the most of his acquaintance with Edward, which had begun with the alphabet, and of the young man's good-natured disposition and inborn intellectual honesty. Henry desired most intensely to put him on his own right path, and to pit himself against a system of belief which Edward had cultivated from his earliest years. This was founded on the example of his home life, fostered by obedience to his parents, and further upheld by the rigour of the law. All of which made it extemely difficult for light of any other kind to penetrate.

As it happened, Henry kept up a siege lasting two years, working on the other by intimate conversation, writing to him, and sometimes by showing him books. The most important of these were the *Confessions* of St. St. Augustine and Thomas à Kempis's *Imitation of Christ*. In the former, Edward came to understand that the great doctor was in agreement with the Catholics. In à Kempis he came to appreciate the four-square conviction of a man whom he earlier regarded as excessively superstitious. There followed Fulke*—a man of his own persuasion— and his reply to Cardinal Allen's book on purgatory, which showed a contempt common in Protestants for the ancient Fathers. It was a letter received from Henry that brought the contest to the desired conclusion.

Although he does not record the arguments he used, or the enthusiasm with which they were written, the letter had so much force that, when it was given to Edward as he sat at table, he got up at once and went to his room in a state of considerable emotion. He put off all doubt about embracing the Catholic faith, and drove from him the fear of offending law and parents. This had held him back. His parents took this issue of their son's conversion so badly that they laid a complaint before a relative in the Privy Council. Henry had to take to his heels in consequence lest he be imprisoned on the authority of a letter from Leicester, Cecil, Walsingham, and Cobham. He thought he would be able to hide for a time in London far from his parents' house. However, there was so much fear everywhere, and the hue and cry was so great that after spending a night in the open country, he decided to go northwards in search of a chance of escape overseas.

Walpole was fortunate in finding a ship well-provided with a crew and carrying no other passenger. This he turned to the best advantage, and disembarked at Le Havre . . . He followed the route from Rouen to Paris, and from Paris to Rheims. There he spent a year on theology, and then set out for Rome to pass another year in the English College. After that, he was received into the Society on 4 February 1584, being 25 years old. So intent was he on the delights of the spirit, that he took little notice of what happened to his body. It was not long before he developed a pain in his chest and stomach which, in the view of the experts, could be cured by no other medicine than a milder climate. He therefore returned to France, and finished the remainder of his training at Verdun. Having shaken off his illness, he went to Pont à Mousson for theology. He received the sub-diaconate at Metz, and was ordained deacon and priest at Paris.

33 bis Alexander, Duke of Parma, who commanded the forces of the Catholic King in Flanders, made use of the services of Thomas de Sailly,* Jesuit, as his spiritual director. His charm of manner and pleasant ways with people, unimportant and important, moved that God-fearing prince to bring in more of the men of his Society to act as chaplains in the camp. Men were specially sought for who were strong in mind and body, and had sufficient knowledge of languages to be of assistance to soldiers of many nationalities. Henry Walpole was proficient in the main European languages—French, Spanish and Italian—and was more than ordinarily endowed with wits, common-sense, and general knowledge. Appointed at the wish of the Jesuit General Claud [Aquaviva], he set out for Brussels. Walpole tackled this difficult task and its attendant dangers with entire concentration of his bodily and mental resources. He fulfilled the complete rôle of a hard-working religious. In the winter months, during which hostilities ceased for most of the time, he was sent to Tournai to do his year's tertianship. It is in this year that the Society tests its men for their final *gradus* in the Order.

While Walpole was returning afterwards to Bruges, he fell into the hands of a Dutch patrol, and was carried off to Flushing. The Dutch do not treat their prisoners-of-war unreasonably. Long experience, and the like necessity on

both sides, had taught everybody that individuals should
be treated in accordance with a soldierly convention.
While ransom money was being got ready, it was possible
for prisoners to spend freely as if guests. But Henry was
handed over, not to the custody of the Dutch garrison,
but to the English. This was engineered by men who
were soldiering among the Dutch at that time under
Leicester [1587]. They thought to indulge the cruelty
of heretic cavaliers in taking it out of an English priest
whom they regarded as a traitor to their country. They
not only believed that nothing they inflicted on him was
harsh enough, but they went about to get him quietly
murdered—they were actually prevented from doing
this by the justice of the municipality of Flushing. Among
the prisoners, they suborned a number of thugs who hoped
to deal with Walpole with impunity by night when he
was all unsuspecting.

Their cruel spite did not long remain hidden from
Walpole. He endured with great patience the necessity
which this situation imposed on him of staying on his
guard for months on end, sometimes only feigning sleep.
At times he had to get up suddenly from sleep to confront
those who came near him . . . Added to his troubles was
the fact that it was wintertime. So intense was the cold
of his comfortless prison that a Protestant captain of the
opposing side could not forbear to show his humanity.
When he visited him for the sake of old acquaintance,
and saw that he was covered with only a thin soutane,
which he had put on for his journey in the summer, he
took off his own silken doublet and put it on him. He
also provided him with means to put up with the other
harsh features of his life more easily. Meanwhile, news
of his captivity had got through to his father's house,
and stimulated his younger brother to see if he could
do something to help him.

Queen Elizabeth, in order to make things difficult for
the Spaniards, helped the Dutch cause with arms and
money. For this purpose, troops crossed over and back
again frequently. Among them was the captain who had

acted as gaoler to Henry. Henry's brother [Michael] attached himself to this man, and together with him crossed to Flushing. The brother-love of both was resourceful and diligent, and had its foundation not only in nearness of blood, but also in the loftiness of their Christian belief. After [Michael] had come to an arrangement for his brother's better treatment, he also pledged himself for the ransom. Part of it was scraped together in Flanders and part in England. After a year of these hardships, and when the ransom was paid, Henry returned to Brussels. He persuaded his brother to put away all thought of going back to his own folk, and to go on to Rome to join the Society. This idea he had conceived from Henry's own example.

He would overcome that fatal procrastination, the enemy of good intentions, by plunging into the enterprise as soon as possible after their happy parting. As things fell out, this proved to be the greatest reward of Henry's labours. Thanks to his own and his brother's deserving, the latter took his vows not long afterwards.

34. The chilliness of prison-life had not cooled the warmth of Henry's desire to endure hardships for the Christian cause. The difficulties endured on alien soil would, he thought, be even more fruitful and worthwhile in his own land. He never ceased reflecting and praying with this hope in view . . . General Claud [Aquaviva] used Robert Persons as his administrator for the English mission. Henry Walpole sent him frequent letters bearing witness to his profound yearning. Persons was then preoccupied with the new seminaries in Spain, and felt that outstanding men with good mental gifts were not less necessary for sowing the seed than in gathering the harvest. He summoned Henry to him with a view to sounding his abilities at first hand. Persons kept him at his side for two months at Seville, and for several more at Valladolid, where he is on record as having performed the offices of minister and confessor to the community. He had made a vow while he was attached

to the military in Flanders never to shrink from any danger
to life while he could do something to serve God. At
Seville he also declared to a familiar friend that unless
some other exceptional service for God presented itself,
he would do everything he could to get himself sent to
England. There in a short time he could accomplish
much . . .*.

35. Since he so earnestly invoked death, it is not surpris-
        ing that he left no stone unturned to get himself
sent over as quickly as possible to where death was to
be found every day by those who adhered to the same
principles . . . It so happened that the seminary recently
founded at St. Omer in Flanders through the industry
of Persons was seeking a subsidy from the king to tide it
over the interval before a maintenance-grant was assigned.
Flanders was overrun by the war being waged simultaneously with the Dutch and French. The taxes on
which the seminary fixed its hope were now insufficient.
Even the great piles of gold and silver which the king
supplied annually from the Treasury of the Indies seemed
inadequate for his government to fill the gaping gulf of
its expenses. Hence the business of administration went
slowly like a clock through many wheels. It almost came
about that a work which began well, thanks to the promp-
titude of the men at the top, was all but suffocated in
its swaddling clothes by reason of the sluggishness of
minor officials who put obstacles in the way.
      Peter Ernest, Count Mansfield, was Viceroy of Flanders
at that time, and enjoyed the widest possible powers.
Henry Walpole was therefore sent to the king, and
managed to get a letter from him to the count and his
lesser officials. In Person's opinion, none seemed more
fitted to finish the work begun in Flanders than the
man who had commenced so auspiciously with his Majesty.
The prospect of getting nearer to England was a factor
which spurred Walpole to his journey and the task to be
done at the end of it. The best enterprises usually meet
with many obstructions. Henry had scarcely put to sea

in the beginning of September [1593], when a fierce
gale blew up which put the ship and those in her in
extreme jeopardy. They shipped an enormous quantity
of water. On land, continuing silence, with no news of
their condition, was taken to confirm disaster. But Walpole
got safely to Flanders, although he was considerably
delayed. He laughingly dispelled deceptive rumour with
the merry quip that the man destined by fate to be hanged
could not be drowned. Walpole made his way to the
court without delay. He delivered the king's letter and
asked for an immediate grant of relief for three months.
This respite sufficed for him to inform Persons of
what he had done. Subsequently, by his authority, and
the energy of our other Fathers in Flanders, it proved
possible to settle with the king for the remaining items
sought for.

Walpole now did everything to speed up his departure
for England. The rumour that the English authorities knew
of his journey did not deter him. Nor did the plague that
was spreading through England. He further refused to be
put off by the short-tempered reluctance of the sailors
to take anyone over lest they be suspected of having
contracted the plague themselves, and so prevented from
entering other ports. There was a ship of Dunkirk which
was about to privateer off the coast of Scotland, and
was said to be on the point of weighing anchor. Walpole
agreed with the Spanish captain of this boat that he
should be taken on board with two companions, and set
down in any part of England where a landing was feasible,
whether openly or by stealth. Walpole then wrote to
thank Persons, as it were on his knees, for the fact that
he had been either author or intercessor so that he could
now fulfil his longing. Henry would disembark all the
more readily where danger loomed more threateningly . . .
He was to experience hostility even from the sea. From
24 November until 4 December, he was tossed about
by dirty weather involving wind and wave of every variety.
On the 10th day day he disembarked at Flamborough
Head in Yorkshire.

The Earl of Huntingdon was the Lord Lieutenant of Yorkshire, a man who was no less a lover of the new religion than proud of an ancient line which stemmed from kings. When he was told that a number of people had made a furtive landing, he sent some of his men to enquire. They ran into Henry at Kilham, fresh from the sea and now a vagrant in those parts. Since he was unable to give a sufficiently ready account of his journey, they conducted him, three days later, to the Earl of York. Landing at a place outside a port was suspicious in itself, but writers are not agreed on the man who first gave Walpole away. Some say that a lady saw him from the window of her house nearby. Others claim that another passenger who happened to be taken on board ship along with Henry was responsible; but his name is unknown to the present writer. Be that as it may, Walpole was delivered up to the Earl. Since it did not prove difficult to find out who he was, and why he had come, he was handed over to the custody of Topcliffe, the pursuivant, while due warning was sent to the Queen.

36. When they got know that a priest and Jesuit had   been taken, some Protestant ministers made haste to find out what the new guest was bringing with him. They asked him about the Church, tradition, the cult of saints, the priesthood, the sacrifice of the Mass, the sacrament of penance, the authentic call of ministers of the Gospel, and of Anti-Christ. Many things said by them less wisely, and with insufficient knowledge, only brought credit to the Catholic champion as he clearly vindicated tradition, the power of priests duly ordained, and the honour due to the saints, especially the Blessed Virgin. He also showed that the other doctrines of the Church were in accord with the written Word of God, to which alone innovators make their appeal, and of which alone a copy was given to Henry in prison for his use.

Walpole startled them in nothing more than when he told them, as they approached him, that he possessed the Catholic faith, and that he was warned by Christ to preserve his faith, once accepted, from false prophets who come in sheep's clothing . . . There was a profound silence for a while on the part of these six or seven men whose manner and demeanour showed serious purpose. At length Remington said, 'We have not come to teach you, but simply to talk with you in a friendly way about your good faith'. Henry was once his student at Cambridge University. He found it pleasing that in a colloquy of this kind they had only his welfare in view. He thanked Remington profusely, recognising that in many things he could still be taught by him. In theological matters, on the other hand, he had gone to school with other teachers; with those, in fact, most learned in Catholic faith . . . The dispute came to an end when a royal injunction arrived that the captive should be transferred to London . . .*.

37. In his letters [to Richard Holtby, Jesuit] Walpole describes much that happened in this prison.* 'Your letters', he says, 'are of the greatest comfort to me. But your presence, if only for an hour, seems more essential to me that I can express in words. I could then be told how and by what means I should deal with my adversaries. It is true, what is impossible for men is possible with God . . . If I was minded to write down all that has happened between me and my adversaries, I would never come to an end, and it would take up very much time. In my examination, I gave a lengthy account in writing of my life overseas; places, doings, intentions. I insisted that I had in mind only God's glory and the dissemination of our faith in all these things. With this in mind, I undertook the return to England. I had a great desire to bring back not only the people to Catholic belief, but more especially the Queen herself and the nobility of England. I openly proclaimed to them that I would be ready to attempt this by every means in my power, with God's grace. I refused to answer questions which touched

the affairs of others. When Topcliffe threatened, I said
that God would not allow me to admit anything from
fear of torture whereby I might offend the Divine Majesty,
my own conscience, and the innocence of third parties.
I have held frequent conference with the Protestants. I
sent all this in writing to the President [of the Council
of the North (?)] since I thought that in the last assizes
held in this city they would have tried me. I added an
essay of appropriate length on our Lord's theme, 'Beware
of false prophets'. One of the divines greatly complained
about me to the president because I had dared to put
such things in writing. But he was not able to refute
them . . . I marvel greatly when I see how near my lack
of merit is brought to the martyr's crown, as some, indeed,
persuade themselves . . . You, most dear Father, are caught
up in the conflict. I in idleness look on at the field of
battle . . . The president asked me who was superior of
the Society in this country. Topcliffe took it upon him
to say that he knew for certain, and named him. I beg
you to share this letter with my brethren . . .

'About half-way through Lent, I expect them to hear
my case; for the Council will then reconvene. Meanwhile,
I have a great opportunity to look to myself, and to await
with mind braced up whatever it shall please God to decide
for me. I beg you to add your holy prayers to my poor
efforts . . . I admitted in my examinations that I worked
for the increase of the two seminaries, that at Seville
and the other at St. Omer; also I thanked the Catholic
King for his exceptional kindness and generosity; again,
that I carried letters to the Governor of Flanders and his
secretary in favour of the seminary. I also insisted that
my actions looked to the good of others and for no one's
disadvantage. This is a summary of what I gave in writing
to the president, and Topcliffe who interrogated me. It
was signed by my own hand. Among other things, it was
enquired what I would do if the Pope happened to declare
war on England. I replied that I would think about that
when it happened. About this and similar matters, more
later . . .'.

38. There were certain Catholics there who, if he wished,
promised Henry their ready help in engineering his
escape. They made this plain through secret letters, and
begged him insistently at least to try it out. At first he was
afraid to lose the chance of martyrdom which lay so near
to hand, and for that reason refused. Before long, lest
he should appear too obstinate, or too much in love with
his own whims, he sent a messenger with a letter to Father
Richard Holtby, and left himself to his decision. For his
own part, he felt certain what he should do . . . Holtby
was struck by the hastiness with which so formidable a
project had been conceived, and after a little prayer
decided that all thought of flight should be abandoned.
This would be an act of outstanding goodness and singularly deserving. His flight, on the other hand, could seem
to not a few like defection from God and the crown of
martyrdom. It could lead his flock to ruin by the example
of a pastor who was afraid to meet death in so sublime a
cause. In any case, all should be carefully prepared beforehand, even if the flight itself were sudden. If he chanced
to be recaptured, his humiliation would be increased.
Finally, even if he escaped to a hide, it would certainly
give the adversary an excuse to begin a more troublesome searching-out of Catholics throughout the land.
This could well be the ruin of many of those taken,
thanks to weakness of purpose. Therefore he deemed that
flight should on no account be attempted. When he
received this, Henry replied by letter in the following
vein:

'I took your letter and advice just as if it had come
from our Lord. I accept it wholeheartedly. Rather similar
reasons moved me to the same conclusion. But what I
might do for other reasons, I was well content to leave
to your decision. For I would not wish to ignore the spirit
of the Society in deliberations of this kind, and I try to
conform to it whenever I can, even in matters which seem
self-evident. I know the angel helped St. Peter to escape
from prison. That befitted the dignity of pastor of the
universal Church . . . Any such consideration is absent in

my case, and therefore this prison remains my Rome and
my "Domine, quo vadis?" . . . The time is at hand not
to fly but to die. Indeed, as the matter is, so I will speak.
I do not see how . . . I could ever be more usefully
occupied, since here there are abundant and effective
means to remind me constantly of what I really am. Therefore, unless a voice from heaven should clearly indicate
the contrary—that is, the word of Christ through holy
obedience—I will not stir from here . . . And because, by
order of the president, five sheets of paper were given me
on which to write down the reasons for my belief, I am
rather more brief in this than I shall be subsequently with
you and with others. If I live, I shall, God willing, write
again about everything. But if I must die, God will provide
for everything more effectively than I can, and I will be
at peace . . . Oremus pro invicem.'

39. By such writings as these, and frequent meetings
      with divines, Henry gradually acquired some
influence with most of them, and a reputation for wisdom,
learning and sincere purpose. In order to defeat this,
Topcliffe and the president set themselves to entangle and
wear him out with fresh questionings. When they saw that
they were wasting their time, they had him brought to
London. Walpole was now forced to undergo a more
severe trial of his resolution than anything he had experienced since his journey began. Topcliffe was given the
task of bringing up the good man, and in accordance
with his savage and brutal turn of mind, he treated him
for the whole distance . . . as if he had already been
convicted of high treason. Topcliffe suborned witnesses
who insisted that Walpole had been responsible for plotting the Queen's death. He resorted so often to sheer
malevolence against priests that he himself lost face by
overdoing it; and so they may have hesitated to include
this among the charges to be laid against Henry. As soon
as Walpole reached London, he was thrown into the
Tower, and in such complete want that he had neither
mattress nor covering. Nothing was provided to protect

him from the bitter cold—it was February—and no food
to relieve his hunger. This exaggerated harshness moved
the Lieutenant of the Tower to pity, so that he ordered
a little straw to be brought to provide rough comfort
for the night. He also gave notice of the essentials Henry
needed in his wretched condition. Such, however, was
the spitefulness of Topcliffe that he not only shut off all
access to assistance of any kind, but by torturing him
most cruelly 14 times, put him beyond hope of helping
himself.

Just as the whole world is the wise man's native land,
so every place is heaven to the religious spirit. As well as
he could, Walpole wrote with a piece of coal or chalk on
the walls the names of the nine orders of angels, and above
them the names of Jesus and Mary, with the name of
God himself in the highest place of all. He did all this in
Greek, Latin and Hebrew. Beneath them all, he added
his own name, what had been inflicted on him in that
dungeon, and the reason for his suffering. He passed a
whole year in this way. The Queen's Council, wearied at
last, decided to summon Henry to their presence . . .
They determined to send him back to York so that, having
found no cause of death in him, it would not be their
responsibility if he were killed by others. Walpole showed
himself the readier to suffer the nearer he approached
his goal. Nor did he relax of his own volition any of the
harshness of life which his enemies' cruelty had forced on
him while at London. During the journey, he lay on
the ground to sleep. Back at York, a plaited mat of straw
three feet long became his only protection. Leaning
on this he passed a considerable part of the night awake
and in prayer. When nature was at length exhausted, he
stretched out on the ground to snatch, rather than take,
his rest.

Assizes were appointed for 13 April [1595], and
Beaumont, Hillyard and Ewens, as the judges, went there
in public procession. A great crowd of gentlemen and
officials crammed the courtroom to utmost capacity.
When it had assembled, Henry, weighed down with leg-irons

and chains, was put in the middle of several criminals to increase his shame. The clerk of the court cried aloud, 'Henry Walpole, raise your hand!'—a trial in England began with the accused declaring himself present, and in full view. After making the sign of the cross, Henry held up his hand. The clerk then proceeded. 'Henry Walpole, you are accused as an Englishman, born in Norfolk County, subject of our Queen Elizabeth, and the eldest son and heir of your father, of leaving the kingdom to go overseas where you assumed the priesthood by the authority of the Roman See. Subsequently, as a traitor and enemy of this realm and her royal Highness, you returned to England against the laws of her kingdom, and entered the township of Kilham where you were taken. Now plead! Are you guilty of these treasons and crimes of *lèse majesté*? Henry pleaded, 'Not guilty of any treason or offence against her Majesty'. The prosecutor: 'To whom, then, will you commit your cause to be tried?' . . .* After some initial hesitation, Walpole recommended his cause to God and his country.

At this point, the sergeant, Saville, began a long oration attacking Roman priests in general and Jesuits in particular, heaping upon them the odium for all the troubles endured by people everywhere, The first and gravest charge against them was that they tried to get everyone to subscribe to the religion and doctrine of the Roman Pontiff. Among them was Father Henry who had seen the Pope, and treated with Persons, Holt and other renegades. He had reformed, nurtured, and founded seminaries. Finally, by his own confession, all this treasonable activity he had undertaken against the laws of his country. Henry asked if he might be allowed to speak. Hillyard, the second judge, giving vent to his spleen, said that so outstanding a contriver of treasons should not be allowed to speak in so honourable a place. As he had admitted so many charges of treason, and his cause had been indicted, he should be sentenced even without his defence being heard. Walpole took exception to this. Opportunity to clear himself had never been denied to a man defending himself

on a capital charge, even the most shameless. Beaumont
allowed this; but he should be brief. Walpole exorted thus:

40. 'My Lords, I am accused on three counts: first, that
I am a priest ordained by authority of the Roman
See. Secondly, that I am a Jesuit. Lastly, because I
returned to my own country to win souls. None of these
things can be in any way connected with treason. As
for the priesthood, you yourselves will readily acknowledge that; nor does it apply to Jesuits, seeing they are
held in honour in every part of the world. No one, indeed,
becomes a traitor by reason of his priesthood or its
functions, but only by an evil designation very far from
priesthood. Nor can the bare fact of my coming home be
represented as treason, provided my return is harmful
neither to my country nor sovereign'. 'It is provided by
law', interjected Beaumont, 'that a priest who returns
from abroad without going before a magistrate within
three days to submit to the Queen's laws is to be held a
traitor'. 'Therefore, I am still untouched', countered
Henry, 'since I was arrested on the very first day I set
foot in the kingdom'.
    At this unexpected argument, the crowd was seen to
stir. Some approved, some laughed, some grew indignant.
Beaumont was merely confused. Ewens, the third judge,
tried to come to his rescue. 'Stop that double-talk', he
said, 'and tell us simply: are you willing to allow the
Queen that authority which the laws of England ascribe
to her? The presiding judge also intervened. 'Walpole,
look how generously you are being treated. We will allow
even so many and such great charges of treason to be
remitted after the simple submission prescribed by law.
If you reject the law's mercy, you must be dealt with
according to the law's rigour'. Henry replied, 'There is
no purely human field, not opposed to God, in which I
will not readily submit. But God forbids me to do anything whereby the divine honour might suffer the smallest
slight. As a faithful subject, I obey and love the Queen my
sovereign. I pray God daily, however, to enlighten her with

His Holy Spirit so that she may follow those counsels in this life which will bring her the glory of life eternal. Further, I call God to witness before all those in whose presence I stand, and especially my accusers, that no less than they, I desire for myself salvation, and fervent regard for the true Catholic faith outside which there can be no salvation'.

By these words, the people were seen to be variously affected. The presiding judge and Beaumont decided, lest the mob become excited, to hurry on quickly with the case. They briefly recapitulated the heads of the accusation, and turning to the 12 jurymen, ordered them to do their duty. After a short deliberation, they plainly declared that Henry seemed to them guilty. The latter, happy at this outcome, thanked God, and waited for his judges to pass sentence. But this was put off till next day. Walpole had his hands tied behind him once again, as though condemned to death, and was taken back to prison. The day after, he was vainly exhorted in his prison to spare his own life. He was again led to the court, and sentenced to the scaffold and customary execution for the day following. Alexander Rawlins was to be his companion in the same punishment. Henry, overcome with joy, fell to thanking the judges. He received very willingly the considerable number of people who went to see him. Quite often he actually fell to hugging Rawlins. They cheered, congratulated and encouraged one another to contest and victory. Furthermore, Walpole wrote to his father asking that, instead of the patrimony due to him as the eldest son according to the laws of nature and the realm, a sum of money amounting to £80 should be given to his guards to divide among them as a present. He signed his letter, 'Your most obedient son, Henry Walpole, prisoner'.

Walpole also wrote another letter to Holtby, the Jesuit, in the following sense: 'Since sentence of death has already been passed on me for tomorrow, I thought it necessary to commend myself to you and all our Fathers and Brothers. I do not doubt that in this my day of need God's

Holy Spirit will have anticipated my letters, and moved your hearts at this time, and those of all Catholics in whose fellowship I rejoice, to pray . . . that He may help my weakness, and strengthen me inwardly with the spirit of endurance . . . All the more because my sentence of death was directly on account of my return to England as a Jesuit priest. No cause on earth could be more glorious than this . . . As regards the vows of the Society—poverty, chastity and obedience—are they not the very same that are taken by all religious throughout the world? Were they not in the hearts of the Apostles as they took them for Christ Himself? . . . Why is this so very treasonable . . .?*

'Certain other matters have been brought forward, namely that I dealt with the King of Spain, and with certain others whom these people regard as traitors. However, they were able to substantiate nothing against me said or done traitorously. Nor did they persist in urging such things. There is therefore no need for me to reply. They pronounced with all eloquence that by force of the statute whereby priests who return to their country are held to be traitors, I stood condemned. I pray God, therefore, that my blood may not be imputed to their charge . . . Certainly, those who devised these traps to catch innocent men will pay an eternal price for it, if they did it on purpose, and after full deliberation, and depart this life impenitent. May God open the eyes of the Queen and her courtiers to see the evil and reform their ways . . .

'I cannot give an account here of my year's testing-time in the Tower of London, nor of many other things . . . This will do, then, written in haste as it is, but with much affection and heartiest goodwill. The time has come to bid my pen farewell, and to pray hard in the presence of Him for Whom I battle, until eventually we meet. I hope tomorrow will unite us . . . This Friday, the fourth in Lent, and so near the Lord's Passion . . . Amen' . . . In the event, Walpole suffered not on the following day, Saturday (8 April 1595), but the Monday after.*

41. When the longed-for day of dissolution dawned, the magistrate was at the prison. Alexander Rawlins was led out first, and at the gates of the prison he lay down on the hurdle on which both would be dragged away. He occupied the left side, saying that he would leave the right to a better than himself. Walpole was held up for more than two hours by a crowd of visitors. Some came to greet him. Other demanded his blessing and effective prayers for themselves. Yet others, on the contrary, were driven by perverse zeal to wear him down in disputation and questioning. He spoke with restraint and in honourable terms of the Queen, testifying his regard and obedient spirit towards her. He prayed that all favour and good fortune might be hers. For this reason, a number of them hastened to the presiding magistrate, and begged him to put the execution off. They were inspired by the delusive hope of shaking his resolution if it were delayed. The magistrate had no power to postpone execution even until next day, nor any hope that Henry would be tripped up by any indulgence or artifice.

In order to concede something to those who made the petition, the magistrate had Henry questioned as to what he would do, and what he advice he would give others, if the Roman Pontiff waged war on the excommunicated Queen. Walpole refused to be drawn by the malice of a personal question of this kind. He would never do anything wrong, he replied: nothing against his office or his conscience. The vain expectation of those who baited him were thus dashed. He was ordered to the hurdle. As Walpole approached him, Alexander welcomed him enthusiastically, and when he lay down, bowed to him. To deprive them even of the comfort they could get from one another's conversation, the officials made them lie different ways on the hurdle. Henry had his head towards the horse while the other was dragged along feet foremost. Hauled half the distance across the city, they arrived at the place of execution. Rawlins was the first to give an outstanding example of courage and fidelity on the scaffold. Walpole was far from being upset by the sight.

Going up spiritedly, he had already mounted the first steps of the ladder when the entire multitude sent up a cry for him, exhorting him to save his life while he still had it. All that was needed to save it was to go some way towards meeting the Queen's wishes, or to agree to a conference with her preachers. He replied he could not conform without fault even in the smallest detail that was against Catholic faith and practice. There would be no point in conferring with those who had talked with him the day before. As he had proved for himself, they had nothing substantial to offer. All he could do was to ask them not to go on making life difficult for him.

There were those who urged him in his extremity at least to consider charity and peace, and join with them in offering to God prayers for his salvation. He said he was already at peace with everybody. He was ready to forgive even those about to kill him, and begged God's mercy for them. To pray with them, however, he could not, since they were cut off from the Church. He besought and exhorted any Catholic present to pray that the rest might receive the light of true faith . . . and that he might persevere to the end . . . He then looked upwards, raising his hands as far as his chains would permit. From a step of the ladder he went through the Lord's Prayer in a clear voice. When he began to add a Hail Mary, order was given to push him off the steps. Shortly afterwards, the rope was severed, and they took up his body to cut it in pieces according to custom. The onlookers were so upset that the majority were unable to hold back their tears. All this happened at York on 17 April (new style) 1595, in his 36th year and 11th in the Society. The number of gentlemen present was so great that the like had scarcely ever been seen . . .

42. Next we must show what fruit was gathered by the surviving Walpoles from the tree thus cut down. As we have said, Henry had been to the rest like a father; and when the parents of Edward, his [cousin], discovered that he too had leanings to Catholicism they summoned

him from London, and by threats and promises tried to turn him back from what he had begun. He was handed over to different Protestant ministers to test his seriousness, but he rose superior to their threatenings and blandishments . . . Although at that time he was unknown to any Catholic priest, he persisted in the faith he had now taken hold of. Love and sorrow mingled with indignation contended in the hearts of his parents. Fear of the law prevented them from showing towards a son who professed the Catholic faith those affectionate attentions due to one's children. After trying vainly many ways to move him from his decision, his mother sent him off with many tears and eight golden crowns as a parting gift. She told him to go where he liked. The lady was well-grounded in earthy practicality, and hoped that when Edward was actually thrown out of his ancestral home he would have second thoughts. He would soften up out of nostalgia for his family—and his considerable inheritance, as compensation for which he only had now a handful of small change.

Edward Walpole, however, put everything in second place to God, and remained undaunted. He lay low for a time with a relative who was also inclined to the Catholics until a suitable day came for trying to quit the realm. He was discovered in the port, taken to London, and led captive before the Privy Council . . . It all became the occasion whereby Edward's late host was restored to his wife's company and bed. He had quarrelled with her a long time before, and now, overtaken by illness, he took the trouble to make his peace with God. Since he was dying without issue, he made Edward his heir . . . Richer by this inheritance, Walpole got leave from the Privy Council to travel for three years. Once a fortune has been uncovered, there are always people to covet. Edward's perseverance in the faith he had received, together with his long absence overseas, inspired in a certain person some hope of winning the Queen's favour. He hoped that Walpole would take Holy Order after the Roman rite, and then never return to his country:

or if he did, it would be easy to dispossess him. First of all, this gentleman successfully petitioned for authority to take over the administration of Edward's property as that of a fugutive. He then sought a verdict that he had adhered to the Queen's enemies and was guilty of treason.*

Walpole had not yet determined which profession he wished to follow. After three years, he returned to England, blissfully unaware of what malicious greed had contrived. He went to his brother, who was staying in London, and at first he was well received. A few days later, the brother changed his attitude, and warned him not to show himself in public. He could not conceal from the justices the appalling crime for which he had been pro-scribed by law. Nor could he allow him what was due to him by right unless he first cleared himself, and in obeying the law made himself a man whom one could assist without peril. So little to be trusted is nearness in blood when it comes to a crisis! When Walpole's return home became generally known, the greater part of the houses in Norfolk and Suffolk were searched, and with a great hue and cry, to find him.

Once again, Walpole went overseas. He first collected a certain amount of money, but was more concerned with preserving his faith and method of prayer than his inheritance. At Rome he occupied himself with higher studies, and was deterred from taking Holy Order only by his poor estimate of himself. While he expressed fitting admiration for the honour of priesthood, he saw nothing in himself that reached the level of so great a responsibility. But a decision that he hesitated to make himself, Providence put into his head on the way to Naples. A fierce storm blew up, and he vowed that when he got back he would put himself at the disposition of the rector of the seminary, and if he judged fit, accept ordination. He called on Richard Smith, his companion on that journey, to witness his vow. Smith was to be well-known later as the Bishop of Chalcedon. Edward Walpole . . . joined the Society of Jesus in 1594 when he was 33 years old. He was sent to Tournai, and after the novitiate there spent another two years at Louvain, Brussels and Antwerp in pastoral work. He went back to England, his old hunting-ground, where he worked on the mission for 40 solid years. He was companionable by nature, and a certain inborn integrity made him welcome to people of every kind. To keep his religion, he relinquished an income of at least £800 a year in our money [1660]. He also abandoned the name 'Walpole', and took another meaning in English 'pauper': this as one who was, and wished to be called, Christ's poor man. He was over 78 when he contracted his last illness, becoming troubled with a persistent bronchial condition whereby he gradually became unable to breathe. At last, after receiving holy communion, he begged for the annointing of the sick . . . Closing his eyes as if going to sleep, he died peacefully on 3 March 1637. He was professed of three vows in 1609.

43. The labours and trials of 40 years during the most difficult times of Queen Elizabeth and King James I could, no doubt, have provided a rich store of historical anecdote for our narrative had not the very dangers precluded the possibility of their description. During all this time no place was safe from the savage horde of pursuivants—no family, no house, not even the deepest cellar at any hour of the day or night. The priest, curled up in some corner of the house, could scarcely breathe, while parents could never be sure of adequate protection for themselves and their families even from their own servants. Everyone had to live in continual suspicion and daily fear. They rightly hesitated to commit to paper matters which could too easily fall into the hands of ill-wishers to the ruin of a whole family. Our men, then, had to live and die in twilight, with none to know all that they endured while they stayed in their houses or went their ways outside . . . Comparatively little escaping the common fire managed to reach Flanders or Rome. Little that passed from hand to hand was snatched from

final oblivion, except transactions which took place in open court. Such things sufficed to make this history something more than nothing at all, but not to provide the illustration its subject merited. The writer thought it advisable to point this out to make it evident to the well-intentioned reader who might want more, and more important things on some matters, whence the dearth arises. Let him measure the story not by its array of deeds and sufferings but by their cause. Now to return to Henry's brothers.

44. We mentioned one warrior [Thomas Walpole] on the King of Spain's pay-roll. Another, after he had helped his brother while he was a prisoner in Zeeland, followed his example and encouragement and joined the Society. This was Christopher, a student of Cambridge University, reconciled to the Church by the efforts of the Jesuit, John Gerard. He also helped him with the expenses of his journey to Holland. Christopher went to Rome and studied for a time in the English College.

He was admitted to the Society, at the age of 24, on 27 September 1592. He was sent to Spain but did not long survive the experience. He died at Valladolid in 1606 while spiritual father there. Richard Walpole, an elder brother of Christoper, proved an excellent theologian according to [John] Pits, although he entered the Society a year later than Christopher. For the most part, Richard directed the students' studies in the English colleges in Rome, Seville and Valladolid. Finally, he ruled the mission as successor to Joseph Creswell.

A certain Edward Squire went to sea with Francis Drake, the well-known pirate. When he was about to carry out raids in the West Indies subject to Spain, Squire was captured in a small ship, with other predators of the same kidney, and taken to Seville. There he was allowed to wander about unhampered; but he gave free rein to his tongue and behaviour, some word of which got back to the judges of the Inquisition. These got hold of him and put him in prison. After a lapse of time, they handed him over to the Carmelites for two years' detention in the hope of bringing him to a better frame of mind. Worn down by solitude, Squire pretended that he wanted to become a Catholic. He had Richard Walpole summoned to him. Walpole had heard much of his untamed temperament although he had never seen him. The priest was rather surprised by the sudden turn of events, and decided to go slowly and carefully. He made his instruction and questioning last many days. Squire complained that he was not trusted. He prayed and besought Walpole to hurry it up: what he had declaimed so bitterly against the Catholics, he said, was really no more than the accusations of those who had claimed with even more bitterness that he had said them. Such things did not correspond with his own meaning. In the end, Richard gave way. Leaving to God the hidden things of the heart, he accepted Squire according to his own confession and gave him absolution. Squire hoped by this stratagem to hasten his liberation. When it was not granted, he secretly made his escape before the year was out. He left a letter in his cell for Richard, making his excuses for going off without saying goodbye.

Although this letter came first to the hands of the Inquisition. It passed through them to Richard. Edward Squire found a ship at San Lucar ready to set sail, and went back to England. At once he renewed his sea-faring life, and sailed with the fleet of the Earl of Essex to harry Terceras [in the summer of 1597]. The reader will remember that at Campion's trial a certain Cradock said that he had been present at a conversation concerning a holy league to subjugate England by force of arms. In this case also, a not dissimilar fable was devised. When Squire got home, he approached a certain nobleman with a view to clearing himself of some suspicion in which he stood according to law since the tale had gone round that he had joined the Catholics. At the magistrate's bidding, he promised to be ready to say that whatever he had pretended to agree to with Walpole was all a joke. The unhappy man had not yet learnt that by whatsoever a

man sins by the same also Providence allows his punishment . . . It was claimed that one of the men who had
been captured with Squire had returned from Spain with
a letter. This letter, using involved language, indicated
that something was to be set on foot by Squire from which
many great issues depended. At first the letter was rejected
as a forgery. Afterwards, it seemed to others that a matter
of such moment was by no means to be neglected.

Squire was called home from the sea. He was examined.
He denied that anything of the kind had ever passed in
his conversations with Walpole. He was put to torture.
Overcome by the ferocity of his torment, he confessed
whatever the wiles of those who had concocted these
stories forced upon him. Thus he confessed to having
received some poisoned compound in a bladder from
Walpole. He was to have smeared it on the Queen's saddle
—this he could easily do by pressing the perforated bladder
on to the saddle. After moving her hand to her nostrils
or mouth in the natural way, the Queen would have taken
it internally, and so died. Nor was it enough for Squire to
say he had received it. He also had to confess that he had
tried it. This also was wrung out by torture, and in
addition, that whatever he had admitted he had signed
with his own hand.

45. When all this got back to Walpole himself, his first
reaction was to laugh at it as the idle imagining of a
lunatic. Then, informed by a series of letters that the affair
was related in earnest, he wrote a letter beginning with
the words of the great Athanasius—'In a voice loud and
clear and with my hand stretched out, I take an oath . . .
that this whole accusation is false. I further protest . . . on
the word of a priest that none of the things objected against
me ever entered my head. I am fully persuaded that this
protestation of mine will amply suffice to convince everyone of my innocence, whose conscience has not been
hardened . . . I will add a few circumstances here to make
it clear that the whole accusation is a trumped-up story

devised by those who do not care how much evil they say
or do provided they damage our Society.

'First of all, then, so slight was the acquaintance between
myself and Squire that he did not even remember my
name properly. For in the accusation I am called William
where I should be Richard. I suppose that those who
fathered this crime on to me will be ready to admit that
I have a brain of some kind. What man, then, having the
slightest degree of common sense, would dream of com-
mitting so grave a matter to a new acquaintance and a
person altogether unknown? This, moreover, was a man
who could be justly supposed capable of betraying a
promise and, indeed, of pretending anything in order to
escape. Added to which, he asked again and again that, if
he should return to England, I would recommend him
to some Catholic who kept a priest in the house. Since he
found I trusted him too little for that, how could it be
supposed that I would confide in him to bring about so
prodigious a crime? Again, he is supposed to have said,
among other things, that I ordered him, should he feel
any hesitation in perpetrating such an outrage, to visit
a certain doctor held among the secular priests in prison.
He named him [Dr. Bagshaw]. Now they also say that
I told our own people of this matter. Why then did I not
send him to our own men rather than to that doctor
who is renowned all over the island as having no love for
the Society? No doubt Divine Providence saw to it
deliberately that something patently absurd should be
mixed in with the rest'.

Finally, there was Squire's first denial, and then, after
five hours' torture, his withdrawal of this admission at
an examination. Again, there is his protestation repeated
before the justices, when his head was at stake, that he
had neither accepted poison, nor attempted any harm
in England against the Queen. All of which shows a man
caught in toils laid by the guile of others. Now he turns
this way, and now that, to get himself out. Although
nothing of all the things he said could be taken as fact,
tossed about on the waves of fear and hope, he eventually

perished by his own irresolution. For although his inquisitors had only wrung from him by torture a confession signed by his own hand, they appeared to inflict a punishment that was not unjust for a liar. But by a torment that was true enough, they attached a shadow of truth to so much falsehood. In this way, the name 'Jesuit' would never be free of odium in the eyes of the people. In this way, also, by guile or gold on the part of men in power, the lives and reputation of others entirely innocent were made sport of . . . and thrown away for purposes preconceived.

46. The entire tragedy was, indeed, a hollow sham apart from the death of Squire which was real enough. Whether it was all concocted by the same Squire to ingratiate himself with the government when he entered the country, or whether it was foisted on him by the witnesses, Stanley, Munday, and Rolle, certainly, there are many factors to help one to a conclusion independently of what Walpole observed. Those who favour the idea of conspiracy say that Squire did not simply escape from Spain, but that an exchange was made with some Spanish prisoners, and in this way he departed. But it is plain from his own letters that he slipped out secretly. Then, they say, when Walpole saw that Squire would not attempt anything in the way of assassination, the Jesuit gave permission to someone returning to England from captivity in Spain to reveal the matter to the government and denounce Squire. As if, indeed, Walpole would have been so careless of his reputation that when he was able to keep such a misdeed hidden, and with nothing to come from it for himself but considerable disrepute, he would allow it to be revealed to a casual traveller. This man, to whom the matter was supposed to have been committed, did not say that he was sent, or allowed to go with that object in view, but that he had stolen from the room certain letters which he carried with him.

It is difficult to make a string of lies hang coherently together. I have not been able to read without wonder—or should I say indignation?—certain things in the report of a man who was on the scene while these things were taking place. When Squire was on trial for his life, he plainly insisted on the fact that he had been torn by five hours of most cruel torture. Thus he had confessed things never said or done by him simply to free himself from the appalling barbarity of his torments. The State prosecution claimed in the same place that he had never been submitted to torture. I leave the solution to the reader. This much seems very clear to me. The affair from beginning to end was carried out with the most blatant collusion of all parties concerned.

Rolle, meanwhile, with whom Squire had got away from Spain, was held close prisoner in the Tower. For if Squire should deny that he had any talk with him about these matters, the capital sentence would be jeopardized. A freer hand was allowed to Stanley and Munday, who were known to be informers, in saddling Squire with any crime they wished. Which artifice is not uncommonly employed by those who think no ugly deed unbecoming provided they can gain their ends. All this took place while Walpole was stationed in Seville.*

END OF BOOK THE FIFTH

BOOK THE SIXTH

1.   [From 1592 to 1594, and 1597], Mutius Vitelleschi
      ruled the English College, Rome.* He it was who
later governed the whole Society for 30 years. He was
a highly cultivated man, and very acceptable to the
Catholic world for more reasons than one. But for all
his pleasant manners and soothing balm, the bitterness
felt towards the Fathers of the Society by certain students
could not, it seems be sweetened. A dubious ideal of
liberty had engendered this attitude among them at that
time. It had been encouraged by the secret malice of ill-
wishers, and strengthened by the fact that it it had lasted
many years. Claud Aquaviva, on the advice of his assistants, was seriously thinking of giving up the management
of that house. He was unwilling to abandon a responsibility once assumed, but without consulting Persons,
he wrote to Spain for further observations, giving an
account of the advice which he had already received
(29 October 1596). Dr. Barret, President of Douai College,
also came to Rome at that time to see if he could do
any good by mediation. After making informal enquiry
into the causes of so much ill-feeling, he offered Pope
Clement the fruits of his experience. He prefaced it with
many things about the good done by the Society for the
English clergy, which they could scarcely conceal or deny
without base ingratitude. He declared that through
quarrels of this sort the religious situation had deteriorated
disastrously; and this was the common opinion of
Catholics everywhere. Only a limited faction of mal-
contents disagreed with it. He thought the situation
had, in all, eight causes which he wrote down on 10 April
1596, and gave to Persons.
    First of all, with the death of Cardinal Allen, studies
had taken a subsidiary place, and the students had become
involved in politics. This was partly in order to get

283

someone else raised to that dignity, and partly because they were intent on getting wider faculties and privileges for themselves. When they found the Society would not go all the way with them, they first reacted with anger, then hatred. They formed factions which looked on the Fathers with jaundiced eye as opposed to their cause and country. The aim of some of the groups was to get the Society out of the college altogether, and its goods administered in the name of the Congregation. They also held out hope to certain of the students that if they joined the insurrection, there would be jobs, rewards, and an easier sort of discipline.

At this point, some were admitted to the college whom [Barret] himself had turned out of the Rheims seminary as trouble-makers. Without injustice, one individual was strongly suspected of dissimulation in coming from England to make his submission. His intention was merely to deceive the unwary behind a mask of piety. The greater number [plures] were, indeed, accepted haphazard out of misguided sympathy, in view of the régime[in England] without any proper examination of their suitability. False rumours about the quarrels between the [secular] priests and the Jesuits in England had, moreover, filled many ears, word of the controversy becoming swollen to enormous proportions. The same faction that had intruded itself in Brussels against the Spaniards, and those who favoured the Spanish crown, insinuated itself also into the seminary. It had support from people who were far from unimportant. Since these matters occupied minds given to the easy life and a good time, it was hardly surprising if, with juvenile energy pushing them, the younger element rushed on to worse things still. Unwilling to put up with any discipline, they wanted to throw over the yoke completely. They were further encouraged by the number of those who agreed to join in, and also by a certain feeling that pardon was now out of the question. Strengthened in their conspiratorial resolve by an oath, they determined to push matters as far as they could rather than go back to any beginning.

2. Barret laid these things before Persons at a time
    when the doctor's journeying to Italy was most
opportune. It was then the way was providentially opened
to reconciliation among the dissidents since six or seven
members of a really obstinate clique had been removed
by death. Claud, the General, then setting out for Naples,
turned the whole affair over to Persons's sensible kind of
piety to look after. He could bring no less benefit by
restoring peace than by founding the college in the first
place: and so Persons entered this thorny business . . . He
put in extremely hard work at his prayers, and made daily
dedication of his toil on behalf of a favourable outcome.
So with the utmost assiduity, he carried out whatever
affection united with wisdom, and sternness not unkind,
could devise by way of remedy. When the gendarmes
picked up some students in a tavern, he got them to agree
to fixing up some cells in the college so that they would
not be carted off in manacles. After that, the culprits
were examined by Accarizio, a canon of the Lateran and
papal attorney. They were found guilty of various squalid
misdeeds, and no less than 10 or 12 were ordered to be
sent away. Persons, however, got them a new suit of
clothes and money for the journey. In the end, the very
men who had ignobly ganged up against him found themselves approving and thanking him for the fact that, with
no word said of former misdemeanours, and with no
heavier punishment, they were allowed to depart with a
certain dignity.

Persons was able to do much subsequently by encouragement and persuasion. He even found praise for some of
the students' own ideas. Already he enjoyed considerable
authority in the Society, and, for the most part, with
leading men. To these advantages he added cheerfulness
of manner and expression, along with a most praiseworthy
prudence in his undertakings. So he was able to bring it
about that those who remained accepted willingly all
that was decided for the future not simply by his decree
but as if he were carrying out their own advice. They also
wrote to General Claud (on 17 May 1597) that nothing

seemed more likely to establish and preserve the longed-
for peace than Persons's prolonged stay among them. In
this way, the man who had restored quiet, and put an end
to ‧quarrelling, by his savoir-faire, moderation, gift for
work, and human kindness would be at hand to confirm
it all for the future . . . Doctor Hill and Doctor William
Gifford, Dean of Lille (in letters of 15 May and 10 July
1597 respectively) both blessed the Deity for sending
Persons in the place of Allen, like Joshua after Moses, and
David after Jonathan. Peace lasted many years. Although
restless spirits afterwards tried to overthrow it, it was by
no means invariably disturbed. But however great and
excellent the success of these efforts to rekindle the right
spirit, it could not be said that the prestige of the priestly
vocation, application to studies, and concern to develop
sound patterns of behaviour, were completely restored
to what they had been.

3.   Persons's journey to Italy was seen to have another
       cause by those who immerse themselves in politics,
and interpret the ends and acts of rulers and ruled by the
tendencies of their own thinking. They were well aware
that Philip II was always ready to listen to him. So much
so, they thought, that when Persons urged or advised
anything at all, it would be willingly accepted. Whatever
he sought he would get without difficulty. They knew
that he had received financial assistance for his journey
to the tune of 500 gold crowns. With the death of
Cardinal Allen, they began to look about for another man
of their own nation to supervise English affairs in a
worthy manner. They were not behindhand in trying to
bring it about that the honour should go to an enemy
of the pro-Spanish party. They were well aware that the
king was not sleeping on the problem; also that he
preferred Persons to any other. With the example of
Cardinal Toletus before them, who had been raised [as a
Jesuit] to that dignity in 1593, it was not difficult to
persuade Pope Clement to put the universal interests of
Church and Christendom before the particular institute

of the Society. And then Persons's good qualities, capacity
for work, enthusiasm, experience of public affairs, and his
widespread renown in all the courts of princes were well-
known throughout the Christian world. This knowledge
served to get going more than a superficial rumour that he
would soon be appointed to the College of Cardinals.
Indeed, some of the Spaniards did not hesitate to exalt
him at that time with the age-honoured title of *'Illus-
trissimus'*.

As soon as word of this got to Flanders, Oliver Manare
and Richard Gibbon, out of concern for the Society's
institute, begged Persons by letter not to allow himself
to be carried away by compliments of this sort from the
way of life which hitherto he had pursued so laudably.
Oliver addressed him thus: 'Reverend Father ... The time
has come for your Reverence to give evidence to the whole
Society, and the world itself, of your integrity and sincerity towards the same Society. When Cardinal Allen
died [16 Oct. 1594] our English gentlemen, priests and
seminaries, laboured no little that you should receive
the Cardinal's hat. With this in view, they got letters from
leading men—the Duke of Feria, and perhaps the Archduke
himself—to his Majesty, his Holiness, and various cardinals.
They also added their own petitions to the Pope sent from
different localities. A movement was also set on foot
with some of our men to turn attention to the most
reverend Bishop of Cassano. It would very much better
serve your Reverence, England, particular individuals
and the seminaries, that you should remain as you are, a
plain religious, rather than be promoted to the dignity
of cardinal. For in the latter case, you would be much
less free than now to maintain contact with all types of
Englishmen, understand secret affairs, and prescribe what
is necessary for individuals, and those with secret com-
missions. Neither could you beg alms from rulers, nobles,
prelates, ecclesiastics, burgesses and merchants, as a
cardinal. As it is, you can do this freely without offence
to any, being a private man and covered by religious
convention.

'You could not change the heart of those hostile to the Catholic faith as you do now. You could not catechise, visit the sick and imprisoned, or go to private houses, or meet English people arriving at the various ports. Finally, you could not administer the sacraments as you do now, and for the maximum benefit and good example of all. You would be obliged to shift your whole attention to church politics, financial affairs, and your own establishment. This would be over-burdened in view of the small income, numerous servants, pilgrims, and poor more numerous still; and there would be the yearning to help them all. How could the honour of being a cardinal help the seminaries? You would have, I would say, an income of 8 or 10,000 ducats. How far would you get in supporting so many people, helping the seminaries, and maintaining a household with the proper decency?

'We put all this to you for your consideration, and we can show that his lordship of Cassano already has a ready and certain income; a greater one than good Cardinal Allen enjoyed. These considerations do not move those good people, for reasons well-known to your Reverence. Your honesty, humanity, knowledge of English affairs, kindness to all, so wins them that they will not listen to any advice but yours. It therefore remains for [you] to do what you would have done without my advice, and to act with complete selflessness, lest the door forced ajar be pushed wider open, and give larger access to some man's ambition. Be careful, however, to see that they do not manage things surreptitiously with the king. Do not let them bring him to the decision which, even if it might help the Society, would not help the common good of the Church and the realm of England. For as his sense of duty is most strong, it is to be feared that he will allow himself to be persuaded. I am quite sure of this, though; there is no one in the Society who can protect it from this misfortune more easily or effectively than your Reverence . . . Brussels, 24 November 1594 . . .'.

4.   Persons was at Seville when he received this letter.

I have not discovered his reply to Manare, but when he sent on his letter to General Claud, he added one of his own:* 'Very reverend Father in Christ . . . That I have written more rarely and briefly to your Paternity these last few months has been caused partly by ill-health, and partly because there was no business of great moment to write about. I have now, thank God, nearly recovered from my quartan fever, even if I am not yet altogether free of it. Further, a very serious matter is now to hand, and so I felt I should write at greater length. After the death of his Eminence, Cardinal Allen, vague rumours began to get about in these parts that a cardinal's hat was in the offing for me. It seemed to me at that time more a case for a smile and a shrug than resistance; for the idea appeared to have no adequate foundation or author. In any case, the matter seemed to be one I could scarcely mention or speak of without embarrassment, lest what I said by way of dissipating the smoke be taken as an intention to fan the flame. However, when I discovered later at Madrid that the topic had come up in the conversation of quite a few people, and was not unheard of even at Rome, I felt myself to be concerned more deeply. Two or three days later, as I remember, I got Father Oliver Manare's letter, of which I send your Paternity a copy herewith. By this I was gravely informed that the matter was being pursued by our Englishmen in Flanders, or at least the good Father thought so—others have more recently written the contrary. So I felt it altogether impossible to stay silent any longer, at any rate to your Paternity . . .

'Firstly, I can most truly assure [you] that the very mention of this subject has been repugnant to me in the extreme. Nothing, indeed, could be further from my way of thinking than that I should be transferred from this steady kind of existence to another sort of life so very different. As I am, I see myself doing at least a small something for God's service . . . and the general relief of my most afflicted motherland. One must admit, that

other life is in itself noble, good and praiseworthy, yet I
feel in myself no aptitude or inclination for it; nor have I
the strength to meet its demands. Having considered the
matter carefully . . . I must say, I think that all the draw-
backs which Father Manare enumerates are most true,
and they would have their effect on our pledged cause
if I were to give up my present way of life. The Spanish
seminaries and those in Flanders would suffer setback.
If now I can give something to individuals, living another
kind of life, I could not be so available. My work is
altogether more useful to my country and countrymen as
it is now—supposing it is useful—than it would be after the
fashion that some would like to thrust upon me . . . Since
all this is most true, I beg your Paternity most humbly . . .
to strive to avert this peril—if any exists. For I have as yet
no certain news. What should be done to bring this about,
your wisdom will best decide. I merely thought it advisable
to bring it to your notice and affectionate concern . . .
Seville, 20 February 1595 . . . Robert Persons' . . .

5.   Persons's attitude becomes much clearer from reading
       a letter of his to Sir Francis Englefield penned some
months later. Englefield had been very intimate with
Persons long before this. He was an out-and-out Catholic,
and altogether devoted to the interest of the Catholic
King. Persons considered him entirely worthy to be raised
to the College of Cardinals, and hoped for it, since he
would be a staunch ally. He had been a member of Philip
and Mary's Privy Council, and was a man of mature judgment, always at hand for any good venture. He had all the
equipment called for in a cardinal. He himself wrote
frequently to Persons asking him to make his mind known
to the Catholic King about finding a successor to Allen.
Persons at last agreed. He wrote to Don John Idiaquez,
a most trusted member of the King's Council, and
explained to him how urgent and necessary it was,
especially at that time, and the qualities with which the
candidate must be endowed. If he should ask subsequently
who were the men suitable, he would refer him to Joseph

Creswell. For one thing, he knew Creswell, and that he was most observant of the Society's rules. When Creswell found out that counsels of this kind were being exchanged among the princes, and that their eyes had fallen on Persons, he replied, as was his custom, in cryptic phrase: 'God is not so short of material that when he wants to make a new suit He has it made from a rough old overcoat!'

Persons was reluctant to name anyone since it seemed to him that among the first to be suggested was Englefield himself. For the sake of their old friendship, however, Sir Francis asked Persons not to let his name be mentioned in this context. After he had acquainted Englefield with all this, Persons told him what he felt about himself as follows:

'I have set out to deal with you plainly and in confidence in this letter. I will go even further and reveal my mind unreservedly . . . First, as you well know, even if the well-being of the whole world depended on my promotion to this dignity which you desire for me . . . I could neither wish nor strive directly or indirectly for such a promotion since I am bound by vow not to seek it . . . Secondly, putting ambition aside, no doubt one could take pleasure in such an advancement, or even long for it. I feel quite free, as I trust, on both counts, and thank God for it. Many attractive ideas occur to one from time to time concerning the great things that fall within the competence of a man in that position. But I say in all sincerity, it seems to me that my present mode of existence is good enough. More especially is this so when I consider more carefully the deceptions which ideas of that sort seen from afar bring with them, and I ponder the uncertain outcome and the dangers and troubles ahead which could be mine in such a way of life. My life is secure enough, and full of compensations; also for me more productive, and perhaps for others. I say all this, bearing in mind certain projects entertained for many years past; such as going through the towns and villages of England teaching the catechism.

'This must be done if England is to be redeemed in my time. I have so little taste for that other way of life that I cannot even bear to think about it, much less hanker after it . . . What is more, I am interiorly drawn . . . to the conviction that this kind of life is, indeed, God's will for me, and not the other . . .

'There follows the third point which you must readily concede . . . It is not only a matter of keeping a vow that I have made, and showing myself faithful to my word, which would suffer by such promotion. I must also beware of danger to my own soul, which ought to be dearer to me than the whole world—indeed, than many worlds. For as we see, entering on dignities of this sort can be gay and pleasant enough, but leaving them at the end, difficult and full of sadness. Nobody noted this more carefully than myself, perhaps, in the case of our late good cardinal . . . If the dignity should be imposed on me by an authority I cannot resist—I hope this will never happen—I also hope that in that case it would be the divine will. It would follow that sufficient grace would be given to sustain the burden for God's glory. The more sincerely one tried to avoid that burden, the more in excess of the task undertaken would be the grace given. This, as we have read, happened to many great servants of God in former times. Here, then, you have all I can say or think on this subject . . . Keep it to yourself, if you please. It is only because I have been worn down by your importunity that I have written this to satisfy you; unless you think it should be shared with any of your intimate friends such as Fitzherbert &c. [*sic*] . . . 10 May 1595'.

6.   You can see how sincere Persons was in this, and quite untouched by any thirst for honours. He got to Rome at the turn of the year to find the rumour gaining ground as it got more talked about. Immediately, he went to the General and the Assistants, saying that he was ready to leave the city at once and secretly, or accept as swiftly anything else they cared to suggest. They

persuaded him to see the Pope and make his excuses,for
he had been told of the reasons why he should reject
that other advice and course. The matter was controversial and beset with difficulties. What if the Pope should
reply that nothing of the kind had entered his head? What
if he should interpret Persons's modest withdrawal as
masked ambition? And if he should think him lacking
in discretion? If he rebuked his haste? What if the king
should think himself rather set aside, with so many marks
of his kindness slighted, if the Pope could come to no
decision without Persons's promptings? Some men, who
were eager hunters after the honour, would say that a
man showed a miserable and abject spirit who preferred
to be blown off course from his greatest hope rather than
do his best to run before a favourable wind to the haven
of this exalted dignity. Persons himself regarded all this
as trivial, provided the danger did not touch the institute
of the Society. On the other hand, it seemed to be prudent
and more advisable to make trial of the ground rather
than by delay allow room to confirm a decision. If the
Pope and king reached agreement, it would be too late
to save either the Society's loss or Persons's integrity.
Since the king admired the Society's institute, it might
not be unwelcome to him to take a stand in some way
on its behalf.

On a day assigned to him according to routine, Persons
approached the Pope and recounted the kind of talk which
was gaining ground in Rome, Spain and Belgium. He
explained why he thought his future work would be more
useful to England if he did it in the kind of dress he wore
rather than scarlet. The demands of the position, keeping
up with competition, various offices and business of all
sorts, would set up an impossible barrier to the sustained
effort which the present state of England called for. Every
day, heretics published many things that were false,
blasphemous, and harmful to the Catholics. All this
demanded a quick and ready pen. It was by the advice
of the late Cardinal Allen himself that he had hitherto
adhered to a programme of writing and working for the

afflicted Church in England. Persons could only beg with
unassuming pleas that he might continue with it. He would
consider it among the greatest benefits possible if, by the
Pope's great favour, he could be allowed to sail his accustomed seas, avoid uncharted waters and nameless reefs.

In reply, the Pope praised the institute of the Society
which cut off the path to coveting honours. He said that
he had received nothing in writing from the king; it was
better to deal with casual talk by ignoring it than by
attempts at suppression. He was pleased with the writing
and other work in which Persons had so far been engaged.
He should hold the same course in his studies for the
future.

In this way, striving for a better reward than any this
world had to offer, he would find God and himself
favourable. Nor would he be lightly interrupted in what
he had so happily begun. This answer gave General Claud
satisfaction, and Persons the respite he had sought from
the untimely chatter about promotion.

7.   Since honourable mention was made of [Thomas]
Fitzherbert in Persons's letter to Sir Francis Englefield, it will be in place to describe at this point what
kind of man and how great he was. He, too, was named
by Persons among those worthy to succeed Allen in the
scarlet. Fitzherbert entered the Society many years before
he died, and among other offices, presided over the English
College, Rome, for a considerable time. His rule was most
peaceful.

Born in Staffordshire [in 1552], he could claim distinction by his ancestry. This distinction he augmented
by his achievements in almost every field of learning,
and added the ultimate embellishment in his sound
character and sturdy devotion to the faith of his ancestors.
He took a wife of equal status, and became the father of
a family which he looked after with no less care for its
religious education than for the maintenance of his home.
When Campion and Persons arrived in England, he received
them cordially and entertained them generously. Later

on, there was a vigorous inquisition for people who would not go to the Protestant churches. Penalties were inflicted on absentees. All were obliged to conform to the law at least in outward appearances. In fact, it was hoped that by regular attendance the minds of Catholics would gradually be induced to think in ways which were anything but Catholic. At all events, the treasury would be filled with the fines of those punished for non-attendance. Fitzherbert was among the first to repudiate this kind of subterfuge and contempt for real religion. He not only stayed away himself, but published reasons why all Catholics should absent themselves, unless they wished to put in jeopardy belief itself and all proper respect for God.

Catholics were not attacked in this way alone. Suspicion was sown in the popular mind of Catholic conspiracy with the Pope and the rest of the princes to invade the realm and disturb the public peace. Leading men, therefore, were coerced, either by imprisonment, or confinement to their own houses and a few miles round about. Something of this kind happened to Fitzherbert. Although he was of the most inoffensive disposition and entirely stable, he was obliged to put up with continual intimidation and harassment. In the end, he bought his freedom and [in 1582] went overseas. He settled first in France, staying there as long as there was any hope for the Queen of Scots. She was then in close confinement in England, but could look for support from the King of France and her relative, the Duke of Guise. At last she died by gross injustice, Fitzherbert's own wife by natural necessity [in 1588], and the Guises by horrible murder. Fitzherbert then transferred himself to Spain. There he did much at the king's court to support the cause of Catholicism in England. At length weary of secular affairs, and desiring a calmer way of living, he departed first of all to Milan with the Duke of Feria. He then went on to Rome, and after taking Holy Order [on 24 March 1602], gave the rest of his life to God and the Church in prayer and writing. He took a place not far from the English College, and governed his own time-table by the college bell,

getting up, praying, going to bed, eating, studying—and
being so careful to exclude distractions that he never
allowed a window which looked on to a house across
the street to be opened!

It was here that he first published his work in Latin
against Machiavelli on the theme, 'Does crime pay?'. This
was a learned work as well as devout. He then published
two books in English on much the same thesis, teaching
that the good citizen or statesman could be of no use to
his country if he did not couple his proceedings with a
true sense of religion.* Subsequently he wrote, 'What
is the true religion?'. Both works were based on numerous
authorities and sound arguments confirmed and illustrated
by examples. In 1613 he openly assumed the dress of a
Jesuit. He then ran the Brussels mission for two years,
and wrote on the controversies of his day, as Alegambe
records. Fitzherbert afterwards filled the post of Rector
of the Roman College for nearly 22 years. Although he
could not altogether prevent the troublesome pranks of
his restless adolescents, however kind and considerate he
tried to be, he was able to keep them within bounds. By
sending some away he managed to keep peace among the
rest. He glided peacefully to his death in his 88th year,
dying on 17 August 1640. The man's memory lives on
to this day, and not only among Catholics . . .

8.   *'I, [Thomas Fitzherbert] am 62 years old at the
      time of writing this, the son of William, and of
Elizabeth Swinnerton, both Catholics. I was born in
1552 . . .'. [He goes on to say that, even as a small boy,
he showed a strong religious sense. While studying at
Oxford as a lad of 16, he attended Protestant sermons.
His confessor connived at this.] He 'was an old man not
very learned. At Oxford he kept out of the way to avoid
the persecution'. [He told Fitzherbert that he could
attend such sermons provided he] 'merely intended to
listen and not to learn. Indeed, at that time, very few
Catholics stayed away from the sermons even if they did
not remain for prayers'. [What he heard drove Fitzherbert

even more strongly towards his own faith. He made no attempt to conceal this, defending his beliefs against Protestant divines, and confirming Catholics in them. Consequently, he was obliged to go into hiding for two years. Eventually he was arrested and imprisoned.] 'It was then that the Fathers Campion and Persons came to England. I joined them, and acted as their executive as far as I could.' [The hunt grew more insistent, and Fitzherbert fled overseas.]

At his wife's death in 1588, Fitzherbert made a 'general confession' to a Jesuit, and after it a vow of chastity. In 1601, while in Spain, he made a further vow to become a priest. On 2 February, the year following, he 'put on the dress of a priest'. On the vigil of the Annunciation he was ordained, and sang his first Mass on the feast. It was not until 15 August 1606, however, that he bound himself by another vow in St. Mary Major's, Rome, to become a Jesuit, if the General would accept him,] 'On 8 September, I was received by him in his room after dinner in the presence of Father Persons. It was thought to be more in the interests of God's glory and the service of the Society that I should neither go to my noviceship nor change to another dress for a time; but Father Thomas Owen, then minister at the English College, was assigned to me as superior. In his presence, I took the three vows of the Society. Relinquishing all I possessed, I tried to observe all the rules of the Society, as far as I could outside its colleges or houses: which meant its prayer times, examination of conscience, spiritual reading, renovation of vows, and giving an account of conscience. Every letter which I wrote or received I showed to my superior; and I spent not a farthing without his particular or general leave, as the same Father can bear witness who is still rector of the college'. [Fitzherbert seems to have been entirely contented in his vocation, and as he himself plausibly claimed and described, enjoyed mystical experience.]

9. The internal discipline of the seminary priests destined to be sent into England was the concern of

concern of their immediate superiors. From the time when they first began, however, a certain general supervision had been entrusted to Persons. Aquaviva wanted this, and the Pope agreed to it. In this way, the man whose labour had brought such substantial aid to Catholic England on the verge of foundering would be able to foster and perfect his work by continuing interest. For most of these years, Persons's efforts were crowned with success. Vindicated by the growth of Catholic faith in the island, Claud conceived the idea that Persons, already rector of the Roman seminary, would effectively establish his authority in every field if he were named Prefect of the English Mission. This headship affected only the Society, more especially its subjects in the seminaries, and in England itself, and Englishmen distributed through its various colleges. Through them, however, it influenced all others who belonged to the seminaries or worked in England, as far as was appropriate. From the beginning of 1590, this supervision was extended for the first time to the seminaries at Valladolid and Seville. In 1596, it assumed the form which lasted and flourished for nearly 30 years; until the beginnings of the newly-erected English Province, in fact. Rules were devised whereby the superior or prefect in Rome, and the vice-prefects in Spain and Belgium, could come to agreement among themselves. With provincials and other superiors they could co-ordinate their efforts for promoting the welfare of this important mission. It seems worthwhile reproducing here a copy of the rules which were ratified in 1606 . . .

'The Office and rules of the Prefect of the Missions both for governing the Mission of the Society, and also the English Seminaries which for their administration are placed under the regimen of the Society.

'Claud Aquaviva, General of the Society of Jesus, to all Provincials, Rectors, and other superiors and religious of the same Society who have occasion to work on the English mission, greeting . . .

'Since the English persecution has been prolonged beyond what was expected . . . and since the Holy See has seen fit to provide by all ways and means possible against the diminution of facilities provided by priests; and lest Catholics, placed in so many dangers, be deprived of the benefit of the sacraments and other ecclesiastical ministrations, it has seemed good to us . . . that these things, in view of the same, should be brought to the notice of provincials, rectors and all other religious of our Society . . .

'We have it specially in view that this mission be stabilised, at least to some extent. Thus our share of a work for many years far from unfruitful, committed to the zeal of the Society by order of the Apostolic See . . . will be advanced towards the goal set before it, as far as this can be done without detriment to other provinces. Therefore, this English mission is to be governed after the manner of a province. At the same time, on account of present persecution, it is scattered among various provinces of our Society, and could not on that account be completely and simply administered by any one provincial. Many things crop up daily in the English seminaries entrusted to the management of the Society calling for solutions which cannot be easily, conveniently or promptly dealt with by [local] provincials and rectors because they are not of the same nation. Matters of this sort include recruiting suitable young men from England, recognising them when they come, distributing them properly in the different seminaries, changing them from one to another for reasons of health or study, or even sending them away altogether. There is also journeymoney to be apportioned and paid out, direction of missions, determining those to be sent, and a good many other items which must all be dovetailed for the glory of God and the maximum advantage of England.

'All these things call for special knowledge of the English scene and particular concern for it. We have therefore seen fit that, quite apart from the care and benevolence which the said provincials and rectors of seminaries exercised in dealing with the English enterprise, some Fathers of our Society of English nationality should be joined with them to share their interest and work. He should be our lieutenant for the more efficient administration of the missions and seminaries, just as we are accustomed to put other provinces under immediate superiors for their better administration. Let provincials and rectors accept by this arrangement not only advice but actual help to lighten their own burden in many fields. We prescribe for him the following rules for the sake of guidance.

'First then, it will be the special care of this Father, who may be called Prefect of the Missions, to see that suitable young men are called at the right time from England and neighbouring places to enter the seminaries. In this way, they will never be short of an appropriate number of students, whatever the difficulties of the times and efforts of others to frustrate them. In order to do this more effectively, he will need to know the ways and means used by others before him to make contact with young Catholics. He will know certain people who can safely be trusted in England, Scotland, Ireland and Flanders whom he may use secretly for this task. He must see to it that all young men coming over, whether by his invitation or for any other reason, are carefully screened either by himself or some other English priest of the Society to obviate fraud or subterfuge. This examination will be according to a prescribed form. Those found suitable, making due allowance for the judgment of rectors and consultors, will be admitted by his arrangement, and similarly removed if need should arise. He must observe what is prescribed elsewhere for the prceise manner of admission. They are to stay in the seminaries; nor shall any scholar once received in a seminary transfer to another or be received in it unless he has letters patent from the prefect.

'The prefect will be much concerned to foster harmony and mutual esteem among the seminaries, removing in time, as far as he can, all pretext for quarrelling and rivalry. He must show himself just and impartial in his dealings with students and in making any kind of distribution which could touch the honour of a college or the convenience of a seminary. We leave it to the judgment of the prefect, making use of the views of rector and consultors, to decide anything concerning courses of instruction in the arts, theology and moral theology; also the number and qualifications of students taking them in any of the seminaries. It sometimes happens that rectors disagree about paying journey-money, or taking students in exchange from one another. The prefect must resolve the difference with all kindness. He must understand that a large part of his office consists in this, namely to solve prudently all the difficulties which can arise among different nationalities, or servants, or students, or even the rectors themselves. He must always warn the provincial when something of more than ordinary importance arises.

'This Prefect of the Missions will be appointed by the general on whom responsibility for the overall welfare of the seminaries devolves, as also the conversion of England. The prefect will be immediately subject to the general since none of the above concern any one provincial; nor can the prefect take up his permanent abode in any one place. If in Spain, he can stay, as affairs demand, at Valladolid, Seville, or sometimes even at the king's court. Whenever he stays in one of our provinces, however, he will be subject to the provincial in everything touching him personally, observing provincial customs and all to do with everyday activity discipline in the Society. He must acquaint the provincial with his principal business, as will be said later. At the same time, he cannot be held up by the provincial in anything that touches his own specific duties. Nor can he be employed in other business without prior consultation with the general.

'Although he is not subject to the rectors of seminaries with whom he stays, he must show them all proper respect, and give them precedence. In such seminaries, he himself will have second place, and be considered a member of the community in both [English] seminaries.

He must not interfere with the régime laid down by rectors, or with day-to-day administration. If, however, anything important in the seminary seems to him to call for reform, he must deal privately with the rector or provincial. He must proceed in this with commonsense and tact so that he no way diminishes the rector's authority with the students, servants, or even externs. He should not easily allow himself to become involved in domestic quarrels if they arise, but in the ordinary way leave it to the rector to settle them. Indeed, he must look especially to the wider needs of the seminaries, and help the rectors to keep things running smoothly, seeing how he can promote good order, good life, and sound studies for the students. He must also—the most significant item, perhaps —look after temporal needs, the discharge of business and building up the missions, as has been indicated.

'For these reasons, the rectors will be very glad to have the prefect with them in the seminaries, and for as long as he can stay with them. They will treat him in all things with the utmost consideration, and share their intentions with him freely, whether in his presence or absence. Nor should rectors or provincials, while dealing with matters involving the seminaries and students, easily allow themselves to do anything of weight without first consulting him; nor proceed in the teeth of his opposition unless they have had the prior consent of the General. This holds especially in what concerns contracts or building about to be undertaken. Likewise, if they wish to make major changes or innovations in anything previously laid down or generally received in the seminaries. If anything is to be introduced for the first time, it should be done circumspectly. It should not be done without first hearing the consultors of the seminary, and having the agreement of the Prefect of the Missions himself: this to avoid the many disadvantages which usually accompany frequent change.

'As far as the temporalities of the seminaries are concerned—which the prefect must especially look after— the rectors must be sure to make a confidential report to the Prefect of the Missions on the state of the colleges fairly often; and this quite apart from the account they are accustomed to give their provincials once a year. They must give details when he requires it of receipts and expenses, indicating or explaining the same. In this way, he will be in a position to offer them more timely help in their needs, as far as he can. In making payments or authorising the same, they should listen willingly to what he has to say, and follow it. If they do not, he must warn the provincial who will apply an effective remedy.

'Since the very foundation of the seminaries and the upkeep of the entire English undertaking depends in a special manner on the royal favour, the prefect will need to go often to court on behalf of the cause. He will determine if either he himself, or some procurator on his behalf and approved by the General of the Society, should take up residence at court both in Spain and Flanders. Without making mention of the necessities of particular individuals, as far as possible—brotherly love should not always be denied even to their needs—he should deal with overall necessities, having regard to the furtherance of the whole Catholic cause, and especially that of the seminaries. He should share his information, as far as circumstances demand it, and he can do so, with the provincial when at hand, and should follow his advice in dispatching business whenever he can. The expenses which the procurator or the prefect find necessary, whether for themselves or in response to requests from different places, should be spread over the seminaries as the prefect sees fit, if they cannot be supplied from somewhere else. This applies whenever such expenses concern the common good of the seminaries, including the cost of journeys which the prefect may carry out on behalf of mission business. He must take care, though, that the seminaries are burdened as little as possible in this way. Rectors, on the other hand, must make ready and generous allowance for what is reasonable and necessary. Nor will they have regard merely to the good of an individual seminary. Again, rather must they keep in mind the Catholic cause as a whole for which the seminaries have been founded.

'Transfer of students from one seminary to another for purposes of study, health, or anything else, is the affair of the prefect, although he should hear what rectors and consultors have to say, when this is called for. This must also be understood to apply to English members of the Society who live in the seminaries, but after previous consultation with the provincials from whose provinces they have been called, and to which they are destined. Because the English seminary of St. Omer in Flanders is to be understood by the terms of its foundation as subject to the Spaniards, the Prefect of the Missions will have the same powers and the right to stay in that seminary also. In his absence, he may appoint an English priest of our Society, having the General's approval, to act as his deputy. He shall conduct himself towards the Rector of St. Omer's, and the rector towards him, in the way explained above. The rector shall also give frequent account to the Prefect of the Missions, in Spain or wherever else he may be, of matters that concern that seminary. The prefect must send on information of everything to the General. In this way, thanks to their closer harmony and common strength, the cause of Catholicism may be promoted through the seminaries. All that has been said here about the vice-prefects in Spain and Flanders must be understood to apply completely to the Jesuit superior in England, to a rector or superior, or the master of novices and noviceship living in Flanders, so that a uniform system of subordination may obtain for all situations everywhere.

'In accordance with the above, the prefect will be allowed to distribute the alms he has solicited sometimes to others, and even to English Catholics in exile if they need it, and his judgment finds it expedient. When extraordinary donations are not forthcoming, he shall have the right to take something from the ordinary income of the seminaries. This he may also do for the journey-money of Jesuit Fathers sent into England, or summoned out of Flanders, Italy and elsewhere. All these things, after all, impinge on the common good of the Catholic cause. For general purposes of this sort he will also be permitted on occasion to entrust money to others, keep it himself, or distribute the same at his discretion, especially those gifts which donors have made to him at his own request.

'When he thinks it desirable, the prefect may summon students whom he thinks suitable from St. Omer's to go to the seminaries in Spain. Nor must those in charge at St. Omer's call them back, or send their young men elsewhere without the express consent of the prefect. For it was the principal intention of the Catholic King in founding St. Omer's, and of those who nurtured and promoted that enterprise, that a suitable posterity should there be reared for the Spanish seminaries. They should be sent on to Spain in due course. As for the expenses demanded by the Spanish journey, the prefect will decide how and how much for those leaving St. Omer's, and what is to be exacted from the other seminaries for which the scholars set out.

'To engender a proper spirit of unity among diverse nationalities, and also to ensure an adequate supply of information on things and persons so that students can be treated with greater understanding, courtesy and consideration, the Prefect of the Missions will see to it, as far as he can, that some of the priests of the Society of English blood, good example and tried goodness, are allocated to each seminary. Thus men will leave it better prepared to go to English mission stations. To get this done more smoothly and in good time, the prefect should deal opportunely with the General on the subject of persons most suitable. In the care of the sick and similar preoccupations of the seminaries, the brotherly love of our Society must be exercised towards the students. Any suitable English coadjutors of the Society, of proved goodness, who chance to be in the various provinces, and who understand the language, customs and needs of the students, should be put to the task of looking

after them with the proper gentleness and care. They are
to be summoned to the seminaries alongside the lay-
brothers of these establishments. Nowhere can they
serve God or the Society more effectively, or give their
labour more usefully. The prefect should deal with the
provincial of the province where the seminary happens
to be about these matters . . . The latter should give him
willing ear, and provide generously and in good time for
the needs of the seminaries. For it is a matter of the
utmost importance that . . . the seminaries be run by men
of suitable character.

'The residences for English priests at San Lucar and
Lisbon . . . were founded in these years, and are decidedly
essential and timely for the English missions. They are not
subject to any of the Spanish seminaries, but serve all
the missions. It falls to the prefect to supervise them,
and ensure that they are staffed as occasion demands by
suitable priests. He may move the same, and send them
on the missions, or recall them to the seminaries, as need
arises . . . The prefect shall also be deemed the superior
of the student while they are in our care, and of English
religious of the Society already appointed to this mission.
He shall supervise those who are occupied in the affairs
of this province [*sic*], and their administration, in England
or abroad, in the seminaries, residences, or anywhere else
for any purpose, if they are engaged in the work of this
mission. He will be able to grant them all that the Holy
See by its authority has granted us, and which we have
committed directly to the provincials and superiors of
other provinces for them to communicate and dispense.
Provided always that they be subject to provincials and
rectors in everything else that concerns common discipline
when they find themselves living outside England . . .

'At the beginning of the year, rectors must send the
vice-prefects lists of all the students of each seminary,
and of English members of our Society in them, with
notification of age, class, studies and abilities, according
to the custom of the Society. They themselves may use
their own judgment as to whether any further observation

should be made, and forward the same to the prefect. They must also write him a succinct summary of the economic as well as the spiritual situation of each seminary. It must be written on separate sheets so that they can be inserted in a book to be kept here, on each college, for the sake of information as need arises. The number of scholars needed in each seminary, of priests ready to be sent to England, together with their names, characters and attainments must also be written on separate sheets for the records. They must not enter on new undertakings or appoint rectors—especially at college expense—or enter on more important contracts—particularly if they involve debt or raising a mortgage on seminary property—without first consulting the prefect. Moreover, rectors and other Fathers, especially the English, should write to the prefect at the commencement of each year a short account in Latin of the principal events occurring in the year just completed. This must be in addition to what rectors and consultors of colleges are obliged to write to us. Let them write what they think essential, so that, if necessary, they can be shown to us.

'These are the arrangements which we have decided to make and acquaint you with for the present. Whatever we determined before on different occasions concerning this office of prefect must be understood as clarified and ratified by these rules. Time and experience will instruct us further. Meanwhile, we offer the above for the observance of the Prefect of the Missions, of those who act for him in the provinces, and also of rectors and provincials. We hope that those responsible for this mission will be encouraged and helped in a fatherly way to do this great work for the glory of God . . . From Tivoli, 15 May 1606. Claud Aquaviva.'

10. Fortified with this authority, Persons set to work zealously to promote and increase efforts for the mission. He took special care to maintain peace lest the over-demanding nature and caustic attitude of the quarrelsome cause enthusiasm for the common purpose

to lose warmth. First of all, he got a papal rescript which ratified and commended to the students careful observance of the rules of the seminaries. Indulgences were to be granted to those who observed feast-days with exceptional devotion. He saw that all the rooms of the students were provided with good meditation manuals properly adapted to the vocation and way of life of secular priests . . . Later on, Thomas Worthington was appointed to succeed Dr. Barret, President of Douai, at his death [20 May 1599]. Worthington was a man in complete sympathy with the society. Other lovers of peace were appointed with him, men as far removed as possible from parties and factions. Further, a Jesuit of worth, living in one of our colleges, visited the seminary every week to hear the confessions of the students, and by exhortation and advice to stifle quarrels immediately they arose.

Finally, so that there should be an adequate supply of books at hand for his fellow countrymen to nourish their religion . . . Persons bought a printing press for St. Omer's with all the accessories. He entrusted it to good Father John Wilson, who had been his secretary in Rome, who would publish the books he received. The precaution was also taken, following the custom of Jesuit provinces, of appointing revisers to look through manuscripts before publication, and send their written opinions to Rome. In this way, truth would be expounded in sound arguments, and provocative speech avoided, it was hoped. Even more important, any indiscreet handling of public affairs would be eliminated lest religion itself suffer setback from the exasperation of principalities and powers. In former years, the Protestants left no stone unmoved to undermine the dignity of the Roman Pontiff, and do away with the veneration in which he was held, for they derived their origin from hatred of the Holy See. Lest England appear to owe as much to the Romans as the Catholics preached, some of their apologists tried to show that the faith in this island was derived in the first place not from Rome, but Greece.

Persons showed how groundless was the above fable by writing a history of England (*A Treatise of Three*

Conversions of England from Paganism to Christian Religion [St. Omer, 1603]), to show that it was thrice converted to those rites which the Catholic and Roman Church always cherished and always will . . . To this he added a refutation of the calendar, or list of martyrs, which John Foxe had previously drawn up . . . Persons produced a work which was a last word; none of his adversaries ventured to reply to it. Scarcely a year went by without something from his pen, or without someone producing a book propounding his views. They brought great advantage to the Catholics, and confusion and compunction to the heterodox. The net result was that the attitude of the more intransigent was mitigated, while the evils which threatened them were removed from the innocent. Our men exerted themselves no less in England itself.

11. While Persons was drawing up his plans in Spain in 1588, John Gerard was allotted to the English vineyard along with Edward Oldcorne. (Gerard was known in Flanders as John Tomson.) He was born in Lancashire of Catholic, upper-class parents. Gerard began his studies at Oxford as a boy of 15, but being unwilling to take part in the Calvinistic celebration of the Eucharist at Easter, he left the university. He stayed at home for a time, and then crossed into France. At Rheims, he heard much about the Society from a man who had been sent away from Rome for health reasons. Gerard therefore transferred himself to Paris in order to learn more of that kind of life. He also wished to take up Latin studies more seriously so as to follow the philosophy course at Clermont College. In his very first year, he contracted a serious illness. When he recovered, he set out with Thomas Darbishire, whom he took as his spiritual director, for Rouen and Father Persons. Gerard told the latter of his keen desire to enter the Society. Persons expressed his admiration for the good disposition of the young man, advised him to convalesce and return to his own country for a while in order to settle things with his friends.

Gerard complied. When he tried to come back at the end of the year, he had to put up with five days' buffeting by the wind which eventually drove him into Dover. He was taken to London, and handed over to his maternal uncle, a Protestant, and then to the Bishop of London, to bring him to another frame of mind. The case was brought before the Privy Council when it was evident that the others had wasted their time. Gerard was put in charge of the captain of the guard for safe keeping. Next year, he was subjected to a fine of 800 crowns, but was able to leave England a free man. He hastened to Rome in the company of William Holt, recently come from Scotland, a future rector of the Roman seminary. By his and Persons's advice, Gerard's effort to join the Society was circumvented for a time. Meanwhile, he prepared himself for very speedy ordination and the next life almost simultaneously, so poor was his health. He heard the lectures on subjects drawn from moral theology. Gerard also served at different times in the seminary scullery, looked after the guests, and did other unspectacular tasks in the company of others with the same object in view as himself. In this way he would not be ignorant of those things which the Jesuits used to test their novices.

A little before the Spanish fleet set sail against England, Gerard set out for Rome with Cardinal Allen's permission and the acquiescence of Claud Aquaviva. He was received into the Society by Aquaviva on 15 August [1588]. One remarkable thing Gerard did was to persuade an apostate priest, originally from Lorraine and a former royal chaplain, to give up his concubine, his reliance on an illicit income, and to reassume the good life. He carried to his bishop the letter Gerard wrote begging pardon. Passing over his activities at Rheims and Paris, we note that Gerard came to Eu. It was open to him, thanks to Persons and Aquiviva, to enjoy a more tranquil existence in the seminary there, but he took ship with Oldcorne and two priests from the Rheims seminary. The latter were subsequently martyred in the north. Gerard disembarked one rainy night towards the end of October. He left his companions, and adopted the rôle of a falconer looking for a bird he had lost. Wandering through lonely places, he thus eluded any watchful eye. Providence in this way sent him by a difficult route to Norwich. There he got new clothes and a horse from a Catholic gentleman, and made his way to London. He reported to Henry Garnet, superior of the Jesuits, for instructions.

On that initial journey, Gerard did not escape danger simply by his own resourcefulness . . . After the first sleepless night spent in the open under the rain in chilly autumn, he had to spend the following day wandering about without food. On the second day, not far from Norwich, he was brought before a local squire for examination. He was, as it happened, in the church listening to a sermon, and ordered Gerárd to be fetched inside. The latter refused to go in. 'What!', they cried, 'don't you want to hear God's Word? This is not the way to get yourself favours! Go in!' Gerard remained obdurate. At length, when the sermon was over, the man came out in some irritation. Looking far from pleased, he asked, 'Where are you from, and why are you here?' Gerard said what seemed necessary for his reassurance, claiming that he was in that place for no other reason than to look for a lost bird belonging to his master. But the gentleman asked him many questions about the house where he was staying, and what he did with himself. In the end, he decided to present him to the justice of the peace. Gerard pretended not to mind if that was unavoidable, but his long absence from home called for haste rather than more delay. The magistrate would be doing him a kindness if he allowed him to depart without further trouble. Admittedly, they were untrusting times, but if he set out for Norwich by a direct route, surely nothing could be suspected against him.

The official gave Gerard a close scrutiny, taking in every detail. Suddenly, he changed his mind. 'Be off with you!', he cried. 'God knows, I would not want to make things difficult for a man who looks genuine enough!' This was the first step to safety. When Gerard came to go away, a man on horseback was on the road some distance ahead of him carrying a pack.* Gerard could not catch up with him even by hurrying. However, the rider's pack fell off. [He stopped to pick it up] and Gerard was able to overtake him. From this man, Gerard learnt much that would be useful if he ever again stumbled into watch or sentry. From him Gerard also got to know of a suitable place at which to say not far from the city gates. It was after he had stayed at this inn a short while that a Catholic of the old persuasion arrived who had endured much for the sake of his religion in the neighbouring prison. He it was who introduced Gerard to the gentleman from whom the priest got his first suit of clothes and horse so that he was able to go to London . . .

Gerard returned to Norfolk at Christmastide. He made Catholics of the brother and two sisters of the man in whose house he had been first received . . . One of the sisters had a very difficult confinement. She was despaired of by the doctors. Hope was held out that health might be restored by Viaticum and the annointing of the sick Within the half-hour . . . she was not only confirmed in the religion she had so recently embraced, but her unlooked-for-recovery persuaded her wondering husband, when he knew the facts, to become a Catholic himself. The other sister, struggling to find the right path to heaven amid so many sects, eventually consulted a well-known savant of Cambridge University (Doctor Pearne). Although he was a Protestant, he whispered in her ear that while she could live more comfortably in this life in the faith which the Queen and most English people professed, if she wanted to make sure of the next, she should die a Catholic. This careful lady, on Gerard's advice, decided that so important a matter was not one to put off to so hazardous a moment. What subsequently happened to the doctor might also occur in her own case . . . That gentleman, delaying the first step along the road which he knew led to Eternity, went to a splendid dinner on a certain occasion with a bishop of the establishment. Pearne dropped dead. Thus he found himself far from the closing scene which he had, no doubt, rightly told the lady would be a happy ending.

Gerard brought back to the Catholic Church more than 20 heads of families in this area, and a very considerable number of less exalted people. He kept open house, so to speak, to all—necessarily so—and stretched himself to the utmost in maintaining a way of life which considered everybody else's time, interests and individual approaches. So it was that, at the right moment, he came across a young gentleman, heir to vast possessions, who had conceived the idea of making the spritual exercises. In order to finish what he had begun with the same man's help, this gentleman got Father Garnet's permission for Gerard to live with him. The responsibility of his previous charge was given to another priest, and Gerard's own timetable thus became more stablised, his studies systematic, and his excursions only at intervals.

Among the results of preaching the spiritual exercises, of which Gerard was a completely convinced devotee and very painstaking, was the birth of a vocation to the Society in Thomas Everard, William Starkey [vere Thomas Wiseman], and Robert Standish [vere John Wiseman]. The latter pair had the same mother but were known under these names to preserve their incognito. They set out for Rome, and were admitted to the noviceship on 26 May [1591?]. Robert did not complete a year in the novitiate before being called to the angels at the age of 21 [1592]. He was a young man of the highest promise. After studying philosophy and the humanities at Cambridge, and nine further years as a lawyer, William sold his valuable estate, and handed over to Garnet £1,000 English. He completed the novitiate, and studied in our college in Rome. To prevent his death from a wasting disease, he was sent to Flanders, but could not get the better of his complaint. He died at St. Omer [1596]. His reputation was not less than the sorrow of all who knew him.

Thomas Everard caught a similar infection but managed to throw it off. For many years, he was minister and procurator at St. Omer's and Watten. He then became socius to the master of novices at Louvain. He was already getting on in years when he carried out his ministry in Norfolk, making circuits through the countryside on foot. The effect of work was added to that of years, but he lived to more than 70, and died a good death. He was a formed co-adjutor from 1613, and after that, endured prison and the hardships of exile. In his later years, he could scarcely read, or even move about thanks to weakness of limbs and eyes. When there were none in the house with whom he could converse, he was accustomed to wile away his loneliness by the continual recitation of the rosary and other prayers, especially the Jesus psalter, which he used from boyhood. The small portion of life left over from apostolic toil he spent in translating spiritual books from various languages. Although our Father Alegambe compiled quite a long list of them, there are more of his surviving works which have not yet been published. He was opposed to every kind of bad habit, but especially to idleness and taking things too easily . . .

Starkey's brother [William Wiseman], whose family was considerable in number and fortune, also succumbed to the exercises.* Starkey prompted him, Father Gerard conducted his retreat, and the good results lasted for many years. [William Wiseman] brought over these Protestants from a mixed household of Catholics and Protestants. This made for peace and safety. To increase the general atmosphere of religious harmony, he gave Gerard as companion to an old priest whom hitherto he had looked after himself. When his previous host was called away by Garnet, Gerard made [Wiseman's] house his third pied à terre so that he could be nearer London, and thus more readily poised to spring to the Society's service. There he introduced frequent recourse to the sacraments and sermons, the practice of mental prayer, examination of conscience, and sometimes spiritual reading aloud during meals whenever the party felt disposed to listen. In order to keep all this going as long as possible, and with maximum freedom from danger, he did not mix with everybody—apart from members of the household—but only with some of the more outstanding Catholics and those whom they felt essential. Nevertheless, opportunities were not lacking for reconciling others to the Church, putting a polish on some by getting them to meditate, sending others abroad for their studies, or to enter religious communities, and finally travelling through areas at some distance from London to hold the Catholics to their faith. In this way, he sent the second daughter of the Earl of Northumberland to Brussels, who subsequently founded the convent of English Benedictine nuns in that city.

At fixed times, Gerard met Garnet to renew his vows and give an account of his conscience; from the performance of which duties, as he said, he emerged greatly heartened . . . What Jesuits devotedly vowed to God for their perfection in the religious life, they repeated twice a year in the presence of witnesses. These two occasions have always been considered of the utmost importance in the mission from the time it was first set up. The meetings have always been held although with prudent avoidance of the risks which usually accompany such reunions. It was not always possible to meet without real danger. Gerard tells how he was once the ninth or tenth to arrive at Garnet's when the question came up as to what should be done if the pursuivants arrived at one of those awkward moments when they were not prepared for them. Garnet said, 'Until the actual renovation of vows is made, I will guarantee your safety. After that, every man must look to himself as best he can'. As soon as the assembly was over, some departed. The rest stayed with Gerard to leave the following day. Scarcely had the day dawned when a peremptory knocking sounded at the door. Four pursuivants of the worst type then tried to break in. Robert Southwell had begun to say Mass. Taking his warning from the untimely din, he slipped quickly out of his vestments and snatched up the equipment from the altar. He then made a grab for his books and travel-gear and dropped into a hole underground made ready for such eventualities. With him were two other Catholics and two secular priests who had come during the night. The search lasted four hours. After that, money was paid out to bring the nuisance to an end. The pursuivants left, and our men came up into the light and made off.*

12. Gerard was not invariably safe even in his own
     domicile. Along with the Catholic servants of the family, the master of the house made great use of the services of a non-Catholic, either because he had been in his service a long time, or because he was industrious and competent. One cannot be sure whether he was after his master's goods or whether he had taken a private dislike to Gerard. Disregarding the risk and embarrassment for his master, he decided to lay a trap for Gerard. He went to Justice Young in London, a long-standing harrier of Catholics. He told him in particular of the three houses which were familiar haunts of Gerard, one in London, and two in the country, all three belonging to his master and the latter's mother. Warrants were sent at once from the Privy Council. Failing to discover Gerard in London— perhaps he had gone elsewhere at Garnet's command— they went to the mother. She was snatched off to prison, while her son was arrested on the highway and put in irons. Meanwhile, Gerard had carried out the rites of Holy Week [1594] in a third house belonging to the son's wife. All this time, the servant remained unsuspected, and going to and fro with letters, had ample opportunity for getting information. The day after Easter, in the course of the morning, two of the leading justices turned up in his company. With them were two pursuivants specially skilled in smelling out domestic hiding-places. Gerard was warned, and hid himself between the walls in a refuge carefully prepared. The pursuivants shut up the servants with their mistress in a small room, and then searched the whole house at their leisure, turning it upside-down. They measured the walls, and broke open places that looked suspicious.

Wearied out by two days of vain searching, the justices ordered the lady of the house to be taken to London with her servants. They went away themselves leaving a few of their co-religionists behind them with the traitor. Even now, the latter was not suspected. Indeed, just before she was due to be taken away from her house, the mistress called him and told him of the closet where Gerard was hiding. She instructed him to go down to him when the rest had left and, calling him by name, warn him that it was safe to leave the empty house. The servant wanted his spitefulness to remain long concealed, so ignoring the wishes of his mistress, he recalled the justices cautiously. He told them about the closed hiding-place, but said nothing further. They used up the next day without result. In order to chase the hours of the night-watch that followed, they lit a huge blaze in the fireplace under which Gerard was hiding. The hearthstone cracked with the heat, and the embers almost fell on the head of the man praying hard underneath. The fellows above noticed the damage but made no attempt to penetrate further. On the fourth day, they chanced upon another hiding-hole in a neighbouring room. Since Gerard was not in it, they gave up the search and made off, leaving behind the lady of the house at whose expense they had made their former decisions. She had imposed upon herself a severe fast, taking nothing in the four days, so that she would have an idea from her own experience how much hunger the other could endure and remain alive. As soon as the departure of the trouble-makers allowed, she went down and called Gerard from his four-day vigil and cramped quarters. He was quite without strength after his long ordeal, for apart from a little biscuit and quince, nothing had been put in the hole. His betrayer was there, concealing his ill-will behind his alacrity in extending the helping hand.

Restored by food and sleep, Gerard went away towards the end of the morning. Not long after, the lady herself departed for her house in London. She made use of the betrayer as her go-between for letter-carrying to old

friends. She wrote to Gerard and awaited his reply. Then
one midnight a fresh horde burst in on them. They took
Gerard with the sleep still in his eyes, and he was thrust
into the constricted and smelly prison-house which was
the Counter.* Irons were put on his feet; but these he
grasped cheerfully, and greeted with a kiss. Examined two
or three times, he replied in writing who he was, who sent
him and why. He had tried to bring men to a knowledge
and love of their Creator. He had taught obedience for
conscience' sake to the laws of God and men. He had kept
out of politics, and had never been in Flanders: nor had
he ever seen Father Holt except when he was at Rome.
Nor did he meet [Sir William] Stanley again after he
left England to fight under Leicester. As he had answered
on these points, so he would on anything else which
concerned himself. Gerard asked them not to put it down
to ill-will or stubbornness if he passed over in silence
whatever he knew concerning Catholics or their servants.
It could accord neither with justice nor decency to reveal
such things. There were many objections against himself
among the items dealt with. Some of his past conversations were brought up by the examiners which none could
have heard apart from that servant whom he had hitherto
considered loyal . . . In addition, this man was ready to
give witness of the very clothes at his master's house which
had belonged to Gerard. It was now only too evident
which renegade had caused the catastrophe. However, it all
served to show Gerard in a clearer light. The experience
brought his example before more people than if he had
preserved longer immunity in the country.

13. Gerard put up with the rigours of the Counter for
three months. Then, with money begged from
friends, he was transferred to the Clink. There he was
fortunate in having a decent gaoler so that he missed out
none of the things he had been able to do in the country.
Some men he brought to believe; for others he opened the
way to life in religion. He allotted to priests newly arrived
on the island places where they could stay, and sent quite

a number of young men overseas to the seminaries. Indeed, he reaped such a harvest that he preferred to stay in that prison than live anywhere else in England. The prison also provided him with a means of doing good to many from the alms with which he himself was very generously supplied. For permission was very easily given to anyone who wanted to talk to him. Gerard also ran a house in the town to put up priests and often enough kept them at his own expense.

Gerard put in charge of this house a good and upright widow by name of Anne Line. Her ultimate reward for so much devotion in running it was to lay down her life for faith and principles . . . After three years of this work, on the Feast of the Purification [2 February 1601], just as everything was ready for the blessing of the candles, the pursuivants broke in. They took everyone by surprise. The priest made a smart exit to a hiding-hole, but the lady was led off to Newgate. So infirm was she in body that she had to be supported on both sides. So tough was her mind that she was more concerned with the priest's safety than her own peril. Apart from bodily infirmity, there were the rigours of the prison. After a few days, she was reduced to the point where, one night as she lay on her bed, she felt herself near to death about 20 times. Providence preserved her, not only to show the strength it can exercise through the weaker sex, but also in order that the whole world should have second thoughts on the subject of our savage-hearted judges. On the 25th of the same month, although the gaoler reported that she could not stand up for want of strength, she was ordered to be brought to court—on a chair. She received the death sentence with all the more satisfaction for knowing that it was passed on her simply for sheltering a priest. Two days later, she was on the hurdle. Her only desire was that for every priest she had received it might have been a thousand. She laid a kiss on the scaffold, signed herself with the cross for reassurance before the rope choked the breath in her throat. Thus she surrendered her courageous spirit.

The priest who escaped when she was taken was Francis Page. He afterwards became a recruit to the Society, and eventually won the proper reward of an old soldier in pouring out his own blood . . . He came of good family, and was trained in English law. As a young man, he worked in the office of a wealthy and skilled exponent of both branches of law. Page shared rooms with a Catholic, who brought him to Gerard as a man unsettled in religion, and he took the Jesuit for his confessor. It was not difficult to bend the malleable mind of the young man towards Catholic faith. Reason persuaded him, and love went on to lead him towards a Catholic girl whom he pursued with the disciplined affection that had marriage in view. But Gerard looked more closely into the young man's cast of mind. He perceived his completely upright disposition and self-control, and put it to him—he did not disagree—that perhaps he deserved something even better than what a woman could bring him, however good she was—or rich. Gerard taught him the principles of religion, and laid the foundations of faith. He then brought him to see the essential uncertainty of the things of this life. This he did by talking to him, lending him books, handing him copies of commentaries on spiritual subjects, and showing him the enduring nature and depth of spiritual things. In this way, he gradually led him on to prefer the single life to marriage, and to win souls rather than cases in court.

The young lady, left high and dry, complained to Gerard for thus turning the thoughts of her Page elsewhere. But Gerard's art and artistry were bent not so much on weddings as on preparing brides for Christ. Certainly, the Lord blessed His dedicated sower. Indeed, the precepts he had sown took such firm root that when Gerard was whisked off to the Tower, as in its place will be described, Page cut himself completely free from temporal entanglements . . . When he saw himself entirely deprived of the help and advice of his instructor, he crossed to Flanders. Drinking in deeply the knowledge required for priesthood, he returned to England as an

ordained priest about 1600. Page had his lodging in
Mistress Line's house mentioned above. There he eluded
the pursuivants when they broke in . . . Anne Line's
companions in her glorious death were Mark Barkworth
and Roger Filcock, the former a son of St. Benedict,
the latter recently received into the Society of Jesus.

14.   Roger Filcock inbibed his theology from the flowing
       springs of Valladolid. In turn, the seminary stood
in his debt for a pattern of decent behaviour, seriousness
of purpose, and many other good qualities. These left
their discernible mark on those who lived with him, and
later bore their ripe fruit when he was in England. In a
letter of Mark Barkworth's* written to a friend from
prison a remarkable testimonial is to be found which is
included below. Barkworth was Filcock's companion
in chains and death . . . The latter took vigorous steps not
long after he landed in England to get himself admitted
to the Society of Jesus. Once accepted, he spent himself
without stint in the service of neighbour as long as he
could. Eventually, he was caught, and put in chains in
Newgate . . . On 23 February 1601, he was called to
defend himself on the charge of receiving a priesthood.
He neither denied nor affirmed it, saying it must be
proved by witnesses on lawful evidence. No witness was
produced, in fact, no other proof.

Two days later, Filcock was again summoned before
the court. The customary form of the indictment was
recited, and he was called on to plead guilty or not guilty.
First, he denied having used those names which were
read out. Hence the accusation was ill-founded. Indeed,
since there was mistaken identity, it had no foundation
at all. Then he refused trial by the jury. He maintained
that innocent men who were either ignorant of the matters
dealt with, or who would produce a verdict merely at the
whim of the judges, should not be saddled with such a
demanding burden and grave responsibility. He recounted
recent examples. Certain men had been proved innocent
in these trials, but the 12 jurymen were ordered by the

justices to return to trial. They had forthwith found the
same men guilty although no new evidence had been
produced. In the end, Filcock made his appeal to the
judges themselves. By their sentence, he was willing to
stand or fall. They understood the law. They could be
moved neither by fear nor favour to work for any man's
destruction.

Since everything was settled and determined for him,
sentence of death was passed in the solemn phrases as on
one who had confessed himself guilty . . . A few hours
before, at a similar trial without witnesses, or the verdict
of a jury, Mark Barkworth, O.S.B., mentioned above,
had also received sentence: a man who commanded
respect for his physical mien no less than for strength of
mind and purpose. Fleming, one of the prosecuting attorneys, objected his priesthood against him. He went on to
say that he bore on his forehead the mark of the beast,
but the athlete in Barkworth remained unconquered.
Those whom God has joined must not be put asunder.
Hence I cannot deprive Barkworth of the great honour
due to him by passing over in silence his replies, especially
as they have come to me in the same manuscript as Filcock's. 'I am a Christian', he said, 'and on my forehead
I bear the sign of the cross. By this sign I am strengthened
against the devil and all who are enemies of God. I am not
afraid of your words or threats . . . For my part, I cannot
serve God except as a Catholic. This I admit . . .!'

Asked how he wished to be tried and to plead, Barkworth rejoined, 'By Christ and the 12 apostles'. For if
he was going to be tried on matters of faith, as a Catholic
he could not submit himself to other arbiters. They
offered him a dozen ministers of the reformed persuasion
by whom he might be tried as by equals before the law . . .
[He refused.] This is how he apostraphised his friend in
the letter I mentioned. 'Don't think too badly of me,
good and Christian friend, for being so determined in this
conflict . . . I have been eight years in another school . . .
First I had for tutor the wise and admirable Doctor Barret.
He was my professor of theology for two years. There

were exceptionally fine confessors there too, Doctors Arrowsmith, Lancster and Bradshaw, men of completely straight character and excellent life . . . It was that holy Father George, a Belgian Jesuit at Douai, who reconciled me to the Church. It is to him I am largely indebted if I have any inkling of spiritual life in theory or practice.

'For the rest, I offer warmest thanks to the Society of Jesus, and to most deserving men in its ranks. I admire them from the bottom of my heart, and always will. I only wish that all would do the same. An especially good and intimate friend of mine, both when I was free and now I am in prison, has been . . . Mr. Arthur (Dominus Arthurus)'—that was the name Roger Filcock assumed— '. . . a pattern on which to shape one's life. He was self-forgetful in the extreme, and a great example of regard for others and dedication. Now he is my companion in chains, and as I suppose, about to die with me. We thought highly of one another in life. Now in death, it seems, we shall not be divided . . .'

15. Barkworth received the death sentence with all cheerfulness. He made the sign of the cross, began a hymn of thanksgiving, and even thanked the judge. He then gave an address to the bystanders, appealing to all who were proud to call themselves Christians to cast away their fear. Let them act as they believed . . . He was sent from the court-house loaded with irons, but carried himself so well through the streets that the people crowding round asked who he was. 'Surely he is one of the men who were close to the Earl of Essex?' 'Not at all!', he replied for himself, 'I am a soldier of Christ; and I am dying because I believe in Him'. The next day, he was stretched on the same hurdle with our own Roger Filcock. It was the customary duet. Barkworth intoned the psalm, 'This is the day which the Lord hath made. Let us exult in it! Let us exult!' Roger made the response, 'Let us rejoice in it!'

You could call it a kind of victory parade with the two victims heralding the restoration of priests leading

processions as they used to before the long intermission.
Filcock and Barkworth were transferred from the hurdle
to a cart to be driven beneath the scaffold. The first
thing Mark did was to kiss the hem of Anne Line's dress,
who was still hanging, while he offered her enthusiastic
congratulations on her happy death. Then he made the
sign of the cross on himself, the wood to which he was to
be tied, and the rope itself. He then kissed each object in
turn and recited one of the joyful psalms. He proclaimed
that he was a monk of St. Benedict's rule, as St. Augustine
once had been: the man sent by Gregory the Great . . . to
plant the faith for which he himself now suffered. He said
that if he had a thousand lives he would pour out all of
them most willingly for the same faith: 'Greater love
than this no man hath, than that a man lay down his life
for his friends'. He also expressed a hope that the Queen
and all those who had had a hand in any degree in his
destruction would come to know eternal happiness with
him. He asked for the prayers of the Catholics.

As the cart was drawn away, Barkworth went on singing
his final anthem until he was left hanging: 'This is the day
which the Lord has made . . .' Barbarity of barbarities!
There was someone at hand to support the weight of the
hanging body so that he might live to be more cruelly
tortured . . . The rope was cut in good time so that the
executioner, who was either sadistic or unskilled, found
himself wrestling with a man only half-dead. As he cut
up his belly, and fumbled in his intestines, the martyr
cried out with his dying voice, 'God have mercy on me!'
Roger had a close-up of it all, and shouted several times,
'Well done, Father! The worse we are tortured, the more
splendid the victory'. It is hard to say who stood in greater
need of encouragement, the man who was now past living
but could not lose his life without the most dreadful
agony, or the other who had before his eyes and senses
in full awareness this appalling scene of butchery which
would be repeated on himself next day. Those scoundrels
were hoping that Roger's endurance would be undermined
by this ghastly scene of torment. Moreover, Filcock was

physically more delicate. His mind, however, was firm and unwavering. No fear of a most frightful death could shake him. So was he able to look on undismayed while his companion was being butchered and so inhumanly mangled. He underwent his own death soon after, and with readiness enough . . .

16. Nearly 14 months had elapsed. Francis Page, who on 2 February [1601], had eluded the pursuivants, now proved incapable of evading the wiles of a woman. Night was closing in, time when for the most part good men go about their works of light more safely amid the children of darkness. Turning his head by chance, Page saw a woman following who was well-known to him. She had once been a Catholic but now made a living out of wantonly betraying priests. Page began to hurry. She did likewise, and called him by name, 'I want you a minute, Sir'. He pretended not to hear. Having no desire to make his way to a Catholic, for which she was hoping, he settled on the first inn he could find in that narrow alley, shut the door after him and went through to the interior. He had not slipped in so furtively, however, that the woman did not notice. With some insistence, Page tried to prevail over the inn-keeper's good nature to let him out by the back. He told him that he was on the run, for there was someone after him to whom he owed money. But the woman now knocked so furiously on the door, and made such a hullabaloo, with her bawling about a traitor and seminary priest, that the entire neighbourhood was roused, and came running to the entrance. A waiter told the inn-keeper that he would see what he could do. He hauled Page back, and handed him over to some watchmen to be handcuffed.

On the occasion of Mrs. Line's execution, certain ladies about the Queen's court pursued Justice Popham with their censures—whether seriously or in jest—because although he had condemned a woman for receiving a priest in her house, the priest himself had not been captured or convicted. When Popham understood, therefore, that this man was a priest, he ordered him to his presence, and after much fruitless questioning commanded him to be thrown into Limbo at Newgate. He was freed from that unhappy fate a short while afterwards, for within a few days he was put on trial; at the next assizes, in fact. He was accused of going overseas and returning as a priest, although he was from this country . . . Page replied by declaring that he was not bound by that law, for he had been born outside the kingdom, at Antwerp in Flanders. It was a legitimate defence which was as true as it was easy to prove: or would have been if the case had not been pleaded before judges who, out of hatred for the priesthood, thought that the slightest delay or postponement would be too much time wasted. In Flanders, indeed, there is a family of the Pages which has English origins, and is proud of its descent. But in vain Page demanded that he should be dealt with by the law of aliens . . . In view of this, Page spurned the jury's verdict, and was sentenced by Justice Popham. He was then taken back to prison.

At that time [1602], Henry Floyd was also detained. He broke down and went on his knees when he met Page coming back from the court, being profoundly upset by so unjust a death-sentence on an innocent man. Page, however, with all kindness, made him get up. 'What is all this, my dear Sir?' he asked, 'Do you really think that my present situation, so very welcome to me, is something for you to complain about? Rather congratulate me. Share my joy in such a happy outcome which opens up the way to unending happiness!' A little while after, they gave one another the consolation of general confession made sacramentally . . . Two days had gone by since the sentence. The gaoler asked Henry to break the news to Page that he must die the next day but one. He disliked the idea of breaking such lugubrious news himself. But Page took it with as much cheerfulness as it if had been a voice from heaven. He got permission to spend his last night with Floyd [19 April]. At the Mass celebrated by the latter, so great was Page's spiritual delight that he

seemed taken out of himself . . . He also said Mass . . .
Floyd used to say afterwards that he got more insight into
divine truth that night than he could possibly have got
from any books or any amount of study . . .

[At the scene of execution, Page showed a momentary
faltering.] He remained for a brief while withdrawn into
himself. The deathly pallor of his face revealed his fear.
He was now on his own, and low moans betrayed his
awareness of the fact as he begged Henry's prayers for
himself. But this agony did not last long. Before the instruments of his execution were laid out in preparation, calm
had returned to thought and expression. This in spite
of the fact that a graceless Protestant minister, who had
jumped up on the cart with him, tried to perplex him with
untimely questions about religion. Page made an open
and spirited profession of faith at the place of execution;
also of the vow whereby he had pledged himself, a little
before, to the Society of Jesus. His end was very tranquil
. . . It will rightly seem to everyone matter for wonder
that men who could derive satisfaction from such slaughter
also found it impossible not to admit their resolution
when they saw them dying; even praising their integrity
. . . They themselves condemned their own sentence when
they proclaimed men as traitors who were only guilty of
becoming priests.

17. [In this paragraph More describes at length, and in
     mystical terms, what seems to have been the severe
state of nerves of Alexander Crow during the night before
his execution on 30 November 1587.]

18. To return to Gerard. When the men who thirsted for
     the blood of Catholics could not find just cause to
injure them, they were prepared to resort to any pretext
at hand. Accordingly, they moved Gerard from the Clink
to the Tower [on 12 April 1597], where they tortured
him most cruelly. There was another priest held prisoner
in the Clink, to whom Gerard had been a benefactor
more than once, and on no small scale. This other priest

had been either too ready to share his knowledge, or
jealous, or carried away by the thought of liberty. He
revealed the facts that Gerard had recently received
letters from Rome and Brussels; that he had given a letter
to his servant to be taken to Garnet; and that this he did
frequently. The justice of peace made a sudden swoop
on Gerard with his strong-arm men. They went through
his room thoroughly. He himself was stripped and his
clothing searched. Not even the hair shirt next to his
skin was overlooked, which they tore off. Gerard had
with him two young men who were under instruction.
These were taken with him. One they put in prison, but
the other managed to escape in time. Nothing was found
to justify the fuss they made, but his captors dragged
Gerard off to the Tower, and pushed him into an underground cell with a little straw thrown in to lie on.

Gerard woke next day to find himself shut up in the
same den that Henry Walpole had occupied. He was the
man who had been tortured 14 times. Walpole had cut
his name in the foot of the wall beneath the names of God
and the angels. Since it seemed likely that he had prayed
at that part of the wall, it became a hallowed place for
Gerard also. From all this he conjectured that he, too,
would be no more leniently treated, and for the same
cause. On the third day, five men presided over his
examination. They had Gerard summoned to a place
deep in the Tower, and there they questioned him: first,
about matters relating to national politics, and then about
the letters he had received; finally, concerning the
whereabouts of Garnet. Gerard replied that he had never
given a thought to the politics of his country. If he had
received letters, they contained nothing that could be
of interest to them. He knew neither where Garnet was,
nor his servant, and if he did he would not say. 'In that
case', they replied, 'you must be tortured, even to your
last gasp! You place this necessity upon us, unwilling as
we are, by your obstinacy. See what you are doing to
yourself!' They showed him the warrant for their
authority, which Gerard read over and replied, 'Do

whatever God allows you. You cannot do more. By His
Grace, I will never say or do anything against the beliefs
and teachings of the Church, or contrary to what is right.
I am confident that God will not allow me to accuse any
innocent person. For the rest, we are all his His hands;
and for that reason I am not particularly afraid of anything you plan to do with me!'

19. In the heart of the Tower there is a cellar lying
      at a great depth. It overawes by its size and darkness.
It is even more frightening for the number and variety of
the instruments devised for torturing the human frame.
The party now went down into the cavern following the
menials who carried torches. They showed Gerard in full
array the different kinds of machine set up for twisting
men apart. Some were for the hands, others for the legs.
In one device the limbs could be forced into a circle;
in another the bones of the neck could be forced downwards. On another gadget the arms could be stretched
upwards; and on yet another, prostrate on the ground,
the limbs, fastened to pitiless rollers, could be stretched,
torn, and rendered useless for every human purpose.
'It will be your lot', they told Gerard, 'to try them all if
you insist on hiding in pig-headed silence matters which
for the realm's safety we cannot have hidden from us'.
He fell on his knees and implored God to help him. They
then put his hands through iron rings which were joined
by an iron bar. This was raised up against a pillar. The
earth was then scooped out to form a hollow beneath
his feet, for he was tall and well-built. The pain in his
hands, arms, chest and stomach became intense. Sweat
poured from his whole body, while voice and breath were
almost choked. After ebbing away thus for an hour, a
basket was put under his feet for him to rest on. This
was done nine or 10 times during the five hours he hung
there . . . Keeping silence, Gerard prayed . . .
    Interiorly strengthened to endurance, he felt the pain
grow less. William Waad, who had taken Justice Young's
place among the persecutors, urged him to say that he

wanted to talk to Cecil, chief man of the Privy Council. Gerard would not consent. 'So then', said Waad, 'you can hang there till you rot!' With that he left. After some further time, however, Gerard was taken down from the column and led back to his room, groaning out at frequent intervals on the way, 'I cannot understand how they can go to these lengths simply to find out where Garnet is', and other comments of this kind. 'Surely they know it was wrong', he said, 'to betray innocent men'. As for Gerard, he would rather die than commit so great a crime. He spoke thus in order to forestall slander: for it is a common trick with persecutors of this sort to put around as already done what they keenly desired should be done. The next day, Waad returned to the Tower. Gerard insisted on Garnet's innocence, so Waad ordered his prisoner to be tortured again in like fashion. When he fainted in his extremity of anguish, they brought him to with a potion forced down his throat. They had scarcely brought him round when he was ordered to be hoisted a third time. It went on until [Sir Richard] Barkeley, Lieutenant of the Tower, sickened by so much cruelty, commanded it to be stopped. Indeed, he is said to have offered his resignation so that he would not have to be present on later occasions as the person responsible for such barbarous and appalling tortures inflicted on innocent victims.

20. The respite snatched from his tortures Gerard devoted to making a spiritual retreat until the use of his limbs returned. He set aside four or five hours of his day for meditation. He also made daily use of the prayers of the Mass, as far as memory would serve him . . . He got hold of his books and papers by bribing his gaoler, and after some 20 days his numbed fingers were able to move as before so that he could add work with his hands to study. He made small crosses out of bits of wood that came his way, and sent them to his former cell-mates in the Clink. On the paper in which they were wrapped, he wrote secret messages in orange juice telling his friends what he wanted. In like manner, replies came back, the

gaoler being quite unaware of this artifice. Through bribery, Gerard was also able from time to time to have visits from some of the Catholics he knew. Their access brought comfort; their trouble, a Mass-set—and eventually a chance of escaping. Opposite the place where Gerard was kept, there is a tower not far from the wall and the moat round the Tower itself. In that tower a Catholic gentleman by name of [John] Arden had been imprisoned 10 years. Gerard bought for a gold piece paid to his gaoler the right to stay with him for a day and a night. His Mass-kit was also surreptitiously brought in, and he celebrated Mass with great satisfaction. He further provided himself with 22 consecrated Hosts for his Communion on the days following. Gerard also noticed that the place was well positioned for an escape. They planned a flight together.

Having determined the method, the day and the way— Garnet also knew of it—Gerard after a few weeks again contrived a meeting with the same man in the same place. That night three men approached quietly in a rowing-boat wearing cloths tied to their chests so that they could be recognised. They were provided with some strong rope, one end of which they tied round a mooring-post on the shore. The other end they weighted with a stone and threw over against the tower. Gerard pulled it up on a piece of string, and tied it to a bronze cannon on top of the tower. Arden slid across first.* Although he wished to give way to Gerard, the latter preferred the safety of his friend and host to his own. Arden had no difficulty in escaping. Gerard, however, found the rope had been slackened by the weight of the first to go, and came down to a point well below the level of the wall so that he was tired out by a long climb up. Indeed, he was only just saved by dint of the efforts and toil put into it by his companions. But saved he was, and restored by a stomach-warming drink which they brought with them. They negotiated the river, and by means of horses ready saddled, Gerard sped off to Garnet.

Before his escape, Gerard wrote three letters: one to the Privy Council, another to the Lieutenant of the

Tower, and a third to his gaoler. The first, to the Council, explained why he thought that his was the course he should follow. He made it clear that he had done it without the knowledge of the Lieutenant or the gaoler lest they become liable to a charge of collusion. The second letter, to the Lieutenant, offered him courteous thanks, and made excuses for the gaoler. In the third letter to the gaoler, he promised that if he followed Gerard's advice, he would be sure of a decent livelihood as long as he lived. The day had scarcely dawned when, from the rope hanging at the side of the tower, it was soon discovered what had happened, although the end of the rope on the shore side had been cut off as they made their escape. It also became quickly evident who was involved. There was a general rush to the cell . . . Everyone searched for the gaoler. He, wise man, had read the letter written to him, and chosen to risk the way of escape offered him. He met a man specially posted by Gerard with horses so that, if he chose, he could use one of them to reach safety. Previously, the warder had been offered 400 crowns, and an annuity of 40 more, which he then refused. Now he accepted it readily enough. It was to affect him for eternity as well as life. As it happened, he got 80 crowns a year to look after himself and his wife. Furthermore, both became Catholics. In this way, they entered on a better kind of life than any they could have hoped for otherwise. And they continued in it. Of the Privy Council, some were astonished at this turn of events. There were those who even admired Gerard's resourcefulness. They were all convinced that it would be useless to go looking for a man who would doubtless elude any who tried to find him now, as easily as he had hoodwinked his keepers in the first place. So his flight made Gerard available to many for a considerable time to come. Moreover, it was effected with only limited harm to very few.

21. John Lilly, Richard Fulwood and one of the warders from the Clink were the men who helped Gerard to

to escape.* Lilly had been a physician before being shut
up in that prison for religion. It so happened that he had
a cell over Gerard's. Hence the latter soon came to know
the man's goodness, and experience his skill. Lilly found
ready opportunity to exercise both on many people in
that place. After Gerard was transferred to the Tower
[and Lilly himself was released by Gerard's efforts],
Lilly went on working for Gerard's release. He was the
man who had contacts, carried secret letters, and won
more ample favours from the warder. He showed Gerard
the danger to life and limb of any other way of escaping,
and that he should trust himself to him alone.

[It was the year 1599.] In a recently-hired house of
some size, three or four men were on the fourth day of
the spiritual exercises, conducted by Gerard . . . Some
inkling of what Gerard was up to was conveyed to the
Privy Council by the treachery or loquacity of one of
his servants. Two justices suddenly appeared at Lilly's
door with their retinue . . . Drawing his sword with every
intention of using it if need arose, Lilly entered the room
in which were Gerard and another Jesuit. Lilly pushed
them into a hiding-hole, refusing Gerard's plea to join
them in hiding. 'Not at all', said Lilly, 'for if I hide, who
is going to say those books or writings are his? They are
a clear indication that someone is hiding in the house.
They will search for days and nights; pull the place apart,
and in the end arrest you. I will stay here. You pray for
me!' Meanwhile, the justices of peace were delayed in a
neighbouring room collecting altar-furniture, which they
had found all ready for use. After picking up their booty,
they banged on John's door. Lilly was now gowned, and
opened up at this later stage quite willingly. 'Who are
you?' they cried. 'A man, evidently!. 'Priest?' 'I wouldn't
say so! It is up to you to prove that! However, I am a
Catholic'. 'Whose are these books and writings?' 'Mine!'
But they all happened to be ritual-books used in the
Society of Jesus by priests, or else elementary and
advanced text-books on the faith and its practice. They
represented the work of 10 years. 'Are these all yours ?

'They are all mine.' Without enquiring further, they took
Lilly away to be handcuffed. As he went along, he greeted
those he met in the hall, and recommended them to the
tender mercies of the justices . . . The next day, his captors
understood that this man had been actively engaged in
medicine for seven years. He had been shut in the Clink
for four, and had been a willing assistant of Gerard's
escape from the Tower. It was the wife of the gaoler who
had fled to safety who told them that. Nor did John deny
it. Next he was dragged off to the Tower where they
inflicted the same kind of torture on him as on Gerard
to tell them where the latter was.

Lilly hung for three hours with no other result than
to prove his patience and endurance. When he had
demolished all hope in his torturers that he would
confess secret matters—it took three months—he was
transferred to another prison. There he helped a priest,
at his suggestion, to escape. He himself got free by the
same stratagem. After this, he lay low for a time at
Garnet's, and then took ship, and went to Persons in
Rome. Lilly was admitted to the Society in 1602, something he had wanted to do for many years. He was not yet
30, but only six or seven years still remained to him,
for he was attacked by a chronic wasting disease which
not even his native air could cure. He [died] in London
in 1609. Lilly had a good head on his shoulders, and was
clever and hard-working in the management of affairs.
Most important, he was a young man of blameless life,
as Gerard bore witness, who lived close to him for six
years. He took great care over his spiritual life. Indeed,
although he lived and rubbed shoulders every day with
men of much less exalted aspirations, he never picked up
any undesirable characteristic to lay him open to a charge
of serious imperfection.

22. After Gerard's escape from the Tower [in October
      1597], Richard Fulwood also had to get out of
the way of the pursuivants. He hid in the cellar of a house
he had made ready· for Gerard's use. One day he was

making his way back to it when he was taken and led off to the Bridewell. Here he was put in a smelly cell crawling with worms, with nothing to sleep or even sit on. For a matter of months, his bed was a stone in the window-place. He lived on black bread, and was kept in solitary confinement. After that, he was brought out for questioning. His previous fidelity in serving now showed to an even greater degree in suffering. His tormentors could wring nothing out of him that was better left hidden. Then came a respite from interrogation, and during the short time available for resting, he found a way to escape. He also stayed with Garnet. When the Privy Council found out, they offered a reward, in an edict, to any person who should take him prisoner. He therefore went overseas, and lived for some years at the mission at Dunkirk making himself extremely useful.

22. The third man who helped Gerard had been one of [bis] his gaolers in the Clink. He had given the priest a helping hand, and was very friendly to Catholics, but was not himself a Catholic. Nor is it certain that he ever came over completely to the Catholics . . . All the same, he twice put his life in jeopardy on Gerard's account. The first night on which they decided to escape, it was made impossible by the unexpected intrusion of a stranger. The boat which Fulwood was rowing span round on itself, and came into collision with a mooring post sticking out in front of the pier. His craft wedged itself in with such force that they could not get it loose, and all three were put in danger of their lives by the strength of the current. [Flung into the water], they cried for help. Meanwhile, two of them were being sucked towards the stones jutting out under the pier. The third swam for dear life as soon as the boat overturned, and only just got away. The next night, Fulwood again looked mortal danger knowingly in the face. This time he won through. Nothing more is told of him. However, the jailer to whom he owed everything for the success of his efforts in the Clink came back to the Church by Gerard's means.

He sold his property and went to Italy. There he decided to withdraw from the world altogether. But he returned to England to settle his affairs, and was captured. He was imprisoned in the same jail where before he had been warder . . .

23.   Among the assistants employed by Gerard in casting Peter's net, Roger Lee must justly be considered one of the most important. He was born in favourable circumstances, and as a young man was welcome everywhere by reason of his lively disposition and well-bred ease of manner. He also tried to combine Catholic faith with the best kind of external devotion. He was on the fourth day of the spiritual exercises when the justices of peace broke in, and Lilly was taken instead of Gerard. By urbanity and aplomb, Lee contrived to go free in view of the fact that he had only recently arrived. He also gave guarantees. He went to another of Gerard's houses to continue the exercises already begun. Once again, suspicion followed, and would have caused serious interruption had he not taken to a previously prepared hiding-hole together with Gerard.

Lee learned from meditation . . . to be more preoccupied with grace than occupied with games, even when he was fowling, or exercising body and relaxing mind by hunting as other people did. He thought constantly about those he could bring to belief, and about those who already believed to higher perfection through Gerard's intervention. So he established friendship with many people . . . In order to get the most out of himself, for his own good and that of others, he went to Rome to study with Thomas Strange, Nicholas Hart and Thomas Smith. All of them, thanks to Gerard's training and influence, hoped to join the Society. After spending some time in the English College, Rome, Lee joined the Society on 27 October 1600. He was then in his 32nd year. He could compete with the best in personal qualities and studies, but he was troubled with some kind of congestion in the lungs. In search of a more congenial climate, he transferred to St. Omer's in Flanders, and became minister at the seminary. In carrying out this function, he skilfully combined the wary eye with forbearance, an attitude of 'no nonsense' with kindness, and an air of authority with friendliness. Thus he showed that there was nothing contradictory in insisting on a high standard of conduct, and at the same time showing everyone deep respect. Since he felt that he and others had derived an enormous amount of help from the spiritual exercises, he got the young men, who were a model body, to make good use of them. The result was that through this kind of influence the first three [to do them] wanted to join the Society. These were Robert Stafford, Thomas Stillington, and Francis Miles. This kind of success was repeated every year so that many followed their example . . . Lee also had not a little to do with increasing the external amenities of the house, for he obtained £500 English to add classrooms to the building.

24. A considerable number of single women up and down Flanders no longer live according to a purely secular way of life but devote their efforts, either privately or living in community, to educating girls.* They give them an education befitting their sex whether they intend to marry or embrace a more austere mode of life. Some of these teaching ladies take no vows; others take a temporary or perpetual vow of chastity. For which reason, they have been dubbed 'devotaries' (Devotarae). This seemed too little for some young ladies from England who, apart from devoting themselves to the education of girls, were aspiring to religious perfection through the additional vows of poverty and obedience. At the same time, they did not wish to be tied to the breviary, or to lived in a fixed house, or to be bound by the jurisdiction of ordinaries, as the phrase is. Rather on the lines of the Society of Jesus, they wished to be free to pursue whatever journeyings or whatever duties neighbourly love demanded. They assumed, as far as was practicable, the name and rule of the Jesuits, as well as the colour of their dress, order of day, and mode of

allotting duties, and also a system of government under one head. The leaders among them fixed on St. Omer as their principal centre, where Bishop Blaise encouraged their beginnings.

In order to give their girls a first-class moral training along with other studies, they made the utmost use of the services of Roger Lee. He always set before himself and others the loftiest standards, and insisted on the highest goals attainable in the service of God. All were agreed that these ladies were endowed with unusual gifts of nature and training, and were not behindhand in the goodness of their lives. For which reason, leading men and women in society were well content to entrust their daughters to them as teachers. For this purpose, they gave them houses in the principal cities of Germany. They spread to Liège, Trèves, Munich, Vienna, Prague, Poznan, Pressburgh and Rome. In time, they might have come to enjoy the full status of a religious order. But they took the Society of Jesus too closely as their model, and tried to be completely self-governing. Roger Lee was said to have been transferred from St. Omer because he did not disapprove of these things; or did not express his disapproval sufficiently. It is certainly true that he went to Louvain and Brussels in search of a remedy for the disease arising from his congestion. Since he failed to find it, he returned to St. Omer in 1615 with the intention of going to England. He died at Dunkirk the day he was due to sail.

25. While all this was going on, the faith continued to take root and flourish in England, thanks to the perspiration of those who lived, and the blood of those who died, for it. The Society was made aware of the more pointed shafts of jealousy directed against it in the person of William Holt . . . Holt came from Lancashire. He received his earliest education at home, and at Oxford University added letters and philosophy to his earlier attainments. He devoted three further years to reading theology. Protestantism lost its hold on him, and he

crossed to Douai in search of something more satisfying to him. After spending another three years there on theology, he was ordained. He then set out for Rome. He was received into the Society on 8 November 1578, ar the age of thirty-three. After his noviceship, and another year's study of theology, came the year when Campion and Persons were sent into England. As they asked for helping hands to gather in the very abundant harvest, Holt joined forces with [Gaspar] Heywood, and likewise sailed to England.

At that time, Mary, Queen of Scots, was kept in close captivity. Amid the difficulties of her imprisonment, she kept among the first calls on her attention her Catholic faith, and the welfare of her son, the prince [James]. She asked for someone on whom she could rely in matters of faith, a right-living man and competent who, if given the opportunity, would see to her arrival at a safe designation as well as look after her son. Holt was a man highly thought of by Persons. Provided with letters from the Queen to the King, her son, Holt got into Scotland. At first he was well received. The courtesy of the leading men roused in him no little hope of gathering much fruit. It soon died. This was due to the persuasions of the more rigorous Calvinists, whom Elizabeth and her supporters encouraged and spurred on from England. Holt was made prisoner, and Elizabeth demanded that he be put to the question. The King refused out of consideration for his mother, and was upheld in his refusal by the French ambassador.

After two years' detention in Scotland, Holt was set at liberty, and told to leave the country. Persons wrote to Ribadeneira in September 1584, 'William Holt has regained his freedom. He it was who, as you understood, was sent from England into Scotland, and suffered imprisonment for a time. Two other Fathers and a lay-brother recently sent to that mission are also at liberty'. In 1586, Holt was summoned to Rome and sent to the English College as rector, a post he occupied for six years. Then he was sent to Flanders, and remained in

Brussels 10 years. His rivals worked in vain to whip up jealousy against him and destroy his reputation. He always managed to evade it, thanks to his exceptional equability and patience that refused to yield.

26. From 1581, Allen and Persons had received a mandate to promote the Catholic cause in England and Scotland by their joint efforts. Among other factors likely to help was one that seemed of more than ordinary importance, namely the liberation of Mary, Queen of Scots, whom Elizabeth had kept prisoner 12 years. Allen and Persons therefore thought good to take Charles Paget and Thomas Morgan into their counsels since they were versed in Scottish affairs. This fact was largely due to the correspondence of the latter with Charles Paget's relatives and friends. However, there arose a difference of view among them from the start. Allen and Persons thought that the matter should be entrusted to the discretion of the Catholic King, the Pope and the Duke of Guise. Paget and Morgan persuaded the Queen that another way should be adopted. The quarrel which began among a few people soon involved nearly everyone. Some supported Allen and Persons, others Paget and Morgan. It lasted until 1587 when, with the death of the Queen, most of the recrimination fell on Morgan and his companions. This was either because he had not trusted some about the Queen sufficiently, or because they had shown a great deal of confidence in others who proved imprudent.

While the quarrel was still going on, Holt was sent to Brussels. Paget and Morgan came there too. Although they were received in kindly fashion, the old distrust still clung to them. They continued to complain that all had been done in accordance with the wishes of Allen and Persons, not theirs. It so happened that letters were found in Morgan's room, written in his own hand, attacking the Duke of Parma, Allen and the King himself. Morgan was therefore expelled from the royal dominions. This result was attributed by Morgan's friends to the Society in the person of Father Holt—indeed, so was nearly everything which happened at the expense of this particular group whatever the ultimate cause might have been in fact. A great deal of work was put in to bring about Holt's expulsion. An accusation with 36 charges was offered to the Cardinal Archduke Albert in which Holt was saddled with threatening the reputations, property, liberty, and even life of certain people: neither was he suitably loyal to the King. Albert put the affair before Oliver Manare [the General's visitor],* and ordered him to examine Holt as to the truth of it all. John Baptist de Tassis, a member of Albert's privy council, was added as umpire. Oliver, dumbfounded by their number, showed the charges to Holt himself. He said that he was very sorry such things had happened, and whatever reply was made, the Society could not come out of it unscathed. Holt felt it keenly. He was grieved that so much could be believed of him before he was even heard, and that prejudice of this sort could be entertained by a man of Manare's calibre. He accepted it, however, and reading through the accusations unravelled everything. 'Father, I will make my reply', he said, 'as clearly and briefly as you could wish. Moreover, from my answer, nothing will be imputable either to the Society or myself that suggests other than upright behaviour, integrity, patience and loyalty.'

27. Some days later, the enquiry was held. Holt asked if he should reply to each item in order or only to the more significant. He was ready to do either. 'Not to each one', said de Tassis, indicating 10 points which he thought more important. When Holt had dealt with them, and wanted to be heard in the rest, they all told him that he had done enough to satisfy on every issue. There was no need for more. It was clear enough to them that he had on many counts been the victim of partisan zeal rather than the object of reasonable doubt. John Baptist de Tassis added that what it amounted to was that certain gentlemen felt that the Society, and those who favoured it, had too much influence with his Highness

and the rest of the Flemish administration. The Jesuits
should wield that influence with discretion. Holt replied
that if he had any such influence he had been moderate
in using it; and, indeed, he would continue to use it
according to the dictates of prudence and decency. He
could not answer for every word or deed of his. *Omnes
enim in multis deliquimus.* But he could give his solemn
assurance that, as for any wrong or affront of a serious
kind, or victimisation in any sense whatever, he had been
guilty of none, nor would be. He had been friendly to
all and helpful—even to those who, from the nature of
the objections, he could guess to be the authors of this
accusation.

'It can be recognised from their common spokesman
(procuratore). It can also be deduced from this reply
of mine. I have been here at Brussels for almost nine years,
and if I have to settle my account with you, I may be
quickly discharged. For you can bear witness that I have
never fallen into any serious fault, and nothing has come
from me that could deservedly be marked as a scandal.
Certainly, I never failed to raise an objection when there
was something to object to. It rarely happens, when
unanimity is absent, that there are not some to make
trouble or simply complain. In any case, the difference
between the parties is not so great as some noisily
proclaim. Nor will future peace be so absolute that there
will never be any contention between the court and the
military on questions of honour and precedence. These
things must be left to Providence: through the trivialities
which more often than not cause men to get excited, this
still controls the most important issues.' De Tassis and
Manare told Holt not to bother himself further, although
he was prepared to say more. He had amply satisfied them
on all points. They said this two or three times and then
the meeting broke up. Oliver, taking the written reply
which Holt held in his hand, threw it on the fire—it was
the fourth Sunday in Advent. Any clear-sighted man, who
was wide awake, would have been ashamed to do less
in such a case. Persons, as he was sailing from Barcelona

to Italy [1597], wrote to Manare on this topic in the following words:

28.   *'. . . I do not expect that the blessings of peace will follow those who want Father Holt removed . . . The experience of many years and the best of reasons convince me that they are not attacking this or that Father but the Society itself . . . The trouble-makers at Rome wanted Father Edmund Harewood removed, the confessor of the English College, and with that they said that the situation would be pacified. When he was transferred, everything became even stormier, because the rowdy element was in open arms against the whole Society . . . The Pope had a conversation with Doctor Barret, rector or the seminary at Douai. From this, significant facts have lately come to light. The same people who now agitate with your Reverence, and the rest of our Fathers, for the removal of Holt for the sake of peace, also wrote then to his Holiness. They attacked not only Father Holt but all the Fathers working in England . . . Of Father Holt I can truly say that in his letters he frequently and strenuously acted in the Spanish court on behalf of the very people who are now attacking him most. But your Reverence ought not to be surprised at this. It concerns nothing less than England's conversion. There also come into it sheer penury, living at a loose end, and much idleness on the part of our afflicted exiles. The heretics use every artful means to keep these quarrels going through their agents . . . It is not remarkable that such things happen . . . Nor should they deceive, or cause any good and sensible man to falter in his tracks. It is enough to distinguish between what comes from reason and what from spleen . . . Since they cannot bring our English Fathers to loggerheads among themselves, they approach Jesuits of other nationalities, who are not so well-informed about us or our affairs . . . These they try to bring by noise, threats, accusations, complaints, or even flattery, into general disagreement with us. They think—and they are right—that nothing could give them

a more effective means of wearing us down than to estrange us from one another.'

So wrote Persons, shrewdly enough to Manare. The latter already annoyed General Claud in giving such easy leave for an external umpire to be admitted to a cause concerning one of our own Society. The reader may have noticed the names Paget, Tresham, and others of the kind which were formerly very well-liked by Campion and Persons even if they were now in disagreement with the Society. The reader must be clear that they were not the same men who in earlier years performed all the offices of friendship towards Jesuits, but only their relatives. The Society was willing to get these others, as exiles, into the good graces of foreign rulers, and to see that their services were employed in public affairs. They themselves lost this favour by their own unwisdom. Whatever the Society did subsequently they interpreted as being in no sense done for them. All leading Catholic Englishmen, however, stood by Holt. A letter of Dr. Barret, President of Douai, signed by seven senior members of the college on 12 November 1596, sufficiently testifies to this. Another letter was sent a month later by Dr. Stapleton, Percy, and Worthington. To this letter more than 100 men besides added their signatures. The letter of Cardinal Allen about these affairs may be justly added to these. It was written to Paget, one of those who had taken the lead in slandering Holt. Allen writes thus on 4 January 1591: *'. . . As for Father Holt, whom you specially charge and insinuate' as guilty, you accuse him of 'foul and shameful matter', but you do not wish to put it on paper. 'If I knew what the matter were, and that it were such as you say, he should neither find favour nor defence at my hands. But things being spoken by you so vehemently, and yet not touched in particular, you must give me leave to suspend my judgment till I see all pretences proved and particularised. [This is what] reason and conscience bind me to do in all men's matters; much more in a man's cause that for honour of religion and particular opinion I have of his honesty and fidelity towards God, as the world. [He] hath been much grateful unto me, and employed by me both in England, Scotland, Italy, and that place always commendably, and to his praise among the principal [men] where he hath lived; and continueth now in very good favour of his Altezza, the present Governor of Flanders, and his councillors. This praise he won not so much from my recommendation as from his own soundness and prudent behaviour. However, they will doubtless listen to your complaints, if they have the serious foundation required, and can be backed up with proof, as you realise . . . Till that be done, you must not marvel that I alter not my meaning and good opinion towards the man . . .'

In order to quieten the clamour, however unjust, Holt yielded his place to William Baldwin, and went to Spain. He died on the journey, having reached Barcelona, in 1599. At his final departure, he said lightly, 'I never lost even one hour's sleep in the midst of all that tumult'. When he was gone, Baldwin was able to see for himself how far from pacific were the men who envied everyone of his own kind . . . In all the 36 heads of the accusation, no mention was made by the rival faction of Queen Elizabeth's destruction with Father Holt's alleged connivance and provocation, as Camden reports. From which it is clear that this was regarded by this time as a dead issue and empty calumny. Camden himself refuted the notion when, knowing nothing about it, he wrote, 'that Holt kissing the Holy Host'—something which is never done!—'swore that the money should be paid as soon as the murder was committed, and that he bound Yorke and Williams by an oath and the Sacrament of the Eucharist to dispatch it. Certainly remarkable at these times . . . was the lewdness of the fugitives in such wicked attempts, while some excited murderers to commit parricide, others, grasping after gain, offered themselves to commit villanies, and being hired with money, presently revealed the same; and some, treacherous among themselves, precipitated others into destruction, as it were acting some other thing, intrapped one another with cunning devices, and sometimes charged one another with false lies'.

29. Holt, then, called to Spain, was also called away to the reward of his life's labours. Almost at the same time, Thomas Hunt, born at Lindon in Rutlandshire, joined our mission after putting in 20 years of varied service in Upper Germany. He was a man of old-style straightforwardness. From his earliest years he had grown up in an uncomplicated kind of piety. His sense of what was due to authority was so great that when as a boy he saw his father blow up with anger, and say something to him not well-considered, or even plain abusive, he would pass a considerable part of the night without sleep. Afraid lest his father die before he had cooled off, he would get up and implore him to calm down, and put himself back on good terms with God so that they could both get some rest! Hunt worked at Dillingen, Innsbruck, and Ratisbon. He took his place in the ranks of formed coadjutors in 1594.

Leaving behind in Germany the reputation of a good man, Hunt crossed to England to acquire the like wherever he went. But if anyone came to consult him on secular business, he used to say he was out of touch with it, for it had nothing to do with his kind of life. Whoever he was with, he eventually brought the subject round to religion, saying something about the saints or their mode of living . . . On Sundays and feastdays, he always took care to see that something was read aloud for the advantage of those who were with him: or he would enlarge on some text of the Gospel himself. He did this with a great deal of skill, although he would announce beforehand that he was not sufficiently clever himself to talk on that subject. He would, therefore, present someone more eloquent to his listeners, namely one of the Church Fathers, or a man who had written more recently on that subject, but with inner understanding. All this seemed a bore to some, but others were greatly taken by the man's candour. Certainly, he came to have the kind of influence with outstanding people in working for their reconciliation which no one else could readily acquire. So it was that sometimes he would order men who were absorbed even more than excessively in gambling, not only to put a stop to it, but actually give something to charity out of their past winnings: and they did not seem to mind. On other occasions, when quarrelling broke out among the players, he would put himslf between them, kneel down, and appeal to them not to make themselves objectionable to one another or to third parties by continuing the brawl. He would tell them not to shout so much, and follow Christ's example in forgiving one another, especially if one of them had gone too far in word or deed. The man's sheer goodness would prevail, and strife would give way to a general shaking of hands.

Two events took place which seem to have accelerated [Thomas Hunt's death]. On one occasion he went about seven or eight miles from his house. Although he took a guide with him, he persuaded himself that he would not need anyone to show him the way home. When he was on his own, he either lost himself, or else wanted to do some praying, and so passed the night in the open. There was a search for him next morning, and he was found not far from the house at which he had arrived only the day before. His servant was very upset by what had happened, but Hunt reassured him that he had never passed a night more pleasant or consoling. Then not long afterwards, when they were in process of disarming Catholics, he consented to go into a garden nearby in order to be out of sight from the searchers. As he sat under a pergola, cold and heavy rain soaked him, and, indeed, they say he was frozen stiff. A few days later, he exchanged this life for a better . . . [This was on Sunday, 10 February, between 1625 and 1628.] *

30. About the same time, two more extremely useful workmen were admitted to the Society, namely the brothers John and Laurence Worthington. They were born at Blainsco in Lancashire. As a boy 12 years old, John was

trapped while he was getting ready to go overseas. He had
to put up with a good deal of discomfort from the Protestant bishop and principal administrators of the region.
They tried to dissuade the boy, who was still immature,
from the truth of his faith, and get him to accept the new
rites. This they did by promises, threats and intimidation.
The youngster's remarkable firmness, and the force of
replies beyond his age, only served to increase the irritation of his opponents, even if it deepened the conviction
of the Catholics. At length John escaped from his captors'
hands by a clever trick. He made Rheims first of all, with
two of his brothers and a paternal uncle. Then he went
on to Eu. There he met Persons, and followed him into
Spain, and as far as Rome. John joined the Society,
being already a priest, on 27 October 1598. After his
years as a novice, and one or two more in the Roman
College, he was sent to Valladolid where he acted as
minister in the seminary. Even John Worthington was
unable to calm down the students who had been stirred
to rebellion at that time, but he did manage to combine
attitudes of sweet reason and no-nonsense so that whatever
he did the students believed he did if for the best. Broken
by the climate and worries of the house, he migrated to
England in 1604 . . . He was the first member of the
Society to fix his abode in Lancashire. By hard work and
application, together with his gift for preaching, he won
the attachment of a great many people, not only there, but
also in neighbouring districts, and opened up a very wide
field for his fellow-Jesuits . . .*

31 to   [These paragraphs deal with that part of John
36.   Worthington's career which lay well outside the
        Elizabethan era. He probably survived until 1652.]

37.   Laurence Worthington, John's brother, was admitted
        to the Society at about the same time, in Spain. After
the novitiate, he spent two years on philosophy at Cordoba and Valladolid. Then he was sent to England in 1612,

and both as a free man and prisoner produced results far
from disappointing . . .*

38. Thomas Worthington, the paternal uncle of the last
     pair, even if he was a long way behind them in the
Society, was the man who persuaded them to undertake
their journey, and made the necessary arrangements. He
was also responsible for their moral training and general
behaviour, and it therefore seems in place that he should
be mentioned with his nephews. Moreover, those who are
called at the 11th hour are the equals of those called first.
He received a good education in the humanities, but he
disliked the reformed doctrines in the midst of which he
passed his adolescence at Oxford University. On his own
inspiration, he passed over to Douai and Rheims. In the
latter place he took his doctorate in philosophy, and was
ordained priest. On the advice of the men at the top,
he went to England, and carried on an extremely useful
ministry for some time. He was betrayed by a young man
whom he had placed under an obligation by many kind-
nesses. Thrown into the Tower as one guilty of every crime
imaginable, he lay in chains, and for some two months
had to go through quite appalling hardships in a subterranean dungeon. When six months were up, he was
deported to France in the company of Gaspar Haywood
and some 20 other staunch champions of Catholicism.
He turned his exile to great advantage for the Catholic
cause, and helped his own country in a variety of ways.
Thus in 1588, at Trèves, he was proclaimed doctor of
sacred theology, and not long afterwards became professor
of moral theology at the English seminary, Rheims.

After that Worthington went to reside at Brussels to act
as adviser, together with Thomas Stapleton, to the apostolic nuncio on affairs concerning England. He then
succeeded Barret on his death as President of Douai
College. He considerably extended the college building,
and brought lustre to the college itself by producing a
translation of the Old Testament into the vernacular,
which he further embellished with reliable notes. He

published other works, as may be seen in Pits and
Alegambe, and was further advanced in dignity by
becoming a protonotary apostolic. When he laid down
the burden of the presidency at a rather advanced age,
he showed a leaning towards the Society—Worthington
had always been one of Persons's close co-operators.
He was actually admitted by the provincial, Richard
Blount. Worthington died in his sixth month of the
novitiate [1626?]. All his life he was a man of high
integrity and purity of intention; but he was chiefly
notable for his learning as a teacher rather than for any
particular skill in administration, maintaining discipline
or forming character.

39. Another Thomas—of the Stanney family—was born
    in comfortable circumstances in the Salisbury
diocese. After two years' philsophy and two more of moral
theology in the English College, Rome, he joined the
Society a year before the two Worthingtons. He was
marked out for England, and shone in the glory reflected
from the crowns of the three lay martyrs, Swithin Wells,
Ralph Miller, and Lawrence Humphrey. These he had
formed in religious spirit and steadfastness. Indeed, he
brought back Catholic faith and its open profession to
some hundreds of people. Thanks to his labours, the places
he had to hide in, and the rigours of his prisons, he was
afflicted with more diseases than one: stone, difficulty in
passing water, rupture, coughing, neuralgia, and gout.
His extraordinary patience rose superior to all his
afflictions.

Exiled in 1606, he went to Flanders and settled at
St. Omer's. A sick man himself, he looked after the sick
there. The office meant not leisure but work for as long
as he could do it, although he would pass his own time
and that of his youthful patients by spinning them yarns
with a moral. He brought alleviation to the anguish of his
gout by prayer, and holy water sprinkled while the
superior prayed! He would not use any other remedy
unless ordered to do so. Stanney also claimed that he

got some relief from his pain by reading the life of St. Ignatius. On 28 May 1617, the general state of health in the place was believed to be perfect—the students' infirmary stood empty. It was when one of the servants came in after a meal to get a purgative that Stanney suddenly collapsed, and vomiting the little he had eaten, remained prostrate on the floor in a faint. The same day, he made his confession and took Viaticum. After being fortified with the sacrament of annointing, his sickness came to an end—in apoplexy. He died next day . . . He was 62 years old, having passed 28 of them with the Jesuits. He had been a formed co-adjutor since 1601.

The years 1598 and 1599 saw many more candidates for the Society, but in view of the shortness of their lives they remained practically unknown. There was John Pole from Spinkhill in Derbyshire, who was sent to Valladolid to be prefect of studies, and to lecture on moral theology in the seminary. He lived his last day at San Lucar in 1604 when he was not yet 30 years old. But he was already a man notable for uprightness and learning. Philip Draycott of Stafford, and William Metcalf of York, barely finished the first year of their noviceship when they were called to the reward of those who aspire after the right things. Henry Floyd, however, was to be preserved for a longer struggle.

40. Floyd [Fludd], as we narrated above, was sent with John Blackfan to Spain [8 May 1589]. He died [in London on 7 March 1641] while he was fulfilling a charge originally received from Persons at the Lisbon foundation [in 1606?]. By many vicissitudes, Floyd came to England [about 1597] and joined the Jesuits [in 1599]. He lived with Sir John Southcote, a man very well known to the Catholics, for 19 years altogether, but with varying fortunes. During his fourth year in England, thanks to the carelessness of one of the servants, the pursuivants rushed in one morning and intercepted him before he had time to get into a hiding-hole. He was thrown into a damp and dismal dungeon in Newgate where

a bench was his bed and his life was shared with criminals. However, he was much more worried about the danger to his host in whose house he was taken than the discomforts of his prison. When he understood his host was safe, he put up with the rest readily enough. However, not long afterwards, he was transferred to a more comfortable place where he had a chance of exchanging courtesies with Francis Page the martyr [on 20 April 1602].

Popham was one of the most important judges at that time. Since he was hankering after Southcote's property, he strove by every shift available to prove that Henry was a priest. This was done by interrogation, drawing him on with fair promises to admit the fact, and also by seeing if there were any false brethren or apostates who knew him. By foresight and wariness, Henry eluded them all, and so he and his host remained safe. Floyd was moved from London to Framlingham Castle in Suffolk, and towards the end of Elizabeth's reign was sent into exile at Lisbon . . .*

41. John was Henry Floyd's younger brother. [He was born in 1572 or 1573], although he was Henry's senior in the Society [which he entered on 1 November 1592]. He learned from experience not only that things are not always what they seem, but they are not always as safe as they seem. He was called to the Jesuit, Father Oldcorne, in Worcester gaol only to be kept there. Nor could he get himself out by plea or fee since he had Popham against him. A year after his exile [1606], he spent a further four years lecturing at St. Omer's. He published a number of things [in the field of controversy] works which won wide approval for their skill and learning . . .*

ENVOI

Book VII: 1. ·Elizabeth reigned 45 years in the midst of plenty and surrounded by every delight. She enjoyed peace at home and a happy conclusion to her foreign wars. With gifted negotiators in plenty, she shone among the ablest rulers of her time through the clear-sightedness of most illustrious councillors, the magnificence of her noblemen, and the wealth of private citizens. Those who consider a people blessed that enjoys such things recall even now the halycon days in which heaven, earth and ocean united to pour out their blessings on a princess who enjoyed the complete devotion of her people; and on a people adorned by all the graces of their sovereign.

James succeeded her, the sixth of that name among the Scots. He owed his right to Henry VII, whose daughter James IV took to wife. Her granddaughter, the only daughter of James V and Claudia of Guise, was married first to Francis II, King of France, and afterwards to Earl Darnley of the house of Stuart. Brought up a Catholic, [Mary] clung steadfastly to the faith she had imbibed with her mother's milk. She tried to communicate this faith to her son, James VI. Thanks to her faith, and the determination and fervour of the Protestants, she was expelled from her kingdom. Seeking a refuge with Elizabeth, she lost first her liberty and then her life. In the event, the claims of the plighted word, the rights of a guest, and the ties of common blood were all set aside . . .

The two grains planted in the island in 1580 had scarcely produced, in all the 20 years, the 20th Jesuit who could be employed in sustaining Catholicism in so great a country. There were others admitted in foreign provinces, or who were not yet sufficiently mature for the work; or else they were doing useful work in the provinces they had joined. This took up some years of their life. It was reasonable enough that when they had done their noviceship and studies with foreigners they should make some return in useful service to those who had trained and maintained them. Furthermore, the seminaries started in Spain and Belgium in these years called away not a few to the varied administration of these houses. Premature death accounted for some members. Among these, apart from Thomas Warcop, who we noted in the first book as dying at Alicante, there was William Sutton and Robert Bennet. They were drowned at sea not

far from the Alicante promontory. They were obeying
a call, in 1590, to the newly-begun house at Valladolid.
The necrology also recalls the name of Paul Tankard who
died at Valladolid on 5 July 1599. He was actually Charles
Tankard who, as a young man of 20, while he was studying
philosophy in the Roman College, set out for Naples.
He was received into the Society in February 1584. After
his theology, he was sent to Seville where he acted as
minister in the English College for a time. He was then
summoned by the Governor of Castile (Don Martin de
Padilla) to be his confessor. He crossed over by sea, and
died at Valladolid in the above-mentioned year . . .

Book VI: 41. All through this [Elizabethan] period, the
(concluded)   English mission experienced the brotherly
                 solicitude of different houses and provinces
throughout the Society, of learned men and steadfast
martyrs. It is ready to acknowledge the source of its distinction, and example worthy to be remembered for
ever by minds overflowing with gratitude. These things
will always be recalled with the utmost satisfaction. It
was because it had these foundations to rest on that the
English mission was later able to stand on its own. Indeed,
it grew into a province . . .

These beginnings, and the growth that followed, owed
their existence not only to neighbouring provinces but to
needed assistance and favour given from farther afield. This
was essential, and indeed, always will be, not only as long
as we lie gasping across the anvil of persecution, but for
as long as the Society itself remains one entity; and for as
long as we hold together in the most complete union possible of all our members. *Pars enim si a parte dissideat quid
consequi potest nisi dolor et interitus?*—If one part disagrees
with another what can ensue but misery and ruin?

END OF BOOK THE SIXTH

APPENDIX A

Books published by Henry More

1. *A Manuall of Devout meditations and Exercises, instructing how to pray mentally. Drawne for the most part out of the spiritual Exercises of B. F. Ignatius. Divided into three bookes Written in Spanish by the R.F. Thomas de Villa-Castin of the Society of Jesus, and translated into English by a Father of the same Society. Permissu Superiorum, S.J. (S. Omer), Anno 1618, 12°, pp. 558,—Dedication to the English novices at Liège and signed: 'I.W.'

*A Manual of devout . . . Drawn for the most part . . . Divided into three books . . . into English by H. M. of the same Society, S.J., 1624, 12°, p. 558.

2. The Happiness of a Religious state, divided in three books written in Latin by F. H. Platus, and new translated into English. Apud Ioannem Cousturier, Anno Domino 1632, 4°, pp. 613.

3. Vita et doctrina Christi Domini notationibus, quae quotidianum divina meditantibus materiam suggerere possunt, explicata: juxta quattuor partes anni Ecclesiastici in Capita distributa per Henricum Morum e Societate Jesu. Antverpiae, apud Jacobum Meursium, 1649, 12°, pp. 617.

The same work was published in English:

4. (i) The Life and Doctrine of our Saviour . . . Ghent, 1656, 8°.

(ii) The Life and Doctrine of our Saviour Jesus Christ. With short reflections for the help of such as desire to use mental prayer. The second part wherein every seventh

Meditation is an application of the former to the most
B. Sacrament. By H. M. of the Society of Jesus, edited by
Rev. C. Bowden of the Oratory (Reprinted from the
edition of 1666) (London, 1880).

5. Historia Missionis Anglicanae Societatis Jesu, ab
anno Salutis M.D.LXXX, ad D.C.XIX et Vice-Provinciae
primum, tum provinciae ad eiusdem saeculi annum XXXV.
Collectore Henrico Moro. Eiusdem Societatis Sacerdote.
Audomari, Typis Thomae Geubels, M. DC.LX. fol.pp. 518.

Notes from C. Sommervogel, S.J.; Bibliothèque de la
Compagnie de Jésus; vol. V (Brussels/Paris, 1894).

APPENDIX B

More's Bibliography

(Based on information supplied by R. K. Browne, Esq., F.L.A.)

BARTOLI, Daniel, S.J.: *Del 'Istoria della Compagnia di Giesú: l'Inghilterra; parte dell' Europa.* (Rome, 1667.)

BOMBINO, Pietro Paolo, S.J.: *Vita et martyrium Edmundi Campiani martyris Angli e Societate Iesu.* (Antwerp, 1618): *Editio posterior ab auctore multis aucta partibus & emendata.* (Mantua, 1620.)
A copy of the Mantua edition, annotated by Bombino is in the Jesuit Archives at Rome.

BRIDGEWATER, John (Aquipontanus): *Concertatio Ecclesiae Catholicae in Anglia adversus Calvino-Papistas et Puritanos sub Elizabetha Regina.* (Trèves, 1588, 1589 and 1594.)

FISEN, Bartholomew, S.J.: *Flores Ecclesiae Leodiensis, sive vitae vel elogia Sanctorum, et aliorum qui illustriori virtute hanc diocesim exornarunt.* (Lille, 1647).

JOUVENCY, Joseph, S.J.: *Historiae Societatis Jesu pars quinta. Tomus posterior ab anno Christi MDXCI ad MDCXVI.* (Rome, 1710.)

ORLANDINO, Nicolaus, S.J.: *Historiae Societatis Jesu: pars prima.* (Rome, 1614; Cologne, 1615; Antwerp, 1620.) References are to book and section numbers.

PITZIUS: PITS, John: *Relationum historicarum de rebus Anglicis. Tomus Primus.* (Paris, 1619.) Only Tomus Primus was published. Frequently cited by the running title: *De illustribus Angliae Scriptoribus.*

POSSEVINO, Antonio: Presumably either *Apparatus ad omnium gentium historiam.* (Venice, 1597), or *Liber decimus sextus de Apparatu ad omnium gentium historiam.* (Venice, 1602.)

PRIMI SAECULI: *Imago primi saeculi Societatis Iesu a Provincia Flandro-Belgica eiusdem Societatis repraesentata.* (Antwerp, 1640.) Compiled by Jean Bolland and others.

RAEMOND, Florimond de (The form favoured by British Museum Cat. and *Biographie Universelle*): Only one of his works seems to fit this reference : *L'Histoire de la Naissance, Progrez et Décadence de l'Hérésie de ce siècle divisée en huit livres.* 2 vols. (Paris, 1605.) Numerous later editions. Latin translation published at Cologne in 1614.

    Catal. of exiles in *Florimondus Raymondus,* part 2, Bk. 2, Ch. 14.

RIBADENEIRA, Pedro de, S.J.: *Historia ecclesiastica del scisma del Reyno de Inglaterra.* (Madrid, 1588.) Numerous subsequent editions.

ZACCHINUS-SACCHINI, Francesco, S.J.: *Historiae Societatis Jesu pars tertia sive Borgia.* (Rome, 1622.) i.e., the third part of ORLANDINO.

APPENDIX C

Original documents or contemporary copies quoted at length, or more fully summarised in More's history, and their present location where known

Copies are contemporary or near contemporary

No.	Correspondents, etc.	Date	Page in More	Location of documents(s)	Page in this Book
1	St. Ignatius of Loyola to Reginald Reginald Pole.	24 Jan. 1555	11	A.R.S.J.* Regest. III. Italia 105, II/III, ff. 6v, 7r. Italian, cf. Monumenta Ignatiana: Series 1a, Tomus 8. vus, Matriti, 1909, pp. 308–311.	
2	Lainez (Polanco) to Francis Borgia.	21 Sept. 1562	12	Ib. Epistolae Nostrae, 55 (Polancus ex Commissione: II. 1556–1563 Trent). ff. 109r–110v.	
3	Lainez to (vere) Rector of Louvain.	7 Nov. 1564	13	Ib. Germania 105, ff. 203v, 204r: Register Copy. Italian.	
4	Same to same	28 Nov.1564 (not 20 Dec.)	13	Ib. f. 221v. Italian.	
5	Same to Everard Mercurian	27 July 1564	13	Ib. ff. 138v. et 139r: Register copy.	
6	Ditto	4 Sept. 1564	13	Ib. f.174v–176r (175v).	
7	T. Stapleton to C. Aquaviva	5 May 1587	29		
8	Polanco to E. Mercurian ..	20 Oct. 1562	31	Ib. Epist. Nostrae, 55, f. 120v.	
9	Mercurian to Thomas Pound	1 Dec. 1578	45/46	Ib. Hist. Flandro-Belgica, 2 (Epist. Gener. 1576–82), pp. 131–2. Register copy.	
10	T. Stephens on Pound ..	1578	47		
11	Robert Persons on Alfonso Agazzari.	17 Nov. 1580	52	Ib. Anglia, 30, I, f. 155 and f. 181. Copy.	
12	R. Sherwin and J. Mush Declaration.	c. 1579	56		
13	Eng. College oath, Rome ..	1580	58	Mount Street Archives, S.J., London, Thorpe Fragments, f. 7r.	

*Archivum Romanum S.J.

No.	Correspondents, etc.	Date	Page in More	Location of document(s)	Page in this Book
14	William Allen to Edmund Campion	5 Dec. 1579	60	A.R.S.J., Fondo Gesuitico, 651, No. 594 (6th letter). Stonyhurst MSS., Anglia, A.I., f. 28 (No. 7). Copy.	
15	Campion to Mercurian	20 June 1580	63		
16	Toletus, Trent assertion ..	14 June 1561 (?)	66		
17	Reply of Trent		69		
18	Edmund Campion to Mercurian ..	1580 (?)	66	A.R.S.J., Fondo Ges∞, 651, No. 612 (2nd letter). No date. No address. Signed holograph.	
19	R. Persons to ?	1580 (?)	78	Ib. No. 596 (2nd letter). Copy.	
20	? to the rector of a seminary	16 June 1581	81/2	Ib. No. 594 (letters 7 and 8: 2 copies).	
21	W. Allen to ?	23 June 1581 (not June 13 1581)	83		
22	E. Campion to Gregory Martin ..	no date	101		
23	R. Sherwin to	Dec. 1581 (?)	103		
24	A. Bryant to the Jesuits ..	Dec. 1581	104		
25	R. Persons to A. Agazzari..	23 Dec. 1581	107		
26	W. Bathe on Persons's De Resolutione.	1582 (?)	112	Stonyhurst MSS., Collectanea, P, f. 293. [W.B.'s writing is not in A.R.S.J., Anglia, 41 (Hibern. Historia 1566, 1591–1692); nor in MSS. Hibernica, 1576–1690, Arch. S.J., Dublin; cf., H.M.C., 10th Report; App. Part V, pp. 340-1. These latter MSS., formerly at Stonyhurst, were transferred to Ireland in 1866.]	
27	R. Persons to Claud Aquaviva ..	21 Oct. 1581	113–21	A.R.S.J. Fondo Ges∞, 651, No. 640 (39 letters, original and copies of R.P. to the General, S.J., and three to R.P.), (3rd letter), copy.	
28	Persons to W. Crichton	1583	122		
29	W. Allen to T. Bayley	Aug. 1584 (?)	123		

No.	Correspondents, etc.	Date	Page in More	Location of document(s)	Page in this Book
30	R. Persons to A. Agazzari..	24 Aug, 1583	123–7	A.R.S.J., Anglia, 30, I, f.287v.: also in Ib., Romana, 156, II, ff. 150r–151v.	
31	Thomas Cottam to T. Pounde	1583 (?)	127		
32.	Gregory XIII to William of Bavaria.	27 May 1580	132–3		
33	Stephen of Poland to Elizabeth I of England.	1585	136	P.R.O., London, State Papers, Poland, 1. f. 61. Original.	
34	L. Kirby to some friends ..	10 Jan. 1582	137		
35	Allen to Agazzari	1582	140		
36	Persons to Pedro de Ribadeneira..	12 Sept. 1584	140	A.R.S.J. Anglia, 30, II, f. 506v; Ib., I, f. 300v. Copies, cf., C.R.S. 39, p. 234. [See R. Persons to General, 15 Sept. 1584, Ib., Gallia, 91, ff. 227r–228v. R.P. mentions having written to Ribadeneira, 'una lettera che scrissi tre giorni sono'.]	
37	E. Mercurian to Thomas Mettam	4 May 1579	140–1	Ib. Historia, Flandro-Belgica, 2, p. 142. Register copy.	
38	Annual Letters (Roman)	1592	141	Ib. Rom. 127, I, ff. 188v, 189r.	
39	R. Persons to A. Agazzari.. ..	17 Feb. 1580	146	Ib. Anglia, 30, I, f. 155. Copy.	
40	Persons to Allen	1592	146		
41	Gregory Martin to E. Campion ..	20 Dec. 1575	148	Ib. Fondo Ges^{co}, 651, No. 636. Letter 2 (seven letters from G.M. to E.C. in all).	
42	George Blackwell to Cardinal Protector of England.	10 Jan. 1596	149–50	Westminster Archives, Anglia IX, No. 9.	
43	Plea against Orders (religious) ..	1587 (?)	151		
44	R. Persons to Henry Garnet ..	24 May 1603	161	P.R.O., London, State Papers Domestic, James I, 1, No. 84.	
45	R. Southwell on suffering		177		
46	R. Southwell to C. Aquaviva ..	23 Jan 1585	182	A.R.S.J., Fondo Ges^{co}, 651, No. 648, 1st letter.	

No.	Correspondents, etc.	Date	Page in More	Location of document(s)	Page in this Book
47	Same to same	16 Jan. 1590	183	Ib., 13th letter.	
48	Same to same	8 Mar. 1590	184	Stonyhurst MSS. Collectanea P, pp. 513–5. Copy.	
49	Same to peregrinating priest ..	1595	189		
50	R. Southwell to his family ..		190	['Letter 37' (More's number): was this letter one of many lost from what is now A.R.S.J., Fondo Ges^{co}, 651, No. 648?].	
51	R. Southwell to his father ..	1589	191		
52	Ld. Burghley on Southwell ..	1595 (?)	193		
53	H. Walpole to R. Holtby ..	Jan. 1594	209		
54	Same to same	1594 (?)	211		
55	Same to same	1594 (?)	215		
56	Same to R. Walpole	Apr. 1595	215–6		
57	R. Walpole to	1598 (?)	221		
58	O. Manare to R. Persons ..	24 Nov. 1594	229–30		
59	R. Persons to C. Aquaviva ..	20 Feb. 1595	230–2	A.R.S.J., Hispania, 138, f. 143	
60	Same to Francis Englefield ..	10 May 1595	232–4		
61	T. Fitzherbert to General, S.J. ..		236–40		
62	Claud Aquaviva's rules for the English Mission, S.J.	15 May 1606	241–8	Ib., Rom. 156, II, ff. 152r and v; 153r–155v; N.B. ff. 191r–197r and ff. 200r–206r. Two copies signed by Aquaviva. Archives du Royaume, Brussels, Jésuites Flandro-Belges, 1085.	
63	R. Persons to P. Ribadeneira ..	12 Sept. 1584	268	Reference as for p. 140 (1660 edition).	
64	Same to Oliver Manare ..	10 (?) Jan. 1597	270	Westminster Arch., main series, vi, No. 4 (p. 13). Copy.	
65	William Allen to Charles Paget ..	4 Jan. 1591	271	Stonyhurst MSS. Collectanea M. No. 129. Copy.	

NOTES ON THE TEXT

*A note is indicated by an asterisk * in the text, and referred to
below by its book and paragraph number.*

*Books mentioned below were published in London unless otherwise
stated.*

Book the First

5. 'Pererebuit' is taken as a misprint for 'praebuerit' in a sentence
which begins obscurely. The title given to Pole in the letter is 'Your
Most Reverend Lordship'—Reverendissima Dominatio Vestra—since
'Your Eminence' was only in use by More's time.

8. Saint Joseph of Arimathea: an academy for the sons of gentle-
men. A marginal reference to the letters of 'Polom' seems to indicate
Polanco who was referred to on page 12 in another note as
'Polaneus'.

16. See H. Foley, *Collectanea*, p. 638. Has More confused Edward
and John Rastall? More relates that John Rastall offered his life to
God for that of his provincial, Paul Hoffaeus, when the latter lay
dying. After making a local pilgrimage, Rastall returned to die of
the same disease from which the provincial soon after recovered.
More saw this as an acceptance by God of Rastall's life for that of
Hoffaeus. More refers to the annual letters from Ingolstadt of 1600
('Annuae Ingolstadii') as his authority; also Sacchini, *History . . .*,
part IV, book 5, no. 107.

18. More's reference to the canonry at Bonn equates it with
worldly success and is at first sight rather slighting. The early Society
reacted strongly against receiving ecclesiastical honours since they
were still not infrequently sought and obtained from less than the
highest motives.

22. 'Post annum sexcentesimum decimum quintum', i.e.,
'some time after 1615'. Foley says *in* 1615 (*Collectanea*).

23. Menochius (Menocchi), John Stephen, was born at Pavia
in 1576. He began his Jesuit novitiate at seventeen. After his studies,
he lectured on Sacred Scripture at Milan, and, after filling a number
of posts, became an assistant to the general. He died at Rome on
4 February 1655. His written works included a two-volume commentary on the Scriptures, a six-volume historical anthology (*Le
Storie overo Trattenimenti eruditi*, Rome, 1646-54), and *De
Republica Hebreorum* (Paris, 1648-52). The latter was a careful
and learned study in two volumes on the manners and traditions of
the ancient Jews. (cf. *Biographie Universelle*.)

363

25. According to Nathaniel Southwell, S.J., in *Bibliotheca Scriptorum, S.J.* (Rome, 1676), p. 402, the first edition of the *Concertatio* was in 1584. This agrees with John Pits. T. W. Lowndes, *The Bibliographer's Manual*, vol. I (1834), makes it 1583. There was an augmented edetion in 1588/9. An edition of 1594, according to J. H. Pollen, S.J., was 'only a reissue of some unused sheets of the 1588 edition with a fresh title-page' (*C.R.S.*, vol. 5, p. 144). It had the same errors, including those resulting from broken type, bad setting and incorrect accents as the previous edition. The three editions appeared at Trèves (Augustae Trevirorum).

26. William Hart's entry is recorded in the *Liber Ruber* of the English College. See *C.R.S.*, vol. 37 (1940), part I, 'Nomina Alumnorum, 1579-1630', p. 10. After William Hart, More gives a brief extract on William Brookesby, whom he takes to be other than Brunsley (see More, I/25). In any case, the terms of reference are so general that they largely correspond with the Brunsley entry.

27. The reference to Langdale is in Persons's 'A Storie of domesticall difficulties', published in *C.R.S.*, vol. 2 (1906), pp. 181 and 182.

28. Referring to Perkins in the same place as Langdale (see I/27), Persons says he was 'made a Doctor'. It seems that Perkins was dismissed from the Society in 1581.

31. The earliest surviving register of novices entering the Society in Rome is still preserved by the Roman Province, S.J. It bears the title *Codex novitiorum Societatis Jesus qui Romae Tirocinium posuerunt ab anno MDLXV ad annum MDLXXXVI* . . . It is now at the Gesù, in Rome (1971). In 1773, the year of the general suppression of the Jesuits, it was transferred to the former building of the Roman College and placed under the care of a representative of the Roman princely house of Mattei: this information is contained in the title-page. More erroneously gives John for Nicholas Owen—'Little John'.

Book the Second

4. Iuvenem Academicum—cf. Gillow, *Biographical Dictionary* . . ., vol. 1, pp. 385-6; At Pont à Mousson, *Edmundi Campiani, S.J., Martyris in Anglia, Opuscula omnia nunc primum e MS edita*, was published in 1622. Bound with it from p. 145 onwards were further *Orationes, Epistolae, Tractatus de imitatione Rhet, (sic)*. However, the 'De Iuvene Academico' was not included but appears in the 1631 edition of Campion's works published by Christopher Plantin at Antwerp (*Edmundi Campiani . . . Decem Rationes propositae in Causa Fidei, et Opuscula eius selecta*) and dedicated to Peter Aloysius Carafa, Bishop of Tricarico and Apostolic Nuncio in Flanders. It appears as 'Oratio III' on pp. 262-97. The first time of

publication seems to have been in the supplement attached to the posthumous works of Robert Turner, an Englishman from Devon and professor at Ingolstadt, which appeared in 1602. The supplement, having its own pagination, bore the title, *Edmundi Campiani Societatis Jesu martyris in Anglia, Orationes, Epistolae, Tractatus de imitatione Rhetorica. A Roberto Turnero, Campiani discipulo, collecta. Et nunc primum e MS. edita . . . Ingolstadii . . .* The oration appears on pp. 29-44. For the *History of Ireland*, see Gillow, *op cit.,* p. 385; also A. C. Southern, *Elizabethan Recusant Prose 1559-1582, passim.* The *History* was reprinted in Dublin in 1809. Three of Campion's letters to R. Stanihurst are published in the 1631 edition (see above) as 'Epistolae II, III and IV' on pp. 347-60. Campion's 1631 letter saying that his history of Ireland has perished is not in the edition. On p. 398 of this edition (Epistola VIII, pp. 396-400) he writes to Gregory Martin, on 17 July 1579, from Prague, 'I wrote to Father Francis Coster, who rules the Rhine province of our Society, that if you would send him my notes (scriptiunculas) on Irish matters which you have by you, he would find a way whereby it could be sent to me here at Prague most safely' (Latin).

As regards the excommunication of Elizabeth, there is reason for thinking that Roberto Ridolphi, who on his own admission later was responsible for bringing in the Bull, was a double-agent working not only for the Pope, but primarily and effectively for Francis Walsingham and ultimately Sir William Cecil. These latter had probably much to do with the publication of the Bull and the time and place chosen. See F. Edwards, *The Dangerous Queen,* 1964, pp. 154, 169-70, 175ff, and 264. Henry More's gross inaccuracy in his account of the northern rising suggests his reliance on secondary continental sources such as Catena, *Vita del . . . Papa Pio V[o]* (Mantua, 1587), who may well have relied in turn on Ridolphi himself. Lord Burghley was at pains to make it appear that the excommunication was timed to help the northern rising. In fact it was drawn up some two months too late, and promulgated in England some six months too late. The northern rising was completely crushed by the end of 1569; Burghley's views in the Council and influence with the Queen were much enhanced by the excommunication.

5. More's marginal note refers the reader to the list of exiles in Florimondus Remondus (Florimond de Rémond), that is, his *Histoire de la Naissance, progrès et décadence de l'hérésie de ce siècle* (Paris, 1605), part II, book II, chapter 14, though More does not name the work. Modern and authoritative works on the subject of the Catholic exiles are Peter Guilday, *The English Catholic Refugees on the Continent, 1558-1795* (1914); Robert Lechat, *Les Rufugiés anglais dans les Pays-Bas espagnols durant le régne d'Elisabeth, 1558-1603* Louvain/Paris (1914); Albert J. Loomie, S.J., *The Spanish Elizabethans* (Fordham, 1963).

6. The letter to Cheney of 1 November 1571, was published in the 1631 edition of the works (see II/4) as 'Epistola V' on pp. 360–79; also in the Campion supplement to the 1602 edition of Turner's works on pp. 56–64.

7. This was undoubtedly Christopher Bagshawe, who later acquired a doctorate somewhat easily in Italy, having himself become a convert to Catholicism and a priest. His career was equivocal in some aspects. The best source on Persons to 1588 is L. Hicks, S.J., *Letters and Memorials of Father Robert Persons, S.J.* (1942) (*C.R.S.*, vol. 39). More gives the text of Persons's resignation from Balliol in full.

10. Wallop (see II/14) was also known as Gallop.

12. Astlow is Latinised by More as 'Ateslous'. See *Letters and Memorials* (*C.R.S.*, vol. 39), p. xi.

14. Daniel Bartoli, S.J. (1608–85), savant, preacher and historian of the Society including the English Province, left behind interesting notes on More's work now in the General's archives in Rome (Anglia 38/I, ff. 433–7). He comments on this passage (on f. 433; More, p. 44), 'Persons in his own life says that he entered the Society on 25 July, feast of St. James. The novices book at Sant' Andrea makes it 4 July 1575. He was 28 years old'.

More further comments, 'Bombino puts Gallop among those who either died for the faith or who achieved renown by wearing themselves out in their labours for it. He is mistaken as to the name. That honour is due rather to Thomas Pounde who sometimes hid himself under the name of Gallop or Wallop, Dukes and Harington . . .'.

The life of Persons is resumed in II/26.

15. Foley translates Mercurian's letter in full; vol. III (*Records . . .*),

16. 'Juris Municipalis praesidiis se praeparavit.'

17. Compare Foley's translation of this letter (*Records*, vol. III, p. 581) which was taken from Cardwell's transcripts from the Brussels Archives (Stonyhurst MSS.: A.IV.13; copy at Mount Street).

19. According to Foley, the 'widow of Newgate' was a kind of leg iron.

20. Principally omitted here are the objects of Pounde's prayer. James I sent the priests into exile in February 1604. Thomas Pounde left a narrative of his sufferings, seemingly addressed to the King himself, or intended to be seen by him (P.R.O., Dom. James I, vol. XXI, no. 48; printed in Foley, *ibid.*, pp. 614–17). The following corrections to Foley should be noted: on p. 614, '. . . Father Thomas Stevens, these 30 years since a famous preacher . . . at Goa, where their College of St. Paul is . . .' p. 615, 'Storforde

Castle' (not Starford) . . . 'My 11th removing from thence—and three more with me, viz., Father Edmonds, Mr. Southworth, and Mr. Archer, priests—I first into the Counter in Wood Street . . .'.

    p. 616, 'which promised more Christianly to protect us'.

    p. 617, 'their obedience to God and His supreme Vicar'.

    N.B.—More gives 'Stephenson' for 'Stevens'.

21. For R. Persons's letter of 17 November 1580, see *C.R.S.*, vol. 39, quoted at p. 48 top, and p. 49, foot. II/22 is devoted to Pounde's letter to Persons of 3 July 1609, from Belmont. This is printed in translation in Foley, vol. III, pp. 611-13. It concerns mainly contemporary details in Pounde's austere life at Belmont, and generalities of about 1609, so it is here omitted.

23. Owen Lewis, Bishop of Cassano: J. Gillow (*Biographical Dictionary* . . ., vol. IV) makes him at one time Canon of Cambrai and Archdeacon of Hainault.

24. In the Stonyhurst Archives (A.IV.29) is an interesting account of the English College, Rome, from 1578 to 1582 (*Breve Ragionamento del Origine e progresso del Collegio . . . dall 'anno . . . 1578*: at the end, 'Il fine A.D. 1582'. This original MS. is in bad condition. A transcript was made by T. W. Murphy, S.J., and is now at Mount Street (7/1). Cf. *Breve Informazione della storia . . .* (Anglia/A/VII, no. 96).

    For the decrees of the second general congregation of the S.J., see *Decreta Congregationum Generalium S.J.* (Rome, 1615) (Brit. Mus., C.25.d.6).

27. The rest of this paragraph is taken up with a long, rhetorical apostrophe as to why the Jesuits should go to England. It adds nothing substantially to the first sentence.

28. More wrongly dates the letter 9 December. The letter is accurately transcribed from Stonyhurst MSS., Anglia A/I/no. 7 in T.F. Knox, *Letters and Memorials of Cardinal Allen* (1882), on pp. 84, 85.

Book the Third

1. More here observed, 'Bombino's memoir concerning the Bishop of St. Asaph and Morton is not confirmed, I find, in any letter or note of Campion or Persons, although perhaps their departure was separated from that of the others by no great interval of time' (Paolo Bombino, *Vita et Martyrium Edmundi Campiani Martyris Angli e Societate Jesu*, Mantua, 1620). Bartoli observes (see note on II/14) 'But it is stated at length in C[oncertatio] A[nglicana], 70A, in the martyrdom of Ralph Sherwin'. It is probable that More was using either the 1588 or 1594 edition of the Concertation in which this fact does not appear in the place cited

by Bartoli. The latter adds (in his notes, f. 433) 'Bombino, p. 62, says that Goldwell and Morton set off before 10 April when Campion and the others set off. The Concert. Anglic. in the said place says that they left in the warm season (tempi caldi) . . . Sacchino . . . says that 13 Englishmen left Rome. Only 12 can be found, as Bombino says: three of our men; four priests from the hospice &c. [*sic*] three student priests; three secular priests. Persons in his MS. says 13 and gives 11 of them. Persons in the MS. of his life says that he and Campion left Rome on Low Sunday, 10 April. Bombino and More say the same. The Red Book of the English College, part II, f. 11, says that they left on 18 April. Sacchino says the same (part IV, book 8, no. 96. Camden, Annals for 1580, puts them in Rome on 14 April, on which day they received from the Pope the "moderation" (Moderatione) of the Bull of Pius V'. [This 'moderation' or 'explanation' suspended the excommunication for all practical purposes.] 'Holinshed, p. 1362, column 2, has the same. He took it from Camden.'

2. This translation of Campion to Mercurian, 20 June 1580, may be compared with Richard Simpson's *Edmund Campion* (1867), pp. 124-5. For George Persons, see *C.R.S.*, vol. 39, *passim*. On the Geneva stay, Bartoli comments (f. 433), 'The Englishman who in Geneva argued with Persons and recognised Campion their friend is called Polaius by Bombino. Sherwin in his letter says that he was called Powell. In many other important matters, Sherwin's letter disagrees with Bombino . . . Sherwin's letter is an original and the English College has it. There is another and one of More closes this paragraph with an introduction to the question of Catholics attending Protestant churches, and the decision of Trent in the matter. Para. 6 gives the letter from persons in England requesting instruction in the same matter. Para. 7 refers to the letter of para 6, and explains why it was not signed by any particular individual since it concerned nearly every Catholic gentleman in England. It was addressed to 'Illustrissima Dominatio'—the Cardinal Protector, seemingly, and his friends at Trent, but admitted, 'perhaps it would be inadvisable (tutum non) to put this question openly in the Counci lest the matter get about and antagonise our Protestants, and increase our danger, unless your wisdom thinks otherwise'. Appeal was rather made for private discussion among the Fathers, and the communication of their conclusions to the petitioners, which would be taken as tantamount to an official and formal decision in the Council. Paras. 8, 9 and 10 (More, pp. 67, 68) give Trent's reply of 1562 to the question. The most operative section, perhaps, is the following: (para. 9) 'it is altogether inadmissible that you should be present at Protestant prayers of this kind, and at their sermons, without sin . . . It is far better to endure every kind of affliction . . . than to consent by any outward sign

in their . . . rites . . . [W]however wrongly obeys the law gives approval to the law, as far as can be, by his tacit consent. He . . . becomes a party to the same schism . . . [Reminds of ancient examples] . . . Think also what grave scandal you could give to those in the same land in whom the light of faith is not completely extinguished! . . .'. The argument is substantially as it was given by Toledo. It stresses the danger of backsliding gradually, and the difficulty of resisting the influence of non-Catholic or anti-Catholic preaching in the long run. Para. 10: More enlarges with quotation on the preferability of going into exile and enduring every hardship at home rather than submit to the laws in England on religion: 'the laws of God must always be preferred to those of men . . .'. Again, 'For the Church of God never lacked ruthless enemies, but it always emerged more splendid and glorious after bearing with evil rather than repelling it by force. It was always an argument for the power of Christ that by the forbearance of the martyrs the strength and might of tyrants was brought low and overthrown' (p. 73). These were the arguments, as More reported them, of the Fathers of Trent.

5. The origins of this resolution of Trent of 1562 are discussed in J. H. Pollen, *English Catholics in the Reign of Elizabeth* (1920), pp. 100-102. The present writer had no more success than Father Pollen in discovering anything that resembled the original reply of Trent in the Vatican Library or Archives. It is likely that the document, if it survives, found its way into the inaccessible records of the Holy Office, more especially since the Holy Office gave a decision in this matter on 11 October 1562 (cf. Pollen, p. 101). This confirmed or rather accepted the decision of Trent. It seems that if Henry Garnet, S.J., had not published this decision as an appendix to his Treatist of Christian renunciation, it would have been lost. He gave it in Latin and English translation. The Treatise was probably written in 1593, but published some years later secretly in England and without date. Garnet referred to the treatise with the appendix in his letter to Persons of 2 June 1601 (Stony-hurst, Collectanea P., no. 553. Copy). More's version (pp. 66-73) follows substantially what was printed by Garnet, although some of More's omissions are significant.

11. For 'Campion's Brag' in full see Richard Simpson, *op. cit.*, pp. 159-61. Also in Campion's 'Ten Reasons proposed to his adversaries for Disputation in the name of the Faith and presented to the Illustrious Members of our Universities', J. H. Pollen edition (1914), pp. 7-11.

12. The letter to Mercurian, which follows in III/13, was probably written in the late November of 1580 when Campion parted with Persons at Uxbridge. It appears in Latin in the 1631 edition of the 'Decem Rationes' and other works (see II/4) as

as 'Epistola X' on pp. 408-19. Translated into English in Simpson, *op. cit.*, pp. 174-7.

15. Persons to Rome, 17 November 1580. Cf. *C.R.S.*, vol. 39, pp. 46-56, especially p. 48, for full letter and translation. It seems that the original is lost. It is not in the more recently discovered Fondo Gesuitico 651 (640) in the General's archives which contains a new group of Persons's letters. There is a copy in the same archive (Anglia 30/I/f. 155). Cf. More, p. 52 (II/21). The omissions from the present paragraph in this translation were substantially supplied there. Printed in Ribadeneira, *Historia Ecclesiastica del Cisma de Inglaterra* (Madrid, 1595 edition) on p. 573; (1786 edition) on p. 265. The sentence, 'Hence they are called recusants' does not appear in the *C.R.S.* version.

By way of note to absence of original, documents in general, the following extracts are of interest, both from Father James Connell to Father Charles Plowden; the first in a letter of 4 August 1792: 'One Kirk, an alumnus of the English College, a great friend, I hear, of Berrington's carried off with him to England a great number of original letters taken out of the archives of the English College: After the abolition [of the Society] orders were given to examine and clear the archives, [and] whole baskets of papers were then thrown out by persons who little knew the value of many of these papers. He selected out those which, as he thought, were worth keeping, and carried them with him to England'. And from a letter written before 6 December, 'Could you think that there be not in the archives of the English College one single letter of Father Persons, and five only of Cardinal Allen, and these to persons in Flanders, after he had transferred his seminary to Rheims . . . Yet it is matter of fact'. Both the Connell letters are in the English Province Archives, Mount Street (vol. 13, Letters of Stone, Sewell and Connell).

For further reproduced original documents and contemporary printed texts on Sherwin and other martyrs mentioned above and below, see, *Sacred Congregation of Rites, Historical Section, 148; Archiocese of Westminster, Cause of the Canonization of Blessed Martyrs . . . Cuthbert Mayne, John Paine, Edmund Campion, Alexander Briant, Ralph Sherwin and Luke Kirby, put to death in England in defence of the Catholic Faith (1535-82).* Official *Presentation of Documents on Martyrdom and Cult.* (Vatican Polyglot Press, 1968), pp. 107-367.

16. This letter of 13 June 1582, was probably to Agazzari, Rector of the English College, Rome. It appears to be lost. The parliament which passed the anti-Catholic legislation of 23 Eliz. Cap. 1 (see *The Penal Laws against Papists and Popish Recusants . . .* [Savoy, London, 1723], pp. 10-15) was that originally summoned on 28 March 1572, and dissolved on 19 April 1583. The 1581 session

lasted from 16 January to 18 March, when it was prorogued until 24 April. See Royal Hist. Soc., *Handbook of British Chronology* (1961); also J. E. Neale, *Elizabeth and her Parliaments, 1559-1581* (1953), pp. 413, 415.

17. More or his printer omitted this number.

20. Campion was taken on the night of 16/17 July 1581. According to Simpson (p. 228), Colebrook was 10 miles from London. Bartoli's note runs (see II/14, f. 433v.), 'Bombino's chronology cannot stand. He tells of the taking of Bryant in the vicinity of Persons's room. He knews what Persons was doing three or four days before being in the wood. He stayed there two more days and then they parted. Campion goes to Lyford and he is taken in that place in less than four days. Now it is certain that Campion was taken on 22 July. The register of the Tower of London does not establish the month but that it was not before July that Bryant was tortured on the rack (?) . . .'.

22. More refers to Yepes's account of Campion's dispute in the *Historia Particular de la Persecucion . . . desde el año . . .1570* (Madrid, 1599), pp. 323-5 and p. 37, para. 1. Alexander Nowell was Dean of St. Paul's; W. Day, Dean of Windsor; Whitaker, Regius Professor of Divinity at Cambridge; Charke, preacher at Gray's Inn; Robert Beale, Clerk of the Privy Council. The latter refers to the conference in his letter to the Earl of Rutland of 18 September 1581: see H.M.C., 12th Report, Appendix part IV (Belvoir Castle MSS., vol. 1), p. 128. More refers also to Ribadeneira, *op. cit.*, Book II, ch. XXXII, adding to his text what is best given, perhaps, as a note. 'Neither Camden in his history of Elizabeth's reign, nor Stowe in his shorter work, nor Holinshed in his more detailed study, nor even, finally, Speed give any record of a victory. At the same time, Stowe describes at some length, and lauds the thrust and parry which took place at, a colloquy in the first year of Elizabeth's reign between Catholic doctors and the men of the reformed religion, as they term it'. More quotes Yepes, *op. cit.*, Book II, ch. 4, no. 1 (edition indicated above, p. 37).

A detailed account from the government viewpoint, of Campion's first Tower conference of 31 August 1581, was published on 1 January 1583, by Christopher Barker, the Queen's printer. It was written by Alexander Nowell and W. Day. On the same day was published, *The three last dayes conferences had in the Tower with Edmund Campion Jesuite, the 18: 23: and 27 of September, 1581, collected and faithfully set downe by M. John Feilde student in Divinitie . . .* (sig. A.i to Gg.i). The disputants were as More gives them, that is, Fulke and Goode.

24. More quotes marginally for his account of the trial, 'From the Acts of Westminster'. See chapter XV of Simpson, *op. cit.*, and the

notes on pp. 384-5. MS. sources include B. M. Lansdowne 33, no. 64 (The Indictment of Edmund Campion . . . for high treason, June 1581; no. 65, Indictment of Allen, Moreton, Parsons, Campion and other Popish traitors, 1581).

30. More's account of Campion's character is based on John Pits and Camden as his marginal note on p. 100 indicates. 'Letter 6': see 1631 edition of the 'works', pp. 380-89. More's quotation begins on p. 381. Much of the quotation has been omitted here since, although it is an excellent example of Campion's polished rhetoric, it contributes nothing to history as such. The quotation beginning, 'Are you making the most of Rome . . .' is mis-indicated in More as from Letter 6. It occurs in Letter 7 which runs from p. 389 to p. 400, in the 1631 edition. More's quotation is on p. 391, or as much as is given here. Letter 8 is on pp. 396-400, and, unlike the others, is dated—17 July 1579 (16.Kal.Augusti). It is from Prague. There are autograph drafts of letters by Campion from this city in the Stonyhurst Archives which run from 1577 to 1579 (Anglia/A/I/nos. 4-6, letters of 1577—and Anglia/A/I/no. 6—five letters of 1579). In *ibid.*, A/II/14, there is the beginning of a Latin life of Campion in Person's hand, dated Sunday, 20 October 1595. Stonyhurst MS. A.IV.12 (2), no. 9, is a transcript of a Latin account of Campion's life and martyrdom transcribed from a MS. at Brussels by Cardwell of 1618.

'The martyrdom of Cuthbert', a reference, no doubt, to the martyrdom of Cuthbert Mayne (29 November 1577) which Campion may have described in his letter to which this replies. No printed work of this name is known (cf. Gillow, Allison and Rogers). An omission by More in the last sentence of his quotation, without indication, has been supplied from the printed works (1631 edition).

31. The quotation from Camden also corresponds with the 1625 Latin edition, p. 377 (An. 27, i.e., 1584/5). More omits mention of Mary Queen of Scots. The second quotation from Camden corresponds substantially, though not always literally, with the 1625 Latin edition (p. 570) from which the present translation is made. Cf. the 1635 English edition, p. 394.

Cradock, or Caddy, was a spy who claimed that the Pope was to sent 200 priests into England to help create a diversion while the Irish invasion proceeded. (See Simpson, *op. cit.*, 1867 edition, p. 310).

32. Sherwin's letter is printed, seemingly in full, in Ribadeneira, *Historia* . . ., Book II, ch. 33 (1786 edition, pp. 283-4). The translation given here is not from More's Latin but from Ribadeneira's Spanish.

34. The account of Bryant's private vow to join the Jesuits may be compared with Foley, *Records* . . ., vol. IV, pp. 356-8, which

translated a copy of a Latin document, the copy being in the Archives du Royaume, Brussels (cf. Cardwell Collections on the martyrs, Stonyhurst MS., A/IV/12 (2), no. 5—Bryant's life and martyrdom). More's account resembles Bryant's life as given in Allen's *A Briefe Historie of the glorious Martyrdom of Twelve Reverend Priests* . . . (Rheims, 1582); reprint edited by J. H. Pollen, S.J. (1908), pp. 46–56. It is given as a quotation in More and here but it may be More's own summary—conventions on quotation in the 17th century were very easy-going in comparison with the best modern standards. More may have followed an independent MS. now lost. Challoner, *Memoirs* . . . (1924 edition), p. 35, *et. seq.* gives a brief extract. Challoner's translation, and also Foley's, corresponds with the Latin version of Bridgewater's *Concertatio* . . . (Trèves, 1594), pp. 74–6. In a marginal note to III/33, More acknowledges his reliance on this source at any rate for his account of Bryant's sufferings in prison. No doubt, More gives Bryant's vow to enter the Society full treatment since some doubt had been cast on whether Bryant did in fact become a Jesuit, or in what sense he was to be regarded as one. Challoner alluded to it but did not give Bryant's letter to the Father of the Society in full.

35. Persons's letter of 23 December 1581, was summarised by Christopher Grene, S.J., in his Collectanea P/I, f. 293 (Stonyhurst MSS.). Grene comments, 'he relateth in one sheet and a half of paper their condemnation and the execution of three of them, which I will not copy out because all may be found in so many printed books, especially F. Bartoli's *Inghilterra*'. Bartoli refers to the letter on pp. 173, 201 (Rome, 1667 edition), but there is no full transcript. Grene's extract is given in *C.R.S.*, vol. 39, p. 123.

36. Challoner's account (edition above, p. 28) makes the interruption by Sir Francis Knollys, Treasurer of the Household from 1572 until his death in 1596. He was Vice-Chamberlain from 1559 till 1570.

37. Gaspar, William and Robert: the first, no doubt, refers to Heywood, who also entered in the summer of 1581 with Father William Holt, probably the second reference. 'Robert' would fit Persons himself.

38. The principal omission here is a pious anecdote related by William Wright, S.J., concerning a certain Baron Mansuander, who was a former pupil of Campion's.

Book the Fourth

1. Persons's published works of this time were *A brief censure uppon two bookes written in answere to M. Edmonde Campion's offer to disputation* (Douai [in fact at the secret Greenstreet press

in England], 1581. This was followed in 1582 by *A defence of the censure, gyven upon two bookes of William Charke and Meredith Hanmer mynysters, whiche they wrote against M. Edmond Campion* (Rouen, 1582). *An epistle of the persecution of Catholickes in Englande. Translated owt of frenche into Englishe and conferred withe the Latyne copie . . . To whiche there is added an epistle by the translator* (Douai, undated, but also of 1582). (See Allison and Rogers.) The Latin copy seems to have been that published as *De Persecutione Anglicana Libellus . . . Romae apud Franciscum Zanettum MDLXXXIII*, dedicated to Cardinal Philip Boncompagno, and given as from the English College, Rome. The first edition of a 'Christian Directory' appeared in Rouen in 1582 as *The first booke of the Christian exercize, appertayning to resolution*. This book, undoubtedly the best-known of Person's works, went through several editions in his own lifetime (see Allison and Rogers). Christopher Grene gives a catalogue of Persons's books in Collectanea P.I, p. 181 (Stonyhurst MSS.). This mentions the fact that the *Epistola de Persecutione* was published at Ingolstadt as well as Rome in 1582.

2. Part of this letter of Persons to Aquaviva was published in W. Forbes-Leith, S.J., *Narratives of Scottish Catholics under Mary Stuart and James VI* (Edinburgh, 1885), pp. 166–74, but with very substantial omissions both at the beginning and end without indication of the fact. Forbes-Leith assigned the date 26 September 1581 to this letter. The late H. Chadwick, S.J., left valuable notes on this letter among which the following may be observed: the probable date is 21 October 1581, for Bartoli (book 2, ch. 9) quotes a passage also found in More (p. 115) and ascribes this date. Aquaviva's reply to Persons of 23 December 1581, answers a letter of 21 October from Persons and deals with some of the points raised therein, which were also included in the present letter.

Persons left England about 12 to 15 August, probably reaching Paris by 21 August; then presumably to Rheims to see Allen (end of August?), but there is no clear record of Persons's interview with Allen or for that matter with Beaton (but see *C.R.S.*, vol. 9, p. 35 and pp. 81–5). Persons went on to Rouen possibly in the first week in September.

Persons's servant was Robert Alfield, brother of the martyr Thomas. Robert later turned traitor (see *C.R.S.*, vol. 4, pp. 48–91), especially p. 54, note.

William Waytes or Watts seems to have been the person specially trusted who was sent to reconnoitre in or near Scotland (cf. More, II/5).

The Earl of Morton was executed on 2 June 1581.

3. The letter of Father William Watts to Persons included in the latter's to Aquaviva of 21 October (?) 1581. The *latter* part of

Persons's letter probably was written or dated 26 September. Seiford is probably Cessford, six miles north-east of Jedburgh, a former seat of the Kerrs. The lairds of Cessford and Ferniehurst were in turn Wardens of the Middle March at this time. The warden in 1581 was William Kerr, or Sir Walter his father (Douglas, *Peerage,* vol. 7, p. 339).

It seems impossible to identify 'Grencknols' with any certainty.

George, fifth Lord Seton, had helped Mary Stuart to escape from Loch Leven, and was at Langside, but his subsequent allegiance was equivocal at times (F. Edwards, *op. cit.,* pp. 405–07). It may be significant that he regained the title of Prior of Pluscardine in July 1581. Chadwick thought 'Baron Geron' was a corrupton of 'Seton', and that 'another letter' with its 'secret signs' may be in the Vatican archives (Misc. de Castello, Addita ad Cap. XV, Arm.15, no. 3).

4. This returns to Persons's letter, and the part which may well have been written on 26 September. The complete absence of any printing press in Scotland at this time seems doubtful. The extreme plight of the English Catholics is described in similar terms by Mendoza, the Spanish ambassador, in his letter to Philip II, 20 October 1581, for example (Spanish Calendar, III, p. 196). Aquaviva decided, 'for grave reasons', not to approach the Pope for money, but he procured a loan of 200 crowns which he said he would send at once to Persons at Rouen (cf. Aquaviva to Allen 23 December 1581; *C.R.S.,* vol. 9, pp. 85–6).

Achilles Gagliardi, S.J. (1537–1606). At this time professor of theology at Rome. Robert Bellarmine, S.J. (1542–1621) was also a professor at the Roman College. Father Ferdinand Capecci was a tutor or 'repetitor' at the English College, Rome (see *C.R.S.,* vol 2, p. 93). The Spaniard referred to was Diego Sanchez (see Sacchini, *Hist. S.J.,* pars V, tom. 1, book 8, no. 156 (p. 404).

5. A number of letters are extant in the Jesuit archives, Rome, which went between Hay, Crichton and the Generals, beginning on 8 May 1564 (Hay to Polanco, the General's secretary) and ending with Crichton to Father Duras (Assistant) on 31 October 1598.

Allen's letter to Thomas Bayley was dated by T. F. Knox, presumably tentatively since he took it from More, August 1587. (*Letters and Memorials . . .,* p. 299). As regards Knox's note (p. 299), 'It does not appear whether these are Cardinal Allen's own words or only a translation of them', More began this extract with inverted commas, and although it is not closed after 'Personius fecit me Cardinalem', the person of More's narrative changes abruptly after this from the first person to the third, so that this cannot be taken as a good example of typographical imprecision; of which admittedly there are examples elsewhere.

6. This letter is given in full in Latin and in translation in L. Hicks, S.J., *Letters and Memorials* . . . (*C.R.S.*, vol. 39), p. 172, *et seq.* It is therefore given here with omissions. Towards the end, occurs a story indicated marginally by More as referring to George Haydock, a secular priest, which appeared in the Annual Letters for 1583 (p. 126): see *C.R.S.*, vol. 39, pp. 181-2.

7. Most of Bartoli's notes (see II/14) emphasise the inaccuracy of Alegambe's entries on Cottam, and at one point a 'falsa narratio' taken originally from the 'book of the Roman seminary', which were used in the *Mortes Illustres et gesta eorum de Societate Jesu qui in odium fidei . . . occisi sunt* (Rome, 1657 [?]). Bartoli's authority was the MS. of Dr. Thomas Worthington's *A Relation of sixtene martyrs: glorified in England in twelve monthes* (Douai, 1601), but Cottam does not appear in the printed version. A MS. seen by Bartoli in the German College, Rome, gave Paul for Thomas (Annales, 1567), but other MSS. in the same college referred to 'Thomas Anglus'. Bartoli further observes that Cottam was 30 years old when he entered Sant' Andrea in 1579, that he was put to teach philosophy, studied theology for two years, and taught grammar and the humanities for three years in England, but precisely when is not clear (d. 435v).

10. More's authorities are Camden, *Annals*, An. 27 (1585) for this, and for the passage on the exile of the 70 priests, Ribadeneira, *op. cit.*, Book II, ch. 38.

11. More was altogether too optimistic in his account of the relationship between Persons and Haywood, although it may have improved with time. An undated document in the General's archives (Anglia/30/I, ff. 118 to 123v), probably drawn up after Haywood reached Rome in 1589, refers to 'Certain things in Robert Persons's government which need to be considered, and committed to the judgment of our Reverend Father General'. The document is too lengthy to give in full but the following is noteworthy: '. . . George Gifford, a wasteful and dissolute young man, stayed at the Queen's court. With him Father Robert Persons dealt with a view to killing the Queen [and] the whole business was entrusted to him so that he should kill her with his own hand. This he took upon him and then betrayed the entire plan. Whether she can by right or not be killed . . . [one word missing] . . . let others judge. How this touches the Society, let our Father General judge' (f. 119). It was not uncommon for 'wasteful and dissolute young men' at that time—and older men for that matter—to turn a dubious penny by acting as *agents-provocateurs* for a government anxious to divide and discredit the Catholics, but this example of one Jesuit retailing a story of this kind against another seems to be unique, at all events for this time and national context. There is no corroboration of the

story by any trustworthy witness that has so far come to light, nor would we expect it. It is unlikely that More saw this document by Haywood.

The annual letters of the Naples Province, S.J., are quoted as the source for Haywood's later years.

The last part of IV/11 is taken up with a refutation of a story related to Rudolph Hospinian's *Historia Jesuitica* . . . (Zurich, 1619), a work hostile to Jesuits which claimed to recount not only their history but also their 'wiles, deceptions, impostures, nefarious crimes and bloody counsels, as also their false, seditious and sanguinary teaching' (title). The author claimed that after 31 years in the Society, and 23 years' profession in it, Haywood wrote to Aquaviva asking for a summons to his presence, when he would say much for the Society's good. Haywood wished to see the weaknesses of the Society corrected before they were publicly proclaimed by some avowed enemy or apostate. Lest the General be tempted to overlook the matter, or regard it as lightweight, the writer sent him a summary of his accusations: all this in 1590. His 11 charges, given as heads in Hospinian, ranged from bad doctrine, and relating false miracles and wonders, to the bad faith of Jesuits, governed and governing, among themselves, and could certainly not be dismissed as light. Haywood wrote more than once, but only received answers that were 'soft' or 'cold', pressure of work and more important people being put forward as excuses for not seeing him.

Owen Lewis, Bishop of Cassano, no friend of the Society, was then in Rome working in the papal curia, and assisting with the visitation and regulation of religious orders. Since Haywood had no satisfaction from his own General, he put his case to Bishop Lewis in whom he found a sympathetic hearer. He further asked the bishop to put the matter to the Pope and get Haywood himself called to Rome from Naples, with the object of airing his problem before the Pope. All must be arranged quickly and secretly lest the Jesuits get in first and mar or debar his entry. Haywood also got Joseph de Costa, a Spanish Jesuit, who had much influence with the nuncio at Madrid, to write to the Pope, and the Duke of Sessa, the Spanish ambassador at the court of Rome, eventually handed the letter to his Holiness. The latter then gave orders for Haywood to come to Rome. Thus far the story is quite plausible, but at this point the familiar tinge of early-17th-century propaganda seems to enter. The Jesuits now managed to cow the nuncio at Naples—indeed, he was 'perterritus'!—into deserting Haywood's cause. The Pope was persuaded that the English Jesuit was out of his mind, and dropped the order for his summons. Haywood consoled himself, as far as he could, by pouring out his soul to the Bishop of Cassano. 'If he had been mad, and they had allowed him to address the Pope, the most wise Pontiff would have found him out at the first meeting, and rejected him, to the great honour of our Fathers and witness to their good faith (conscientiae). He would have established the fact that they were so innocent that they had no one to condemn them save a madman'.

It is scarcely the Pope's function to grant interviews to decide whether a man is mad or not. The essential task of subordinates is to save their superior's time for tasks only he can do. But More does not argue from much knowledge or very credible reasons when he rejects the whole story out of hand. His strongest point is that, if Hospinian saw these letters to Cassano, and presumably had copies (but did he?), why had they not been published in the considerable interval since Hospinian had published his history? One could think of a number of answers to More, the most obvious being that he would not wish to compromise the bishop to that extent. More makes much of Hospinian's errors of fact, but this would not make him wrong in everything or in this; although it must be admitted that Hospinian, following the polemical standards of his age, was more concerned to discredit the Jesuits than to tell the truth. At the same time, More's argument that Haywood would not have done such a thing must carry little weight when we think of the gravity of at least one of the charges which he made against Persons, as we have seen, without any serious attempt at proof. The subject remains one for further research.

12. For an account of the projected disputation see Challoner, *Memoirs . . .* (1924 edition), p. 31. He gives November, not September.

13. This mention of Hart occurs in Luke Kirby's letter of 10 January 1582, to some of his friends, which was published in the *Concertatio Anglicana* (1588 edition), pp. 92v–93.

14. The General's archives contain much of interest on the English College, Rome, among which may be mentioned reports on it for 1582 (Anglia/30/I/ff. 247–70); a Latin narrative of troubles in the college from 1580 to 1596 (*ibid.*, II/ff. 318–34v), Latin annals for 1583 (*ibid.*, ff. 481–6); letters of Richard Barret, President of Douai, for 1583 to 1598 (Anglia/37/ff. 10–17—from Grene's collection); the visitation of the English College in 1585 (*ibid.*, ff. 20v–22). A letter of the students to Aquaviva of 17 May 1597, in admiration of Father Persons (Fondo Gesuitico/651/613); Edmund Harvard/ Harwood to the General, 21 August 1595 (*ibid.*, no. 626). At Stonyhurst, Grene's *Collectanea N.I.* contains seven transcripts devoted to the history, martyrs and other worthies of the English College. The Vatican archives include undated letters and addresses from both priests and students to the Pope or Cardinal Aldobrandino of about this time (Fondo Borghese/III/124 C, ff. 118–20v and 127–8v).

There is still no adequate survey of the Elizabethan spy system available in print, although the material to hand in archives private and public is vast in bulk. Worthy of special mention in this context are the special studies of L. Hicks, S.J., in *The Mnnth* on 'An Elizabethan Propagandist: Solomon Aldred', p. 181, *et. seq.* (1945); and in *Studies*, 'The strange Case of Dr. William Parry', vol, 37 (1948); more recently, *An Elizabethan Problem* (1964). Concerning the priests, Dr. Bagshawe was, perhaps, the sharpest thorn in the side of the Jesuits. A study on him is in active preparation. See also Godfrey Anstruther, cf., *The Seminary Priests*, vol. I (Ware/Durham, 1968).

15. More dates Person's letter to Ribadeneira 15 September 1584 (17 Kal. Octobris). Is this the same letter as that published in *C.R.S.*, vol. 39 on pp. 227–35? This is also dated 15 September. Seemingly not, since the present passage cannot be identified in it. L. Hicks's note, p. 227 (1), mentions various MS. copies. Only a fragment of the original seems to have survived (Westminster Arch., Main Series, III/9), also indicated in the note. More's quotation may be simply a mistake as far as date and addressee are concerned.

N.B.—More's numbering omits any paragraph 16.

17. The use of Wisbech Castle as a prison for recusants was first mooted in 1572, and put into effect for the first time in 1580. The most recent and scholarly study on the subject is *The Wisbech Stirs, 1595–1598* (*C.R.S.*, vol. 51), edited by Miss P. Renold, which reproduces 38 documents and includes a short but informative introduction. T. G. Law's *A Historical Sketch of the Conflicts between Jesuits and Seculars in the Reign of Queen Elizabeth with a Reprint of Christopher Bagshaw's 'True Relation of the Faction begun at Wisbech', and illustrative Documents* (1889), is also valuable especially for the reprint and the documents which, together with Law's *The Archpriest Controversy* (Camden Society, London, 1896 and '98: two vols.), present largely the anti-Jesuit side of the case. The Jesuit William Weston's autobiography was first published by John Morris, S.J., in *The Troubles of our Catholic Forefathers . . . Second Series* (1875), pp. 3–284. For the continuation, see *C.R.S.*, vol. 1 (1905). See also P. Caraman's translation, *An Autobiography from the Jesuit Underground,* by William Weston (New York, 1955). The jealous man referred to before, who played a leading role in anti-Jesuit activities at Wisbech and elsewhere, was undoubtedly Dr. Christopher Bagshaw. Ralph Ithell, another of this party, subsequently apostatised, while Dr. John Nordon, the 'doctor of medicine', died suddenly.

18. Persons's letter to Agazzari was dated 17 November 1580, not September, as More says. See also pp. 52 and 78.

20. Gregory Martin's letter was of 20 December 1575.

21. This letter from the archpriest, as he became by Cardinal Cajetan's appointment on 7 March 1598, was dated 10 January

1596 (draft in Westm. Arch., Main Series, Anglia IX, no. 49—the volumes Anglia VIII and IX were formerly in the Stonyhurst Archives but went to Westminster by exchange in February 1921). After 'how much money' comes, in the Westminster document, 'out of their own patrimony (for what comes to them from alms is very small— . . .'.

Apart from this, More follows the above original accurately down to 'patefacta rerum veritas dissipet' (blown away by truth), after which it beomces largely précis until the closing sentences. This letter may be compared with what Blackwell wrote to the Pope from London on 22 October 1600. After declaring that the 'heretics are making a furious search for me especially, and for the Father Superior of the Society of Jesus, whom they mark down among other of our brethren and fellow priests, for death and destruction', he refers to 'the indispensable help of the Fathers . . . who are reliably at hand to give hospitality, to take part in the warfare and stand in the line of battle, a strong bulwark against those who threaten the peace of the Church; for they are always endeavouring to bring back to the obedience of your Apostolic See those who are troubled in spirit and disturbed in their minds . . .' (Vatican Arch., Fondo Borghese III, 124.G.I., f. 49: Latin).

The amount of paper covered, both manuscript and printed, on the archpriest controversy was very considerable. The greater part of what exists has not yet been published. Most of what has been published gives the view of the anti-Jesuit party (cf. M. A. Tierney's, *Dodd's Church History of England* (1839–54) (5 vols.), appendices; T. G. Law, *op. cit.*).

24. The latter part of this paragraph is a good example of the writer's more obscure style. One Ciceronian sentence runs for some 10 lines. It appears to allow of a translation which suggests that a few of the Jesuits' adversaries were seeking after honours, but what is given appears to be the more obvious meaning of the Latin.

Book the Fifth

1. D'Espernon, Duc, Jean Louis de Nogaret de la Valette (1554–1642). His military career began at the siege of La Rochelle in 1573, and over the years he became a leading figure among the Catholics and a great favourite of Henry III, who heaped honours upon him, although at the cost of rousing much envy. De Nogaret acquired his duchy in 1581.

Philippe de Mornay, Seigneur de Plessis-Marly, was a leading Calvinist politician, writer and opponent of the Catholic League formed in 1576. He was the author of *Vindiciae contra Tyrannos*, a work defending tyrannicide. After the wars of the League broke out in 1584, de Mornay soon came to the front as the right-hand man of Henry of Navarre (later Henry IV of France). Agreement was reached between the Huguenot party and the French court after the murder of the Duke and Cardinal of Guise and other of their supporters in 1588. One condition of the peace was that Saumur should be given to Henry of Navarre as a cautionary town with the further condition that it was governed by de Mornay. See *Biographie universelle*; Anselme and de Fourny, *Histoire généalogique et chronologique de la Maison royale de France*, tome VI (Paris, 1730), p. 283/ix; Raoul Patry, *Philippe du Plessis-Mornay . . . 1549-1623* (Paris, 1933), ch. vii, p. 319.

4. The letter from Seville to Clement VIII is quoted extensively if not in full in Yepes, *op. cit.*, Book VI, p. 767, of the 1599 edition. The translation given here is from Yepes rather than from More.

5. Camden, *Annales . . .* (Latin edition of 1625), pp. 620-21; (English edition of 1635), p. 428, for the reference to 'Doleman's' book. For a discussion of authorship, see L. Hicks, S.J., 'Father Robert Persons, S.J., and *The Book of Succession*', article in *Recusant History*, vol. IV, no. 3 (Oct. 1957), especially pp. 126-8. The letter of 24 May 1603, referred to by More, was written to Garnet (see L. Hicks' article, p. 127).

6. For these beginnings of St. Omer's, with further reference to Archduke Ernest, Governor of the Netherlands, see H. Chadwick, S.J., *St. Omers to Stonyhurst* (1962), ch. 2, especially p. 27.

7. Foucart was relieved of his post in July 1601, when Giles Schondonck succeeded him. (See Chadwick, *op. cit.*, p. 42.) Omitted at the end of this paragraph is a certain amount of information on rectors whose period of administration fell well outside the Elizabethan era.

8. The at first sight scarcely credible story of Cornelius's degree of abstraction becomes more plausible when it is remembered that the students would probably proceed from one place to the other in 'crocodile'.

10. N.B.—Foley presented this (*Records . . .*, vol. III, p. 467) as if Cornelius asked to be tried by men chosen by priests or by Oxford academics. According to More, Cornelius asked for trial by priests (lectis e Clero Catholico sui similibus) or by men from Oxford (ex academicis Oxoniensibus).

11. Omitted is a story from John Gerard's repertoire concerning a certain nobleman in Staffordshire whose ghostly presence returned to haunt his widow until his unquiet soul was at last laid to rest by the saying of a number of Masses (p. 172 in More).

12. More put Horsham St. Faith's three miles from Norwich. Samuel Lewis's *Topographical Dictionary*, vol. II (1849), is here followed.

For Southwell's 'Lament' see Foley, *op. cit.*, vol. I, pp. 305–7. The pious passages and prayers omitted here are also included in Foley: e.g., Athony Sucquet's rather pessimistic prayer of self-abasement (Foley, *op. cit.*, p. 310).

15. Anthony Sucquet, *Viam Vitae Aeternae* (Antwerp, 1620): in three parts, corresponding to the three spiritual paths of beginners, proficients, and the perfect. Sucquet was a Belgian from Mechlin, born 1574; died 1626. He entered the Society on 27 April 1597, was ordained in 1607, and became provincial of the Flemish province in 1619. See N. Southwell, S.J., *Bibliotheca Scriptorum S.J.* . . . (Rome, 1676), p. 85.

16. In a letter to L. Hicks, S.J., of 23 January 1932, Alfred Poncelet, S.J., pointed out that More was in error in sending Southwell to Tournai since the Jesuits were expelled from this place on 3 June 1578, to which they did not return before 29 November 1581, with the support of Alexander Farnese. Novices were not received again before April 1582. The few who were received between 1578 and 1582 were sent to Trèves or St. Omer. Poncelet published *Nécrologe des Jésuites de la province Gallo-Belge* (Louvain, 1908); *Histoire de la Compagnie de Jésus dans les anciens Pays-Bas* . . . (Brussels, 1927), and *Nécrologe des Jésuites de la Province Flandro-Belge* (Wetteren, 1931).

19. There are omissions in More from this letter of 16 January 1591, which are not indicated in the text (p. 182–3). It was copied by Grene in his Collectanea P. II (Stonyhurst), pp. 521, 522. A Spanish summary of this letter was printed by Yepes (*op. cit.*, pp. 647–8). It may have been this summary further summarised which was translated once again into his own Latin by More. This would explain considerable differences at times between More's version and Grene's transcript which was presumably from the original. Yepes and Grene give 1590 as the year for this letter—which corresponds also with the date of a letter in the General's archives in Rome—following the continental style, while More followed the English: another point made by Grene. The translation given here is from Grene, not from More, although the differences between them scarcely amount to contradiction. Omitted are several stories of extraordinary and portentous natural phenomena common in the literature of the age.

Grene, in a marginal note, suggests that Christopher Bales was one of the priests taken. He was executed on 4 March 1590. See also Nieremberg. The letter of 8/18 March 1590/1, is in Collect. P. II, pp. 513–15. It is noted by Grene (Coll. p. II, p. 516) as occurring in Yepes (p. 648) and that More translated it thence into Latin (p. 182–3).

20. In describing the hardships of life in a great Catholic house, More, no doubt, is dealing with the complaint made by some against

the Society that it chose such houses leaving others to the hardship of life elsewhere in the mission.

More erroneously gives 1573 as the year of the fourth Duke of Norfolk's death. For a study of his last years, see F. Edwards, *The Marvellous Chance* (1968). The plot of the gentlemen—More's 'nobilium'—was doubtless the Babington Plot. For Philip Howard, Earl of Arundel, 1557-95, see *C.R.S.*, vol. 21, *English Martyrs*, (1919).

More gives a marginal reference to a eulogy of Southwell by Cornelius a Lapide in his commentary *Ad Hebreos*, 10.v.34.

21. The greater part of this paragraph is omitted (from top of p. 186 to nearly halfway down p. 188). It deals with Southwell's spiritual precepts and teachings.

22. The main omissions in the letter to the peregrinating priest are further aphorisms on the lines of those given. For a full translation, see Foley, *Records . . .*, vol. I, pp. 338-9. More was Foley's principal source for these letters of Southwell, seemingly.

23. For the full version of the letter to his father as given in More, see Foley, *op. cit.*, pp. 339-47. Further details on 'Saint Peter's Complaint' and 'Mary Magdalen's Tears' are given in Pierre Janelle, *Robert Southwell the Writer* (1935), ch. VIII.

Omitted at the end of this paragraph is part of the writer's summary of Southwell's thoughts on time.

24. Omitted is a long, rhetorical page on the sufferings of the martyrs in general terms.

25. Burghley's admiring words with regard to Southwell seem decidedly aprocryphal. The Lord Treasurer allowed himself no high opinion of those who opposed or disobeyed him.

27. For Yorke and William's plot of 1594, see Thomas Fitzherbert's *An Apology of T. F. in Defence of himself and other Catholyks . . .* (Antwerp (?), 1602), ch. 15. This little treatise by Thomas Fitzherbert (not mentioned as such in Allison and Rogers catalogue [Bognor Regis, 1965]) was bound with—at least in the copy at Mount Street—*A Defence of the Catholyke Cause . . .* (Antwerp, 1602). (See Allison and Rogers.)

William Hacket was a puritan fanatic executed in 1591. See Conyers Read, *Lord Burghley and Queen Elizabeth* (1960), pp. 470-1.

Popham's quotation of the 'true bill' as reported by More may be compared with the same as it appears in the Middlesex Sessions Rolls of 2 December 1595 (see J. C. Jeaffreson, *Middlesex County Records*, vol. 1 (Clerkenwell, 1886 [?]), p. 207.

29. Thraso: a braggart soldier in Terence's 'Eunuch'.

30. More mentions 'MSS. Gerardi' (marginal note, p. 200) as a source for the Southwell legend. Foley (*Records . . .*, vol. 1, pp. 364–75) gives an English narrative from Stonyhurst (Anglia A/II), dated marginally 26 February 1595. This is a translation, seemingly of an Italian account in this volume dated marginally 21 February 1595. There is also a Spanish account dated marginally 21 February 1595, but shorter and different in content from the two other accounts. All have been numbered (1) in the volume, seemingly by Foley, as also the copy of a Latin letter from Henry Garnet to Claud Aquaviva of 25 February 1595, which also deals with Southwell's execution. A Spanish translation of this letter also appears under (1). A reasonably full report of Southwell's trial and execution is in the General's archives, Rome (first part in Anglia 31/I, ff. 70–83; second part in *ibid.*, 30/II, ff. 508–16). Letters of Henry Garnet to the General on the subject, at least *inter alia*, of Southwell's martyrdom are also in *ibid.*, 31/I, ff. 107–8 (22 February 1595); ff. 109–114 (17 March); ff. 115–116v (22 February); on ff. 117–119v (7 March), all apparently old style. Stonyhurst MS., A.IV, 12 (1), a volume on the martyrs, includes a life of Southwell; A.V, 4 is a volume of autograph writings and poems, as is also if not quite so certainly MS. A.V, 27. The letter from Garnet to Aquaviva translated in Foley (*Records*, vol. I, p. 376) is a fragment and not the whole. A relation of Southwell's execution by Thomas Leake from Stonyhurst Anglia A/VI, no. 24, was printed in *C.R.S.*, vol. 5 (1908).

32. This declaration is given in translation in Foley, *op. cit.*, vol. I, pp. 316–7.

33. William Fulke, D.D., *A Rejoynder to Bristowe's Replie in Defence of Allen's Scroule of Articles and Booke of Purgatory: also the Caviles of Nicholas Saunders about the Supper of our Lord* (1581): see W. T. Lowndes, *op. cit.*, vol. II.

33 (bis). Thomas de Sailly, S.J. (died 1623), was founder of the 'missio castrensis' or chaplaincy to the forces fighting under the Catholic rulers in the Low Countries, the direction of which he held for 20 years. He was also confessor to Alexander Farnese, Duke of Parma, and later rector of the Jesuit college in Brussels. His eulogy was written by Charles Scribani, S.J. (MS. 654, pp. 289, *et. seq.* in Bibliothéque royale, Brussels). See also *Biographie nationale* (Belgium), vol. 21, cols, 46–50. Information from A. Poncelet, S.J., *Nécrologe des Jésuites de la Province Flandro-Belge* (Wetteren, 1931), p. 33.

34. Much of paragraph 34 is taken up with Walpole's pious reflections, as reported by More, on the desirability of martyrdom.

· **36.** Much of this paragraph deals with Walpole's theological debate with the divines.

37. Richard Holtby, S.J. (1552/3–1640), came to England in 1589, and was appointed superior of the Jesuit mission after Garnet's death in 1606. For a reliable brief biography, correcting More in some points, see John Morris, S.J., *The Troubles of our Catholic Forefathers* (1877) (Third Series), pp. 105–17. Walpole's letter to Holtby, written most probably towards the end of January 1594, was published seemingly from a copy seen by Challoner at St. Omer's in his *Memoirs of Missionary Priests* (1924 edition), pp. 221–4. Note More's version adds an important sentence after the first missing from Challoner's copy: and also from A. Jessop, *One Generation of a Norfolk House* (1879) (pp. 236–9), who followed Challoner in this. Jessop, apart from this work which is largely a life of Walpole, published *Letters of Fa. Henry Walpole, S.J.* (Norwich, 1873), from the original letters at Stonyhurst in Anglia A/I, except no. 49.

39. At this point More makes general observations on the English usage of the sworn jury for such trials. He goes on to observe what may be included as a note: 'If anyone refuses to submit to trial in this way, he is penalised by being laid with his loins on a sharp stone. A weight is then placed on him, and he is pressed until he faints. Some prefer to undergo this torture to make sure that their possessions will pass to their heirs. Otherwise they are forfeit to the royal treasury. If a poor man refuses to plead, he is considered to have pleaded guilty, and is killed by the usual punishment of hanging. This happened to most priests at this time'.

40. See also Jessop, *One Generation . . .*, pp. 277, 278. 7 April, 1595, was a Friday, not a Saturday, as More says, if this was, as is generally accepted, the day of the execution.

42. The man unnamed by More who had his eye on Walpole's property seems to have been Arthur Gregory—an expert in the art of resealing broken letters after interception and examination by the government (see A. Fraser, *Mary Queen of Scots* (1969), p. 483). Gregory wrote to Sir Robert Cecil on 17 March 1596/7, 'For Walpole's land, I protest I knew it not until Ballard told me that he had acquainted your honour therewith, But seeing it is as it is, I desire your honour to let me know how far I may deal therein with your good allowance . . . For as I am I cannot long live in London with so great charge, being already far indebted and my estate engaged' (Salisbury MSS., 39/24: *Calendar*, part vii, p. 118: cf. also H. Foley, *Records . . .*, vol. II, p. 262, no. 15).

46, 47. Omitted is an account of Richard Walpole's part in the conversion of Pickering, son of Baron Wotton, in the autumn of 1605.

48. This paragraph deals briefly with Michael Walpole, Henry's brother, who succeeded him as prefect of studies at Valladolid, and later became superior of the Jesuit mission in England, and died at Seville in 1620.

Book the Sixth

1. More gives 1595 as the year of Vitelleschi's rule in the English College. According to a note by Christopher Grene (General's archives, Anglia/37, f. 142v), Vitelleschi began as rector on 16 April 1592; handed over to Alfonso Agazzari on 17 May 1596. R. Persons succeeded him for a month on 25 May 1597, but Vitelleschi returned on 29 June 1597. Persons was made rector on 13 December 1597, and continued in office until his death in 1610: 'and so it is quite evident that Father More was in error at the beginning of book vi when he says that the rector in 1595 was Father Mutius' (Latin).

4. More gives Persons's letter to the General very faithfully with only one minor omission and one or two alterations of words, which might have been the printer's errors as much as More's. Along with this letter in the General's archives (Hispania/138, f. 143, holograph) is preserved a covering letter in Spanish of the same date (*ibid.*, f. 142). This letter reiterates his small personal desire for the proposed honour, but he did not reject it on his own inclination alone. 'When . . . I got Father Oliver's letter, I thought it my duty to consult the superior and five or six of the fathers most looked up to. They were of the opinion that I ought to write what I have written to your Paternity, and also to the Fathers in Madrid, asking them to use their utmost influence. This I am doing, and have done as well as I can everything possible, without making a stir and bringing the matter back to life . . . The Fathers did not think the time had yet come for me to write myself to the king or his councillors, but your Paternity may rest assured that for my part I shall not fail to do everything possible to put a stop to this business . . .': from the L. Hicks collection of Person's letters at Mount Street.

7. T. Fitzherbert's English works to which More refers would appear to be, *The First Part of a Treatise concerning Policy and Religion* (Douai, 1606), and *The Second Part of a Treatise concerning Policy and Religion* (Douai, 1610). The Latin work was *An sit utilitas in scelere vel de infelicitate Principis Machiavelliana* . . . (Rome, 1610). Cf. Allison and Rogers, *op. cit.*; De Backer, *Bibliothèque des Ecrivains de la Compagnie de la Compagnie de Jésus* (Liège and Paris, 1869), vol, 1, col, 1873, 4.

8. This is a summary of a spiritual diary written in the first person, and so printed in Foley, *Records . . .*, vol. II (series II, III and IV) (London, 1875), on pp. 207-13. Given in full here is an important omission from Foley, to be added on p. 209 and immediately after the signature following the vow-formula.

11. The episode of the man with a pack is so condensed in More's Latin as to be quite obscure. The meaning becomes clear from the translation of Gerard's autobiography in John Morris, S.J., *Life of Father John Gerard* (1881), p. 41. Morris's life of Gerard, like the more recent translation by P. Caraman, S.J. (1952), was based on a contemporary or near-contemporary copy of a MS. formerly in the Roman Jesuit novitiate. This copy is at Stonyhurst (MS. A.V.22), and carries the title—in Latin like the narrative— 'Narratio Patris Joannis Gerardi de rebus a se in Anglia gestis. Authentica apud Sanctam Andream in manibus Patris Sacchini' (qv. in More's bibliography, p. 357).

In a marginal note, More refers to William and Robert Wiseman as the two brothers, but what is given seems more accurate: cf. Foley, *Collectanea*; also *Necrology English Province S.J., 1561 to 1937* (Roehampton, 1938). For Gerard's stay with the Wisemans of Braddocks, see the autobiography, chapter 6. Gerard's previous host was Henry Drury.

For the incident of the pursuivants' interruption of Southwell's Mass, More gives a marginal reference to a 'Southwell letterbook V, no. 19', which would appear to have been lost; but this incident is also included in Gerard's autobiography: cf. Morris edition, ch. ix, pp. 108-10.

12. Two London prisons went by the name of 'The Counter', one in Wood Street and another in Southwark. According to Stowe's survey of London, 'on the west side of Bread Street, amongst divers fair and large houses for merchants, and fair inns for passengers, had ye one prison-house, pertaining to the sheriffs of London, called the Compter in Bread Street; but in the year 1555, the prisoners were removed from thence, to one other new Compter in Wood Street, provided by the city's purchase, and builded for that purpose' (London, 1603, p. 667). It is not clear in which Counter Gerard was held. See Morris, *op. cit.*, p. 186, note 1.

14. Mark Barkworth is given in More as St. Mark Barkwith. The *Necrology of the English Congregation of the O.S.B., 1600 to 1883* (1883), by Rev. T. B. Snow, M.A., gives the name as it is also found in Gillow (*op. cit.*) and so rendered here.

20. More than one Catholic Arden was imprisoned in the Tower during the period. Morris identified the Arden who shared Gerard's adventure as John (*op. cit.*, p. 277, note 1). John Arden was in the Cradle Tower, Gerard in the Salt Tower (see *ibid.*, p. 292).

21. Some of the sentences in the early part of this paragraph concerning John Lilly are written in More's most obscure and condensed style.

24. More is here referring to the institute of Blessed Mary Ward, one of the most remarkable women of her generation by any standard. Jesuits were roughly divided in their attitude according to those who felt that they should help an institute whose early struggles and ideals so much resembled their own; and those on the other hand who were uneasily aware that their own Society was not sufficiently accepted in all quarters to enable them to help dubious causes without bringing all parties in jeopardy. John Morris and J. H. Pollen, Jesuits, collected a volume of transcripts of *Documents concerning the Institute of Mary, 1593–1909* bound up 1910 and preserved in the English Province archives, S.J.

26. Oliver Manare: b. Douai, 1522, d. at Tournai on 28 November 1614, after 62 years as a Jesuit. He was provincial of France and of the Rhine Province, and of the Belgian before a crisis took place in 1578 which led to the separation of the region into French and Flemish-speaking Jesuit provinces. Manare was visitor for a number of provinces and for more than one General. He was vicar-general of the Society at the death of Mercurian. Cf. A. Poncelet, *Nécrologe . . . Flandro-Belge* (Wetteren, 1931), p. 25; *Histoire de la Compagnie de Jésus dans les Pays-Bas* (Brussels, 1927), *passim.* For a scholarly account of the Paget/Morgan faction see L. Hicks, *An Elizabethan Problem.* (See note IV/14 above.)

28. The date of this letter is 10 January 1597. The original letter seems to have perished but there is a contemporary or near-contemporary copy in Westminster Archives, main series, vol. VI, no. 4, p. 13. It was partly printed in Tierney-Dodd, *Church History . . .,* vol. III (1840), p. lxxxiv. More's version is given here, but it abbreviates considerably the Westminster version. The omissions from the latter in More are indicated by dotted lines. Minor word changes appearing in More are retained, but they hardly alter the meaning of the Westminster text. It is probable that More was working from the original.

The letter of Allen to Charles Paget, dated 4 January 1591 (1592 in Grene's Collectanea M), is given in full (?) by Grene (no. 129), and in the original English. T. F. Knox in his *Letters and Memorials of Cardinal Allen* gave part of this letter (p. 319), but omitted all reference to Holt without any indication of the fact. R. Persons's *Apologie . . .* gives a summary (pp. 36, 37) of the letter. Grene's Collectanea M omitted passages which More included. The extract of the letter as given here is made up from Grene, where possible, and from More for the omissions, giving *in toto* substantially as much as More gives.

William Camden's charge against Holt in the *Annals . . .* is given here from the third edition, in English, translated by R. N. Gent and published in London in 1635 (pp. 440, 441). A fuller quotation is given here than appears in More, who incidentally renders Gent's 'of the fugitives' as 'hominum'.

29. The omitted passages of Thomas Hunt deal with his personal piety which, *inter alia*, regarded dancing as an invention of the devil.

30. The remainder of this paragraph deals in a general way with the spiritual side of John Worthington's work, which scarcely differed from that of his brethren. Parts of the narration fall well outside the Elizabethan era.

37. The number of this paragraph is misprinted 'XXXIII'. Foley reproduces a long letter written by Lawrence Worthington from the Gatehouse in 1616 describing his experiences (*Records* . . ., vol. II, pp. 96–100).

40. Henry Floyd returned to England about 1607, working mainly in the London district where he died at the age of seventy-eight.

41. Paragraph number misprinted as 'LIX'. John's career also extended into the Commonwealth, and More's account is here much abbreviated. John Floyd died on 16 September 1649.

INDEX